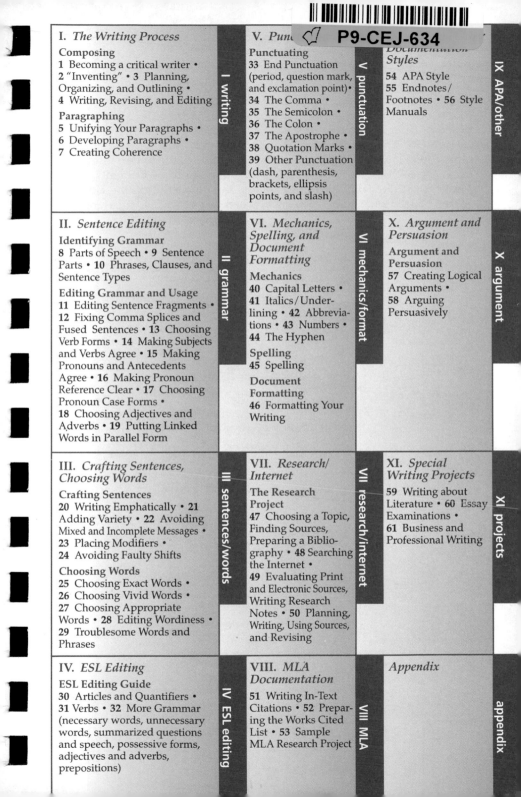

P9-CEJ-634

How to Find What You Need
in *The Ready Reference Handbook*

You can find information in *The Ready Reference Handbook* in a number of ways. Look for your topic in the **Tab Guide** on the reverse of this page, the **Brief Contents** section at the front of the book, or the **Index** at the back of the book. Scan the **Writing Processes chart** inside the front cover to locate a "How To" box that fits your writing situation. Once you've found the topic you're looking for, use the **Tabbed Dividers** to flip to the section you need. On each divider you'll find a **Detailed Table of Contents. Topic Markers, Chapter and Section Numbers,** and detailed **Running Heads** at the top of each page will let you know when you've reached the right spot.

Chapter numbers and sections

Running heads indicate the subject discussed on this page.

Topic markers and correction symbols

"How To" boxes provide immediate help for most writing processes.

Cross-references show where to find related information elsewhere in the book.

Computer tips provide ways to use computers to facilitate the writing process.

Section headings describe guidelines for writing, revising, and editing.

Handwritten corrections show how to revise and edit in a given situation

Bracketed explanations show the reasons for the changes.

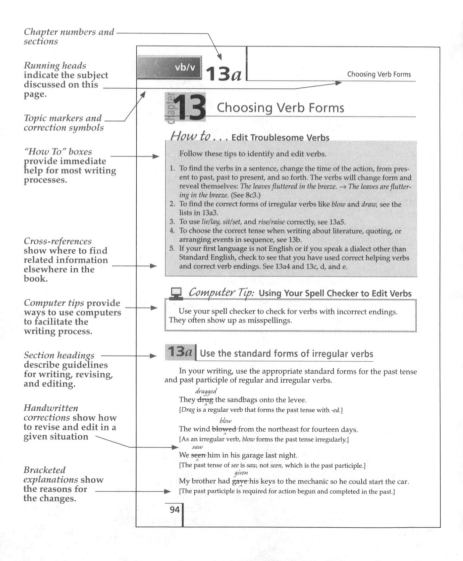

vb/v **13***a*

Choosing Verb Forms

13 Choosing Verb Forms

How to . . . Edit Troublesome Verbs

Follow these tips to identify and edit verbs.

1. To find the verbs in a sentence, change the time of the action, from present to past, past to present, and so forth. The verbs will change form and reveal themselves: *The leaves fluttered in the breeze.* → *The leaves are fluttering in the breeze.* (See 8c3.)
2. To find the correct forms of irregular verbs like *blow* and *draw*, see the lists in 13a3.
3. To use *lie/lay, sit/set*, and *rise/raise* correctly, see 13a5.
4. To choose the correct tense when writing about literature, quoting, or arranging events in sequence, see 13b.
5. If your first language is not English or if you speak a dialect other than Standard English, check to see that you have used correct helping verbs and correct verb endings. See 13a4 and 13c, d, and e.

🖥 *Computer Tip:* Using Your Spell Checker to Edit Verbs

Use your spell checker to check for verbs with incorrect endings. They often show up as misspellings.

13*a* Use the standard forms of irregular verbs

In your writing, use the appropriate standard forms for the past tense and past participle of regular and irregular verbs.

dragged
They ~~drug~~ the sandbags onto the levee.
[*Drag* is a regular verb that forms the past tense with *-ed.*]

blew
The wind ~~blowed~~ from the northeast for fourteen days.
[As an irregular verb, *blow* forms the past tense irregularly.]

saw
We ~~seen~~ him in his garage last night.
[The past tense of *see* is *saw*, not *seen*, which is the past participle.]

given
My brother had ~~gave~~ his keys to the mechanic so he could start the car.
[The past participle is required for action begun and completed in the past.]

94

The
Ready Reference Handbook

Writing, Revising, Editing

SECOND EDITION

Jack Dodds
William Rainey Harper College

Allyn and Bacon
Boston ■ *London* ■ *Toronto* ■ *Sydney* ■ *Tokyo* ■ *Singapore*

Editor-in-Chief, Humanities: *Joseph Opiela*
Developmental Editor: *Donna de la Perrière*
Series Editorial Assistant: *Mary Beth Varney*
Executive Marketing Manager: *Lisa Kimball*
Composition and Prepress Buyer: *Linda Cox*
Manufacturing Buyer: *Suzanne Lareau*
Cover Administrator: *Linda Knowles*
Editorial-Production Administrator: *Susan Brown*
Editorial-Production Service: *Matrix Productions*
Text Designer: *Carol Somberg/Omegatype Typography, Inc.*

Copyright © 2000, 1998, 1997 by Allyn & Bacon
A Pearson Education Company
Needham Heights, MA 02494
Internet: www.abacon.com

Between the time Website information is gathered and then published, it is not unusual for some sites to have closed. Also, the transcription of URLs can result in unintended typographical errors. The publisher would appreciate notification where these errors occur so that they may be corrected in subsequent editions.

Library of Congress Cataloging-in-Publication Data

Dodds, Jack.
    The ready reference handbook: writing, revising, editing / Jack Dodds. — 2nd ed.
        p.   cm.
    Includes index.
    ISBN 0–205–30020–0
    1. English language—Rhetoric—Handbooks, manuals, etc.
    2. English language—Grammar—Handbooks, manuals, etc.   I. Title.
PE1408.D595   1999
808'.042—dc21
                                                                99-11167
                                                                CIP

Printed in the United States of America
10 9 8 7 6 5 4 3 2   03 02 01 00 99

A Brief Contents and Browsing Guide

Preface

Poet, journalist, and teacher Donald Murray once remarked that a wise composition instructor looks for what is best in students' writing and then shows these developing writers how to make their best even better. The students, teachers, and reviewers who have made suggestions for the second edition of *The Ready Reference Handbook* have done me that favor. In the first edition, I aimed for a book easy to use, practical, and as comprehensive as possible for a brief handbook. Their comments and suggestions have shown me how to make this new edition easier to use, more practical, and more comprehensive.

An easier-to-use design

- The binding makes the book sturdier for everyday use and preserves the lie-flat, ready-reference format.
- Twelve tabbed dividers organize *The Ready Reference Handbook* into the quick-access topics student writers need to consult most often as they write and revise.
- A more open page layout makes individual sections easier to locate and examples easier to see.

More practical advice for practicing writers

- The "How-To" boxes (see inside cover) that students and teachers have found so useful for guiding the writing process have been simplified and focused to provide essential tips, guidelines, questions, and checklists when and where writers need them most.
- New "How-To" boxes provide advice on critical thinking and reading, annotating a text, profiling an audience, peer reviewing, proofreading a final draft, writing summaries, searching the World Wide Web, and evaluating sources.
- "Computer Tip" boxes are placed throughout *The Ready Reference Handbook* to provide students with advice for doing efficient word processing and for using the computer as a critical-thinking tool.
- Chapters on composing, grammar, usage, and style have been sharpened to provide students with the most practical advice possible for inventing, drafting, revising, and editing—without, however, sacrificing the user-friendly tone of that advice, which students have found encouraging.
- Increased coverage is given to the key rhetorical choices that direct a writer's writing: analyzing an audience, crafting thesis statements to fulfill specific rhetorical purposes, and writing effective introductions and conclusions.
- Increasingly, students are becoming multi-media learners and writers. To meet their needs, this edition of *The Ready Reference Handbook* uses visuals to illustrate critical reading and online research. For their own writing, students are provided with illustrations of frequently used graphics.
- An Appendix provides a topical list of URLs helpful to students learning Internet research.

More comprehensive coverage

- A new first chapter, "Becoming a Critical Writer," provides an important frame of reference for all that follows in *The Ready Reference Handbook*. The critical-thinking skills of analysis, interpretation, evaluation, and synthesis aid students as they investigate a topic, read, plan for readers, write, and revise.
- In chapters on the research paper, discussion of computerized research has been expanded with additional guidance to library search tools, Boolean searching, and note taking.
- A new Chapter 48, "Searching the Internet," gives a clear, non-jargon, step-by-step introduction to the possibilities and challenges of Internet research.
- Chapter 48 and 46e introduce students to communicating online, observing Internet "Netiquette," and creating their own Web sites.
- In Chapter 49, the new mnemonic "CASE" method for evaluating sources (currency, authority, suitability, and ease of use) provides students with a comprehensive yet easy-to-remember procedure for judging the quality of their reading.
- Chapters 51–56 provide the latest guidance for online documentation using the MLA, APA, CMS, and CBE documentation styles.

Other helpful features of *The Ready Reference Handbook*

- The insides of the front and back covers give writers an overview and access to key features: the "How-To" boxes, the tabs leading to each section, the book's reference features, and common correction symbols.
- Section numbers and letters provide rapid references to headings and subheadings that summarize practical writing guidelines.
- *The Ready Reference Handbook* emphasizes all stages of the writing process, gives developing writers pract ical activities to meet their objectives at each stage, and provides numerous options so that writers can tailor their writing to their own styles or to the requirements of a particular situation.
- Students will find thorough introductions to the common forms of academic and public writing: the essay, formal report, and business writing.
- Special projects—argument, persuasion, the literary essay, and the essay exam—are covered in depth and detail.
- Problems of grammar are treated not only as errors but also as unsuccessful strategies in specific rhetorical situations. The best solutions are shown as process-oriented responses to these situations.
- An ESL editing unit and brief notes throughout the handbook offer pointed advice for writers whose first language is not English.
- Annotated, full-length student writing samples illustrate an informative essay, MLA-style research project, formal report (APA), persuasive essay, literary essay, business letter, résumé, and memo.
- Throughout, the user-friendly tone, numerous examples, and positive advice encourage writers to practice and experiment until they discover what to say and the best way of saying it.
- A separately published *Exercise Book* keyed to this handbook offers students additional practice in critical thinking, composing, grammar, usage, punctuation, style, research, and argument.

- A Test Bank/Diagnostic Test with two 50-item diagnostic tests and additional test questions is available in printed or computerized (Windows or IBM) formats.

Acknowledgments

To all those who assisted with the second edition of *The Ready Reference Handbook* I offer my heartiest, most grateful thanks. Many friends and colleagues at Harper College gave me much support: Peter Sherer, Joseph Sternberg, Barbara Hickey, Xilao Li, Richard Johnson, Kurt Neumann, Julie Fleenor, Pauline Buss, Andrew Wilson, and Fran Martin. I am also thankful for the insightful suggestions provided by my colleagues at other colleges: Claire Berger, Camden County College; Jane Chapman, Metropolitan State College of Denver; Ray Dumont, University of Massachusetts, Dartmouth; Mary J. Flores, Lewis-Clark State College; Loretta Gray, Central Washington University; Maureen Morley, Cuyahoga Community College; and Nancy Prosenjak, Metropolitan State College of Denver. Special thanks to all at Allyn & Bacon who have encouraged and guided this project: Joe Opiela, Vice President for Humanities, who encouraged me to write and enthusiastically guided me along the way; Mary Beth Varney, his assistant, who helped with reviewing; Merrill Peterson and Matrix Productions, who provided thoughtful, careful editorial assistance; production administrator Susan Brown, who guided the project through the design and production processes with skill and aplomb; and especially Donna de la Perrière, a tireless, tenacious, imaginative—and patient—editor. And throughout, my wife Judy's support has nourished body, mind, and spirit.

JD

Credits

Dillard, Annie, excerpt from "In the Jungle" from *Teaching a Stone to Talk* by Annie Dillard. Copyright © 1982 by Annie Dillard. Reprinted by permission of HarperCollins Publishers, Inc.

Durning, Alan Thein, "The Consumer Society," excerpt from *How Much Is Enough? The Consumer Society and the Future of the Earth* by Alan Durning. Copyright © 1992 by Worldwatch Institute. Reprinted by permission of W. W. Norton & Company, Inc.

Ehrlich, Gretel, "Rules of the Game: Rodeo," from *The Solace of Open Spaces* by Gretel Ehrlich. Copyright © 1985 by Gretel Ehrlich. Used by permission of Viking Penguin, a division of Penguin Putnam Inc.

Eiseley, Loren, "The Cosmic Prison." Reprinted with the permission of Scribner, a Division of Simon & Schuster, from "The Cosmic Prison" in *The Invisible Pyramid* by Loren Eiseley. Copyright © 1970 by Loren Eiseley.

Haines, John, excerpt from "Snow." Copyright 1989 by John Haines. Reprinted from *The Stars, The Snow, The Fire* with the permission of Graywolf Press, Saint Paul, Minnesota

Hayakawa, S. I., "How Dictionaries Are Made." Excerpt from *Language in Thought and Action*, Fourth Edition by S. I. Hayakawa, copyright © 1978 by Harcourt Brace & Company, reprinted by permission of the publisher.

Hoffman, Banesh, "Unforgettable Albert Einstein." Reprinted from the January 1968 *Reader's Digest*. Copyright 1967 by The Reader's Digest Assn., Inc.

Hubbell, Sue, "Summer," *A Country Year*. Copyright © 1983, 1984, 1985, 1986 by Sue Hubbell. Reprinted by permission of Random House, Inc.

IAC InfoTrac® Search Bank information © 1998 Information Access Company.

Leopold, Aldo, *A Sand County Almanac: And Sketches Here and There*. New York: Oxford University Press, Inc., 1987.

Marius, Richard, adapted from "Writing Drafts." *A Writer's Companion*, 2nd ed. New York: McGraw-Hill, 1991. Reprinted with permission of The McGraw-Hill Companies.

Maslow, Abraham H., data based on hierarchy of needs from *Motivation and Personality* by Abraham H. Maslow. Revised by Robert Frager, James Fadiman, Cynthia McReynolds, and Ruth Cox. Copyright © 1954, 1987 by Harper & Row, Publishers, Inc. Copyright © 1970 by Abraham H. Maslow. Reprinted by permission of Addison-Wesley Educational Publishers Inc.

Merriam-Webster's Collegiate® Thesaurus. © 1988 by Merriam-Webster, Incorporated. Reprinted by permission of Merriam-Webster, Incorporated.

Milgram, Stanley, introduction to "Some Conditions of Obedience and Disobedience to Authority." From *Human Relations*, Vol. 18, No. 1, 1965, pp. 57–76. Copyright © 1972 by Stanley Milgram.

Miller, R. Keith, "The Idea of Children." *Newsweek* 27 August 1979.

Murray, Donald, "Tricks of the Nonfiction Trade." Reprinted by permission of Roberta Pryor, Inc. p. 12.

Orwell, George, excerpt from "Shooting an Elephant" in *Shooting an Elephant and Other Stories* by George Orwell. Copyright 1950 by Sonia Brownell Orwell and renewed 1978 by Sonia Pitt-Rivers, reprinted by permission of Harcourt Brace & Company.

Park Net home page courtesy of The National Park Service.

Rodriguez, Richard, "Aria: A Memoir of a Bilingual Childhood," "*Hunger of Memory*" by Richard Rodriguez. (Boston: David R. Godine, Publisher, 1981) Copyright © 1981 by Richard Rodriguez. Reprinted by permission of Georges Borchardt, Inc. for the author.

Sanders, Scott Russell, excerpt from "The Men We Carry in Our Minds." Copyright © 1984 by Scott Russell Sanders; reprinted by permission of the author and Virginia Kidd, Literary Agent.

Stafford, William, "Traveling through the Dark." Copyright 1962, 1998 by the Estate of William Stafford. Reprinted from *The Way It Is: New & Selected Poems* by Jane Kenyon with the permission of Graywolf Press, Saint Paul, Minnesota.

Statistics on U.S. National Parks visitation and funding in Chapters 46 and 53 from the Natural Resources Defense Council, based on statistics from the National Park Service Office of Public Affairs and Budget Office.

Teale, Edwin Way, *Wandering Through Winter*. Copyright © 1990 by Edwin Way Teale. From *Wandering Through Winter* by Edwin Way Teale. Reprinted by permission of St. Martin's Press, Incorporated.

Thomas, Lewis, "Social Talk." Copyright © 1972 by The Massachusetts Medical Society, from *The Lives of a Cell* by Lewis Thomas. Used by permission of Viking Penguin, a division of Penguin Putnam, Inc.

William Rainey Harper College computer catalog screen used by permission.

PART **I.**

The
Writing
Process

Composing

Paragraphing

Composing

The Ready Reference Handbook is designed for college writers and for anyone else who wants practical suggestions for writing effectively. What follows is based on the experience of writers of all kinds. At the outset, you should have some basic understanding about writers and the writing they do.

Writers write. Some people assume that writers are different from everyone else. They are inspired, they have a touch of the poet, at least they have the gift of gab. But the truth is that writers are simply people who write. If they are inspired, they have worked hard for that flash of insight. If they sound poetic, they probably had writer William Zinsser's experience of "endlessly rewriting what I had endlessly rewritten." When *you* write, you too are a writer.

Writing is a process. Writing is not the straightforward transcribing of your thoughts. That would be dull work. It's a more exciting and experimental process of creating thoughts through written words. The process is exciting because it involves discovery; writers don't always know what they'll say when they begin writing. It's experimental because writers play with words and ideas until they find what they want to say.

Writing is more than communication. Successful writers write first for themselves, to see what they think, and then for their readers, to communicate. Your writing will always be read by someone, of course. Even if you write only in a diary, you write for an audience of one—yourself. But before it is communication, writing is exploration, discovery, and self-expression. Successful writers almost always work in this two-step way: first finding something to say and then finding a way to communicate it.

Good writing satisfies both writers and readers. Good writing is more than good grammar or impressive-sounding words. Yes, most successful public writing is polished, well laid out, and correct. But it also carries the sound of a writer's voice speaking to readers, it contains good ideas worth writing and reading about, and it is written with power and conviction.

There are many ways to write well. You might think that a book like this preaches one right way to successful writing, but it doesn't. Every successful writer has personal habits and techniques. Some writers are genuinely quirky. Ernest Hemingway sharpened precisely eight pencils before he began each writing day, and a French writer required the smell of apples rotting in his desk drawer to set him to work. Most successful writers, however, have more practical ways of doing their writing. This book describes many of these strategies. Consider them options. Explore and experiment to find what works for you.

1 Becoming a Critical Writer

For many people, "critical" is a word with a bad reputation, associated in their minds with faultfinding, nit-picking, and negativity. But it has a much broader meaning, one important to writers of all kinds. *Critical* comes from a Greek word meaning "to discern or perceive, to separate, to understand." To be critical, therefore, means to look carefully at something, to discover its parts and what it's made of, and then, sometimes, to evaluate—positively or negatively.

In this day of political "spin doctors" who twist the truth, of computer-manipulated images, of competing authorities with conflicting opinions on nearly everything, it's sometimes difficult to tell fact from fiction, the virtual from the real. Skepticism and common sense may not be enough for deciding what to believe, whom, or how much. What can help are the methods of critical thinking, reading, and writing described in this and the following chapters.

1*a* Think critically about information, ideas, and opinions

What goes into your writing may come from your own knowledge, imagination, or observation, or from a book or some other source. Whatever their source, facts, ideas, and opinions will come to you in clumps or in bits and pieces, and you may be uncertain about their meaning or doubtful about their value. To sort things out, see the connections, and decide what things add up to, you'll use four methods of critical thinking: analysis, interpretation, evaluation, and synthesis. In school and out, in research papers and other academic writing, in job applications, in business and professional writing of all kinds, even in your personal writing, you'll use these methods. This chapter introduces them to you and provides critical questions for you to ask as you think about a topic and prepare to write about it. Later chapters will show you how to apply these methods in specific kinds of writing. (See Chapters 2–4, 47–50, 57–61.)

1 Analyzing

When you analyze something, you take it apart and describe it, according to some specific interest, in order to understand it. If a literature teacher asks you to analyze a short story, you may describe the roles that each of the characters plays, divide the plot into a series of related events, or explain why the characters behave as they do. Your interest in character relationships, the action of the story, or human motivation determines what you see as you make your analysis.

How to . . . **Think Critically**

From the following list, choose relevant questions to ask about the topics of your writing. If necessary, reword the questions to fit the topic and your interests, and then look for answers. Study the examples to see how to modify the questions.

1. What are the parts of (your topic)? How do they fit or work together? What larger topic is (your topic) a part of? How is it similar to or different from other topics?

   In Charlotte Perkins Gilman's short story "The Yellow Wall-Paper," what are the traits of the narrator's relationship with her husband? [a question about parts]

   How do the effects of visitor overcrowding compare to other environmental threats to US national parks? [a question of comparison]

2. What is the environment or background of (your topic)? Where does it come from?

   What is the history of government aid to dependent children in the United States?

3. What is happening to (your topic)? What are the causes of its change? What are the effects of this change? Who is affected? How? What will stop the process?

   What causes the narrator's insanity in Charlotte Perkins Gilman's "The Yellow Wall-Paper"?

   How have poor people in the United States been affected by reform of the welfare laws? Who has benefited most from welfare reform? Who has benefited least?

4. What is known for a fact about (your topic)? What do the experts or eyewitnesses think? What assumptions or biases influence their view of the facts? Where do they disagree? Which opinions are best supported or most reasonable?

   Who are the homeless in the United States?

5. What is missing from the information about (your topic)?

   Why does the narrator of William Stafford's poem "Traveling Through the Dark" display so little feeling when he discovers the dead deer on the highway?

6. How are you involved with (your topic)? What bias might influence your thinking?

   Why do I automatically become suspicious and skeptical when supposedly homeless panhandlers ask me for spare change?

7. What should be done about (your topic)? Who will do it? What will it cost?

   What will repair the environmental harm caused by visitors to US national parks?

- *Descriptive analysis.* When you describe the roles played by the various characters in a short story, you're making a descriptive analysis. You are assigning each character a part in the story and describing how that character plays his or her part, based on the contents of the story. A botanist who describes a newly discovered plant species part by part—root, stem, leaves, and flower—is also making a descriptive analysis.

- *Process analysis.* To divide an event or activity into stages or steps and then describe their relationships is to make a process analysis. A recipe for chicken enchiladas is a kind of process analysis: first do this, then this, then this. A sports reporter who writes a quarter-by-quarter account of a basketball game is writing a process analysis.

- *Causal analysis.* To examine events as patterns of cause and effect is to make a causal analysis. A naturalist who sets out to explain why the forests of Shenandoah National Park are slowly dying and discovers the reasons in automobile air pollution has made a causal analysis, reasoning backward from effects to causes. An urban planner who considers the traffic consequences of a new highway is reasoning forward, from causes to their potential effects.

When you want to analyze a topic, think of the parts, steps, stages, causes, or effects of that topic. To begin thinking analytically, choose from questions 1, 2, and 3 in the "How to Think Critically" box (p. 3). As you analyze a topic, be sure to describe *all* of its parts and to apply your interests—your principles of analysis—consistently. For example, your analysis of the death of a forest would be incomplete and ineffective if you failed to mention some of the regions affected or some of the causes, or if you confused the effects of automobile pollution with those of harmful insects.

2 Interpreting

To interpret means to explain or bring to light. When analysis alone doesn't produce understanding, interpretation becomes necessary. When you interpret something, you're reading between the lines, whether those "lines" are the actual lines of a difficult short story or poem, the confusing behavior of a person you know, or the reasons for some mysterious phenomenon. You're looking for "hidden meanings" that will remain hidden until you reveal them through interpretation. Where are you likely to find these hidden meanings?

- *Assumptions.* To read printed texts—or people—successfully, try to discover their assumptions, the basic, often untested beliefs that influence their outlook and behavior. A person who argues that "The US government should temporarily halt legal immigration because our economy cannot absorb any more new immigrants" is assuming but not actually saying that immigrants drain economic resources rather than adding to them or having no effect.

- *Patterns.* When you're trying to understand something, look for patterns—regularities or repetitions in information, design, language, or occurrence. Patterns often reveal the meaning of what you're studying. Imagine an acquaintance who, you have noticed, speaks constantly about money: how much he has or doesn't have, other people's salaries, the cost of this or that, the dangers of inflation. You probably would base your interpretation of his personality on his overriding concern with money, guessing his values and predicting his future behavior accordingly.

- *Implications.* An implication is a connection, usually unstated, between one thing and another. Often printed texts and people don't come right out and say exactly what they mean. Instead, they imply something—that is, they suggest or point in a certain direction. To discover implications, ask yourself, "Where is this train of thought going? What is the next logical step?" What, for example, are the implications of a national welfare policy that requires single parents to look for a job in order to qualify for financial aid but does not provide day care funds for the children of those parents?

When your subject matter requires interpretation, choose from questions 2 through 7 in the "How to Think Critically" box (p. 3). You'll express the results of your interpretation as an **inference**—that is, a statement of meaning based on your understanding of the available information. To state—or "draw"—an inference, you bring together all assumptions, patterns, and implications to see what they add up to. Using reasoning, you state an idea that didn't exist or wasn't apparent before your interpretation. For example, in a literary essay interpreting a poem (see 59g), student Leslie Kelly investigates the language, assumptions, and actions of a character in the poem to discover why he commits what appears to be a cold, heartless act. What she discovers (her interpretation) is summed up in her inference about what motivates his behavior.

3 Evaluating information and opinions

When you evaluate, you do more than state your personal opinions or subjective preferences regarding a topic—a movie, an automobile, a book, a political speech. When you evaluate, you measure something against widely shared **standards of value** that indicate whether it is good or not so good. To write effectively, you'll evaluate all that goes into your writing to see that it is useful and trustworthy.

- *Facts and statistics.* A fact is something that can be verified. The statement "State governments used public lotteries during the American

Revolution to fund the Continental Army" sounds like a fact, as does "Per capita sales of lottery tickets are higher in poor, urban neighborhoods than in the suburbs." You can check these statements in history books and public records to see whether they're true. To decide whether you and other writers are using facts effectively, apply these four standards (known as *Rules of Evidence*): (1) **sufficiency**—are there enough facts to support the point being made? (2) **relevance**—do these facts actually apply to the situation being considered? (3) **timeliness**—are these facts up-to-date information? (4) **variety**—do these facts come from or are they verified by a variety of sources? The fourth standard acknowledges that people who disagree are likely to disagree about the facts. When such is the case, the more sources that accept something as true, the more confident you can be that it is.

- *Opinions.* Consider these two statements: "Gambling causes an increase in the same hormones in the blood that are seen in drug addicts. Obviously, gambling, like drug usage, is addictive." Both statements sound like facts. The first can be verified by observation and is a fact. The second, however, is an inference—an opinion— based on the first. An opinion is a statement of belief or a conclusion. In your writing, you'll use both facts and opinions, and you'll have to distinguish between them. When you identify an opinion, evaluate its usefulness with these questions: (1) Is this opinion supported by sufficient facts? Mistrust any opinions that aren't. (2) Is the source of this opinion an expert or eyewitness? Be careful with opinions from unqualified sources. (3) What are the opinions of other experts or eyewitnesses? See how they compare.

- *Examples and anecdotes.* An **example** describes one member of a group in order to explain the whole group (see also 6b5). Here is an example of an example: In order to explain the economic effects of state lotteries on poor people, a writer focuses on one state, Illinois, as an example. By showing what happens in Illinois, the writer intends to suggest what occurs in other states. An **anecdote** is a brief story that makes a point. Examples and anecdotes are vivid ways to explain or support a point because they help readers see what you mean. To use them effectively, ask yourself this question: Does my example or anecdote really represent what it is supposed to illustrate? Now take another look at the example at the beginning of this paragraph and ask yourself: Is Illinois really like other states in its lottery-marketing expenditures, in the amount of money that poor people spend on the lottery, and in the social and economic effects of this type of gambling?

When you write about important topics, you'll evaluate frequently, both information and the sources of information. Questions 4, 5, and 6 in the "How to Think Critically" box (p. 3) will help you begin. To evaluate the sources of information, follow the guidelines in 49a and b. For more on evaluation, see 57c1 "Testing an argument" and 59c "Writing about literature: The review."

4 Synthesizing

When information and opinions come from a variety of sources, you have to synthesize them to make them useful to you. *Synthesis* comes from a Greek word meaning "to put together, to integrate, to blend." When you synthesize facts, ideas, and opinions, you choose among them and put together your choices to express *your* ideas and support *your* opinions. *Your* thinking becomes the focus.

To prepare a research paper on overcrowding in US national parks, student Eric Martin (see Chapter 53) read books, articles, and Internet sources, interviewed US Park Service officials, and drew on his own experiences. He gathered information about the effects of visitors on the environment, on park facilities, and on one another. He also gathered a variety of opinions, some conflicting, about what should be done about these crowds. He didn't reject conflicting opinions or eliminate those he disagreed with. He evaluated them, selected the best supported and most reasonable, and showed what was wrong with the others. From all his research, he drew inferences and formed his own opinions about the most economical, efficient solutions to the problem. Like most research papers, his is the result of synthesis.

To synthesize effectively, follow these guidelines:

- *Make a working bibliography.* When you take materials from two or more sources, make a list of your sources, including complete publication information (see 47e2). You may make this list an annotated bibliography by adding brief statements about the content and quality of each source (see 47e3).

- *Compare sources.* Notice similarities and differences in your sources' use of key terms, in their thinking, and in their uses of facts and opinions. Try to classify or group your sources. To help yourself make useful comparisons, ask question 4 in the "How to Think Critically" box (p. 3).

- *Choose the best sources.* Use the guidelines in 49a and b. Consider how your readers will respond to the sources you've chosen. Decide how to respond to sources you disagree with.

- As you write, blend your sources smoothly, so they support your ideas and opinions clearly and coherently (see 50c and e).

A note on the differences between synthesis and summary: When you synthesize, you gather information from a variety of sources to support your ideas. When you summarize, you present a brief digest of another person's ideas in your own words. A good synthesis makes frequent use of summary. (See also 49e2.)

1b | Read critically

Some reading you can do in the relaxed, casual way you watch television. But the reading you do for school, on the job, or about important issues calls for greater attention and care. Ideas won't leap off the page with dramatic clarity, and you won't always be able to tell at a glance whether something that looks plausible really is.

1 Previewing

Before you begin reading a book, article, or other source, look it over briefly to get a sense of its content and to see whether it meets your needs. Previewing will help you read with efficiency and understanding. Look for the following:

- The major topics of the source.
- Patterns of organization. Common patterns of organization are time order, part by part or step by step, comparison, thesis/support, problem/solution.
- Information about the author. Try to discover the writer's experiences, opinions, or organizational affiliations that reveal point of view or possible bias.
- The purpose of the source and whether it suits your purpose.
- Quality indicators that reveal whether the source is trustworthy and whether readers will respond favorably to it if you refer to it in your writing. Evaluate a source according to the guidelines in 49a and b.

How to . . . Preview Your Reading

To preview a source effectively, follow these tips:

1. Skim titles, prefaces, introductions, headings, boxed text, graphics, and captions for information about a source's subject matter, author, and organization.
2. Check title pages, headnotes, endnotes, and book jacket biographies for information about the author.
3. If a source is lengthy, challenging, or controversial, take extra time to read about the author in periodicals like *Current Biography*. Read reviews of the source in *Book Review Digest* or *Book Review Index*. Your librarian will direct you to these and other review sources.

2 Reading to understand

If you read in the active, attentive way recommended here, you'll be doing the analyzing, interpreting, evaluating, and synthesizing described earlier in this chapter. Use the questions in the "How to Think Critically" box (p. 3). Be especially aware of whether you're reading facts, opinions, examples, or anecdotes, and whether they support the author's ideas. Listen for the charged words, name-calling, irony, or sarcasm that signals possibly unfair bias. Would you trust the following opinion? "The nervous nags spinning their broken records on gun control haven't the foggiest notion about the importance of handgun ownership in the control of crime." Do you hear the bias in *nervous nags, broken records,* and *foggiest notion*?

While reading your source, you also should be reading yourself. The material before you, no matter how fair or objective its author may be, has been selected and organized to represent a point of view or support an opinion. It is not neutral, and neither are you. When you read, you don't merely absorb the meaning of a source; you select and organize the materials to make them meaningful to you. And you use your own assumptions, outlook, knowledge, and opinions to help you make this meaning. Therefore, as you read, you should pay close attention to your responses and to what is causing them. Note what you don't understand, where you agree or disagree, whether your responses are emotional or intellectual. Ask yourself whether your thoughts and reactions are fair, relevant, and complete.

3 Annotating your reading

People who do a lot of reading know that the way to read for greatest understanding is to annotate what they read—highlighting important passages and jotting brief notes. True, they don't annotate everything they read, but if it's important or challenging, they do. If you annotate what you read, you begin a dialogue with the authors that will deepen your understanding of their words and ideas. You'll find that your annotations—the record of your critical thinking—will be useful to you when you borrow materials from a source to include in your own writing.

Certainly, you won't write in library materials or other people's books. Notes for these sources you might jot on a sheet of paper, a note card, a "stickie pad," or a computerized notes file. But if you own the source, if it's a photocopy or a computer file, you should annotate it. You don't have to be elaborate or use colored highlighters, but you should keep a record of your understanding of a source and your reactions to it.

On page 10 is an example of an annotated reading. In a composition class emphasizing research, student Eric Martin investigated problems of overcrowding in US national parks. While doing his research, he learned of a controversial proposal to build a new community, Canyon Forest Village, to accommodate the increasing number of visitors to Grand Canyon

http://www.gcvsb.com/   A Village in the Forest   Wednesday, October 31, 1998

A Village in the Forest
A Brighter Tomorrow for Grand Canyon National Park

A Time of Crisis: A Park in Peril   Grand Canyon National Park, the crown jewel of America's national parks, faces an awesome crisis.

- Park visits have exploded by 85% since 1985 to over 5 million a year, 27,000 per day during peak season.
- By 2010, 7 to 11 million visitors will throng the park.
- Visitors wait in mile-long lines to enter the park, clog park roadways, are often turned away from motels and campgrounds.
- Local community services and retail facilities are unequipped to handle this crush of visitors.
- Federal budget cuts have left park facilities crumbling, park workers live in dilapidated housing they refer to as "dumpsters."

Park Superintendent Robert Arnberger declares, "We are under siege." What can be done to preserve America's most beloved national park?

The Best Solution: Canyon Forest Village   An ecologically designed gateway community one mile from the south entrance to Grand Canyon National Park, Canyon Forest Village is the result of six years of effort by a public/private partnership. No tax dollars will be spent in its construction.

- Nestled on 300 acres in the pines of Kaibab National Forest, Canyon Forest Village will be a sustainable development community.
- Canyon Forest Village will double the number of locally available hotel rooms and add nearly 300,000 square feet of retail space.
- The community will offer visitors a year-round conference center and a 300,000 square foot museum.
- Parking spaces for up to 10,000 cars will be provided.
- New homes, condos, and time shares will increase the recreational possibilities of the region.
- New housing will be provided for up to 3,000 employees.

Your Support for Canyon Forest Village   Join National Park Service and Forest Service employees and the members of 9 environmental groups in supporting Canyon Forest Village.

Grand Canyon Visitor Services Bureau—Last updated: October 25, 1998

This solution to over-crowding in the Park may only increase the problem by attracting visitors more interested in the resort than in the park. [Interpretation]

Note charged language. [Evaluation]

What other solutions have been offered? [Interpretation]

What do these terms mean? [Analysis]

Who is involved in this "partnership"? [Analysis]

What will be the ecological impact of creating a town ½ mile square with this many people in a region with scarce water resources? [Analysis]

What are their reasons for supporting this solution? [Analysis]

Does this organization have a relation with the Park Service or Canyon Forest Village? [Analysis]

National Park. Looking into the debate over this proposal, he discovered a Web site supporting the construction of this community.

Consider how Eric's underlining and marginal notes reveal his critical thinking as he analyzes, interprets, and evaluates the information in this document. He raises questions for further investigation, notes charged language that adds an air of urgency to the document, looks for relationships and bias in the various organizations involved, and considers the consequences of the proposed community. Through annotated reading and the critical thinking it stimulates, this student comes to a deeper understanding of his topic and begins to form opinions that he may present in his own writing. Annotating your reading will help you prepare to write as well.

How to . . . Annotate Your Reading

Highlighting. Use the following symbols to highlight sources you own, photocopies, and, when possible, computer files.

_____	Underline key words and phrases. Also underline "clue" words and phrases that indicate relationships between ideas, suggest the importance of a passage, or indicate the author's evaluation: *to conclude, fortunately, in all fairness, on the other hand,* and so forth.
|	Draw a vertical line next to important passages that you may want to quote or summarize in your own writing.
?	Place a question mark next to unfamiliar words or passages you don't understand.
+ or −	Use a plus or minus sign for passages you agree or disagree with.
*	Use an asterisk for passages an author wants you to respond to.
1, 2, 3, etc.	Number ideas in sequence or use arrows to connect related ideas.
Z	Identify where your attention drifts or you lose interest, and ask yourself why.
X-ref	Note cross-references to other sources containing related ideas. Marginally note the author of the cross-reference or other identifying information.

Notes. In the text's margins or elsewhere if the source does not belong to you, jot brief summaries of important passages, questions you have, musings, reactions, ideas about how you'll use information from your reading in your writing.

🖥 *Computer Tip:* Annotating Computer Files

Print out Internet files; then annotate them as you would a photocopy. Or, copy and paste Internet files into a word processing file. Then you can open them and add highlighting symbols or insert notes as you would to any other text file. However, be sure to use some clearly identifiable method of separating your words from your source's words, such as a row of asterisks (********) or some other keyboard symbol typed at the beginning and end of a note. If you wish to take detailed notes, create a second file and divide your computer screen into two windows to switch between, one containing your source, the other, your notes. Some word processing files even have "stickie pad" utilities you can use to attach notes to computer files.

1c Write critically: survey the writing situation

When you have a writing project, make preliminary plans by looking carefully at what you need to do. Ask yourself these questions to help you analyze and evaluate a project before you actually begin writing. You may not be able to answer them all at once, and some of your answers may change as the project unfolds. That's natural. But use the answers to guide your writing.

1 The subject and the assignment

- Has your topic been given to you as part of an assignment? Can you adapt the topic to your interests? If you have to choose a topic, what is suitable for the assignment?

- What kind of writing does the assignment require: a letter, essay, report, review, or some other form?

- What is the scope of the assignment? Do you have to cover a broad topic? How focused must your writing be because of reader interest or length and time restrictions? How much detail will you have to use? *A note on college writing:* Most college writing assignments ask you to focus on a limited, specific topic and provide as much detail as the allotted time or space allows.

- What do you know about the topic? According to the assignment, what kinds of information should be included: personal experience, facts and figures, or expert opinion? Where will you get your information: from memory, observation, reading, discussion? What experience or bias may affect your view of what you find? If you borrow others' words or ideas, what system of documentation are you required to use?

2 Your purpose and role

- What purpose does the wording of the assignment set for you? Consider instructions such as "Write a personal narrative," "Write an informative essay," "Explain," "Evaluate," and "Take a position." (To learn to interpret the instructions given in writing assignments, see 60a.)

- What writer's role have your knowledge and personal experience prepared you for? Can you play the role of an **autobiographer** writing about yourself, a **reporter** informing readers, a **teacher** explaining ideas or procedures, a **critic** making an evaluation, or a **persuader** arguing for a position, or some combination of these? Deciding on the appropriate role to play in your writing will help you find your writer's voice, strike the appropriate relation with your readers, and choose appropriate strategies for writing.

3 Audience

When you were younger, your teachers may have instructed you to write for a "general audience." This is good advice for writers first learning to write publicly. But frequent, successful writers know that no audience is "general." Audiences may be large or small, one or a million readers, but all members of an audience bring to their reading specific knowledge, expectations, opinions, and experiences that influence what they read and how they respond. As you plan your writing, envision the people in your target audience: Who are they? What do they know about your topic? What do they want or need from you? Ask the questions in the "How to Profile an Audience" box (p. 14). Then use your answers to plan how you'll express your ideas to meet your audience's interests and needs.

Consider the informative and argumentative essay on bicycle commuting written by John Chen, a student (see 4f). He knew that most individuals in his college audience would be motorists, and so, as he planned his writing, he had to consider the opinion of many that bicycles and motorists cannot share the same road safely. In his essay, he had to show that the two really could travel safely together. So, too, Eric Martin, the writer of a persuasive essay on overcrowded national parks (see 58d), had to consider his audience as he prepared a solution to his problem and then pose something his college-age readers would accept and act on.

A cautionary note: Sometimes, it's not wise to think too much about your audience early in a project, when you're exploring a topic or trying to discover your opinions. Doing so may cramp your reasoning or creativity. But as soon as you begin thinking of the actual writing you'll do, think carefully about your readers. Your supporting details, focus, organization, style, and word choice—all these depend on who your readers are and the response you want from them.

How to . . . Profile an Audience

As you begin planning your writing, answer these questions to help you envision your readers and plan how to communicate with them.

1. How can you classify your readers? Are they (1) **allies** who will accept almost anything you write, (2) **potential allies** who need only to be informed to accept your ideas, (3) **disinterested observers** who want information above all else, (4) **skeptics** who expect careful reasoning and detailed support, (5) **opponents** who require abundant proof and may not accept your ideas even if you provide it?
2. What do these readers know about your topic? What assumptions, biases, or knowledge gaps will influence their responses? What illustrations will help them understand?
3. What do readers expect from you: personal experience, information, explanation, evaluation, proof, entertainment? What writing style is appropriate for addressing them, informal or formal?
4. What do these readers believe about your sources of information? Which ones will they accept as authoritative? Which might they reject as superficial, biased, or inaccurate?

4 The final draft

- Are there length specifications?
- When is the final draft due? How much time do you have for each stage of your writing: gathering materials, planning, writing, revising, typing, and proofreading?
- What is the appropriate format for your final copy? (For academic writing, see 46a; for business writing, see Chapter 61.)

🖥 *Computer Tip:* Creating Templates

You can create a master computer file, called a **template,** that lists all the questions you'll need to ask yourself as you survey a writing assignment. Use the questions here in 1c, or make shorter files focusing on a specific set of questions about, for example, your audience. Then, at the beginning of a writing project, open this master file and answer the questions. Be sure to save your file of answered questions under a new and appropriate file name, such as "Survey#1" or "Audience: Autobiography."

2 "Inventing" Your Writing

Writers, like inventors, create their work not all at once but in stages, through trial and error, reflection, and discovery. As you begin this creative process, guide your writing by making the critical survey recommended in 1c. Then use the tips and options in this chapter to turn the results of your survey into the actual subject matter of your writing. Because this process differs from one writer to another and one kind of writing to another, you'll want to practice and experiment to discover which invention strategies are right for you and the writing you do.

Computer Tip: Writing Successfully with Computers

Computers are an especially powerful tool for doing the exploratory, multistage writing recommended here. To write successfully with computers, use the tips offered here and throughout *The Ready Reference Handbook.*

- *Saving your work.* Save your writing frequently. If you lose power or your program crashes, anything not saved into permanent memory—on floppy or hard disk—will be lost.
- *Backing up your files.* To protect against damaged disks, save files on backup disks.
- *Making templates.* For frequent assignments, make templates. These are files that you create to reuse every time you begin a new project. They may contain questions or other prompts that guide you through each writing project. Consider templates for audience profiles, questions to answer about your topics, note-taking formats, outline formats, thesis or purpose statements, revision and editing checklists, formats for final drafts. Once you've created and saved an empty template file (named "Outline," for example), all you have to do is open it and begin typing at the appropriate prompt. If you want to save your work, save it under a new file name (for example, "Outline 1"). The original, empty template will stay in place for your next project.

2a | Explore possible topics

As you make a critical survey of a writing assignment and begin to see what to do (see 1c), create choices for yourself. The British novelist E. M. Forster once asked, "How can I know what I think till I see what I say?"

Help yourself see what you think about possible topics by doing exploratory writing. Examine the following kinds of exploratory writing, and adapt them to your style and habits. Some may be more useful than others or appropriate only for certain kinds of writing.

1 Keeping a journal or diary

These daily records of experience, reflection, and opinion can be a valuable source of personally important topics that you may decide to transform into public or academic writing.

2 Brainstorming

To brainstorm, simply make free-association lists. Start with a topic or whatever first comes to mind. Follow wherever your mind leads. Don't worry if you can't think of much the first time. Lists should be easy and fast. When you finish, underline key words or phrases to explore further.

Brrr! Cold outside

Almost too cold to bike to school this morning--

Snow on the way home--

Wisconsin last spring, caught in a freak April storm

"Just look at you!" cried the woman at the quick mart where I stopped--snow mounded on my helmet, me covered with slush, soaking wet, shaking in the cold

<u>Drivers' strange looks</u> when it's this cold--disbelief, mostly: "What are you doing out there?" their eyes ask.

Actually, I'm doing okay--<u>feeling good</u> in the crisp air. Toes don't get cold till I'm almost to school or home. Easy trip unless there's rain, snow, or headwind.

Pedal, pant, puff--<u>endorphins flowing,</u> a steady 17-18 mph this a.m.

In all that traffic, I'm getting where I'm going just about as fast as the cars are, backed up one after another in endless traffic jams.

Honk, inch ahead, stop, honk, inch ahead

Commuting--<u>bicycle commuting</u>

good for <u>health, fitness</u>

good for everybody's <u>health--less pollution,</u> one less car--

This brainstorm may make little sense to anyone but the writer, but if you look, you can see several topics that the writer might explore further, expand, rearrange, and turn into the materials for a full-length writing project.

2a `dev`

3 Topic mapping (clustering and branching)

If you like to visualize what to say before you write, draw a **topic map.** Put a topic in the middle of a sheet of paper, draw a circle around it, and then draw branches that lead to related topics and subtopics. Leave room in case you think of other branches and topics to add later.

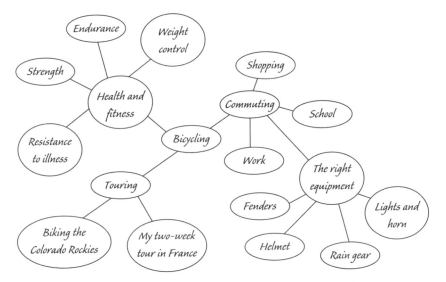

4 Freewriting

Like brainstorming and mapping, **freewriting** is free association on paper. The difference is that, for most people, freewriting expresses thoughts more fully in sentence- and paragraph-length statements and may lead more deeply into a subject. Many writers find it a useful activity throughout the writing process as a way to explore new or challenging ideas. In freewriting, your aims are to loosen up your mind, go where it leads you, and record what it gives you.

Looping, an expanded form of freewriting, will help you focus your thinking and narrow a topic. When you finish a freewriting, read it and look for the central thought or most interesting point. Use that as the opening for a new freewriting. When you finish this second exploration, look again for the central thought or most interesting point. Use that to begin a third exploration. Sometimes you'll circle around a topic, examining it from different perspectives; at other times you'll spiral into a topic, probing it more deeply each time you write.

17

How to . . . Explore a Topic

Follow these tips for doing exploratory writing. Notice that some tips apply to some kinds of exploration more than to others.

1. You can do exploratory writing in two ways. In unfocused explorations, write whatever comes to mind, whether everything connects or not. In focused explorations, try to focus on one topic, unless you get pulled to something more interesting.
2. Set a time limit, usually 7 to 15 minutes. Start writing about whatever comes to mind the moment you begin. Write by hand, on a typewriter, or at a computer.
3. Don't stop. If your mind suddenly goes blank, write "blank, blank, blank" or repeat your last word until thoughts begin flowing again.
4. Don't censor. Write whatever comes to mind, however strange it sounds. It may lead to something important or powerful. If you don't like what you've written when you finish, you can throw it away.
5. Don't change anything. If you write something one way and think of another way, make a slash (/) and then write the second version.
6. Don't stop to correct mistakes. Don't worry about them. You're only exploring.

5 Choosing a topic

If you've surveyed the writing assignment (see 1c) and explored possible topics, you'll probably see what's best to choose. Or, if you already have a topic, you'll see more clearly what is most interesting about it. A good writing topic has these characteristics:

- It is important. A good topic is important to you and your readers.

- It is fresh. A good topic is new to you or your readers, or your approach to a familiar topic is fresh. Don't reject topics that at first seem quirky or strange. They may inspire your freshest writing.

- It is challenging. Choose topics that challenge your thinking, curiosity, or feeling. Easy topics may lead to boredom for you and your readers.

🖥 *Computer Tip:* Exploratory Writing

If you're having trouble getting started, try darkening the screen and writing out your thoughts without looking at them. Or try online brainstorming through e-mail, Internet chat rooms, or networked computers; toss ideas back and forth with other people to see how they evolve.

2b | Focus your writing

Most topics first come to you as an inviting—sometimes perplexing—array of possibilities. They are open-ended, broad, general—unfocused. **Focusing** a project means becoming clear about your subject, what you want to do with it, and the point you want to make. *A reminder:* You may not be able to decide everything at once. In fact, if you focus on too much too soon, you may not see important parts of your topic. But before you begin a first draft, try these strategies.

1 Narrowing your topic

Most topics discovered in exploratory writing or listed in assignments are too broad for you to cover them adequately in the space and time available. Therefore, focus on one narrow but important part of your topic and on the significance of that part.

BROAD TOPICS				NARROW TOPICS
My life on the move: from the city to the suburbs	→	What I learned moving 5 times in 18 years	→	What moving has taught me about good people and good communities
My grandmother	→	My grandmother, an old-fashioned artist	→	My grandmother's lost art: bobbin lace making
Bicycling	→	Bicycle commuting	→	How to increase bicycle commuting
America's national parks		Overcrowding in America's national parks		The environmental consequences of over-crowding in America's national parks
Charlotte Perkins Gilman's short story "The Yellow Wall-Paper"	→	The symbolic wallpaper	→	The wallpaper as a reflection of the narra-tor's state of mind

2 Writing a purpose statement

After surveying the requirements of the assignment and exploring your ideas, write a tentative **purpose statement.** Briefly tell yourself what you want to accomplish in your writing. This purpose may change as your project unfolds, but writing it out early will guide you.

I want to inform urban and suburban readers that, for many, bicycling is a solution to the frustrations of rush-hour commuting.

This writer's purpose is to inform; the writer's roles are to act as a reporter and a teacher.

3 Asking questions

Jot down questions based on the reporter's *who, what, when, where, why,* and *how,* or use the critical thinking questions listed in the "How to Think Critically" box (p. 3). Ask other questions relevant to your topic. Your answers might become the materials for your project.

Who should become a bicycle commuter?

What problems do bicycle commuters face?

What are the benefits of bicycle commuting?

What are the best conditions for bicycle commuting?

Why do some motorists object to sharing the road with bicyclists?

How can a cyclist begin commuting by bicycle?

How can a community or business begin to encourage bicycle commuters?

2c | Consider your voice (persona)

Everything you write has a **voice,** also called a **persona.** Whether your writing is personal or public, informal or formal, opinionated or objective, whether you appear in your writing (as "I") or not, your writing speaks with your voice. Readers hear it in your words and sentences, in your attitude toward your subject, and in your relationship with these readers. This voice is the written expression of your personality, and you should write and revise to express that personality. Creating a voice is one of the great pleasures of writing.

But just as you modify the way you speak to suit various occasions, so should you adapt your persona, adjusting it as you would adjust the volume, tone, and balance on a stereo to produce the best sound. Each of these features of a writer's voice can be adjusted toward one or the other end of a spectrum:

Formality	Informal vocabulary	←•→	Formal vocabulary
Tone	Negative attitude	←•→	Positive attitude
Balance	Understatement	←•→	Overstatement
Manner of Address	Irony, sarcasm, indirectness	←•→	"Straight talk"

How to . . . **Create Your Persona**

Follow these guidelines as you write and revise.

1. Your writing should sound like you, speaking in a way suitable to the occasion, formal or informal (see 27a–d). Writing and speaking are different, but good writing almost always sounds like speech. "Talk" to readers as you write.
2. Choose words true to your knowledge and experience. Don't worry about writing impressively. What will impress is your accuracy, honesty, and command of the facts.
3. Choose positive, negative, or neutral words that accurately express your feelings but that also express the amount of objectivity appropriate to the occasion.
4. As you revise, read aloud and listen to your sentences. If necessary, rewrite sentences so that they emphasize your most important words and have the rhythms of speech (see 21a–f).

1 The persona for formal writing

In formal academic and professional writing, aim to sound fair, objective, and relatively serious. Generally, make your style straightforward and to the point. Use "I" to refer to yourself if necessary, but focus on your subject. Avoid slang and most contractions, but don't sound pompous or stuffy. Whatever you write should sound like you speaking in a voice suitable to the subject and occasion. (See also 27a1 and 2.)

2 The persona for personal or informal writing

The more personal your subject, the more informal you can be. In informal writing you have lots of room for variety in vocabulary, attitude, and style of expression. But keep in mind the knowledge and interests of your readers.

$2d$ Write a tentative thesis

When you know enough about the subject and purpose of your writing, write a tentative statement of the point you want to make—your **thesis.** Usually a sentence but sometimes longer, the thesis in its final form will be the primary controlling idea or opinion holding your writing together, the basic message you want your writing to express. It may be any kind of assertion: a factual statement, a generalization, a cause-and-effect statement, an evaluation, a prediction, or a proposal. Consider these thesis statements:

- An informative thesis (an evaluation):

  Bicycles are a safe, practical, economical solution to the problems of rush-hour commuting.

- The theme of an autobiographical essay (cause and effect):

  Moving five times in eighteen years, from a housing project to an apartment building to a house in the suburbs, has given me invaluable knowledge about getting along with people and what makes for good communities.

Whatever its topic or assertion, a thesis is usually the most important statement in a piece of writing. At the beginning of a project, it will help you decide what to say. In a later, more detailed version based on the information you've gathered, it will act as a point-to-point map to keep you on course as you write a draft. Still later, as you revise your project, you'll compare your thesis to what you've actually written to see whether your point has remained the same or changed. If it has changed, you'll rewrite the thesis to fit your new discoveries. In the final version the thesis will help readers answer the one question they almost always ask: "So what's the point?"

How to . . . Write a Tentative Thesis

Early in a writing project, use the following formula to write a tentative thesis. Begin with the words *My point is that,* and then follow with a statement that identifies your topic and makes an assertion about it.

My point is that to ease the problems of commuting, federal highway funds and state gasoline taxes should be used to create bicycle lanes on city streets and wide shoulders on secondary roads.

If you can't write a thesis early in your project, because you don't yet know enough about your topic, write it later, after you've learned what you need to know.

1 Guidelines for writing an effective thesis

As your knowledge grows and your thinking changes, rewrite your thesis following these guidelines:

- *Making assertions instead of asking questions.* Write a sentence that makes a point or, if necessary, several sentences, but not a question. If all you can write is a question, you're not ready to write a thesis. Answer your question first. Compare these original and revised statements:

Original *Are home-schooled students as well educated as students who attend public schools?*

Revised *Standardized test scores and college graduation rates indicate that home-schooled students are as well educated as students who attend public schools.*

[The revised version is an assertion that answers the question in the original version and identifies the subject matter the writer will cover in her essay.]

- *Writing a thesis instead of a purpose statement.* Be sure to write a thesis statement rather than a purpose statement. A **thesis statement** focuses on your topic and says something about it. A **purpose statement** focuses on your paper and says something about it rather than your topic. Compare these statements:

Purpose *In my paper I intend to examine the case against the death penalty.*

Thesis *The death penalty does not deter murderers from their crimes, and it is unfairly applied to the poor and minorities.*

[The purpose statement focuses primarily on the writer and his paper rather than the topic of the paper. The thesis statement makes two assertions that the writer will attempt to prove. The thesis gives his paper focus and direction.]

- *Avoiding "So?" statements.* A "So?" thesis is a statement that prompts readers to ask, "So? What's the point?" Do more than announce your topic or state a fact. Make a complete assertion about your topic. Compare these thesis statements:

So? *Mercury poisoning kills many people each year.*

Revised *The many deaths each year from mercury poisoning can be prevented by more detailed consumer education, extensive employee training in the handling of mercury, and stricter regulation of mercury waste disposal.*

[The first sentence may state a tragic fact, but it lacks a point. The revised version makes three assertions—or points—about how to prevent this tragedy.]

- *Using accurate and specific words.* Replace broad, vague words with specific words that say precisely what you mean. Compare the original thesis and a revised version:

Original *In Charlotte Perkins Gilman's "The Yellow Wall-Paper," the narrator's doctor-husband does many things that drive her crazy.*

Revised *The narrator of Charlotte Perkins Gilman's "The Yellow Wall-Paper" is driven insane by her doctor-husband's misdiagnosis of her depression and by his indifference to her need for intellectual and social stimulation.*

[In the original version, the words *many things* and *crazy* are broad and vague. They do not tell readers what the husband does and whether his wife is merely angry or actually insane. The language in the revised version is both specific and accurate.]

- *Matching your thesis and supporting information.* Be sure the facts and other details you've gathered support your thesis. Revise the thesis and the body of your writing until they fit each other point by point.

- *Writing a reader's thesis.* After writing your essay, cut the *My point is that* formula as you revise, keeping only your actual assertion. The formula helps you make a point, but readers won't need it to get your point. With the formula removed, the thesis in the "How to Write a Tentative Thesis" box (p. 22) becomes

To ease the problems of commuting, federal highway funds and state gasoline taxes should be used to create bicycle lanes on city streets and wide shoulders on secondary roads.

2 Unwritten thesis statements

In some kinds of writing the writer decides not to state a thesis directly. It may be unnecessary, impossible, or unwise to state a point, so the writing makes an implicit point. Readers will still "get the message," because everything supports that unwritten thesis, develops a dominant mood, and fulfills the overall purpose. Note, however, that in most academic writing you will be expected to state your thesis clearly and explicitly.

3 Placement of your thesis

Thesis statements usually appear early in a writing. If they're clear and especially dramatic, they may come in the first sentence. But more often they appear at the end of an introduction, after the writer prepares readers for the main point. Placed in the introduction, the thesis acts to guide writers as they write and readers as they read. (See the introduction to student John Chen's essay in 4f.)

Sometimes the thesis doesn't appear until the conclusion, revealing an important discovery or summing up what has come before. If you place a thesis at the end of a paper, your introduction must point the way to it, perhaps hinting at its message, describing the problem it solves, or posing the question it answers. (See the conclusion to the sample report in 54d.)

4 Other thesis-like statements

Thesis statements are usually associated with informative and explanatory essays. But other kinds of writing also depend on thesis-like statements to give them unity, focus, and direction. Most of the writing you do will make a point of some kind or other.

- **Personal narratives** frequently contain a **discovery statement** to sum up the meaning or lesson of the experiences that the writer describes. Often this statement appears near the end of the story, at a moment of discovery or revelation.

- **Reviews** generally contain a **dominant impression statement** that gives the reviewer's overall judgment of the movie, book, product, or other topic under review. This statement may appear at the beginning or the end of the writing.

- **Arguments and persuasive writing** contain a **claim** that the writer intends to prove or to demonstrate as plausible. (See 57a.)

- **Reports** contain a **conclusion** that sums up the meaning, significance, or uses of the information in the body of the report. (See 61d2.)

2e Gather the materials for your writing

Gather the information for your project by remembering, reflecting, observing, reading, or discussing. If the project will be brief, you can keep most of your ideas in your head or jot down a list of points to cover. But if your subject is complex or unfamiliar—as is likely in most college writing projects—you'll have to take notes (see 49d and e). Here are ways you can approach a topic. The types of information you end up using will depend on your purpose and your readers' interests. (See 6b.)

- Gather facts and figures to inform, evaluate, or argue. (See 6b4.)

- Quote or summarize eyewitnesses, experts, or others involved with your subject. Use quotations to add life, variety, and authority to your writing. (Be sure to credit your sources when you borrow words or ideas. See 50e.)

- Describe scenes, people, features, traits, processes, and events in autobiographical and informative writing. (See 6b3.)

- Tell stories or anecdotes to inform, evaluate, or argue. (See 6b1.)

- Give examples (6b5), compare and contrast (6b6), classify (6b9), and define (6b10) to inform, evaluate, or argue.

- Explain. Restate unfamiliar ideas in familiar words, give instructions, or add details to expand a subject and make it clear.

- Create metaphors and similes to dramatize feelings and ideas. (See 26c.)

- Interpret your subject. State its meaning or significance and describe its implications—where it leads. Draw conclusions that tell what everything adds up to.

💻 *Computer Tip:* A Template for Taking Notes

Use the columns or tables feature of your word processing program to create a note-taking template. Adjust margins and spacing so you can take several notes on each printed page. As you begin taking notes for a new project, save your file under an appropriate name—for example, "Notes1," "Notes: Res.Paper." Be sure to document the sources of your notes (see 49d). When you finish taking notes, print the file and cut the pages into individual slips that you can arrange and rearrange to help you organize your ideas.

3 Planning and Organizing

3a Refocus your writing

Because writing is a process of discovery, your topic and what you intend to say about it will probably change as you prepare to write. New information will lead to new ideas, perhaps a new thesis; your original purpose may change; you may change your relations to your audience. Therefore, before you begin a first draft—or later, after completing a draft—pause, step back, and reconsider your project in light of all you've learned. Compare what you have so far with the survey you made as you began (see 1c). Answer these questions:

- At this point in your project, what is your exact subject?

- What will your paper contain: facts, feelings, opinions, personal experiences or observations? Are they reliable and suitable to the occasion? For most kinds of serious informative writing, personal experience or observation may not be suitable or sufficient. Consider your audience's interests and needs.

- Do you have what you need to fulfill your purpose? If you do not, should you gather more information or change your purpose?

- Do you have enough information to support your point (your thesis) and communicate its message? If you do not, what do you need? Should you rewrite your thesis to fit what you've found?

3b Plan a communications strategy

Experienced writers usually make detailed plans for communicating with readers. You'll write more effectively if you plan a communications strategy that includes the following elements.

1 Organization

Arrange the content of your essay to fulfill your purpose and satisfy readers' needs. You can organize your writing to:

- Tell a story (personal narrative, how-to writing, steps in a process). (See 6b1 and 2.)
- Present causes and effects. (See 6b8.)
- Describe (scenic arrangement, part-by-part analysis). (See 6b3.)
- Compare or contrast (point-by-point or the block method). (See 6b6.)
- Classify. (See 6b9.)
- Emphasize what is most important (organizing from least to most important or from most to least).
- Give the pros and cons of an issue and then state your opinion.
- Explain a problem and pose a solution.

For additional organizing patterns, see the research project (50b1), the argument (58a3), and the report (61d2).

2 Introduction

Think of an opening to attract and focus your readers' interest. (See 6c.) It should identify your topic, suggest your purpose, and, usually, state your thesis.

3 Lead

As you plan an introduction, try to think of an opening line, your **lead,** to start you writing and draw readers into your introduction.

4 Title

Think of an original title that is informative, intriguing, or both, but don't make it a baffling mystery. Come up with a word or phrase that arouses curiosity and, if possible, suggests your topic or even your thesis.

5 Conclusion

Good writing doesn't abruptly stop, nor does it slowly unravel. Bring your writing to a satisfying close that ties up loose ends and leaves readers feeling that everything has come together. (See 6d.)

3c | Write an outline, if necessary

For many kinds of writing, especially on difficult or unfamiliar topics, outlines are almost essential. Especially for informative, technical, and research writing, you can use outlines to organize ideas, guide your writing, and later reveal the actual design of various drafts. Depending on your project, you may write three related kinds of outlines, each a version of the others: a sketch, working, and final-draft formal outline. For some papers, a sketch outline is all you'll need; for others, you'll need all three.

1 Sketch outline

A **sketch outline** is little more than a list of major points in the order you want to cover them. As you begin organizing, experiment with sketch outlines until you find one that is right for your ideas and purpose.

Bicycles are a safe, practical, economical solution to the problems of rush-hour commuting.

I. The myths and realities of bicycle commuting in America
   A. Bicycling as a safe means of transportation
   B. Bicycling as a practical means of transportation
II. Becoming a bicycle commuter
   A. How to get started
   B. The benefits of bicycle commuting

2 Working outline

A **working outline** is developed from a sketch outline and is divided into topics and subtopics. It is the most detailed of the three outlines and will function as a map to follow as you write. As a kind of rough draft of a rough draft, a good working outline has a place for almost everything:

- Introduction
- Thesis or main idea
- Major topics and subtopics, including facts, key details, illustrations, explanations, and quotations
- Major transitional statements
- Conclusion

You will, no doubt, think of other things to say while drafting, but the clearer and more detailed your plans now, the easier your first draft will be to write.

How to . . . Organize Your Ideas and Write an Outline

To organize your writing, choose from these tips.

1. Look for organizing clues in key words, in the sequence of ideas in your thesis, or in the list of questions readers might ask about your topic.
2. If your exploratory writing doesn't follow a logical sequence, number the topics in the order you'll write about them.
3. Jot down a list of topics you'll cover (a sketch outline).
4. Draw a **flow chart,** a conceptual diagram showing relations and connections. Put topics in boxes arranged in sequence and connected by lines that trace the path of your writing. Use other boxes and lines to insert advice to yourself about details to remember, quotations, facts, transitional statements, and ideas about introductions and conclusions.
5. Create a working outline that includes most of what you want to say:

   - Sort your materials to see whether everything fits under the major headings of a sketch outline. Revise your sketch outline if necessary.
   - Then arrange your materials in the order you want to follow as you write your paper. Write a detailed working outline that reflects this order.
   - Look for relationships among ideas, and group them as subheadings under headings. Beware of long "shopping lists" of topics.
   - If you can't decide where to put something, put it in two or more places in your outline and trust your writing to show you where it belongs.
   - If an important idea doesn't fit, write a new outline with a place for it. If you're uncertain whether an element is necessary, write a reminder to see whether it belongs after you've written a draft.

3 Final-draft formal outline

Your instructor may require you to hand in a **formal outline** with the final draft of some projects. Base the outline on the organization of your finished paper. It probably will be longer than a sketch outline but shorter than a working outline, often about a page. Include your thesis statement, list your major topics, and follow the guidelines for formal outlines listed below and illustrated in 3c4.

   - Be sure at least two subheadings follow each heading. Because subheadings divide the ideas in a heading, you must have at least two subheadings under each heading. You can't divide a topic into only one subtopic. If you have only one subheading, you may have simply restated the original heading.

- Be sure your subheadings are logical. Because subheadings break up or divide ideas in the headings they stand under, they must reflect the ideas and even the language of those broader headings.

- Be sure your headings are grammatically parallel. If heading *I.* is a complete sentence, headings *II.* and *III.* must also be complete sentences. If *A.* under heading *II.* is a noun phrase, *B.* must also be a noun phrase, and so forth. (See Chapter 19.)

- Use standard outline subdivisions.

    I.
       A.
       B.
          1.
          2.
             a.
             b.
                (1)
                (2)
                   (a)
                   (b)
    II.

💻 *Computer Tip:* **An Outline Template**

Create an outline template to use whenever you write an outline. Use the correct numerals, letters, and spacing for the standard outline subdivisions (see 3c3). Include enough subheading numbers and letters for a lengthy, detailed outline. Later, as you use the template to outline a project, cut unnecessary subheadings. Save each new outline under an appropriate file name.

4   Sample formal outline

Notice how the example follows the guidelines for formal outlines given above in 3c3. (For a sample formal outline arranged in the format for a typed paper, see Chapter 53.)

Thesis statement	Thesis: Bicycles are a safe, practical, economical solution to the problems of rush-hour commuting.
Logical subdivisions: Every heading has two or more subheads clearly related to the headings.	I. The myths and realities of bicycle commuting in the United States
	A. Bicycling is a safe means of transportation.
	1. The fears motorists have about bicycling safety
	2. The facts of bicycling safety
	B. Bicycling is a practical means of transportation.
	1. Motorists' objections to bicycle commuting
	2. Widespread support for bicycle commuting
Parallel grammatical form: Coordinate headings are grammatically parallel. For example, I and II are noun phrases; IA and IB are complete sentences.	a. Numerous bicycle commuters
	b. Business support
	c. Federal, state, and local government support
	II. Becoming a bicyle commuter
	A. How to begin bicycle commuting
	B. The benefits of bicycle commuting

chapter

4 Writing, Revising, and Editing

4*a* Write a first draft

Like experienced writers, you should expect to write more than one draft of important, complex projects. Each revision provides an opportunity for rethinking, rearranging, and rewording based on the discoveries of the preceding draft. When you write a first draft, let yourself go; you don't have to get everything right the first time. If you have the information you need and have planned your project, writing a first draft should feel almost like doing a freewriting once you get going.

If you're struck by writer's block as you stare at that blank first page, try these tips:

- Reread your plans and start your writing with the first thing that comes to mind, as if you were doing a freewriting. The words and ideas will start to flow.

- If you can't begin at the beginning, begin in the middle. Come back and write your opening later, after you're warmed up.

- Instead of beginning your project, write a letter to your audience. Tell them what you'd like to write about. Or write a letter to yourself about what you want to say and your frustrations.

- Try visualizing something to do with your subject. Start by writing about what you see.

- Write an advance summary of your project: "In this essay I have tried to . . . " Pretend you're finished. Describe what you would like to have written.

How to . . . Write a First Draft

Follow these tips for writing a successful first draft.

1. Write major sections or a complete draft at one sitting. Give yourself time to get warmed up.
2. Whether you write by hand, typewriter, or computer, leave lots of room to revise. Double-space or triple-space, and leave wide margins.
3. Don't bother editing or correcting. If you're unsure of a word or phrase, write out several versions separated by slashes (/). Put a checkmark (✓) in the margin to mark passages to fix later.
4. Use a blank line or row of asterisks (******) to mark easy-to-find places to fill in missing words or information as you revise a draft.
5. If you have to stop, give yourself a thread to pick up when you return. Start writing a sentence or paragraph that you know how to finish, and then stop in the middle of it.

🖥 *Computer Tip:* Writing a First Draft

Write revision notes to yourself surrounded by the pound sign (######) or another easy-to-see symbol. Your word processing program may even have a "stickie pad" feature, enabling you to attach notes to your text. Or you can create a "Notes" file as you draft, split your computer screen, and switch between your draft and your notes. If you're unsure whether to keep something you've written, cut and paste it to the end of your file, where you can reconsider it as you revise.

4b Revise to say what you want to say

Novice writers think they're nearly finished when they complete a first draft. For them, revision is correcting or touch-up work. Experienced writers, however, know that a single draft rarely says all they want it to say or says it in the best way. The discovery process they began with exploratory writing continues as they revise. For them, revision means "reseeing" and then rewriting based on what they've seen. How to revise? Consider these strategies.

1 Letting your writing cool off

Don't confuse the elation you feel when you finish a draft—or your frustration—with a judgment of the quality of your writing. If you can, wait awhile before you revise. Your perspective and objectivity will improve.

2 Identifying the status of your draft

Ask yourself, "Is this draft a dress rehearsal, complete except for finishing touches? Is it exploratory, still searching for a point or something to hold it together? Is it experimental, trying out topics and styles?" Your answers will help you see what to do next.

3 Considering the big picture first

Imagine you're a camera with a telephoto lens. Look at the big picture first. Decide on the status of major elements such as your thesis, its support, and your overall design. Add information, cut, rearrange, condense, or substitute to make your point and fulfill your purpose. When you're satisfied with the big picture, zoom in and focus on individual paragraphs, sentences, and words. Don't waste time fixing small problems before you fix the big ones.

4 Comparing plans and results

- Compare the draft of your paper to the original plans you made as you first surveyed the assignment (see 1c). Did you fulfill the requirements of the assignment or meet your reader's needs? Revise accordingly.

- Compare your original thesis with what you've written in your conclusion. Look for "Aha!" statements. Often, near the end of a draft, writers write something that makes them say "Aha!" They think they've found a conclusion, but what they may have found is the real point of the paper—a new thesis, different from the original. If you find such a statement, rewrite it as your new thesis, move it to the introduction of your essay, and revise to support it.

- Compare your outline to your draft. If the two are different, which makes more sense of your ideas?

🖥 *Computer Tip:* **Revising with a Computer**

(1) Revise on hard copy. Experienced computer users move from "on-screen" text to printed "hard copy" of their writing when they begin revising. Revision is easier when you can lay your projects out before you, page by page, rather than scrolling back and forth through a document on-screen. Revise and reprint as often as necessary.
(2) Save multiple versions. If you make significant changes to a draft but are unsure whether they're the right ones, save several versions of your draft under different file names—for example, "Essay 1a" and "Essay 1b." Compare printed versions and choose the best.

4c Use peer review to help you revise

Professional writers have reviewers to help them evaluate their writing. You should, too. In many college classes peer review is a frequent activity. On your own you can form readers' groups to share and improve your writing.

1 Reading as a peer reviewer

When you review another person's writing, your most valuable traits will be honesty, tact, sensitivity to your experiences of reading, and awareness of the writer's purpose. Your aim is not to tell the writer how you would write but to help the writer say what he or she wants to say. As a reviewer, you may play three roles:

- As a **respondent** you give the writer feedback about your experience of reading. Tell what you thought and felt as you read, what you understood or didn't, where you followed or lost the writer's thread. This role helps writers see the impact of their writing.

- As an **editor** you show the writer how to fulfill his or her intentions. If asked, you may give advice about subject matter, organization, style, and grammatical matters. Be specific, detailed, and practical.

- As a **critic** you evaluate. The best critics are the most descriptive and factual, describing what something is or is not, what it does or doesn't do, rather than whether something is good or not. To paraphrase a famous poet, your aim is to tell the truth in the kindest

How to . . . Make a Peer Review

Use these questions to help you review others' writing—and your own. Tell reviewers which questions to answer about your writing, or ask them to respond to the ones they think important. First consider the project as a whole.

1. What is the subject? Does it change from one page to the next? If it does, which subject is right for this project? (See 2a5 and 2b1.)
2. Is the purpose of the writing autobiographical, informative, persuasive, or critical? Does it change? If it does, what purpose is appropriate? (See 1c2 and 2b2.)
3. Given the content, who is the audience for this project? Are readers supposed to respond with sympathy, understanding, evaluation, agreement, or enjoyment? Will this project achieve its purpose? What changes would make it more effective? (See 1c3.)
4. Does this project have a thesis, main idea, or overall mood? Point it out or describe it. Does the writing provide enough detail to illustrate, explain, or support its point? What should be added? (See 2d and e.)
5. Can you follow this project from start to finish? What reorganization would make its ideas clearer or easier to follow? (See 3b and c.)

When the project seems to say all that is necessary to fulfill its purpose, consider how effectively it will communicate with its intended audience.

6. Does the project have a distinctive writer's voice? What changes would make this voice more emphatic or appropriate? (See 2c.)
7. What does the opening do to attract readers and help them predict the project's subject, purpose, thesis, organization, or style? What changes would make the opening more interesting to readers? (See 6c.)
8. Consider whether each paragraph focuses on a single topic and says all that needs to be said about it. What changes would improve the paragraphs in this project or make them fit more smoothly with preceding or following paragraphs? (See Chapters 5–7.)
9. Are any sentences hard to follow? What additions, cuts, or rearrangements would make them clearer or more emphatic? (See Chapters 20–24.)
10. Are any words inaccurate, vague, abstract, or ambiguous? Are any charged with inappropriate feeling or bias? What are better alternatives? Can any words be cut without loss of meaning or feeling? (See Chapters 25–29.)
11. Does the project appear to be correct in grammar, punctuation, and spelling? Is it appropriately formatted? What changes are necessary? (See Chapters 11–19 and 33–46.)

words possible. Play this role only when asked by writers you know well. Tell writers what you see as the status of their writing. Is it a dress rehearsal, nearly finished? Or does it seem exploratory or experimental? Explain your answer.

2 Sharing your writing with peer reviewers

If you share your writing with readers outside class, check with your instructor for a definition of fair editorial assistance. If you know what you want, ask for specific feedback. But don't talk too much, don't explain, and don't apologize for what you've written. If you do, you'll color readers' views and prevent them from giving honest responses. As you listen, remember that this is your paper and you have the final say. If their advice makes sense, use it. If it doesn't—well, thanks, but no thanks.

3 Creating a discussion agenda for peer reviewers

The following list will direct you to "How to" lists of questions that will help you read as a peer reviewer or provide reviewers with questions to answer about your writing.

- General questions for revision and editing. See "How to Make a Peer Review," p. 35.
- Research projects. See "How to Revise and Edit a Research Project," p. 335.
- Argument and persuasion. See "How to Revise and Edit Persuasive Writing," p. 406.
- Writing about literature. See "How to Revise and Edit a Literary Essay," p. 418.

4d Edit for your readers

1 The aims of editing

When you revise, you're focusing primarily on your ideas and message. When you edit, you're focusing on your readers and rewriting to help them get your message. Editing is a paragraph-by-paragraph, line-by-line process. Consider the edited paragraph about bicycle commuting that follows. The student writer, John Chen, made typical editorial improvements—the kinds you'll make in your writing:

- Improving accuracy and brevity. The writer cut and added words to increase accuracy and brevity.

- Adding important information and details. He inserted additional information and details to develop and clarify his proposal.
- Adapting the content for the intended audience. He cut a sentence that might offend readers who are motorists.
- Increasing precision and vividness. He cut vague, general words and substituted descriptive details.
- Rearranging for clarity and emphasis. He moved one passage earlier in the paragraph to reorganize for emphasis.

What will end commuters' rush-hour nightmare
~~The cycling solution to the problem of commuters' gridlock already~~
solution for all, however.
~~exists in sketch form. What it consists of~~ is not a single ~~one-way for~~

~~all plan~~ Commuting problems and needs differ from community to

community, region to region. The best solutions will be local. Each will

specific
have a number of parts, and each part will solve a local travel problem.
All that may be needed is public service announcements to encourage bicycle commuting.
In some communities, few changes are required. In other communities,

⌣ *ways*   *park paths or*
converting abandoned railroad lines to green ~~paths~~ or improving other off-road

bikeways is the right solution. In others, parking might be restricted along

busy streets during peak travel times. ~~The police might begin ticketing~~

~~and the courts prosecuting drivers who harass bicyclists exercising their~~

-s,
~~right to the road.~~ In still other communities, ~~where highways have long~~

repaved with widened
~~been crumbling, aging~~ highways might be ~~widened to provide wide~~
dangerous sewer grates might be removed, and high curbs eliminated. Larger,
shoulders, ~~or eliminate high curbs. Clearer,~~ more frequent signs would

well-placed
guide motorists and cyclists alike. In almost every community, bicycle
would   *commuting.*
racks and storage facilities ~~will help~~ encourage more bicycle ~~commuters,~~

~~as will public service announcements to promote bicycle awareness.~~

2 Editing symbols

As you edit, use the following copyediting symbols to make your final draft easier to prepare.

insert

add space

delete letter or ~~word~~

close up

tranpsose

let it stand as written: *stet*

start a new paragraph: ¶

remove paragraph: *no* ¶

cAPITALIZE A LETTeR OR word

LOwercase a Letter or WORD

move left:

move right:

🖥 *Computer Tip:* Editing with a Computer

Use these tips to make your editing easier and more effective.

- *Hard copy.* Edit your writing on a printed—hard—copy of your draft, using the editorial symbols in 4d2. Then transfer these changes to your computer file. Changes on hard copy are easier to see than changes on screen.
- *Find commands.* Use Search and Replace or Find commands to locate words, punctuation, blank lines, or symbols such as asterisks that you inserted at places where you want to add or change things.
- *Grammar checkers.* Beware of relying too heavily on grammar or style checkers. They can identify repeated words, clichés, wordy or vague phrases, big words, and long or short sentences. But they can't read your intentions, don't know your audience, and can't detect the feelings you want to convey. Be sure a recommended change will actually improve your writing before you accept it.
- *Spell checkers.* Spell checkers can't identify confused words such as *threw* for *through*, *there* for *they're* or *their*, *see* for *sea*, *so* for *sew*. If you misspell a word by typing another, correctly spelled word—*ad* instead of *and*—your spell checker can't identify that error either. Use your spell checker but proofread afterward.
- *Manuscript form.* For information about the manuscript form of computer-produced papers, see 46a1.

3 How to know when you've finished revising and editing

You may have to write several drafts before you say what you want to say in the way you want to say it. But some writers tinker and tinker, changing and changing, never sure when they've finished. When your changes aren't making your writing noticeably better, you're finished; you've written as well as you can.

4e Prepare and proofread your final draft

As you prepare your final draft, use the appropriate manuscript form. (See 46c for the Modern Language Association format for writing in the humanities and 46d for the American Psychological Association format for writing in the social sciences.)

Proofread your final copy slowly and carefully. When many writers proofread their own writing, they miss spelling errors and other typos because they read as they normally do, for the meaning, or in anticipation of parts they like.

How to . . . Proofread a Final Draft

Follow these tips for effective proofreading.

1. Read your final draft aloud, slowly pronouncing each word as it appears on the page. Use a pencil eraser to point at each word, or lay a ruler beneath each line to guide your eyes.
2. After you spot and correct an error, return to the beginning of the line and begin proofreading anew in case you missed a second error on that line.
3. If you find it hard to focus on the spelling of your words or if you're a poor speller, read your writing backward, word by word. Use a dictionary to verify the spelling of any word you don't write frequently (see Chapter 45).

🖳 *Computer Tip:* Effective Proofreading

Proofread on printed copy. If you proofread on screen, errors will be hard to detect.

4f Sample student essay

The writer of the following project was instructed to "write a 3–5 page informative and explanatory essay about a topic many people misunderstand." An **essay** (a frequent college assignment) is generally a brief piece of nonfiction on one subject unified by a specific purpose, thesis, or mood. The writer of this essay on bicycle commuting describes the myths of bicycle dangers, evaluates the feasibility of bicycle commuting, and explains how to become a bicycle commuter. For other sample essays, see the research project (Chapter 53), the persuasive essay (58d), and the literary essay (59g). The writers of these essays followed the Modern Language Association format for papers in the humanities (46c).

Chen 1

John Chen

Professor Sternberg

English 101–015

September 10, 200–

The Highway My Way

For most residents of America's cities and suburbs, the worst part of any weekday is the excruciating time spent trapped in rush-hour traffic. Morning, night, and sometimes even at noon, I watch my fellow commuters lined up, scowling, inching, and honking their way to work or school. I used to share their fender benders, foul air, fouler tempers, frazzled nerves, clenched jaws, high blood pressure, higher insurance premiums, the same old tunes on the radio, the wasted time, and boredom. But no more. Not since I parked my car and began commuting by bicycle. What I've discovered in the process is that bicycle commuting is a safe, practical, economical, and enjoyable alternative to short-trip car travel. If other motorists joined me, we could bring an end to this commuting misery.

Many drivers, however, think of cycling, especially commuter cycling, as anything but safe. To them, people who put their fragile bikes and bodies on rush-hour streets and highways risk instant destruction by 4,000-pound cars and 40,000-pound trucks and buses. How could a bicycle commuter survive even one rush hour, they wonder.

The truth is that cars, trucks, buses, and bicycles can safely share most roads and streets. As reported in <u>Bicycling</u> magazine, fewer than twelve percent of cycling accidents involve cars or other motorized vehicles (Drake 18). With increased enforcement of traffic laws, roadway redesign, the creation of more off-road bike paths where appropriate,

Modern Language Association format (see 46c)

Standard heading information

Centered title

Double-spacing throughout

Dramatic introductory description to attract reader interest

The writer's informative thesis

Transition to the first part of the essay: the myths and realities of bicycle commuting

A topic sentence: the realities of bicycle safety

4f

and improved driver and cyclist education, the incidence of these accidents will be even lower. If millions upon millions of bicycle commuters can pedal their way safely along the narrow, densely crowded streets and roads of Mexico, the Netherlands, Sweden, India, China, and many other countries, cyclists can easily be accommodated on the United States' wider streets and roads.

Information that supports the topic sentence

Even so, many will object, what happens elsewhere is no guide to the future of America's roads. Large-scale bicycle commuting would be impractical. In America, the car is king. Highway redesign and modification to accommodate cyclists would be too complex and expensive. Another bureaucracy would be created, they argue, and one more governmental body would lean on us for taxes. Where would we begin?

Transition and topic sentence: objections to the practicality of bicycle commuting

The truth is that we have already begun. Already seven percent of Americans bicycle or walk to work (Pena 38). Many businesses now encourage bicycle commuting by providing bicycle parking and employee clean-up facilities. In all fifty states, bicycles have for years had the same legal status as motor vehicles, and cyclists have had the same legal rights and responsibilities as motorists. In 1998 Congress reauthorized the Intermodal Surface Transportation Equity Act (ISTEA), which provides $3.3 billion to state and local governments to develop more ecological modes of transportation, including bicycles. The American Association of State Highway and Transportation Officials has already produced a <u>Guide to the Development of Bicycle Facilities</u>, with highway redesign recommendations that will enable bicycles and other vehicles to coexist safely. The federal government and most state and local governments already have officials to oversee the integration of bicycles

Parenthetical in-text documentation of borrowed information (see Chapter 51)

The reality of bicycle commuting as a practical alternative

Chen 3

into transportation programs. And many municipalities--such as San Diego, Denver, Minneapolis, Chicago, and Philadelphia--have already laid out networks of bike routes to aid bicycle commuters. Some, such as Portland, Seattle, and Washington, DC, equip buses with bike racks to expand the possibilities for bicycle commuters (Cormeny).

This kind of business and government support makes it easy for other commuters to do as I did: park their cars and ride their bikes instead. Most of the trips we take by car are under ten miles. Most of the routes we drive are bicycle accessible. These are trips we could take most of the time in most weather by bicycle. Many of us already own bicycles. A call to our local government or a visit to a bike shop will give us routes and maybe even maps. What else do we need?

-A bicycle tune-up

-A review of the rules of the road (We have to follow the same regulations motorists do.)

-A few articles of clothing and equipment (a helmet for sure, bike shorts perhaps, baskets or bags, rain gear, lights for night commuters, possibly fenders, and a horn or bell)

- Cycling companions to share the ride with us

It takes only a little imagination to see the benefits of bicycle commuting. Those who must drive because of health, their route, or the distance will benefit from reduced traffic and commuting times. Bicyclists will benefit from increased exercise, and the money they save on gasoline and insurance can be put to better uses. Businesses will benefit. According to <u>Bicycling</u> magazine, U.S. businesses now pay $1,035 per employee per year "to compensate for lost productivity of workers stuck in traffic" (28).

Margin notes:

Transition to the second part of the essay: becoming a bicycle commuter

A list for emphasis

Topic sentence

Introduction of a source of information and in-text parenthetical documentation of the page number

4f ms

Bicycle commuters are money in the bank. Finally, all of us
will benefit from the cleaner air that results from fewer cars
and trucks. According to that same issue of <u>Bicycling</u>, a week
of bicycle commuting by one person (a five-mile round-trip)
eliminates 1.5 pounds of carbon monoxide from the air (28).

Imagine a morning or afternoon when the sky is not brown
with smog. Imagine broad, open streets easy and safe to travel
any time of day. Imagine the scent of flowers and trees instead
of gasoline and rubber. Imagine the songs of birds instead of the
blare of horns, the rumble of engines, the screech of tires.
Imagine feeling relaxed and exhilarated at the end of a commute,
instead of frustrated, tense, angry. This is what a bicycle rush hour
would be like. Instead of the worst part of the day, it just might
be the best.

Descriptive conclusion that contrasts with the introduction and dramatizes the writer's thesis

Works Cited

<u>Bicycling</u> Mar. 1993: 28.

Cormeny, Sara. "Commuting by Bicycle." <u>WashingtonPost.com</u>
20 Sept. 1996. 28 Oct. 1998 <http://washingtonpost.com/
wp-srv/local/longterm/commute/bicycle.htm>.

Drake, Geoff. <u>Bicycling</u> May 1996: 18.

Pena, Nelson. "Brothers in Arms." <u>Bicycling</u> Mar. 1993: 38.

An alphabetical list of the sources of information for this essay (see 52a)

Paragraphing

Ancient Greek writers drew a mark, called a *parágraphos*, to divide man-
uscripts into distinct and manageable parts. In the same way, **paragraphs**
signal changes of subject or purpose and thus make writing and reading
easier. Your paragraphs contribute powerfully to the success of your writing when they unify ideas, develop subjects effectively, and flow coherently from one to the next.

5 Unifying Your Paragraphs

A good paragraph is like any piece of good writing. It has a purpose, focuses on a single topic, and has an overall design. In a word, a good paragraph is *unified*. To write unified paragraphs, do as you would in any writing.

5a Write topic sentences to focus your paragraphs

A **topic sentence** resembles the thesis statement of an essay. It announces a topic or makes a point. Just as everything in an essay supports
its thesis, everything in a paragraph supports its topic sentence. Consider
this example:

> Topic sentence — Calf ropers are the whiz kids of rodeo: they're expert on the
> horse and on the ground, and their horses are as quick-witted.
>
> Cowboys as expert riders — The cowboy emerges from the box with a loop in his hand, a
> piggin' string in his mouth, coils and reins in the other, and a
> network of slack line strewn so thickly over horse and rider,
>
> Cowboys and horses working together — they look as if they'd run through a tangle of kudzu before ar-
> riving in the arena. After roping the calf and jerking the slack
> in the rope, he jumps off the horse, sprints down the length of
> nylon, which the horse keeps taut, throws the calf down, and
> ties three legs together with the piggin' string. It's said of Roy
>
> A supporting example — Cooper, the defending calf-roping champion, that "even with
> pins and metal plates in his arm, he's known for the fastest
> groundwork in the business; when he springs down his rope
> to flank the calf, the resulting action is pure rodeo poetry."
>
> A concluding evaluation — The six or seven separate movements he makes are so fluid
> they look like one continual unfolding.
>
> (Gretel Ehrlich, "Rules of the Game: Rodeo," from
> *The Solace of Open Spaces*)

Topic sentences may appear early in a paragraph, as in the preceding
example, or later, to sum up preceding information, as in the following:

> Transitional phrase to link paragraphs — Girls, on the other hand, play in small groups or pairs; the
> center of a girl's social life is a best friend. Within the group,
> intimacy is key: Differentiation is measured by relative close-

Details about girls' play

ness. In their most frequent games, such as jump rope and hopscotch, everyone gets a turn. Many of their activities (such as playing house) do not have winners or losers. Though some girls are certainly more skilled than others, girls are expected not to boast about it, or show that they think they are better than the others. Girls don't give orders; they express their preferences as suggestions, and suggestions are likely to be accepted. Whereas boys say, "Gimme that!" and "Get outta here!" girls say, "Let's do this," and "How about doing that?"

A topic sentence explaining girls' play

Anything else is put down as "bossy." They don't grab center stage—they don't want it—so they don't challenge each other directly. And much of the time, they simply sit together and talk. Girls are not accustomed to jockeying for status in an obvious way; they are more concerned that they be liked.

(Deborah Tannen, "It Begins at the Beginning," from *You Just Don't Understand*)

How to . . . Write Topic Sentences

Follow these tips to write effective topic sentences.

1. As you organize your writing, consider items in outline headings or in lists you have made as potential topic sentences. Compose headings that you can later expand into topic sentences.
2. As you write a first draft and indent for new paragraphs, think of sentences to announce your topics. Where will you put them for best effect? At the beginning, to launch your paragraph? Or at the end, as a destination to aim for?
3. As you edit, look for topic sentences in your writing. They should appear regularly, but sometimes a topic sentence in one paragraph will announce a topic for several paragraphs. Sometimes you can imply your point rather than state it explicitly.
4. Reread your writing from your readers' point of view. If you suspect they might ask, "So, what's the point here?" add topic sentences to answer their question.

One key to successful paragraph design is the placement of the topic sentence. Organize your paragraphs to follow from the topic sentence or to lead to it, as in the preceding examples. Another key is emphasis. Whenever possible, put the most important information early in your paragraph, an arrangement known as **dramatic order,** or late, known as **climactic order.** In the following example, the writer opens with a topic sentence but saves her most important example for the end of her paragraph.

Topic sentence

Neat people are especially vicious with mail. They never go through their mail unless they are standing directly over a trash can. If the trash can is beside the mailbox, even better. All ads,

Clarifying
description

Supporting
examples

Most important
example

catalogs, pleas for charitable contributions, church bulletins
and money-saving coupons go straight in the trash can without
being opened. All letters from home, postcards from Europe,
bills and paychecks are opened, immediately responded to,
then dropped in the trash can. Neat people keep their receipts
only for tax purposes. That's it. No sentimental salvaging of
birthday cards or the last letter a dying relative ever wrote. Into
the trash it goes.

(Suzanne Britt, "Neat People vs. Sloppy People,"
from *Show and Tell*)

5b Adjust paragraph length to express your purpose and suit your audience

1 Paragraph length, purpose, and audience

Paragraphs may be almost any length. Some are necessarily short to set
them off or signal changes in topic or purpose: speeches in a dialogue, a
paragraph to set off a thesis, transition statements, or emphatic paragraphs.
These may be only a sentence or two—or even less. Paragraphs that present
and develop ideas, such as introductions, body paragraphs, or conclusions,
may be much longer.

In any case, you should write paragraphs for your readers' eyes as
well as their brains. Too many short paragraphs will make your writing
look choppy and disconnected even when it isn't. Too many long paragraphs may make readers think, "I can't read this; it's too difficult." Paragraphs should look readable.

2 Paragraph length and content

Paragraphs must not only look readable but be readable, fully expressing their topic and purpose. Adjusting paragraph length involves
more than combining short paragraphs and dividing long ones. As you
adjust length, be sure each paragraph connects to the preceding one, that it
clearly announces its topic or purpose, and that it is complete. A paragraph may contain six kinds of sentences. Not every paragraph contains
every kind of sentence, but a good paragraph has all the sentences necessary to make its point and connect it to surrounding paragraphs:

- *Transitional* sentences linking one paragraph to another
- *Introductory* sentences
- *Topic* sentences
- *Supporting* sentences that present a topic or prove a point
- *Clarifying* sentences that explain or restate
- *Concluding* sentences

As you adjust paragraph length, check to see that each paragraph has all the sentences it needs. Individual sentences may perform more than one function. But each paragraph has to have the sentences necessary to do its job.

💻 *Computer Tip:* Editing for Paragraph Unity and Length

If you're unsure whether a passage belongs in a particular paragraph, select it, cut it, and paste it temporarily at the end of your paper. Read the paragraph without it. If it belongs, move it back. Otherwise, move it to a suitable spot in another paragraph or delete it.

How to . . . Adjust Paragraph Length

Follow these guidelines to write paragraphs of appropriate length.

1. To divide a paragraph that seems too long, look for break points at shifts in time or place, between subtopics, or before sentences that signal logical shifts.
2. In double-spaced typescript, common in college writing, break for a new paragraph one to three times per page—every 100–200 words or so. Break more often to increase the pace of your writing or for special-purpose paragraphs.
3. In single-spaced typescript, common in business letters, make your paragraphs from four or five to nine or ten lines long. Break more frequently if your information is complex or if your readers may only be skimming your writing for its main ideas.
4. If you are writing in columns, as in technical writing and journalism, break up long paragraphs to make them look readable, usually one to three sentences in length.
5. If you are writing by hand, divide once or twice per page.

6 Developing Topics and Paragraphs

6a | Include details to support your topic sentence

"God is in the details," said architect Mies van der Rohe. As in a well-designed building, the power of a well-designed paragraph lies in its details. If you're writing to readers familiar with your topic, you may not need to say much. However, in most public writing, especially in college writing, readers want enough detail to understand fully the main idea of your topic sentence. That means writing well-developed paragraphs.

How to . . . **Write Well-Developed Paragraphs**

Follow these tips to write well-developed paragraphs.

1. Do exploratory writing or take notes before beginning a first draft. Give yourself things to put in your paragraphs before you write them.
2. As you revise, see that the points in your topic sentences are fully supported by the body of your paragraphs. Add details to prove your points or express your ideas.
3. Read your paragraphs from your readers' viewpoint. Do they answer readers' questions and satisfy their interest in your topic? Add details where necessary.

6b Choose appropriate methods of paragraph development to present a topic

The methods of paragraph development illustrated in this section will enable you to communicate information, experiences, feelings, ideas, and opinions. Sometimes, when an idea needs several kinds of support, you'll combine more than one method in a paragraph, as in the paragraph about calf-ropers earlier (see 5a), in which the writer combines narration, description, and example. Sometimes, when subjects are complex or your readers' need for information is great, you may extend one method of development over several paragraphs, all unified by one topic sentence. You may even use one method throughout an entire piece of writing, unified by a thesis statement.

The method you choose will depend on your purpose and your readers' needs. Although each method can serve a variety of purposes, writers customarily use specific methods for specific ends, as the following examples indicate.

1 Narration

Narration organizes events in chronological order to tell a story. Use it in personal-experience writing and to illustrate a point in explanatory writing or argument. As in the following example, narrative paragraphs almost always include description to make actions clear and vivid.

Event 1: action and reaction

When I pulled the trigger I did not hear the bang or feel the kick—one never does when a shot goes home—but I heard the devilish roar of glee that went up from the crowd. In that instant, in too short a time, one would have thought, even for the bullet to get there, a mysterious, terrible change had come

Dramatizing
description

over the elephant. He neither stirred nor fell, but every line of his body had altered. He looked suddenly stricken, shrunken, immensely old, as though the frightful impact of the bullet had paralysed him without knocking him down. At last, after what seemed a long time—it might have been five seconds, I dare say—he sagged flabbily to his knees. His mouth slobbered. An enormous senility seemed to have settled upon him. One could have imagined him thousands of years old. I fired again into the same spot. At the second shot he did not collapse but climbed with desperate slowness to his feet and stood weakly upright, with legs sagging and head drooping. I fired a third time. That was the shot that did for him. You could see the agony of it jolt his whole body and knock the last remnant of strength from his legs. But in falling he seemed for a moment to rise, for as his hind legs collapsed beneath him he seemed to tower upward like a huge rock toppling, his trunk reaching skywards like a tree. He trumpeted, for the first and only time. And then down he came, his belly towards me, with a crash that seemed to shake the ground even where I lay.

Event 2: a
second shot
and its effects

Event 3: a third
shot and its
effects

(George Orwell, "Shooting an Elephant," from
Shooting an Elephant and Other Essays)

2 Process

Like narrative paragraphs, **process** paragraphs are organized in chronological order. But they emphasize the sequence of events as much as they emphasize the events themselves. Process paragraphs are used frequently to explain steps or stages in informative and how-to writing.

Step 1

Step 2

Step 3

To define a word, then, the dictionary editor places before him the stack of cards illustrating that word; each of the cards represents an actual use of the word by a writer of some literary or historical importance. He reads the cards carefully, discards some, rereads the rest, and divides up the stack according to what he thinks are the several senses of the word. Finally, he writes his definitions, following the hard-and-fast rule that each definition must be based on what the quotations in front of him reveal about the meaning of the word. The editor cannot be influenced by what he thinks a given word ought to mean. He must work according to the cards or not at all.

(S. I. Hayakawa, "How Dictionaries Are Made,"
from *Language in Thought and Action*)

3 Description

Description adds sensory details to personal and informative writing—whenever it is important for writers to "see" a subject. Descriptive paragraphs are usually organized in spatial order: left to right, front to back, top to bottom, and so forth. The following paragraph is organized from the center to the margins of a scene.

<table>
<tr><td>Topic sentence</td><td rowspan="2">There once was a town in the heart of America where all life seemed to live in harmony with its surroundings. The town lay in the midst of a checkerboard of prosperous farms, with fields of grain and hillsides of orchards where, in spring, white clouds of bloom drifted above the green fields. In autumn, oak and maple and birch set up a blaze of color that flamed and flickered across a backdrop of pines. Then foxes barked in the hills and deer silently crossed the fields, half hidden in the mists of the fall mornings.</td></tr>
</table>

Visual details

Color

Sound

> (Rachel Carson, "A Fable for Tomorrow," from *Silent Spring*)

4 Facts and figures

Factual paragraphs present **facts or statistical information** in some clear pattern to provide information or prove a point in an argument. The following paragraph is organized according to the ways bats are both familiar and strange to human beings.

Facts that make bats familiar

Facts that make bats strange to human beings

Bats are mammals like we are. They suckle their young, and have such wizened ancient-looking faces that they seem strangely akin and familiar. Yet they find their way and locate food by using sound that we cannot hear. They hunt by night, and in cold weather some migrate and others hibernate. They are odd and alien to us, too, so much so that we have made up fancies about them—that they are evil and ill-omened, or at the very least will fly into our hair. Anyone who has read *Dracula* will remember that young ladies should not moon around graveyards at night, or they will be in big trouble with bats.

> (Sue Hubbell, "Summer," from *A Country Year*)

5 Examples

An **example** uses individual members of a group (people, events, conditions, objects, ideas, and so forth) to explain or illustrate the whole group. Explanatory writing and argument frequently depend on examples. Occasionally, they are introduced by signal phrases: *for example, for instance,* or *such as.*

Topic sentence and the group to be explained: visible symbols of the consumer society

Since its birth in the United States, the consumer society has moved far beyond its American borders, yet its most visible symbols remain American. The Disneyland near Tokyo attracts almost as many visitors each year as Mecca or the Vatican. Coca-Cola products are distributed in over 170 countries. Each day, a new Mc-Donald's restaurant opens somewhere in the world. Singaporean

Examples   youngsters can brush their teeth with the Teenage Mutant Ninja Turtle Talking Toothbrush, which says "Hey, Dudes!" in Malay. The techniques of mass marketing first perfected in the United States are now employed on every continent, teaching former East Ger-

Signal phrase   mans, for example, to "Taste the West. Marlboro."

(Alan Thein Durning, "The Consumer Society,"
from *How Much Is Enough?*)

6 Comparison/contrast

Comparison/contrast presents subjects according to similarities and differences in order to explain a subject or make an evaluation. Comparison/contrast paragraphs may be organized in two ways. In **block comparison,** as in the first paragraph that follows, one subject is presented and then the other, subject A and then B. In **point-by-point comparison,** as in the second paragraph, the comparison moves back and forth, first to one point of comparison, then to a second, and so forth, $A_1 B_1$, then $A_2 B_2$, and $A_3 B_3$.

Block contrast

Custer's knowledge of his society

Crazy Horse's knowledge of his society

[George Armstrong] Custer's society was specialized. Thus, despite his range of choices, once Custer settled into an occupation, he knew relatively little about what other men in his society did for their daily bread. After becoming a soldier, Custer knew almost nothing about medicine or law or manufacturing. He never really understood how his society worked. [The Sioux warrior] Crazy Horse knew how to do everything required to make his society function. He could put up a tipi, kill buffalo, skin animals, cook, make war, treat injuries or illness, and so on. Put Crazy Horse down naked and alone on the Great Plains and within a month he would have a full set of weapons, shelter, stocks of food, and be in good shape to face the future.

Point-by-point comparison

Differences in dress

Differences in bearing

Two similarities

Beyond their bravery, Custer and Crazy Horse were individualists, each standing out from the crowd in his separate way. Custer wore outlandish uniforms, let his hair fall in long, flowing gold locks across his shoulders, surrounded himself with pet animals and admirers, and in general did all he could to draw attention to himself. Crazy Horse's individualism pushed him in an opposite direction—he wore a single feather in his hair when going into battle, rather than a war bonnet. Custer's vast energy set him apart from most of his fellows; the Sioux distinguished Crazy Horse from other warriors because of Crazy Horse's quietness and introspection. Both men lived in societies in which drugs, especially alcohol, were widely used, but neither Custer nor Crazy Horse drank. Most of all, of course, each man stood out in battle as a great risk taker.

(Stephen Ambrose, from *Crazy Horse and Custer:
The Parallel Lives of Two American Warriors*)

7 Analogy

As a form of comparison, **analogy** uses something simple or familiar to explain something complex or unfamiliar. To help explain what can be observed in newly fallen snow, the writer of the following paragraph compares snow to a book.

Topic sentence	To one who lives in the snow and watches it day by day, it is a book to be read. The pages turn as the wind blows; the characters shift and the images formed by their combinations change in mean-
The wind = pages turning	ing, but the language remains the same. It is a shadow language, spoken by things that have gone by and will come again. The same text has been written there for thousands of years, though I was not here, and will not be here in winters to come, to read it. These seemingly
Physical details = the language of the book	random ways, these paths, these beds, these footprints, these hard, round pellets in the snow: they all have meaning. Dark things may be written there, news of others' lives, their sorties and excursions, their terrors and deaths. The tiny feet of a shrew or a vole make a brief, erratic pattern across the snow, and here is a hole down which the animal goes. And now the track of an ermine comes this way, swift and searching, and he too goes down that white shadow of a hole.

(John Haines, "Snow," from *The Stars, the Snow, the Fire*)

8 Cause/effect

Cause/effect paragraphs divide events into causes and effects in order to explain relationships within a process. They may be organized in two ways: *causes → effects* or, as in the following example, *effects → causes*. Notice how the writer arranges causes into a *causal chain*, from immediate to underlying causes.

Topic sentence: an effect (literacy)	Fortunately, there are many children who manage to become literate despite the way in which they are taught reading. They do so because they are highly motivated by their home environ-
Two chief causes: home and school	ment or because of an attachment to their teacher. Studies show that nothing correlates more highly with a child's future academic success than the academic achievement of his parents. The reason for this is not just that the parents are committed to the
Underlying causes: observation and experience	merit of reading, a commitment which they pass on to their children, but also that from an early age the child can observe how important reading is to his parents and how much they enjoy it. Additionally, parents who are avid readers are more likely to read often—and with enjoyment—to their children. So the child becomes convinced that reading is important and enjoyable long before he is confronted for the first time with a primer in school. And he is then able to distance himself from the stupidity of the primers, since he knows not all books are like those. Still, many

Two additional effects of these causes	years later, that child will remember how disgusted he was with the books he had to read in early grades.

(Bruno Bettelheim, from *Johnny Wants to Read*)

9 Classification

Classification divides subjects into classes according to characteristics shared by the members of each class. Classification paragraphs are often used in informative and evaluative writing to show how things differ or fit together. They may include examples or description to distinguish the members of one class from another.

Topic sentence	There are three kinds of book owners. The first has all the standard sets and best sellers—unread, untouched. (This de-
Class one	luded individual owns woodpulp and ink, not books.) The second has a great many books—a few of them read through, most
Class two	of them dipped into, but all of them as clean and shiny as the day they were bought. (This person would probably like to make books his own, but is restrained by a false respect for their physi-
Class three	cal appearance.) The third has few books or many—every one of them dog-eared and dilapidated, shaken and loosened by contin-
Descriptive details	ual use, marked and scribbled in from front to back. (This man owns books.)

(Mortimer Adler, "How to Mark a Book," in *Saturday Review,* July 6, 1940)

10 Definition

In explanatory writing and argument, **definitions** explain what something is. There are several methods of definition.

- **Formal definition** puts something into a class of related items and then distinguishes it from other words in that class.
- **Functional definition** tells how something works.
- **Etymology** traces the history of a term to its origins.
- **Giving synonym**s compares words with similar or related meanings.
- **Providing examples** defines by illustrating the term.

Definition by origin, by synonym	"Niche" is a word ecologists have borrowed from church architecture. In a church, of course, a "niche" means a recess in the wall in which a figurine may be placed; it is an address, a location, a physical place. But the ecologist's "niche" is more than
Definition by contrast	just a physical place: it is a place in the grand scheme of things. The niche is an animal's (or a plant's) profession. The niche of the wolf spider is everything it does to get its food and raise its ba-
Example and functional definition	bies. To be able to do these things it must relate properly to the place where it lives and to the other inhabitants of that place.

Everything the species does to survive and stay "fit" in the Darwinian sense is its niche.

> (Paul Colinvaux, "Every Species Has Its Niche," from *Why Big Fierce Animals Are Rare*)

6c Write introductions that attract reader interest

Professional writers frequently spend a lot of time on openings. They know that a good lead will take them in the right direction as they begin a draft. They also know that they have to arouse interest within the first two or three sentences or risk losing their readers. And they know that effective introductions are sometimes challenging to write because these introductions must do several things at once:

- Identify the writer's topic and, often, the purpose of the writing
- Stimulate reader interest
- Create the writer's personality and style
- State the writer's thesis or main idea
- Provide a bridge to carry readers into the body of the writing

Consider how the following introduction attracts reader interest and then focuses it on the thesis statement.

Dramatic quotation to create interest
Explanation that announces the writer's topic
Thesis statement

"A name is a prison, God is free," once observed the Greek poet Nikos Kazantzakis. He meant, I think, that valuable though language is to man, it is by very necessity limiting, and creates for man an invisible prison. Language implies boundaries. A word spoken creates a dog, a rabbit, a man. It fixes their nature before our eyes; henceforth their shapes are, in a sense, our own creation. They are no longer part of the unnamed shifting architecture of the universe. They have been transfixed as if by sorcery, frozen into a concept, a word. Powerful though the spell of human language has proven itself to be, it has laid boundaries upon the cosmos.

> (Loren Eiseley, "The Cosmic Prison," from *The Invisible Pyramid*)

1 Strategies for introductions

The following strategies for introductions are appropriate in many kinds of writing. Choose the one that fits your topic, purpose, and audience expectations.

- Begin with a **dramatic quotation,** as Loren Eiseley does. Be sure to tell who is speaking and, if necessary, provide explanation to help readers understand how the quotation introduces your topic. (See Chapter 53, the sample research project.)

- Open with **dramatic details or description.** (See 58d, the sample persuasive essay.)
- Open at a dramatic point **in the middle of things** (also referred to as *in medias res*); then flash back to the beginning.
- Write a **strong statement:** a warning, something that at first seems puzzling or contradictory.
- Pose a **problem** to solve **or question** to answer. (See 4f, the sample essay, and 54d, the sample report.)
- Open with an **analogy or comparison** that describes or illustrates your topic. (See the example paragraph in 6b7.)
- Tell an **anecdote**—a brief story—that illustrates your point. For example:

> He was one of the greatest scientists the world has ever known, yet if I had to convey the essence of Albert Einstein in a single word, I would choose *simplicity*. Perhaps an anecdote will help. Once, caught in a downpour, he took off his hat and held it under his coat. Asked why, he explained, with admirable logic, that the rain would damage the hat, but his hair would be none the worse for its wetting. This knack for going instinctively to the heart of the matter was the secret of his major scientific discoveries—this and his extraordinary feeling for beauty.
>
> (Banesh Hoffman, from "Unforgettable Albert Einstein")

2 Introductions, purpose, and audience

Although the introductions in 6c1 are suitable for almost any kind of writing, the beginnings of certain kinds of writing usually do certain specific things for their readers.

- *Autobiographical and narrative writing.* Good stories usually begin at a point when something dramatic or important is about to happen. The introduction creates tension or expectation about the events soon to occur. Consider:

> The last inch of space was filled, yet people continued to wedge themselves along the walls of the Store. Uncle Willie had turned the radio up to its last notch so that youngsters on the porch wouldn't miss a word. Women sat on kitchen chairs, dining-room chairs, stools, and upturned wooden boxes. Small children and babies perched on every lap available and men leaned on the shelves or on each other.
>
> The apprehensive mood was shot through with shafts of gaiety, as a black sky is streaked with lightning.
>
> "I ain't worried 'bout this fight. Joe's gonna whip that cracker like it's open season."
>
> (Maya Angelou, from *I Know Why the Caged Bird Sings*)

As this scene is set, readers are interested to read on, as interested as the listeners in the story to hear whether "Joe," the great boxer Joe Louis, will indeed win the fight that is about to begin.

- *Informative and explanatory writing.* Good introductions to informative and explanatory writing do whatever is necessary to help readers understand the information about to follow. They may put the topic in some larger context, describe the background, define key terms, identify the writer's point of view, present a problem to be solved or questions to be answered, state the purpose of the writing, or review what is already known about the topic. Consider this opening to a formal research report:

> The situation in which one agent commands another to hurt a third turns up time and again as a significant theme in human relations. It is powerfully expressed in the story of Abraham, who is commanded by God to kill his son. It is no accident that [Danish philosopher Søren] Kierkegaard, seeking to orient his thought to the central themes of human experience, chose Abraham's conflict as the springboard to his philosophy.
>
> War too moves forward on the triad of an authority which commands a person to destroy the enemy, and perhaps all organized hostility may be viewed as a theme and variation on the three elements of authority, executant, and victim. We describe an experimental program, recently concluded at Yale University, in which a particular expression of this conflict is studied by experimental means.
>
> In its most general form the problem may be defined thus: if X tells Y to hurt Z, under what conditions will Y carry out the command of X and under what conditions will he refuse?
>
> (Stanley Milgram, from "Some Conditions
> of Obedience and Disobedience to Authority")

In three brief paragraphs, this researcher puts his study in religious, philosophical, and cultural context, announces his topic and purpose, and poses the question he will try to answer. His readers have been prepared for his information.

- *Argumentative and persuasive writing.* Frequently, writers who intend to change readers' thinking or behavior begin by establishing a bond with their readers, earning their trust, and presenting their credentials for making the case that they do. (For persuasive introductions, see 58b.)

6d Write conclusions that create a feeling of completeness

Conclusions are more than stopping places. For writers and readers alike, they create a sense of fulfillment and wholeness. They are not only your final words; they are your final opportunity to fulfill your purpose

6d ¶ dev/det

for your writing. Consider how this conclusion to an essay celebrating America's cultural diversity leads in the final sentence to a restatement of the writer's main point.

Two examples that illustrate the writer's thesis

Rhetorical questions that explain the examples

Answers that restate the thesis

One of our most visionary politicians said that he envisioned a time when the United States could become the brain of the world, by which he meant the repository of all of the latest advanced information systems. I thought of that remark when an enterprising poet friend of mine called to say that he had just sold a poem to a computer magazine and that the editors were delighted to get it because they didn't carry fiction or poetry. Is that the kind of world we desire? A humdrum homogeneous world of all brains but no heart, no fiction, no poetry; a world of robots with human attendants bereft of imagination, of culture? Or does North America deserve a more exciting destiny? To become a place where the cultures of the world crisscross. This is possible because the United States is unique in the world: The world is here.

(Ishmael Reed, "America: The Multinational Society," from *Writin' Is Fightin'*)

1 Strategies for conclusions

As the preceding example illustrates, effective conclusions restate, provide food for thought, and challenge reader thinking, feeling, or action. Create a conclusion appropriate to the topic and the occasion.

- Conclude with **your thesis** or other unifying statement. Organize your writing so that it leads naturally and inevitably to your point.
- Conclude by asking a **rhetorical question** for which the body of your paper has suggested the answer.
- Conclude by **challenging readers** to new thinking or action.
- Conclude with a **quotation.** Introduce and explain it if necessary.
- Conclude with an **anecdote** that summarizes your thinking.
- Conclude with a **hook.** Unify your writing by returning to—hooking up with—the subject of your opening and commenting on it in light of what you've written in the body of your paper.

2 Conclusions, purpose, and audience

Like introductory strategies, the preceding conclusion strategies may be adapted to almost any writing situation. But certain kinds of writing tend to do certain things as they close in order to emphasize or achieve the writer's purpose.

- *Autobiographical and narrative writing.* These kinds of writing often end with a discovery the writer has made. The story just completed has brought changes of understanding, outlook, or action, and the conclusion announces or dramatizes them.

- *Informative and explanatory writing.* These kinds of writing often end by telling readers what can be done with the information they've just received. These conclusions may state the meaning or significance of the information, offer proposals for action, describe the benefits of action, or predict the consequences of action or inaction. (See 4f and Chapter 53.)

- *Argumentative and persuasive writing.* These kinds of writing often end with an emotional appeal, an attempt to rouse readers' desire to agree with the writer. (See 58c and d.)

How to . . . Revise Introductions and Conclusions

Follow these guidelines for effective introductions.

1. Avoid repeating your title in your opening line; doing so may make your introduction sound monotonous or unimaginative.
2. Cut unnecessary background or warm-up writing that you used to get yourself started. Advice for movie directors is also good for writers: "Cut to the chase." Open where your readers are, with what will interest them.
3. Although purpose statements are often appropriate in reports and scholarly articles, they are usually unnecessary in essays whose introductions contain a thesis statement. At the beginning of essays, don't tell your readers what you'll do; just do it.
4. Beware of mysterious openings. It's one thing to stimulate curiosity, quite another to mystify readers or plunge them into the dark. Your introduction should help readers make sound predictions about your topic—and even about your design and style.
5. Beware of overworked openings such as "Webster's defines . . ."

Follow these guidelines for effective conclusions.

1. Be sure your conclusion flows smoothly from the body of your writing. If necessary, write transitions or repeat key words.
2. If you choose to state your thesis in your conclusion, do more than merely reword the thesis that you wrote in the introduction.
3. Avoid stock phrases that tell the obvious, such as *In conclusion, In closing,* and *In summary.*
4. Do not introduce new topics. Refocus attention on your original topic.
5. Be sure your readers will understand a closing quotation. Identify the speaker and, if necessary, explain its point.

7 Creating Coherence

Effective writing is **coherent,** meaning that all of its parts fit snugly together. A more descriptive word is **fluent.** Effective writing flows from idea to idea, paragraph to paragraph, sentence to sentence, and so is easier to read than incoherent writing. Writing unified by a single topic and overall design already has the essential features of coherence. Following are other features of coherent writing and ways to create them.

7a Repeat key words and their synonyms

Some writers believe that repeated words are a sure sign of uninspired, monotonous writing. But key words that name your topics are worth repeating, especially key words from your thesis and topic sentences. Readers depend on them just as they depend on highway route markers to tell them they're on the right road. For example, consider the following paragraphs in which Pulitzer Prize–winning poet and journalist Donald Murray explains how experienced nonfiction writers create voice. Notice how often Murray repeats the word *voice* and related words (emphasis added).

> Experienced writers rarely begin a first draft until they **hear** in their heads—or on the page—a **voice** that may be right. **Voice** is usually the key element in effective writing. It is what attracts the reader and communicates to the reader. It is that element that gives **the illusion of speech. Voice** carries the writer's intensity and glues together the information that the reader needs to know. It is the **music** in writing that makes meaning clear.
>
> Writers keep rehearsing possible first lines, paragraphs, or endings, key scenes or statements that will reveal how what is to be **said** may be **said** best. The **voice** of a piece of writing is the writer's own **voice,** adapted in written language to the subject and audience. We **speak** differently at a funeral or a party, in church or in the locker room, at home or with strangers. We are experienced with using our **individual voices** for many purposes. We have to learn to do this same thing in writing, and to **hear a voice** in our head that may be polished and developed on the page.
>
> The **voice** is not only rehearsed but practiced. We should **hear** what we're writing as we write it. I **dictate** most of my writing and monitor my **voice** as I'm **speaking,** so that the **pace,** the **rhythm,** the **tone** support what I'm trying to **say.**
>
> ("Tricks of the Nonfiction Trade," *The Writer,* July 1985)

From paragraph to paragraph, sentence to sentence, repeated key words lead readers from a definition of voice to a description of its effects and the way it is created.

How to . . . Edit for Coherence

Follow these editing tips to evaluate your coherence.

1. Look at your writing. Be sure you've written topic sentences and necessary transitions. If not, add them.
2. Mark key words and their synonyms. If you've written coherently, you'll see these words repeated frequently. If you have marked many different key words, you may have too many topics, and your writing may be disunified or incoherent. Refocus, reorganize, and rewrite to support your thesis and topic sentences.
3. Reread from the beginning of a paragraph. When you finish rewriting a paragraph, go back to its beginning and reread. If your rewrite fits coherently, your original and revised sentences will flow together smoothly.
4. Reread at your readers' pace. Writers read their writing more slowly than readers, pausing frequently to consider and evaluate. At this slower pace, transitions and repetitions may seem appropriate. But if you reread at your readers' swifter pace, you may discover that your momentum will carry you smoothly from one idea to the next without transitions or repetition. Cut unnecessary words.

Computer Tip: Checking Coherence

As you revise a rough draft, use your word processor's style features (underlining, italics, boldface, even alternative type fonts and sizes) to highlight topic sentences, key words, synonyms, pronouns, and transitions. You can see at a glance whether you've written coherently. Be sure to reformat your final draft before you print it. (See 46a1.)

7b | Write transitions to connect ideas

Coherent writing not only repeats key words to develop its subject; it also links topics, sentences, and paragraphs with **transitions.** The word *transition* comes from a word that means "going across." Transitional words, phrases, and sentences are like bridges that enable writers and readers to "go across" from one idea to the next. They make the following connections:

- Addition: *additionally, again, also, and, as well, equally important, first (second, third), for one thing, further, moreover, next,* and so forth
- Alternation: *or, otherwise, nor, rather, instead*

- Comparison: *also, in the same way, likewise, similarly*
- Concession or agreement: *granted, it is true, of course, to be sure*
- Contrast: *after all, and yet, but, conversely, even so, however, in contrast, instead, nevertheless, nonetheless, on the contrary, on the other hand, yet*
- Examples: *as an illustration, for example, for instance, specifically*
- Explanation and logical relation: *as a result, because, consequently, for, for this reason, so, that being the case, therefore, thus, since*
- Place: *above, at this point, below, beyond, close, elsewhere, farther, here, near, next, on the other side, opposite, outside, within, there*
- Summary, emphasis, or conclusion: *accordingly, in conclusion, in other words, in short, in summary, indeed, on the whole, that is, therefore, thus*
- Time: *after, as, at last, at once, at the same time, by degrees, eventually, gradually, immediately, in a short time, in the future, later, meanwhile, promptly, soon, simultaneously, suddenly, then, when, while*

Consider transitions in the following excerpt, in which the writer uses his childhood to make a point about the value of living with risks. Transitions weave action and description into a story, compare the past to the present, and signal conclusions. (Transitions linking paragraphs, sentences, and clauses are emphasized.)

Time transition	**When** I was a boy skating on Brooks Pond, there were no grown-ups around. Once or twice a year, on a weekend day or a holiday, some parents might come by with a thermos of hot cocoa. Maybe they would build a fire (which we were forbidden to do), **and** we would gather around.
Addition	
Contrast	**But for the most part** the pond was the domain of children. In the absence of adults, we made and enforced our own rules. We had hardly any gear—just some borrowed hockey gloves, some hand-me-down skates, maybe an elbow pad or two—**so** we played a clean form of hockey, with no high-sticking, no punching, and almost no checking. A single fight could ruin the whole afternoon. **Indeed,** as I remember it, thirty years later, it was the purest form of hockey I ever saw—until I got to see the Russian national team play the game.
Logical relation	
Emphasis	
Time, contrast	**But before we could play,** we had to check the ice. We became serious junior meteorologists, true connoisseurs of cold. We learned that the best weather for pond skating is plain, clear cold, with starry nights and no snow. (Snow not only mucks up the skating surface but also insulates the ice from the colder air above.) **And** we learned that moving water, even the gently flowing Mystic River, is a lot less likely to freeze than standing water. **So** we skated only on the pond. We learned all the weird whooping and cracking sounds that ice makes as it expands and contracts, **and thus** when to leave the ice.
Addition	
Logical relation	
Logical relation	
Question link	**Do kids learn these things today?** I don't know. How would they? We don't let them. **Instead** we post signs. Ruled
Contrast	

Contrast by lawyers, cities and towns everywhere try to limit their legal liability. **But try as they might,** they cannot eliminate the underlying risk. Liability is a social construct; risk is a natural fact. When it is cold enough, ponds freeze. No sign or fence or ordinance can change that.

Conclusion   **In fact,** by focusing on liability and not teaching our kids how to take risks, we are making their world more dangerous.

Time   **When we were children,** we had to learn to evaluate risks and handle them on our own. We had to learn, quite literally, to test

Logical relation   the waters. **As a result,** we grew up to be savvier about ice and ponds than any kid could be who has skated only under adult supervision on a rink.

> (Adapted from Christopher B. Daly, "How the Lawyers Stole Winter," *The Atlantic,* March 1995)

7c Link sentences with pronouns

Pronouns substitute for nouns and noun phrases—the antecedents of pronouns (see 8b). The result is smoother reading. In the following example, consider how pronouns substitute for key words and, by so doing, link one sentence to another. Also imagine how much choppier the paragraph would seem if the writer had used only nouns. (Pronouns and antecedents are emphasized.)

> In the folklore of the country, numerous superstitions relate to winter weather. Back-country **farmers** examine **their** corn husks—the thicker the husk, the colder the winter. **They** watch the acorn crop—the more acorns, the more severe the season. **They** observe where white-faced **hornets** place **their** paper nests—the higher **they** are, the deeper will be the snow. **They** examine the size and shape and color of the spleens of butchered hogs for clues to the severity of the season. **They** keep track of the blooming of dogwood in the spring—the more abundant the blooms, the more bitter the cold in January.

> (Edwin Way Teale, from *Wandering Through Winter*)

7d Write "old/new" sentences: include material from preceding sentences in each new sentence

Fluent sentences repeat "old business" from earlier sentences—words, ideas, or structural patterns—and add "new business" to develop a topic one step further. Read the following paragraph and consider how each sentence is linked to those that precede it. (Sentences are numbered; "old business" in each sentence is emphasized.)

> (1) Be willing to make radical changes in your second draft. (2) If your thesis **changed** while you were writing your first draft, you will base your **second draft** on this new subject. (3) **Even if your thesis** has not **changed,**

you may need to shift paragraphs around, eliminate paragraphs, or add new ones. (4) Inexperienced writers often suppose that **revising** a paper means **changing** only a word or two or adding a sentence or two. (5) **This kind of editing** is part of the writing process, but it is not the most important part. (6) **The most important part of rewriting** is a willingness to turn the paper upside down, to shake out of it those ideas that interest you the most, to set them in a form where they will interest the reader, too.

(Adapted from Richard Marius, "Writing Drafts," from *A Writer's Companion*)

Sentences 1 and 2	*Changes/changed* [. . .] *second draft* are key words used in both sentences.
Sentences 2 and 3	*If* [. . .] in sentence 2 is grammatically parallel with *Even if* [. . .] in sentence 3 (parallel structure), and the words *thesis* [. . .] *changed* are key words used in each sentence.
Sentences 3 and 4	*Revising* in sentence 4 connects with *shift paragraphs around, eliminate paragraphs, and add new ones* in sentence 3 (key words).
Sentences 4 and 5	The key words *This kind of editing* in sentence 5 refer to an activity described in sentence 4.
Sentences 5 and 6	In sentence 6, *The most important part* repeats key words from sentence 5, and a dramatic description of revision reminds readers of the key words *radical changes* in sentence 1.

As you rewrite, examine your sentences to see whether they repeat words, ideas, and patterns from earlier sentences. Without these links, your sentences will seem to jump around, disconnected. With them, your sentences will flow.

A note on needless repetition: If you repeat words or sentence patterns unnecessarily, your writing will sound choppy or wordy. (See 21b and 28a–c.)

How to . . . Link with Transitions and Pronouns

Follow these guidelines to use transitions and pronouns effectively.

1. Use transitions sparingly. If you organize effectively, your writing will lead naturally from one topic to the next. You'll need few transitions; more would be distracting.
2. Choose transitions that accurately signal the relationship between ideas and paragraphs—not ones that mean almost what you intend. For example, *and* may mean either "in addition" or "consequently."
3. Choose transitions that suit the formality of your writing. For example, you may use *so* or *but* in informal writing and *therefore* or *nevertheless* in more formal writing.
4. Repeat pronouns frequently to substitute for nouns and noun phrases. As reminders, occasionally repeat the nouns or phrases to which pronouns refer.

PART II.

Sentence Editing

Identifying Grammar

Editing Grammar and Usage

II grammar

Identifying Grammar

Grammar describes how native speakers and writers of a language produce their sentences. It is not so much a list of do's and don'ts as it is a portrait of the way people speak and write. But this description is not what people have in mind when they say, "Watch your grammar!" What they mean is a set of language rules known as usage. **Usage** refers to the conventions and language etiquette that the members of specific language groups follow. Grammar says, in effect, "This is what a native speaker or writer *does*." Usage says, "This is what a speaker or writer *ought* to do."

The grammar presented in the following pages is actually a combination of the grammar and usage for one version or dialect of English, **Standard Written English.** This is the dialect generally written in schools, the professions, the business world, and the media. It is worth knowing because it is so widely shared. It is also worth knowing because it will give you editorial skills useful for improving your writing.

 chapter **8** Parts of Speech

The term **parts of speech** refers to a system for classifying English words according to their functions in sentences. Traditionally, words have been divided into eight parts of speech: nouns, pronouns, verbs, adjectives, adverbs, prepositions, conjunctions, and interjections. But some words change classes as their functions change. Consider the word *present.*

- A verb that describes action: *A geologist will present the next report.*
- A noun that describes an object: *Larry gave his sister a present.*
- An adjective that describes a feature: *This verb is in the present tense.*

65

How to . . . Identify Nouns and Verbs

Use the following tips to help you identify nouns and verbs as you edit your sentences.

Nouns
1. Nouns may be preceded by *a, an,* or *the*: *a computer, an apple, the president.*
2. Most nouns may be singular, plural, or possessive: *horse* [singular], *horses* [plural], *horse's* [possessive].
3. Nouns formed from other words end in *-ance* (*guidance*), *-ation* (*donation*), *-dom* (*freedom*), *-ence* (*reference*), *-hood* (*neighborhood*), *-ice* (*justice*), *-ion* (*incision*), *-ist* (*tourist*), *-ity* (*generosity*), *-ment* (*judgment*), *-ness* (*business*), *-ship* (*friendship*).

Verbs
1. If you change the time of an action, a verb changes its form (known as **tense**) and reveals itself: *Aaron opened the book. Aaron is opening the book.* (For more on tense, see 8c3.)
2. Verbs formed from other kinds of words end in *-ize* and *-ify*: *realize, identify.*

A note on adverbs: The adverbs *already, always, ever, not, often, only,* and *very* are sometimes placed in the middle of verbs to provide additional information: *Larry has already written the report.* Do not mistake adverbs for verbs.

8a | Nouns

Nouns name persons, places, and things, including ideas, activities, qualities, conditions, and materials. There are several kinds of nouns.

1 Proper nouns and common nouns

A **proper noun** is capitalized and names a specific person, place, or thing: *Harriet Beecher Stowe, the Sudan, the Holy Grail.* (See also 40b.) A **common noun** names a general category of person, place, or thing: *pilot, desert, gemstones.*

2 Abstract nouns and concrete nouns

An **abstract noun** names an intangible, something that we cannot perceive with our five senses: *joy, mercy, prudence, democracy.* A **concrete noun** names something that we can perceive with one or more of our senses: *glove, computer, book, mountain, voter.* (See also 26b.)

3 Count nouns and noncount nouns

A **count noun** names something that can be counted: *an apple, twenty-nine cents, three cookies, billions of stars.* (See also 30a.) A **noncount noun** names a mass or quantity that cannot be counted: *pepper, snow, air, iodine, peace.* (See also 30a and b.) *An ESL note:* Do not omit the *-s/-es* endings of plural count nouns: *suits, potatoes.*

4 Collective nouns

A **collective noun** names a group acting as a unit: *jury, class, team, community.* (See also 14g and 15c.)

5 Compound nouns

A **compound noun** consists of two or more words and may be written as separate words (*attorney general*), as one word (*makeup, grandfather*), or as a hyphenated word (*brother-in-law*). (For more on hyphens and compounds, see 44b.)

8b Pronouns

A **pronoun** refers to a noun, called its **antecedent,** that gives the pronoun its meaning. Pronouns change form to signal their function in a sentence.

| | personal | possessive | reflexive |
| antecedent | pronoun | pronoun | pronoun |

The little boy boasted that he could tie his shoes for himself.

1 Personal pronouns

Personal pronouns refer to specific persons, places, or things. (See also 17a–d.) Singular: *I, me, you, he, she, him, her, it.* Plural: *we, us, you, they, them.*

2 Possessive personal pronouns

In contrast to possessive nouns, **possessive personal pronouns** have no apostrophe. Singular: *my, mine, your, yours, his, her, hers, its.* Plural: *our, ours, your, yours, their, theirs.* (See also 17d; for ESL, see 32d.)

3 Demonstrative pronouns

A **demonstrative pronoun** (*this, that, these, those*) points to the noun it replaces.

pronoun   antecedent

These are the grapes my mother uses to make jelly.

4 Indefinite pronouns

An **indefinite pronoun** refers to a nonspecific person or thing. (See also 14f and 15d.)

all	anything	everyone	nobody	several
another	both	everything	none	some
any	each	few	no one	somebody
anybody	either	many	nothing	someone
anyone	everybody	neither	one	something

5 Interrogative pronouns

An **interrogative pronoun** begins a question: *who(ever)*, *which(ever)*, *whom(ever)*, *whose*, *what(ever)*. *Who wrote this poem?*

6 Relative pronouns

A **relative pronoun** (*who, which, whom, whose, that, whoever, whomever*) connects a relative clause to a noun in the main clause. (See also 10b3 and 16d.)

antecedent   relative clause

pronoun

We asked directions from a man who was selling newspapers.

7 Intensive and reflexive pronouns

Intensive and **reflexive pronouns** consist of a personal pronoun plus *-self* or *-selves*: *myself, yourself, himself, herself, itself, ourselves, yourselves, themselves*. (See also 17g.)

- An **intensive pronoun** emphasizes a noun: *Joan designed the house herself.*

- A **reflexive pronoun** identifies the receiver of an action as identical to the doer of the action: *Peter rewarded himself with a day off.*

8 Reciprocal pronouns

A **reciprocal pronoun** (*each other, one another*) refers to an individual part of a compound subject: *Pedro and Jack read each other's essays.*

8c Verbs

Verbs express action or a state of being: *run, wish, is, appear, become, taste.*

Carol Morales **is campaigning** for a seat in the legislature.

He **seems** content.

1 Helping verbs

Twenty-six **helping verbs** (also called **auxiliary verbs**) help to complete the meaning of a main verb: *They have arrived. They may arrive.*

HAVE, DO, BE	MODALS
have, has, had	can, could, may, might, must, shall,
do, does, did	should, will, would, ought to, had better, had to
be, am, is, are, was, were, being, been	

The verbs *have, do,* and *be* may also be the main verb of a sentence: *I had the answer. They were amazed.* **Modals** act only as helping verbs: *We might leave early.* (See also 13d; for ESL, see 31a–c.)

2 Main verb forms

Except for the verb *be,* the main verb of a sentence has five forms:

- Base or infinitive form: *I often (play, speak).*
- *-s/-es* or third-person form: *He often (plays, speaks).*
- Past tense: *Then I (played, spoke).*
- Past participle: *I have (played, spoken) before.*
- Present participle: *I am (playing, speaking) now.*

A note on participles: When accompanied by helping verbs, participles act as verbs: *They are playing my song.* When they stand without helping verbs, participles act as nouns or as adjectives: *Playing is sometimes hard work. Playing softly, the guitarist sang a sad song.* (See 8c5 and 10a2; for ESL, see 31f.)

3 Tense

Helping verbs and main verb forms combine to indicate **tense,** the time when an action occurs. Standard English has six tenses, and each of these tenses has a progressive *-ing* form to indicate continuous action. (See also 13b; for ESL, see 31a.)

- **Present tense:** action taking place now. *I sigh. He speaks. You/we/they are working.*

- **Past tense:** past action. *I sighed. He spoke. You/we/they were working.*

- **Future tense:** action that will take place. *I will sigh. He will speak. You/we/they will be working.*

- **Present perfect tense:** past action continuing or completed in the present. *I have sighed. He has spoken. You/we/they have been working.*

- **Past perfect tense:** past action completed before another past action. *I had sighed. He had spoken. You/we/they had been working.*

- **Future perfect tense:** action that will begin and end in the future. *I will have sighed. He will have spoken. You/we/they will have been working.*

4 Transitive, linking, and intransitive verbs

Verbs can be classified by their function in a sentence.

- A **transitive verb** acts on someone or something, called the **direct object.** (See 9c.)

  transitive verb   direct object
  The player kicked the ball into the net.

- A **linking verb** links a subject to a noun, pronoun, or adjective, called the **complement,** that describes the subject. (See also 9d1 and 14c.) Common linking verbs are *be, appear, become, feel, grow, look, remain, seem, smell, sound,* and *taste.*

  linking verb   complement
  Abidjan is the capital of the Ivory Coast.

- An **intransitive verb** does not require an object or complement to complete its meaning, although it may be followed by other words.

  The engine **hummed.** The mechanic **hummed** softly.

5 Verbals

A **verbal** is a verb acting as a noun, adverb, or adjective.

- A **gerund** is the *-ing* verb form standing alone and acting as a noun: *Writing is both a craft and an art.* The gerund *writing* is the subject of the sentence. (See also 10a2; for ESL, see 31f.)

8d

- A **participle** is the verb form ending with *-ing, -d, -ed, -en, -n,* or *-t.* When a participle stands alone, it acts as an adjective to modify or provide information about nouns and pronouns. (See also 10a2.)

Please give me **written** instructions.

Writing rapidly, she completed the letter in fifteen minutes.

- An **infinitive** consists of *to* plus the base form of the verb: *to write.* It may act as a noun, adjective, or adverb. (For ESL, see 31f.)

infinitive as a noun (the subject of the sentence)

To write effortlessly is the goal of every writer.

infinitive as an adjective modifying *assignment*

Here is your assignment to write for next week.

infinitive as an adverb modifying *use*

Use a computer to write your essay.

6 Two-word verbs

A **two-word verb** (also called a **phrasal verb**) consists of a verb and a preposition-like word called a **particle.** The meaning of a two-word verb differs from the meanings of its individual words: *Please put out* [extinguish] *your cigarette. I put the book away* [*put away* means to remove to a proper place]. *Let's put off* [postpone] *our date until next week.* (For ESL, see 31g.)

8d | Adjectives and articles

An **adjective** modifies a noun or pronoun. It answers the questions *which one, what kind,* or *how many.* (See also 18a–d; for ESL, see 32e.)

which one   how many

That rock contains three fossils.

what kind   what kind

The dark clouds warned of a dangerous storm.

A note on articles: The **articles** *a, an,* and *the* are considered adjectives. *The* is a **definite article** referring to specific persons, places, or things: *the dancer, the house. A* and *an* are **indefinite articles** referring to indefinite persons, places, or things: *a lawyer, an apple.* (For ESL, see Chapter 30.)

A note on adjective series: Two or more adjectives used together and not separated by commas must be arranged in a particular order. (See 32e3.)

8e Adverbs

An **adverb** modifies verbs, adjectives, and other adverbs. It answers the questions *how, when, where, why, under what circumstances,* and *to what extent.* (See also 18a and c; for ESL, see 32e.)

adverb modifying the adverb *softly:* how

The old man whispered very softly.

adverb modifying the verb *revise:* when

Revise your paper later.

adverb modifying the verb *are camping:* where

The scouts are camping nearby.

8f Prepositions

A **preposition** usually precedes a noun or pronoun called the **object of the preposition.** Together the preposition and its object form a **prepositional phrase,** which modifies other words in a sentence. (See also 10a1; for ESL, see 32f.)

preposition object   preposition object

The children ran into the room and knelt before the fire.

As the following list indicates, some prepositions consist of two or more words.

COMMON PREPOSITIONS

about	before	down	of	till
above	behind	during	off	to
according	below	except	on	together with
to	beneath	for	opposite	toward
across	beside	from	out	under
after	besides	in	over	underneath
against	between	in addition	past	unlike
along	beyond	to	regarding	until
among	by	in spite of	respecting	up
around	concerning	instead of	round	upon
as	considering	into	since	with
as many as	despite	like	through	within
as well as	different	near	throughout	without
at	from	next		

8g Conjunctions

A **conjunction** links words, phrases, or clauses and signals their relationship as grammatically equal or unequal.

1 Coordinating conjunctions

Coordinating conjunctions (*and, but, for, so, or, nor, yet*) link grammatically equal words and word groups. (See also 11b6, 14d, 15a, and 19a; for ESL, see 32b3.)

Kim **and** Jean played their best tennis of the season, **but** they lost to superior opponents.

2 Correlative conjunctions

Correlative conjunctions are word pairs (*both/and, either/or, neither/nor, not/but, not only/but also, whether/or*) that link grammatically equal words and word groups. (See also 14e, 15b, and 19c.)

Both the Earl of Oxford **and** Ben Jonson have been proposed as the true author of William Shakespeare's plays.

3 Subordinating conjunctions

Subordinating conjunctions begin adverb clauses and link them to independent clauses. (See also 10b2.)

In the following example, the subordinating conjunction *after* introduces an adverb clause that tells when the action of the main verb (*began*) occurs.

┌────── subordinate clause ──────┐ ┌────────── independent clause ──────────
After they finished breakfast, the campers began loading their gear into the canoes.

COMMON SUBORDINATING CONJUNCTIONS

after	even if	since	until
although	even though	so	when
as	how	than	where
as if	if	that	wherever
as though	in order that	though	whether
because	rather than	till	while
before	once	unless	why

4 Conjunctive adverbs

A **conjunctive adverb** is used with a semicolon to link independent clauses. (See also 12b3 and 35b.)

It rained five inches in the last week; **however,** the drought is far from over.

COMMON CONJUNCTIVE ADVERBS

also	furthermore	likewise	otherwise
anyhow	hence	meanwhile	similarly
anyway	however	moreover	still
besides	incidentally	nevertheless	then
consequently	indeed	next	therefore
finally	instead	nonetheless	thus

8*h* Interjections

An **interjection** is a strong expression of feeling or a call for attention, followed by a comma or exclamation point: *Oh, I'm sorry to hear that. Ouch! I've pinched my hand in the door.*

9 Sentence Parts

A sentence has two parts: a subject and a predicate. Together they make a complete statement, question, exclamation, or command. In most commands, the subject *you* is not stated.

- Statement: ⌐subject ⌐ ⌐ predicate ⌐
The sonnet has two forms, the Italian and the Elizabethan.

- Command with unstated subject *you*: ⌐ predicate ⌐
Be sure to bring the volley-ball to the picnic.

9*a* Subjects

The **subject** of a sentence names the person, place, or thing that acts, is acted on, or is described. The subject may precede or follow the predicate but usually precedes it.

She works as a pathologist.

Algae produce their food through photosynthesis.

The batik technique for dyeing fabric was developed in Malaya.

In a box under the porch slept **four tiny kittens.**

How to . . . Identify the Subjects of Sentences

Use the following tip to help you identify the subjects of sentences and other clauses.

Ask *who* or *what* + the verb + the remainder of the sentence: *Algae produce their food through photosynthesis.* What produce their food through photosynthesis? *Algae.* Note that not all sentences open with the subject: *Into the room walked the President of the United States.* Who walked into the room? *The President of the United States.*

1 Simple subjects

The **simple subject** of a sentence is a noun or pronoun by it-self, without modifying words, phrases, or clauses: *she, algae, technique, kittens.*

2 Complete subjects

The **complete subject** is the noun or pronoun and all of its modifiers: *algae, the batik technique for dyeing fabric, four tiny kittens.*

3 Compound subjects

A **compound subject** consists of two or more simple subjects linked by a conjunction.

Muscle **strength and** aerobic **efficiency** are essential to physical fitness.

9*b* | Predicates

1 Simple predicates

The **simple predicate** of a sentence consists of a verb and any helping verbs.

The locksmith **is resetting** the tumblers of the lock.

2 Complete predicates

A **complete predicate** consists of the simple predicate and all words associated with it: modifiers, objects, and complements.

┌── verb ──┐┌──── object ────┐
The locksmith is resetting the tumblers of the lock.

3 Compound predicates

A **compound predicate** consists of two or more predicates with the same subject.

```
      ┌── subject ──┐ ┌────── predicate ──────┐    ┌── predicate ──┐
```
The locksmith reset the tumblers of the lock and made a new key.

9*c* Objects

1 Direct objects

A **direct object** is the person, place, or thing that receives the action of a verb. (See also 8c4.)

```
      ┌── verb ──┐ ┌── direct object ──┐
```
Judy is growing a new variety of hosta in her garden.

2 Indirect objects

An **indirect object** is the person to whom or for whom an action occurs.

```
  subject    verb    indirect object    direct object
```
Dr. Watson gave Sherlock Holmes a clue.

9*d* Complements

Complements complete the meaning of a verb and provide additional information about a subject. (See also 14c and 18b.)

1 Subject complements

A **subject complement** is a noun or adjective that renames or describes the subject of a linking verb, such as *become, be, feel, taste.* Subject complements are also called *predicate adjectives* or *predicate nouns.* (For more on linking verbs, see 8c4.)

```
          subject complement: adjective
```
The sunset is beautiful.

```
                  subject complement: noun
```
The prince will soon become king.

2 Object complements

An **object complement** is a noun or adjective that follows a direct object and renames or describes it.

subject   verb   direct object   object complement: noun

The proud parents named their daughter Stephanie.

subject   verb   direct object   object complement: adjective

The jury found the defendant guilty.

9e | Basic English sentence patterns

English sentences can be grouped into five basic patterns according to their parts. Knowing these patterns will help you construct effective sentences. (For more on writing effective sentences, see Chapters 20 and 21.)

Pattern 1: Subject + verb

subject   verb

Writers write.

Pattern 2: Subject + verb + direct object

subject   verb direct object

Some writers write books.

Pattern 3: Subject + verb + indirect object + direct object

subject   verb indirect object direct object

Many writers write their friends letters.

Pattern 4: Subject + verb + subject complement

subject verb subject complement

Writers are creative.

Pattern 5: Subject + verb + direct object + object complement

subject   verb   direct object   object complement

Envious writers call successful writers lucky.

chapter 10 — Phrases, Clauses, and Sentence Types

To add detail to your writing, you can use single words, phrases, and clauses to expand the five sentence patterns described in 9e.

10a Phrases

A **phrase** is a grammatically related group of words lacking a subject, a verb, or both. Within a sentence a phrase may act as a noun, verb, adjective, or adverb.

> phrase as a noun | phrase as an adjective
>
> Kevin's decision to return the lost wallet was not very difficult to make.

1 Prepositional phrases

A **prepositional phrase** consists of a preposition plus a noun or pronoun (the object of the preposition) and any modifiers. (See also 8f; for ESL, see 32f.)

> preposition modifiers object
>
> at the morning roll call

Prepositional phrases may act as adjectives (telling *which one* or *what kind*), as adverbs (telling *how, when,* or *where*), or as nouns.

> prepositional phrase as an adjective: which one
>
> The man in the gray suit is my father.

> prepositional phrase as an adverb: where
>
> Sally is studying in the biology lab.

> prepositional phrase as a noun: subject complement
>
> The best time to see your instructor is before class.

2 Verbal phrases

A **verbal phrase** is a verb and its related words acting as a noun, adjective, or adverb. (See 8c5.) There are three kinds of verbal phrases.

- A **gerund phrase** consists of the *-ing* form of a verb (the present participle) and any related words: *campaigning for office, swimming in the ocean, exercising regularly.* In a sentence, a gerund phrase acts as a noun. (For ESL, see 31f.)

> gerund phrase as a subject
>
> Campaigning for office requires energy and money.

gerund phrase as a direct object

I enjoy swimming in the ocean.

gerund phrase as a complement

One key to good health is exercising regularly.

- A **participial phrase** consists of the present or past participle of a verb and any related words. A participial phrase always acts as an adjective modifying a noun or pronoun. (See also 8c5 and 11b2.)

participial phrase modifying a subject

Gazing at the painting, she recalled the house where she was born.

participial phrase modifying a direct object

The soldier put on a uniform covered with ribbons and medals.

- An **infinitive phrase** consists of the word *to* plus the base form of the verb plus any related words. It may act as a noun, adjective, or adverb.

infinitive phrase as a noun: direct object

Paul wanted to learn silk screening.

infinitive phrase as an adjective modifying *place*

Unfortunately, the library is no longer a place to find peace and quiet.

infinitive phrase as an adverb modifying *use*

Use a spell checker to help you proofread your writing.

3 Appositive phrases

An **appositive phrase** renames or describes a preceding noun or noun phrase. It usually acts like a noun or noun equivalent.

noun   appositive phrase

Shiraz, the ancient capital of Persia, is now a pilgrimage center for Shiite Muslims.

4 Absolute phrases

An **absolute phrase** consists of a noun or noun phrase plus the present or past participle of a verb and is preceded or followed by a comma. An absolute phrase modifies an entire sentence or clause.

Hands waving, the children clamored for the teacher's attention.

The sailors raised the sails eagerly, **their minds filled with dreams of home.**

10*b* Clauses

A **clause** is a group of words with a subject and a predicate: *roses are red, where the buffalo roam, which is best.*

- An **independent clause** (often called a **main clause**) can stand alone as a complete sentence: *Roses are red.*
- A **dependent clause** cannot stand alone: *where the buffalo roam, which essay is best.* Within a sentence a dependent clause may act as a noun, an adjective, or an adverb: *We were told to decide which essay is best.* The dependent clause *which essay is best* acts as a noun, the direct object of the sentence.

(To distinguish between independent and dependent clauses, see the yes/no question test in the "How to Edit Sentence Fragments" box, p. 82.)

1 Noun clauses

A **noun clause** may act as a subject, object, complement, or appositive. Noun clauses usually begin with *how, that, which, who, whoever, whom, whomever, what, whatever, when, where, whether, whose,* or *why.*

```
       ┌── subject ──┐
```
Where he went is a mystery to me.

```
                       ┌── direct object ──┐
```
Researchers have discovered what causes depression.

2 Adverb clauses

An **adverb clause** (often referred to as a **subordinate clause**) begins with a subordinating conjunction such as *after, because, since, when* (see 8g3 for a list). Adverb clauses modify verbs, adjectives, or adverbs, and tell *how, when, where, why,* or *under what conditions.* (See also 11b3.)

```
┌adverb clause that tells *when*┐
```
After the hailstorm ended, the farmers inspected their damaged crops.

3 Adjective clauses

An **adjective clause** (also called a **relative clause**) begins with a relative pronoun (*who, whoever, which, that, whose, whom, whomever*) or, occasionally, with the adverbs *when, where,* or *why*. Relative clauses act as adjectives and tell *which one* or *what kind*. (See also 11b4.)

> We plan to hire someone **who can do technical writing.**

> The land **where the buffalo roam** has been shrunk to a few national parks and preserves.

$10c$ Sentence types

Sentences can be identified by the clauses they contain or by their purposes. Knowing these sentence types will help you create sentences that are emphatic, varied, and interesting to read. (For more on emphasis and variety, see Chapters 20 and 21.)

1 Classifying sentences by their clauses

- A **simple sentence** has one independent clause and no dependent clauses. It may have a compound subject and compound predicate and one-word or one-phrase modifiers.

  ┌──────────── independent clause ────────────┐
  The Roman poet Virgil is the author of the *Aeneid.*

  ┌─────────────────── independent clause ───────────────────┐
  Adam a ¹ Eve left the Garden of Eden and entered a treacherous new world.

- A **compound sen. nce** has two or more independent clauses and no dependent clauses. Its clauses are linked by a coordinating conjunction (*and, or, but, yet, so, for, nor*) or by a semicolon. (See also 34a and 35a.)

  ┌────── independent clause ──────┐ ┌────── independent clause ──────┐
  A penny saved may be a penny earned, but the earnings don't amount to much.

- A **complex sentence** has an independent clause and at least one dependent clause.

  ┌────── dependent clause ──────┐ ┌────── independent clause ──────┐
  When the wind changed direction, the temperature began to drop.

- A **compound-complex sentence** has at least two independent clauses and at least one dependent clause.

  ┌────── independent clause ──────┐ ┌────── independent clause ──────┐
         ┌── dependent clause ──┐   ┌── dependent clause ──┐
  Imran knew that he should help, but he wasn't sure what he should do.

2 Classifying sentences by their purpose

- A **declarative sentence** makes a statement: *Bumblebees hummed in the doorway of the abandoned house.*

- An **interrogative sentence** asks a question: *Where is Lake Agassiz located?*
- An **imperative sentence** issues a command, makes a direct request, or gives advice: *When you come to the meeting, bring your copy of the annual report.*
- An **exclamatory sentence** makes an exclamation of excitement or emotion: *That's the best performance of* Othello *I've seen!*

Editing Grammar and Usage

 chapter

Editing Sentence Fragments

How to . . . **Edit Sentence Fragments**

To identify sentence fragments, follow these tips as you reread your writing.

Reading from the end of your paper. Begin at the end of your paper and read each sentence aloud. Isolating each sentence in this way will help you hear the incomplete thoughts that signal fragments.

Using the yes/no question test. If you're unsure whether a word group is a complete sentence, try the yes/no question test. If a word group is not already a question, turn it into a yes/no question. Rearrange words if necessary.

She is going to buy a new computer → Is she going to buy a new computer?

If the word group contains a single-word verb, add a helping verb. Change verb forms as necessary to complete the question.

She bought a new computer → Did she buy a new computer?

If the yes/no question makes sense and sounds complete, as in the preceding examples, the original word group is an independent clause, which can be punctuated as a complete sentence. Otherwise, the word group is a sentence fragment.

Because she is going to buy a new computer → Is because she is going to buy a new computer?

[The question doesn't make sense; therefore, the original is a fragment.]

Buying her first computer, a laptop → Is buying her first computer, a laptop?

[The question sounds incomplete; therefore, the original is a fragment.]

Looking for clue words. Look for clue words that sometimes signal sentence fragments: (1) present participles (the *-ing* verb form) without helping verbs (see 11b2); (2) a subordinating conjunction, such as *although, because, when, after,* or *if* at the beginning of a word group (see 11b3); (3) a relative pronoun—*who, which, whom,* and so forth—at the beginning of a word group that is not a question (see 11b4).

Fix fragments by connecting them to nearby complete sentences or by rewriting them as complete sentences, with subjects, verbs, and, if necessary, helping verbs. (See 11a.)

🖥 *Computer Tip:* Using Search and Replace to Find Sentence Fragments

Use the Find or Search and Replace command of your word processing program to look for clue words that sometimes signal sentence fragments (see the "How To" box above).

11*a* Connect fragments to complete sentences or rewrite them as complete sentences

A **sentence fragment** is an incomplete sentence. To be complete, a sentence must have an independent clause—a subject and verb that can stand alone. (See 9a and b, 10b.) In the following examples, fragments are italicized.

The individual most responsible for making Texas part of the United States was Sam Houston. *War hero, president of Texas, and its first senator.*

[The italicized word group is a series of noun phrases without a verb.]

Last night I opened my window to enjoy the autumn air. *Which unfortunately was filled with ragweed pollen from the vacant lot next door.*

[The italicized word group has a subject and verb, *which . . . was filled,* but the relative pronoun *which* cannot be the subject of an independent clause.]

If you sometimes write fragments, you can teach yourself to identify and rewrite them as complete sentences. (See the "How to Edit Sentence Fragments" box, p. 82.) Most fragments can be fixed in one of two ways.

1 Connecting fragments

Connect the fragment to a nearby complete sentence. Repunctuate if necessary. Use this method if your main idea is expressed in the complete sentence rather than in the fragment.

The individual most responsible for making Texas part of the United
States was Sam Houston. *War* hero, president of Texas, and its
[with insertion: , *war*]

first senator.

2 Rewriting fragments

Rewrite the fragment as a complete sentence. Add words or change word forms; if necessary, rearrange for clarity or emphasis. Use this method to emphasize an idea in the fragment or to create two sentences where one would be too long.

Last night I opened my window to enjoy the autumn air. ~~Which unfor-~~
[with insertion: *Unfortunately, it*]

~~tunately~~ was filled with ragweed pollen from the vacant lot next door.

[The relative pronoun *which* cannot be the subject of a sentence. The revision substitutes the personal pronoun *it*, which can be a subject, and rearranges for emphasis.]

11b Learn the clues that signal sentence fragments

Certain word groups are sometimes written and punctuated as if they were complete sentences. Learn to recognize them as sentence fragments.

1 Appositive phrases without verbs

Look for noun phrases—**appositive** phrases—that describe a word at the end of the preceding sentence. An appositive phrase standing alone, without a verb, is a fragment. Usually you can attach these fragments to the preceding sentence with a comma. (See also 10a3.)

The first African American to earn widespread fame as a novelist was
Richard Wright. ~~Author~~ of *Native Son* and *Black Boy*.
[with insertion: , *author*]

[Use the yes/no question test to identify the fragment: *Has the author of* Native Son *and* Black Boy? This sounds incomplete and is therefore a fragment.]

2 Phrases with present participles and no helping verbs

Phrases with -*ing* verbs—present participles—and no helping verbs are participial phrases, which cannot be punctuated as complete sentences. They lack subjects and complete verbs. (See 10a2.) Usually you can connect these fragments to the preceding sentence.

The greatest environmental threat to equatorial Africa is the
, *spreading*
Sahara/~~Spreading~~ southward during ten years of severe drought.

[Use the yes/no question test to identify the fragment: *Is spreading southward during ten years of severe drought?* This sounds incomplete and is therefore a fragment.]

3 Word groups beginning with subordinating conjunctions

Subordinating conjunctions, such as *after, because,* and *when,* link dependent to independent clauses. (See 8g3 for a list.) A dependent clause has a subject and verb, but its subordinating conjunction prevents it from being a complete sentence. A dependent clause standing by itself is a fragment. Connect it to a sentence nearby. If necessary, move it next to the words it modifies, as in this example.

Because his paintings appeal to nostalgia and sentimentality,
∧Norman Rockwell is an artist admired by many. ~~Because his paintings~~

~~appeal to nostalgia and sentimentality.~~

[Use the yes/no question test to identify the fragment: *Is because his painting appeals to nostalgia and sentimentality?* The result is a nonsense question, and the original is therefore a fragment.]

A note on punctuation: Introductory phrases and clauses are usually set off from the main part of the sentence with a comma. (See 34b.)

4 Word groups beginning with relative pronouns

Relative pronouns (*who, whom, which, that*) link a group of words—an adjective clause—to an independent clause. (See 10b3.) A relative clause has a subject and verb but is not a complete sentence. If you find a capitalized relative pronoun at the beginning of a word group that is not a question, you may have found a fragment.

, *who*
Each judge gave a long speech praising the contestants/~~Who~~ stood near

the podium, smiling nervously, waiting for the winner to be announced.

[Use the yes/no question test to identify the fragment: *Is who stood near the podium smiling nervously, waiting for the winner to be announced?* The result is a nonsense question, and the original is therefore a fragment.]

5 Lists punctuated as sentences

Connect fragmentary lists to the clause that introduces them. Use a colon, a dash, or an introductory phrase such as *for example, such as,* or *including.* (See 36a and 39a3.)

Plans for rehearsing the play should be precise/~~Two~~ weeks for

: two

memorizing the script, two weeks for learning the music, one month for

practicing the dance routines.

[To identify the fragment, apply the yes/no question test to the list.]

6 Disconnected compound predicates

One part of a compound predicate (see 9b3) separated from the other part and punctuated as a complete sentence is a fragment. Connect the fragment to the preceding sentence.

Most viewers praise the artistry in <u>Birth of a Nation</u>/~~But~~ condemn the

but

movie for its racism and distortions of American history.

Their engines groaning, several cars slowly climbed the steep mountain

road/~~Then~~ disappeared over the summit.

, then

[To identify the fragments in these examples, apply the yes/no question test to each group of words punctuated as a sentence.]

7 Long prepositional phrases

Look for phrases beginning with *during, concerning, except, in addition to, instead of.* (See 8f for a list of prepositions.) A phrase that is not connected to an independent clause is a fragment. Connect it to the preceding sentence.

The senator from Ohio proposed that all welfare recipients receive job

training or education/~~In~~ addition to welfare checks.

in

[To identify the fragment, apply the yes/no question test to each statement punctuated as a sentence.]

11*c* | Occasionally use fragments for special effect

Most writing for school, business, and the professions requires complete sentences. But occasionally, in personal, informal, or emotionally charged writing, you may use fragments to emphasize an idea, avoid repetition, or duplicate speech rhythms. To decide whether a fragment is appropriate, consider whether the situation permits informal or emotionally charged writing. Use fragments sparingly. (Fragments are italicized in the following examples.)

1 A fragment for emphasis and economy

A beautiful woman, we say in English. *But a handsome man.* "Handsome" is the masculine equivalent of—and refusal of—a compliment which has accumulated certain demeaning overtones, by being reserved for women only.
(Susan Sontag, "A Woman's Beauty: Put-down or Power Source?")

2 Fragments for emphasis, feeling, and speech rhythms

Family language, my family's sounds: the voices of my parents and sisters and brother. Their voices insisting: You belong here. We are family members. *Related. Special to one another.* Listen! *Voices singing and sighing, rising and straining, then surging, teeming with pleasure which burst syllables into fragments of laughter.* At times it seemed there was steady quiet only when, from another room, the rustling whispers of my parents faded and I edged closer to sleep.
(Richard Rodriguez, "Aria: A Memoir of a Bilingual Childhood," *American Scholar*)

12 Fixing Comma Splices and Fused Sentences

12a | Fix comma splices by repunctuating or rewriting

A **comma splice** results when two or more independent clauses (grammatically complete word groups) are linked by a comma. They are spliced together as if they were parts of one sentence instead of being punctuated as the separate statements they actually are—for example,

Ramon performed well on the first test, he expected to do even better on the second.

[*Ramon performed . . . test* is one independent clause with its own subject and predicate; *he expected . . . second* is another.]

In Standard Written English, independent clauses are not joined by only a comma. Learn to identify and fix comma splices. Choose the solution that helps you emphasize the point you want to make.

A note on ESL and dialects: Some languages and English dialects permit comma splices; Standard Written English does not.

How to . . . Edit Comma Splices

To identify comma splices, apply the yes/no question test to word groups preceding and following a comma. (The yes/no question test is explained in the "How to Edit Sentence Fragments" box, p. 82.) If these word groups make sense and sound complete by themselves, they are independent clauses linked by a comma: a comma splice.

John had told a lie, he knew he had to apologize. → Had John told a lie? Did he know he had to apologize?

> [The two questions make sense and sound complete, so they are two independent clauses linked by a comma: a comma splice.]

Because John had told a lie, he knew he had to apologize. → Had because John told a lie? Did he know he had to apologize?

> [The first question doesn't make sense, so it is not a complete sentence. The first word group is a dependent clause followed by an independent clause. Therefore, the example is a complete sentence, not a comma splice.]

The weather forecaster predicted sunshine for our picnic, however, it rained all day. → Did the weather forecaster predict sunshine for our picnic? Did it rain all day, however?

> [The yes/no question test identifies two word groups linked by a comma and the conjunctive adverb *however* that make sense and sound complete. Even with the adverb, they are independent clauses linked by a comma: a comma splice.]

Eliminate comma splices by repunctuating with a period, semicolon, colon, or dash. Or rewrite, turning one independent clause into a dependent clause or a phrase. (See 12a.)

Having told a lie, John knew he had to apologize.

The weather forecaster predicted sunshine for our picnic; however, it rained all day.

---

1 Repunctuating

- Use a **period** to make each clause a separate sentence.

  Ramon performed well on the first test/ he expected to do even better on the second. . He

- Use a **semicolon (;)** to join related independent clauses when they are nearly equal in importance. (See 35a.)

  Ramon performed well on the first test/ he expected to do even better on the second. ;

- Use a **colon (:)** to join independent clauses when one clause introduces or explains the other. (See 36a.)

  Professor Li is the best instructor I've had⸱ he knows his subject and how to present it in an imaginative way.

- Use a **dash** to join independent clauses when the second clause makes a surprising or abrupt response to the first. (See 39a.)

  Alison asked Betsy if she knew where the car keys were—she didn't.

2 Adding a coordinating conjunction

Add a coordinating conjunction (*and, but, or, nor, so, yet, for*) after the comma that joins two independent clauses. The result is a compound sentence. (See 10c1.)

and
Ramon performed well on the first test, he expected to do even better on the second.

3 Rewriting to create one complete sentence

- *Adding a subordinating conjunction.* Add a subordinating conjunction (*because, although, when,* and so forth) to one clause to connect it grammatically to the other. (See 8g3.) The result is a complex sentence that emphasizes one clause and deemphasizes the other. (See 10c1.)

  Because
  Ramon performed well on the first test, he expected to do even better on the second.

- *Turning a clause into a phrase.* Turn one clause into a phrase that modifies the remaining independent clause. The result is a simple sentence. (See 10c1.)

  After performing   *Ramon*
  ~~Ramon performed~~ well on the first test, ~~he~~ expected to do even better on the second.

12*b* | Learn the clues that signal comma splices

1 Independent clauses on both sides of a comma

Examine the words on both sides of a comma. If you can put a period after both word groups, you have two independent clauses incorrectly connected with a comma. Fix the comma splice by repunctuating or rewriting.

I'm not going to college because my parents told me to; there are specific

subjects I want to study.

[To the left of the comma, *I'm not going to college* is an independent clause; to the right, *there are specific subjects* is an independent clause.]

To identify independent clauses, use the yes/no question test. (See the "How to Edit Sentence Fragments" box, p. 82.) The first word group in the preceding example becomes *Am I going to college because my parents told me to?* The second becomes *Are there specific subjects I want to study?* Both questions sound complete and make sense; they are, therefore, independent clauses joined by a comma—a comma splice.

2   A second clause that begins with a pronoun

In some comma splices the subject of the second independent clause is a pronoun referring to the subject of the first.

Julian refused the award for heroism. He said he had only done what

anyone would.

[The *he* following the comma is the subject of the second independent clause; it also refers to the subject of the first, *Julian*.]

3   Independent clauses joined by a comma and a transition or conjunctive adverb

Transitions and conjunctive adverbs link words and word groups (see 7b and 8g4).

COMMON TRANSITIONS AND CONJUNCTIVE ADVERBS

accordingly	conversely	in fact	otherwise
after all	even so	in other words	similarly
also	finally	in the first place	specifically
anyhow	for example	likewise	still
anyway	for instance	meanwhile	subsequently
as a matter of fact	furthermore	moreover	then
as a result	hence	nevertheless	therefore
at any rate	however	next	thus
at the same time	indeed	now	that is
besides	instead	of course	
certainly	in addition	on the contrary	
consequently	in conclusion	on the other hand	

These words seem similar to the coordinating conjunctions (*and, but, for, nor, or, so,* and *yet*) but are grammatically different. Joining independent clauses with a comma plus a transition or conjunctive adverb produces a comma splice. Use a semicolon instead.

Mass transit offers many environmental benefits/ for example, the

nitrogen emissions responsible for smog are greatly reduced.

[The linking of two independent clauses with a comma and the transition *for example* produces a comma splice. To join independent clauses, use a semicolon before a transition.]

John did not enjoy mathematics/ however, if he was going to study

economics, he had to understand statistics.

[The linking of two independent clauses with a comma and the conjunctive adverb *however* produces a comma splice. To join independent clauses, use a semicolon before a conjunctive adverb.]

A note on other uses of conjunctive adverbs: A comma plus a transition or conjunctive adverb does not always signal a comma splice: *Both parents may work part-time, however, to share the care of their children.* The word group before *however* is an independent clause; the word group after *however* is a phrase. The commas before and after *however* signal a pause within a single independent clause. (See also 34f.)

12c Fix fused sentences by punctuating or rewriting

A **fused sentence,** sometimes called a **run-together** or **run-on,** results when two or more grammatically complete sentences are joined with no punctuation between them. They are joined—fused—so tightly that they appear to be a single sentence, not two sentences.

Consider this example:

Soon the holidays will be here once more many will miss an opportunity to share themselves and their possessions with the less fortunate.

Did you stumble as you read this example? If you did, you experienced the effect of fused sentences. Learn to identify and rewrite fused sentences, usually by adding punctuation or making one sentence subordinate to the other.

1 Adding punctuation

■ *Periods.* Use a period to separate one independent clause from another.

. *Once*

Soon the holidays will be here once more many will miss an opportunity

to share themselves and their possessions with the less fortunate.

[In this example, *the holidays will be here* is one independent clause; *many will miss an opportunity* is the second.]

- *Semicolons and colons.* Use a semicolon to link related independent clauses roughly equal in importance. (See 35a.) Use a colon to link independent clauses when one clause introduces or explains the other. (See 36a.)

The Grand Canyon is not the first choice of travelers familiar with

canyon scenery ;that honor goes to Zion National Park or Bryce

Canyon.

It all began like this: I had a new computer and needed help installing

the software.

How to . . . Edit Fused Sentences

Follow these tips to identify fused sentences.

1. Reread your writing aloud at a steady pace. If you have written a fused sentence, you may stumble where two separate thoughts blur together. Pause and study your words. Divide them into separate word groups.

   In 1900, there were few forests in Vermont now the state is covered with woodlands. → [1] In 1900, there were few forests in Vermont [2] now the state is covered with woodlands.

2. Can each word group be punctuated as a complete sentence? To find out, use the yes/no question test (see the "How to Edit Sentence Fragments" box, p. 82).

   Were there few forests in Vermont in 1900? Is the state now covered with woodlands?

   [The yes/no question test reveals two word groups that sound complete and make sense: independent clauses that could be punctuated as complete sentences. Linking them without punctuation creates a fused sentence.]

   To fix fused sentences, put a period, semicolon, colon, or dash between independent clauses. Or rewrite to create two complete sentences.

   In 1900, there were few forests in Vermont. Now the state is covered with woodlands.

- A comma + a coordinating conjunction. Insert a comma before a coordinating conjunction (*and, but, or, nor, so, yet, for*) to link related independent clauses.

  I enjoy cooking**,** but cleaning up afterward is another matter.

- *A semicolon plus a transition or conjunctive adverb.* Insert a semicolon before a transition or conjunctive adverb linking independent clauses. (For a list of transitions and conjunctive adverbs, see 12b3.)

  The Jensens knew that starting a business would not be easy**;** however**,**

  they did not imagine how difficult it would be.

  [The semicolon links two independent clauses; the comma is added following *however* to signal a pause. For more on punctuating transitional words and phrases, see 34f.]

2 Rewriting to make one clause subordinate to the other

Add a subordinating conjunction (*because, although, when, since,* and so forth) to an independent clause to make it a dependent clause. Connect the dependent clause to the remaining independent clause to make one complete sentence. (For a list of subordinating conjunctions, see 8g3.)

The witness did not understand the lawyer's question about South
because
Carolina he had never been to South Carolina.

[Adding the subordinating conjunction *because* turns the second independent clause, beginning with *he had,* into a dependent clause.]

3 Compressing two independent clauses into one sentence

Omit words or change word forms to make one shorter sentence out of two independent clauses.

Travelers
~~The Grand Canyon is not the first choice of travelers~~ familiar
                                                         prefer
with canyon scenery ~~that honor goes to~~ Zion National Park or
        to the Grand Canyon
Bryce Canyon.

The Jensens ~~knew that starting a business would not be easy however~~

~~they~~ did not imagine how difficult it would be/ *to start a business.*

13 Choosing Verb Forms

How to . . . Edit Troublesome Verbs

Follow these tips to identify and edit verbs.

1. To find the verbs in a sentence, change the time of the action, from present to past, past to present, and so forth. The verbs will change form and reveal themselves: *The leaves fluttered in the breeze.* → *The leaves are fluttering in the breeze.* (See 8c3.)
2. To find the correct forms of irregular verbs like *blow* and *draw*, see the lists in 13a3.
3. To use *lie/lay, sit/set,* and *rise/raise* correctly, see 13a5.
4. To choose the correct tense when writing about literature, quoting, or arranging events in sequence, see 13b.
5. If your first language is not English or if you speak a dialect other than Standard English, check to see that you have used correct helping verbs and correct verb endings. See 13a4 and 13c, d, and e.

💻 *Computer Tip:* Using Your Spell Checker to Edit Verbs

Use your spell checker to check for verbs with incorrect endings. They often show up as misspellings.

13a Use the standard forms of irregular verbs

1 Identifying main verb forms

Except for the verb *be,* the main verb of a sentence has five forms:

- Base or infinitive form: *I often (play, speak).*
- *-s/-es,* or third-person form: *He often (plays, speaks).*
- Past tense: *Then I (played, spoke).*
- Past participle: *I have (played, spoken) before.*
- Present participle: *I am (playing, speaking) now.*

2 Identifying regular and irregular verbs

Regular verbs form the past tense and past participle in predictable ways, by adding *-d* or *-ed.* **Irregular verbs** form the past tense and past participle in various unpredictable ways.

	PRESENT TENSE	PAST TENSE	PAST PARTICIPLE
Regular verbs	play	played	played
	believe	believed	believed
Irregular verbs	begin	began	begun
	eat	ate	eaten

The past-tense forms of regular and irregular verbs can stand alone, without any helping verb, as the main verb in a sentence: *The pianist played softly. The pianist began her solo.* The past participles of regular and irregular verbs cannot stand alone as the main verb in a sentence; they need a helping verb like *is, has, had, were,* or *does* to complete their meaning: *She had played this song many times before. The concert has begun.*

3 Identifying frequently used irregular verbs

If you're unsure about the form of an irregular verb or about whether a verb is irregular, consult this list of frequently used irregular verbs or your dictionary.

PRESENT TENSE	PAST TENSE	PAST PARTICIPLE
awake	awoke, awakened	awakened
be	was, were	been
beat	beat	beaten
begin	began	begun
bend	bent	bent
bite	bit	bitten, bit
blow	blew	blown
break	broke	broken
bring	brought	brought
build	built	built
burst	burst	burst
buy	bought	bought
catch	caught	caught
choose	chose	chosen
come	came	come
cost	cost	cost
do	did	done
draw	drew	drawn
drink	drank	drunk
drive	drove	driven
eat	ate	eaten
fall	fell	fallen
find	found	found
flee	fled	fled
fly	flew	flown
forget	forgot	forgotten
freeze	froze	frozen

PRESENT TENSE	PAST TENSE	PAST PARTICIPLE
get	got	gotten
give	gave	given
go	went	gone
grow	grew	grown
hang (to suspend)	hung	hung
hang (to execute)	hanged	hanged
hear	heard	heard
hide	hid	hidden
hold	held	held
keep	kept	kept
know	knew	known
lay (to place something)	laid	laid
lead	led	led
leave	left	left
lend	lent	lent
lie (to recline, to rest on a surface)	lay	lain
lose	lost	lost
pay	paid	paid
ride	rode	ridden
ring	rang	rung
rise	rose	risen
run	ran	run
say	said	said
see	saw	seen
set (to place)	set	set
shake	shook	shaken
shrink	shrank	shrunk
sing	sang	sung
sink	sank	sunk
sit (to be seated)	sat	sat
slide	slid	slid
speak	spoke	spoken
spend	spent	spent
spring	sprang	sprung
stand	stood	stood
steal	stole	stolen
strike	struck	struck
swim	swam	swum
take	took	taken
teach	taught	taught
tear	tore	torn
tell	told	told
throw	threw	thrown
wear	wore	worn
weave	wove	woven
write	wrote	written

4 Avoiding switched verb forms

A note on dialect: Some speakers of English use verb forms different from those of Standard English. They add regular endings to irregular verbs (*blowed* instead of *blown*), treat regular verbs as if they were irregular (*drug* instead of *dragged*), or use the past participle in place of the past tense (*seen* instead of *saw.*)

NONSTANDARD ENGLISH	STANDARD ENGLISH	NONSTANDARD ENGLISH	STANDARD ENGLISH
brung	brought	drived	drove
binded	bound	drug	dragged
blowed	blew	growed	grew
catched	caught	snuck	sneaked
creeped	crept	sweared	swore
costed	cost	had went	had gone
drawed	drew		

In your writing, use the appropriate standard forms for the past tense and past participle of regular and irregular verbs.

        dragged
They ~~drug~~ the sandbags onto the levee.
[*Drag* is a regular verb that forms the past tense with *-ed.*]

        blew
The wind ~~blowed~~ from the northeast for fourteen days.
[As an irregular verb, *blow* forms the past tense irregularly.]

    saw
We ~~seen~~ him in his garage last night.
[The past tense of *see* is *saw*, not *seen*, which is the past participle.]

        given
My brother had ~~gave~~ his keys to the mechanic so he could start the car.
[The past participle is required for action begun and completed in the past.]

5 Using *lie/lay*, *sit/set*, and *rise/raise* correctly

The words in each of these pairs are often confused. One is an intransitive verb, the other a transitive verb (see 8c4). **Intransitive verbs** do not require direct objects; they indicate states of being or conditions: *The basket is sitting on the table.* **Transitive verbs** take direct objects; they do something to someone or something: *The boy set the basket on the table.* Avoid confusing one kind of verb with the other.

- *Lie, lay, lain, lying* (intransitive) means "to rest on or to recline": *He lay down to take a nap. The book is lying on the table. The cat had lain in the basket for an hour.*

- *Lay, laid, laid, laying* (transitive) means "to put or place something": *I will lay the pillow on the bed. He laid the book on the table.*

- *Sit, sat, sat, sitting* (intransitive) means "to be seated": *She sat down at the piano.*

- *Set, set, set, setting* (transitive) means "to put or place something in a particular position": *The student set the pen on the desk.*

- *Rise, rose, risen, rising* (intransitive) means "to get up from a lying, sitting, or kneeling position": *She rose from the chair.*

- *Raise, raised, raised, raising* (transitive) means "to move something or someone to a higher position": *He raised his hand to speak.*

6 Spelling irregular verbs correctly

Because of their similarity to other words, the following irregular verbs are sometimes misspelled.

- *Laid/"layed."* The past tense of the verb *lay* is *laid,* not "layed."
  He ~~layed~~ the book on the table. *(laid)*

- *Led/lead.* The past tense of the verb *lead* is *led,* not "lead."
  The leader ~~lead~~ the soldiers into battle. *(led)*
  [When *lead* is pronounced like *led,* it refers to the soft gray metal or to pencil lead.]

- *Lose/loose. Lose* is a verb; *loose* is an adjective.
  If he doesn't improve his grades, he may ~~loose~~ his scholarship. *(lose)*

- *Paid/"payed."* The past tense of the verb *pay* is *paid,* not "payed."
  The workers were ~~payed~~ weekly. *(paid)*

13*b* Choose verb tenses that put events in sequence

Tense is the time when the action of a verb takes place. Verbs change form to indicate tense: present (*she is studying*), past (*she studied*), and so forth. Sometimes it is difficult to know which tense to use to describe an action, especially if there is more than one action involved. The following guidelines will help you decide. (To review the six tenses of English verbs and the way to create them, see 8c3; for ESL, see 31a.)

1 Using the present tense in special situations

- *Writing about literature.* Authors of fiction, poetry, and nonfiction usually write in the past tense—for example: *When Paul went down to dinner, the music of the orchestra came floating up the elevator shaft to greet him* [Willa Cather]. But to summarize action in a literary paper, use the present tense. (See 59f2.)

  goes   *hears*
  When Paul ~~went~~ down to dinner, he ~~heard~~ the orchestra through the

  elevator shaft.

- *Introducing quotations, summaries, and paraphrases.* In research writing, use present-tense verbs such as *reports, suggests,* and *argues* in signal phrases that introduce quotations, summaries, and paraphrases. Follow this convention whether the writer you cite is living or dead. (See also 50c1 for a list of these verbs.)

  argues
  In the essay "Violent Crime," Bruce Shapiro ~~argued~~ that current

  anticrime legislation is based on "a delusion, a myth" about criminals.

  A note on APA style: If you include a date in the text of your writing, as the American Psychological Association style requires, use the past tense to introduce your borrowing: *In the essay "Violent Crime," Shapiro (1995) argued that current anticrime legislation is based on "a delusion, a myth" about criminals.* (See also 54a1.)

- *Describing scientific principles and general truths.* Use the present tense to describe accepted scientific principles or general truths.

  describes
  Ohm's law ~~described~~ the amount of resistance in an electrical circuit.

  declares   *are*
  The Declaration of Independence ~~declared~~ that all people ~~were~~ created

  equal.

2 Using the present perfect tense to describe past action continuing in the present

Use the present perfect tense (*has/have* + the past participle: *has laughed, have eaten*) when actions begin in the past and continue in the present or occur at no specific time.

have never forgotten
I ~~never forgot~~ my mother's words of wisdom.

[Because the writer still remembers these words, the present perfect tense is appropriate.]

3 Using the past perfect tense to describe past action completed before some other past action

Use the past perfect tense (*had* + the past participle: *had laughed, had eaten*) when a past action begins and is completed before some other past action.

The police officer stated that my brother ~~was~~ *had been* in an accident.

[The accident occurred before the officer informed the writer.]

When the hikers reached the lake, they found that someone *had* camped there recently.

[Others had camped there before the hikers arrived.]

4 Using infinitives and participles in a sequence of events

Use infinitives and participles to refer to actions that are related in some way to the action expressed by the main verb.

- *Simultaneous actions: the present infinitive.* Use the present infinitive (*to* + the base verb form: *to laugh, to eat*) for actions occurring at the same time as or immediately after the action of the main verb.

  Park officials tried to ~~have~~ *spray* ~~sprayed~~ for mosquitoes after every rain.

  [The action of the infinitive *to spray* occurred at the same time as the action of the main verb *tried.*]

- *One action and then another: the present perfect infinitive.* Use the present perfect infinitive (*to have* + the past participle: *to have laughed, to have eaten*) for actions occurring before the action of the main verb.

  The mayor would like to ~~give~~ *have given* a speech before the council voted on the resolution.

  [The speech would have occurred in the past before the mayor's wish. Therefore, the present perfect infinitive (*to have given*) is required.

- *Simultaneous actions: the present participle.* Use the present participle (*-ing*) for an action occurring simultaneously with that of the main verb: *Pulling into the parking lot, he saw a thief smashing a car window.*

- *One action and then another: the past participle or present perfect participle.* Use the past participle (*laughed, eaten*) or the present perfect participle (*having* + the past participle: *having laughed, having eaten*) for an action occurring before that of the main verb.

  ~~Finishing~~ *Having finished* his exam before the period was half over, Kim asked to be excused.

13*c* | Use *-s/-es* endings on present-tense verbs that have third-person-singular subjects

A note on dialect and ESL: Some speakers of English drop the *-s* or *-es* from third-person-singular verbs in the present tense: *he works* becomes *he work.* In your writing, take care to add *-s* or *-es* to third-person-singular verbs following the types of words listed below.

- Singular nouns: *Joan hikes. The baby cries.*
- Singular personal pronouns: *She hikes. He sings. It flies.*
- Indefinite pronouns, which are usually singular: *Everyone hikes. Each sings. No one qualifies.*

tries *keeps*
He ~~try~~ to come home early, but his job often ~~keep~~ him out late.

13*d* | Use the Standard English forms of the verbs *be, have,* and *do*

A note on dialect: Some speakers of English use the forms of *be, have,* and *do* in ways different from Standard English. In your writing, use Standard English verb forms.

1 *Be*

The eight forms of *be* (*be, am, is, are, was, were, been, being*) make it the most complex English verb.

	SINGULAR	PLURAL
First person	I am/am being/ was/have been	we are/are being/ were/have been
Second person	you are/are being/ were/have been	you are/are being/ were/have been
Third person	he, she, or it is/is being/ was/has been	they are/are being/ were/have been

To use *be* in its Standard English forms, follow these guidelines:

- *Events in progress or habitual events.* Use the third-person-singular *-s* form (*is*) plus the present participle (*-ing*) to indicate events in progress and habitual or continuous events: *is laughing.*

is
He going to school.
[He is on his way to school.]

is
He ~~be~~ going to school.
[He is currently attending school.]

- *Using* am, is, *and* was *with first-person-singular and third-person-singular verbs.* Use *am, is,* and *was* with first- and third-person-singular verbs. Otherwise, use *are* and *were.*

  was
  She ~~were~~ trying to get her essay published in the campus magazine.
  ^
  [The third-person-singular pronoun *she* takes a third-person-singular verb, *was.*]

- *Omitted verbs.* In informal Standard English, forms of the verb *be* are sometimes shortened and combined with their subjects: *I'm, you're, she's, we're, they're.* But these verbs must not be omitted entirely. (See also 31a2.)

  'm
  I working forty hours a week.
  ^

  is
  The actress on stage now.
  ^

2 Have

Use the -s form *has* for the third-person singular (*John has*). Use *have* for all other present-tense and present-perfect forms (*we have*). Do not omit *has* or *have* when these forms are used as helping verbs: *John has worked, we have lived.* (See also 31a2.)

has
She ~~have~~ come to every meeting of the drama club.
^

has
He been a successful businessman for twenty years.
^

have
They been going to Canada every summer for five years.
^

3 Do

Use the -es form *does* for the third-person singular (*she does*). Use *do* for all other present-tense forms. (See also 31b.)

doesn't
Merrilee ~~don't~~ want to go to the party this weekend.
^

Does
~~Do~~ he ever consider other people's feelings?
^

13*e* Beware of omitting or misusing verb endings in words like *used to, supposed to, asked,* and *would have*

Influenced by the sound of spoken English, writers occasionally omit or confuse verb endings. Follow these guidelines to Standard English verb endings.

1 *Used to* and *supposed to*

"Use to" and "suppose to" are nonstandard. Write *used to* and *supposed to*.

supposed
Polly was ~~suppose~~ to fly to Memphis at the beginning of the month.

used
Scientists ~~use~~ to believe that outer space was filled with ether.

2 Past and past perfect endings

The *-d* and *-ed* endings signal the past and perfect tenses of regular verbs.

frightened
The little boy ~~frighten~~ the ducklings.

asked
My mother has ~~ask~~ me to call her every week.

developed
Robert Goddard was the American who ~~develop~~ the rocket engine.

3 *Would, could, should*

"Would of," "could of," and "should of" are nonstandard. Write *would have* or *would've, could have* or *could've, should have* or *should've.*

have
We would ~~of~~ won the tournament if we had practiced harder.

13f Use the subjunctive mood for wishes and other nonfactual statements

The **mood** of a verb is a verb form that indicates how the writer or speaker views the action expressed by the verb. The **indicative mood** is used to make statements of fact and to ask questions: *She looked happy. They would have won. Are you sad?* The **imperative mood** is used for commands or direct requests: *Come home. Try again.*

The **subjunctive mood** is used for statements contrary to fact: wishes, speculations, assumptions, recommendations, indirect requests, and hypothetical situations.

To form the **present-tense subjunctive,** use the base form of the verb (*be, give, arrive*).

It is important that everyone arrive by nine o'clock.

To form the **past-tense subjunctive,** use *were,* not *was.*

If I were better organized, I would get more done.

Though slowly disappearing from English, the subjunctive is still used in certain phrases and situations.

1 Wishes and desires

Use the subjunctive to express wishes and to follow verbs expressing a wish or desire: *ask, insist, move, recommend, request, suggest,* and *urge.*

We recommend that the dean ~~awards~~ *award* an honors certificate to Carlos

Montoya.

[present-tense subjunctive]

Gena wished that the instructor ~~was~~ *were* finished with his lecture.

[past-tense subjunctive]

2 Nonfactual statements

Use the past-tense subjunctive after *if* or *as if* to express hypothetical or nonfactual situations.

If I ~~was~~ *were* you, I would study harder for tomorrow's quiz.

3 Indirect requests

Use the subjunctive to express indirect requests.

It is important that you ~~are~~ *be* in your seat before the concert begins.

[present-tense subjunctive]

4 Speculation

Use the subjunctive to make a speculation.

If James ~~was~~ *were* going with us, he would be here by now.

[past-tense subjunctive]

14 Making Subjects and Verbs Agree

Agreement is the correspondence of one word to another in number, person, and sometimes gender. Subjects and verbs must agree in number (singular or plural) and person (first, second, and third), as in the following examples.

	SINGULAR	PLURAL
First person	I run	we run
Second person	you run	you run
Third person	he/she/it runs, Pauline runs	they run

18 Choosing Adjectives and Adverbs

chapter

How to . . . Edit Adjectives and Adverbs

Follow these tips to identify and edit adjectives and adverbs.

1. Adjectives answer the questions *which one, what kind, how many*. They modify (provide information about) nouns and pronouns. Adverbs answer the questions *how, when, where, why*. They modify verbs, adjectives, and other adverbs. (See 18a.)
2. Look for linking verbs (*be, appear, become, feel, grow, look, prove, remain, smell, seem, sound, taste, turn*) that are often followed by complements, words describing the subject of the sentence. Be sure that these complements are adjectives or nouns, not adverbs. (See 18b1.)
3. Look for the verbs *call, consider, create, elect, find, keep,* and *make*. Use adjectives, not adverbs, to modify their direct objects. (See 18b2.)
4. Look for *good, bad, well, badly*. Use *good* and *bad* as adjectives, especially after linking verbs like *be, look,* and *smell*. Use *well* as an adjective to refer to health; otherwise, use *well* as an adverb. Use *badly* as an adverb.
5. Look for comparative statements. Use comparative forms (*-er, more, less*) to compare two subjects; use superlative forms (*-est, most, least*) to compare three or more. Use one comparative form at a time, *-er* or *more, -est* or *most*. (See 18d.)
6. Look for absolutes, words like *unique, perfect,* or *priceless*, which cannot be compared. Omit the comparative or superlative or rewrite to make your meaning clear. (See 18d4.)
7. Look for negative words. Use one negative word at a time. (See 18e.)

18*a*   Use adjectives to modify nouns and pronouns; use adverbs to modify verbs, adjectives, and other adverbs

1 Using adjectives

Adjectives modify—provide information about—nouns and pronouns and indicate *which one, what kind,* or *how many*. (See 8d.)

which one   what kind
That tall, heavyset man is an excellent dancer.

A note on adjectives in sequence: Two or more adjectives with no commas separating them must be arranged in a specific order. (See 34d; for ESL, see 32e3.)

2 Using adverbs

Adverbs modify verbs, adjectives, and other adverbs and indicate *how, when, where, why,* or *under what conditions: She spoke enthusiastically.* (See 8e.) Many adverbs, as in this example, end in *-ly,* but not all: *always, here, nearby, there,* and *very.* And some *-ly* words are adjectives: *friendly* and *lovely.*

In casual speech adjectives are sometimes substituted for adverbs, usually by dropping the *-ly* from the end of an adverb. In writing, however, use adverbs to modify verbs, adjectives, and other adverbs.

Stock market investors in 1929 ~~sure~~ *surely* did not expect the market to crash.

[The adverb *surely* is necessary to modify the verb *expect.*]

Second-parent adoption is a ~~rapid~~ *rapidly* growing phenomenon.

[The adverb *rapidly* is necessary to modify the verbal adjective *growing.*]

It was a ~~real~~ *very* beautiful morning, perhaps the best of the summer.

[In casual speech *real* is sometimes used to modify adjectives like *beautiful.* But in Standard English use *very.*]

18b | Use adjectives as complements

Adjectives usually appear before nouns. But they may also follow certain verbs as complements, words that complete the meaning of a noun or pronoun.

1 Using adjectives as subject complements

Subject complements describe or rename the subjects of linking verbs such as *be, become, feel, look, smell, seem, sound,* and *taste* (see 9d1). Use an adjective as a subject complement following a linking verb.

She *became* **angry**; he *felt* **sick.**

Does anything smell as ~~sweetly~~ *sweet* as a freshly mowed lawn?

[*Sweet,* an adjective, modifies the subject *anything,* not the linking verb *smell.* It describes a thing, not an action.]

2 Using adjectives as object complements

Object complements give information about the direct objects of verbs such as *call, consider, create, elect, find, keep,* and *make.* (See 9c1 and 9d2.) Use adjectives to modify noun and pronoun direct objects.

A safe-deposit box will keep valuable papers **secure.**

The personnel manager considered the applicants ~~equally~~.
equal

[*Equal* is an adjective describing the direct object *applicants.* In the original sentence, *equally* modifies *considered* and describes the action of the manager.]

18c Use *good/well* and *bad/badly* correctly

Some writers find these words troublesome because of the influence of casual speech; others try too hard to use them correctly. Follow these guidelines to the correct use of *good, well, bad,* and *badly.*

1 Using *good* and *bad* as adjectives

Use *good* and *bad* as adjectives after linking verbs (see the list in 18b1): *The fresh bread smelled good. The music from those speakers sounds bad.*

As the coach studied her players, she thought how ~~well~~ everyone
good

looked.

[*Good* is a subject complement accompanying the linking verb *looked* and describing the appearance, not the health, of the subject *everyone.*]

Bill felt ~~badly~~ about his behavior.
bad

[Following the linking verb *felt, bad* is an adjective, a subject complement describing the subject *Bill.* It does not describe the act of feeling.]

2 Using *well* as an adjective or an adverb

Use *well* as an adjective to refer to health or well-being. Otherwise, use it as an adverb modifying verbs, adjectives, and other adverbs.

After three weeks' rest, I feel ~~good~~ again.
well

[Here *well* is an adjective following a linking verb and modifying the subject *I.*]

After its tuneup, the car runs ~~good~~.
well

[Here *well* is an adverb modifying the verb *runs.*]

3 Using *badly* as an adverb

Use *badly* as an adverb: *The team played badly.*

18*d* Use the comparative and superlative forms of adjectives correctly

1 Forming comparatives and superlatives

Adjectives and adverbs have three forms to indicate degree or intensity: **positive, comparative,** and **superlative.**

POSITIVE	COMPARATIVE	SUPERLATIVE
good	better	best
bad	worse	worst
happy	happier	happiest
beautiful	more beautiful, less beautiful	most beautiful, least beautiful

To form comparatives and superlatives, follow these guidelines:

- *One-syllable adjectives and adverbs.* One-syllable adjectives and adverbs generally use *-er* and *-est* (*taller, tallest; faster, fastest*).
- *Two-syllable adjectives.* Two-syllable adjectives accented on the first syllable generally use *-er* and *-est* (*happier, happiest; lovelier, loveliest*).
- *Three-syllable adjectives.* Three-syllable adjectives use *more/most, less/least* (*more beautiful, most beautiful; less beneficial, least beneficial*).
- *Two- and three-syllable adverbs.* Two- and three-syllable adverbs, especially those ending *-ly,* use *more/most, less/least* (*more slowly, most slowly; less happily, least happily*).
- *Irregular adjectives and adverbs.* Memorize these irregular words: *good/better/best; bad/worse/worst; far/farther/farthest; far/further/furthest; little/less/least; many/more/most.*

2 Choosing between comparative and superlative forms

Use the comparative form to compare two things, the superlative to compare three or more.

Although Ernest Hemingway and William Faulkner are considered
major novelists, Hemingway has been ~~most~~ *more* influential.
[Two writers are compared; the comparative form is necessary.]

My chores were weeding, planting, and, ~~worse~~ *worst* of all, emptying garbage.
[Three activities are compared; the superlative form is necessary.]

3 Avoiding repetition of comparative or superlative forms

Use either *-er/-est* or *more/most,* not both.

Increasing the number of pedestrians will lead to a ~~more~~ healthier environment.

That was the most ~~unkindest~~ *unkind* remark I have ever heard.

4 Avoiding comparison of absolutes

Absolutes are words describing characteristics that cannot be compared. *Unique,* for example, means one of a kind; something cannot be more unique ("more one of a kind") or most unique ("most one of a kind"). Other absolutes: *absolute, boundless, circular, complete, definite, empty, eternal, enough, favorite, final, full, inevitable, mutual, perfect, perpendicular, priceless, round, square, sufficient, supreme, total, triangular, universal, vacant.* Avoid the comparison of absolutes.

Your story will be ~~more~~ complete when you add an exciting ending.

Of all the old jazz bands, the Count Basie Orchestra is my ~~most~~ favorite.

18e | Avoid double negatives

A note on dialect: A **double negative** says *no* twice and seems to contradict itself: *Eighteen-year-olds without jobs don't have nothing to lose by joining the army.* A logical person might say that if these young people do *not* have *nothing* to lose, then they must have *something* to lose.

Of course, no one misunderstands double negatives in this way, and in many dialects of English the double negative is a way of saying *no* emphatically. But Standard English tends to be logical. Therefore, avoid double negatives in writing. Avoid using *not, never,* or *no* with other negative words, such as *no one, nobody, neither, none, nothing, barely, hardly,* and *scarcely.*

Eighteen-year-olds without jobs ~~don't~~ have nothing to lose by joining the military.

She ~~can't hardly~~ *can barely* swim a stroke.

Despite what some may think, welfare recipients don't live ~~no~~ *a* life of ease.

An exception: You may use a double negative to soften the intensity of a positive statement or to suggest irony: *Karen was not unhappy to learn she would graduate with honors.*

^{chapter}19 Putting Linked Words in Parallel Form

Parallel form (also known as **parallelism or parallel structure**) refers to a similarity in the grammatical structure of two or more words, phrases, or clauses that are linked by coordinating conjunctions or in some other way. In the phrase *Rosario or Maria, Rosario* and *Maria* are parallel nouns linked by a coordinating conjunction. Similarly, *revise and edit* is a pair of linked, parallel verbs. Abraham Lincoln's *government of the people, by the people, for the people* is a series of parallel prepositional phrases. And from President John Kennedy's inaugural address, *ask not what your country can do for you—ask what you can do for your country* is a pair of parallel clauses. Parallelism is a way to join and emphasize equally important ideas.

Faulty parallelism occurs when linked words do not have the same grammatical form. *To hike or skiing* links a verb and a noun. *Tall, dark, handsome, and with a sly wit* links three adjectives to a prepositional phrase. To make your sentences emphatic and grammatical, put linked words in parallel form. (See also 20c.)

How to . . . Edit for Parallel Form

Follow these tips to identify and fix faulty parallelism:

1. Look for the conjunctions *and, or, but, yet, so, for, nor.* Be sure the linked words before and after them are parallel in form. (See 19a–c.)
2. Look for comparisons. Be sure that the items being compared have the same grammatical form. (See 19d.)

⌨ *Computer Tip:* Using Search and Replace to Edit for Parallel Form

Use the Find or Search and Replace command to locate conjunctions. Then determine whether the linked words are parallel in form (see item 1 in the "How To" box above).

19*a* Make words linked by a coordinating conjunction parallel in form

Coordinating conjunctions (*and, but, yet, for, so, or, nor*) link grammatically equal words. (See 8g1.) Use parallel forms before and after these conjunctions.

jogging
Among her favorite sports, Jill likes ~~to jog~~ and racquetball the most.
^

[In the original, the verb form *to jog* is linked to a noun, *racquetball*. The revision links a noun to a noun.]

having
Nearing thirty-five and ~~with~~ only a high school diploma, Alan is
^

pessimistic about his future.

[In the original, an adjective phrase, *nearing thirty-five*, is linked to a prepositional phrase, *with only a high school diploma*. The revision links two adjective phrases, *nearing thirty-five* and *having only a high school diploma*.]

19b | Make words in a series or a list parallel in form

Words in series may be linked by a conjunction, or they may be a list. In either case, make each item in the series grammatically parallel to the others.

As I plan this semester, I am dividing my life into three categories:
school
~~academic~~, work, and pleasure.
^

[In the original, the adjective *academic* is linked with two nouns. The revision links three nouns.]

Representative Cairns criticized her opponent as soft on crime,
quick to raise taxes
indifferent to voters, and ~~a tax-and-spend politician~~.
^

[The original links two adjective phrases (*soft on crime, indifferent to voters*) to a noun phrase (*a tax-and-spend politician*). The revision links three adjective phrases.]

19c | Make words linked by a correlative conjunction (*either . . . or*) parallel in form

Correlative conjunctions are linking phrases that come in two parts: *either . . . or, neither . . . nor, not only . . . but also, both . . . and, whether . . . or.* (See 8g2.) Make words linked by correlative conjunctions grammatically parallel. Do not use a comma after the first part.

When it comes to fast food, I love not only old favorites like hamburgers

but also ethnic foods like falafel ~~make my mouth water~~.

[The original links a noun phrase *old favorites like hamburgers* to a clause *ethnic foods like falafel make my mouth water*. The revision links two noun phrases, *old favorites like hamburgers* and *but also ethnic foods like falafel*.]

camping
Cassie was undecided whether to go white water rafting or ~~camp~~.
^

[The original links a verbal noun—the gerund *rafting*—to the verb *camp*. The revision links two gerunds, *rafting* and *camping*.]

19d | Make comparisons using *than* or *as* parallel in form

to compose
Many students find it easier to write a research paper than ~~composing~~ a

poem.

[The original links the infinitive *to write* and the gerund *composing*. The revision links two infinitives, *to write . . . than to compose*.]

the Acropolis
The Anasazi ruins of Mesa Verde are as impressive as in Athens ~~at the~~

~~Acropolis.~~

[The original links the noun phrase *the Anasazi ruins* to a prepositional phrase, *in Athens at the Acropolis*. The revision links two noun phrases.]

19e | Repeat function words to achieve parallel form

Readers depend on function words to signal grammatical forms and relations. Function words are prepositions (*to, by, in,* and so forth), articles (*a, an, the*), the infinitive *to,* and introductory words at the beginning of clauses (*that, who, which, because, when, if,* and so forth). If readers are likely to misunderstand you, repeat function words before parallel statements. To see the effect of repetition, read the following examples in their original versions and then in revision.

The climbers deserved praise for risking their lives to save their injured

for
friend but not the recklessness that led to his fall.

The keys to academic success, Jana decided, were to attend class as if she

to
were going to work and study as if she were playing a sport.

that
Senator Cohen said that he opposes the Cartwright Dam project and the

Fremont River must remain unobstructed.

PART III.

Crafting Sentences, Choosing Words

III sentences/words

Choosing Words

III sentences/words

Crafting Sentences

20 Writing Emphatically

In emphatic sentences, important ideas stand out. Not only do they appear where readers expect them, they have been arranged to attract attention. The following guidelines will help you give your sentences this kind of impact.

How to . . . Edit for Emphasis and Variety

To make your sentences clear, emphatic, and interesting to read, follow these guidelines.

1. Place important ideas at the end of a main clause or the end of a sentence. (See 20b and e.)
2. Deemphasize less important ideas in subordinate phrases or clauses. (See 20b.)
3. Link related important ideas in a coordinate structure. (See 20c.)
4. Repeat important words for emphasis. (See 20d.)
5. Count the number of words in your sentences. If you find passages in which sentences repeatedly have nearly the same number of words or sentences that all have the same structure, you may have found a choppy or monotonous passage to rewrite. Vary the length and structure of your sentences. (See 21a–c.)
6. Look for words to cut, such as forms of the verb *be* and needless repetition. Look for sentences in which you can compress a wordy phrase to fewer words yet say the same thing. (See 28a–c.)

20*a* Use the active voice when possible

Voice refers to verb forms that show whether a subject performs an action or is acted on. In the **active voice,** an active subject—an actor—performs the action of a transitive verb.

subject verb   direct object
Jane mailed the letter.

In the **passive voice,** a passive subject receives the action of the verb.

subject   verb
The letter was mailed.

1   Using the active voice for emphasis

In the active voice, a sentence becomes a little story: *Jane heaved a sad sigh and dropped the letter in the mailbox.* Someone or something does something. This kind of sentence is usually the simplest to write, the shortest, and the easiest to read. And simplicity and brevity usually make main ideas stand out.

As you edit your writing, look for forms of the verb *be* (*be, am, is, are, was, were, being, been*) and passive voice sentences. If a sentence lacks action or fails to emphasize what's most important, rewrite it. Choose an action verb, make the actor the subject of the sentence, or, if necessary, identify the actor.

This award ~~is in recognition of~~ *recognizes* your months of hard work.

[The revision moves the action of the sentence to the verb.]

The Board of Trustees is considering tuition ~~Tuition~~ increases of ten percent ~~are being considered~~ for next year.

[The revision adds the actors who perform the action of the sentence.]

2   Using the passive voice effectively

Two situations require the passive voice:

- When actors are unknown or unimportant, use the passive voice.

  Nearly half of the world's fresh water **is locked** in the Antarctic ice sheet.

- When actors are the most important information, use the passive voice to move the actor from the beginning of the sentence to the end, where it will receive the greatest emphasis.

  During the last Ice Age, the landscape of Wisconsin and northern Illinois **was gouged and shaped** by a gigantic moving ice sheet.

To put a verb in the passive voice, use a form of the helping verb *be* plus the past participle of the main verb: *is mailed, was loved, will be chosen.* Don't confuse voice and tense; the passive voice may appear in any tense. (See also 31d.)

20*b*   Subordinate less important ideas

To emphasize important ideas, put them in an independent clause, the main part of a sentence. To deemphasize less important ideas, subordinate them in dependent clauses or phrases connected to the independent clause. What you choose to emphasize will depend not only on what is most important about your topic but also on the way one sentence fits with the sentences that precede and follow it. (For more on subordination, see 21b and 28c.)

1 Subordinating with dependent clauses

You can deemphasize an idea by expressing it in a **dependent clause,** a group of words with a subject and verb that cannot stand by itself as a complete sentence.

- *Dependent clauses beginning with subordinating conjunctions.* Add a subordinating conjunction, such as *after, although, because, when,* and so forth, to create a dependent clause. Connect it to a related independent clause. (For a list of subordinating conjunctions, see 8g3.)

Because
  ₍ₐ₎Oahu was once a social center for Hawaii's kings, ~~so~~ it is now called

"The Meeting Place."

[By subordinating the first half of the sentence as a dependent clause, the revision emphasizes the title given to Oahu.]

- *Dependent clauses beginning with relative pronouns.* Add a relative pronoun, such as *who, which,* and *that,* to act as the subject of a dependent clause. Use it to modify a word in the main clause or to act as part of the main clause. (See also 10b1 and 3.)

  , which
  Oahu‿was once a social center for Hawaii's kings, ~~so it~~ is now called

"The Meeting Place."

[The dependent clause deemphasizes the history of Oahu; the independent clause emphasizes the title based on that history.]

2 Subordinating with phrases

You can reduce the importance of an idea further by putting it into a **phrase,** a word group lacking a subject, a verb, or both.

- *Appositive phrases.* Put a less important idea in an appositive, a nounlike word or phrase that describes a nearby noun.

  Oahu‿,~~was~~ once a social center for Hawaii's kings, ~~so it~~ is now called

"The Meeting Place."

- *Participial phrases.* Put a less important idea in a phrase headed by the *-ing* or *-ed* participial forms of the verb. Put the phrase near the noun or pronoun it modifies.

Called "The Meeting Place,"
  ₍ₐ₎Oahu was once a social center for Hawaii's kings,‿~~so it is now called~~

~~"The Meeting Place."~~

[By deemphasizing the second half of the sentence in a participial phrase, the revision emphasizes Oahu's history, now part of an independent clause.]

20c | Use coordination to emphasize equal ideas

Coordination (also called **parallel form**) refers to linked words having the same grammatical form (see Chapter 19). It is a way to emphasize the equality of related words and ideas.

1 Coordinating with a conjunction or with a comma and coordinating conjunction

- Use a coordinating conjunction (*and, but, or, so, for, yet, nor*) to link and emphasize equally important words and phrases.

  ┌— linked words —┐
  Horns and sirens announced the ship's arrival.

  ┌————————— linked phrases —————————┐
  The violin evolved from ancient Asian fiddles and medieval stringed
  instruments.

- Use a comma and coordinating conjunction to link equally important independent clauses. (See also 34a.)

  , but its
  The old cabin looked warm and cozy. ~~Its~~ roof leaked even in a gentle rain.

2 Coordinating with a semicolon and a transition or conjunctive adverb or with a semicolon alone

- Use a semicolon and a transition or conjunctive adverb such as *however* or *therefore* to link related and equally important independent clauses. (For a list of transitions and conjunctive adverbs, see 12b3; see also 35b.)

  ; however, they
  Some say American workers are unproductive. ~~They~~ now work more
  than forty-five hours per week.

- Use a semicolon standing alone to balance equally important clauses that are similar in structure. (See 35a.)

  ; artificial
  Natural air pollutants include dust, gases, spores, and pollens. ~~Artificial~~
  air pollutants include smoke and gases from industries, vehicles, and
  households.

A note on faulty coordination: Avoid stringing coordinate word groups together into loose, rambling, unemphatic sentences. (See 21c.) Also avoid the faulty parallelism that occurs when grammatically unequal words are linked. (See 19a–c.)

20d Repeat key words to emphasize ideas

To affirm your beliefs, express feelings, or give special emphasis, repeat key words in grammatically equal (parallel) structures. Parallel structures are italicized in the following passages.

> If all you saw of life was the Iowa State Fair on a brilliant August day, when you hear those incredible crops ripening out of the black dirt between the Missouri and Mississippi rivers, you would believe that this is surely the best of all possible worlds.
>
> You would have *no* sense of the destruction of life, only of its rich creativeness: *no* political disasters, *no* assassinations, *no* ideological competition, *no* wars, *no* corruption, *no* atom waiting in its dark secrecy to destroy us all with its exploding energy.
>
> (Paul Engle, "The Iowa State Fair," *Holiday,* emphasis added)

> Twice in my life I have seen the expression on the face of a person who was soon to die by suicide. *It was* not the look of depression or despair. *It was* more the look of a person watching life from a great distance. *It was* an absorbed attention, as if the person were reviewing an elaborate show, of which he or she had once been the star. I hope I never see it again.
>
> (Hugh Drummond, "The Masked Generation," *Mother Jones,* emphasis added)

In the first example, each repeated *no* helps emphasize just how safe the writer believes Iowa to be from the threats of the modern world. In the second, the repeated *it was* links the ideas in three sentences and emphasizes the contrast between the despair readers might expect to see and what the writer actually saw.

A note on excessive repetition: Excessive repetition will make your writing sound choppy or overemotional. (See 21b and d.)

20e Place important ideas in emphatic positions

Beginnings and endings—especially endings—are emphatic positions. Consider:

> Stars, like people, do not live forever. But the lifetime of a person is measured in decades; the lifetime of a star in billions of years.
>
> (Carl Sagan, from *The Cosmic Connection: An Extraterrestrial Perspective*)

The writer might have begun *Like people, stars do not live forever.* But because he is more interested in the age of stars than of people, he begins and ends with stars and their lifetime.

1 Putting emphasis at the beginning

To emphasize a topic at the beginning of a sentence, make it the subject and open with the main clause. Compare these examples:

The lightning was no longer forking now but illuminating the entire sky, flashing a dead strobe white, turning the bay fluorescent and the islands black, as if in negative.

(Joan Didion, from *Miami,* emphasis added.)

[In the main clause that opens the sentence, the topic—*the lightning*—is the subject and the compound verb—*no longer forking now but illuminating*—states the main idea, which is then described in modifying phrases at the end.]

~~The truck swerved and hit the~~ *The* ancient elm standing in front of my house *was hit by a swerving truck.*

[The revision makes the direct object of the original sentence—*the ancient elm*—into the subject.]

2 Putting emphasis at the end

- Design your sentences so that the main idea comes in the final phrase or word. Compare these examples:

    Having laid waste the wilderness, skunked the waterways with toxics, and decimated animal and Indian alike in the name of economic progress, *we now indulge ourselves in an orgy of sentimentalism for whatever comes labeled "natural."*

    (Jonathan Evan Maslow, "Stalking the Black Bear," *Saturday Review,* emphasis added)

    The transformation of American horror movies began with Alfred Hitchcock's <u>Psycho</u> ~~began the transformation of American horror movies~~.

- To develop suspense in a series, place the most important item last. To protest boxing's brutality, the writer of the following example builds to a final italicized description of a boxer punishing his injured opponent.

    It is nonsense to talk about prize fighting as a test of boxing skills. No crowd was ever brought to its feet screaming and cheering at the sight of two men beautifully dodging and weaving out of each other's jabs. The time the crowd comes alive is *when a man is hit hard over the heart or the head, when his mouthpiece flies out, when blood squirts out of his nose or eyes, when he wobbles under the attack and his pursuer continues to smash at him with poleax impact.*

    (Norman Cousins, "Who Killed Benny Paret?" *Saturday Review,* emphasis added)

21 Adding Variety

21*a* Vary the length of your sentences

Effective writing is like music. Repeated words and sentence patterns create an emphatic rhythm, and varied patterns make a melody that adds surprise, moves readers ahead, and prevents monotony. One of the most important creators of this musical style is variety in sentence length. Consider the following example. The numbers to the left indicate the number of words per sentence:

19 The point of going somewhere like the Napo River in Ecuador is not to see
8 the most spectacular anything. It is simply to see what is there. We are here on
18 the planet only once, and might as well get a feel for the place. We might as
60 well get a feel for the fringes and hollows in which life is lived, for the
Amazon basin, which covers half a continent, and for the life that—there, like anywhere else—is always and necessarily lived in detail: on the tributaries, in the riverside villages, sucking this particular white-fleshed guava in this particular pattern of shade.

> (Annie Dillard, "In the Jungle," from *Teaching a Stone to Talk*)

As you write and revise, do as the writer of this example has done. Use short sentences to emphasize important ideas. The topic sentences of paragraphs are often shorter than those that follow; so are emotionally charged sentences and climactic sentences that make a closing point. Use longer sentences to explain, describe, and restate. The following guidelines will show you how to create this variety.

21*b* Combine short, choppy sentences

One or two short sentences will emphasize important ideas, but several choppy ones may create a monotonous, singsong effect. To combine choppy sentences, do the following: eliminate unnecessary words, reword, rearrange, and repunctuate.

1 Subordinating less important ideas

Combine choppy sentences by reducing one sentence to a subordinate phrase or clause. (See 20b.)

Although many ,
ₐ ~~Many~~ people try to avoid jury duty~~.~~ ~~But~~ those who serve often praise

for the
their experience~~.~~ ~~They speak of~~ new insights into human nature they

have gained.

[The revision combines three sentences into one, subordinating the first sentence as a dependent clause and the third as a phrase.]

2 Coordinating equal ideas

Use parallel forms to coordinate related, equally important ideas. (See 20c.)

Most high school students watch television several hours a day. They

spend little time on homework. They seldom read and never write for

pleasure.

[The revision eliminates pronouns and repunctuates to link the uses of high school students' time into an emphatic series.]

21c | Divide loose, rambling sentences into two or more separate sentences

Carefully crafted long sentences can be as clear, emphatic, and easy to read as shorter sentences. But long, rambling sentences may obscure important ideas and be tiresome to read.

1 Dividing loose sentences at conjunctions or transitions

Omit conjunctions or transitions if possible. Then check to see that your revised sentences are varied and emphatic.

Some cigarette advertisements use cartoons to make smoking a playful

activity; and others present attractive models to make smoking

glamorous. But if you examine these ads closely, you will discover more

complicated messages about smoking.

2 Dividing sentences at subordinating conjunctions or relative pronouns

Too many dependent clauses in a sentence make reading difficult, especially when they come at opposite ends of the sentence. Rewrite dependent clauses as complete sentences.

As the soil of privately owned tree farms in the Pacific Northwest has

become less fertile, lumber companies have turned to federal lands and

their prime stands of old-growth timber. Once logging begins,

however, these forests will last less than a decade.

[To create two sentences, the revision omits a subordinating conjunction, *although,* and adds a conjunctive adverb, *however,* as a transition.]

21d Vary your sentence types

Sentences can be classified according to the clauses they contain: simple, compound, complex, and compound-complex. (See 10c1.) Varying sentence types will help you emphasize important ideas and vary sentence length and rhythm. Consider the varied sentences in the following example.

Compound	The Puritans were a daring lot, but they had a mean streak.
Simple, simple	They hated the theater and banned Christmas. They punished
Complex	people in a cruel and inhuman manner. They killed children who
	disobeyed their parents. When they came in contact with those
Complex	whom they considered heathens or aliens, they behaved in such a
	bizarre and irrational manner that this chapter in the American
	history comes down to us as a late-movie horror film. They exter-
Compound-complex	minated the Indians, who taught them how to survive in a world
	unknown to them, and their encounter with the calypso culture of
	Barbados resulted in what the tourist guide in Salem's Witches'
	House refers to as the Witchcraft Hysteria.

(Ishmael Reed, "America: The Multinational Society," from *Writin' Is Fightin'*)

21e Vary the structure of your sentences

1 Varying sentence openers

Most sentences, like this one, open with their subjects. But too many of these sentences in a row can be monotonous. Vary your sentence openers occasionally to create new rhythms and to direct readers to the ideas you want to emphasize.

- *Adverbs and adverbial openers.* Adverbs can appear almost anywhere in a sentence.

Slowly, the
~~The~~ bicyclist pedaled ~~slowly~~ up the steep hill.

When runners   exercise, they
~~Runners~~ and bicyclists should not wear portable stereos ~~when they~~

~~exercise.~~

- *Participial openers.* Open with a participial phrase beginning with the *-ing* or *-ed* form of the verb. Follow it with the noun or pronoun that it modifies.

Churning the brown river, the
~~The~~ paddle-wheel steamer ~~churning the brown river~~ pulled away from

the dock.

- *Prepositional phrases.* Open with a prepositional phrase, often a modifier of the main verb of the sentence.

In November, the
^The city of Bloomington opened its first homeless shelter ~~in November~~.
                                                                          ^

- *An appositive.* Open with a noun or noun phrase that modifies a nearby noun.

The loneliest of athletes, ultramarathon   *compete*
^~~Ultramarathon~~ runners ~~are the loneliest of athletes, competing~~ in events
                                                                        ^

with few prizes and even fewer spectators.

- *An infinitive phrase.* Open with a *to* verb and its related words.

To study unwritten languages, linguists
^~~Linguists~~ go to Alaska, Africa, and South America ~~to study unwritten~~
                                                        ^

~~languages.~~

2 Inverting sentence order

The most common English word order is subject plus verb plus object, complement, or verbal modifier. If you invert this order, putting the verb or other later words before the subject, you will change the rhythm of a sentence and create variety.

On the east wall hung a
^~~A~~ small painting of a French river ~~hung on the east wall~~.
                                         ^

[This revision moves the verb and a prepositional phrase to the beginning.]

Among
^~~The Chippewas of central Minnesota are among~~ the first Native
                                                are the Chippewas of central Minnesota
Americans to govern themselves outside federal government authority.
                                                                    ^

[This revision moves the subject and verb to the end of the sentence.]

A note on overusing the inverted order: Too many inverted sentences will make your writing sound awkward or pretentious.

21f Ask an occasional question

Most sentences you write are declarative sentences that provide information. (See 10c2.) You can increase sentence variety and attract readers if you alternate declarative sentences with questions. This strategy is italicized in the following examples.

1 Using a question to begin a paragraph

Placed at the beginning of a paragraph, questions give direction to your writing and involve readers in a search for answers.

But does imprisonment deter crime? Deterrence requires that potential offenders think about the consequences of their actions, as many fail to do. More important, deterrence requires that those who do think about the consequences see some real risk that they will be caught and punished—a risk that must outweigh the benefits they expect from the crime. Unfortunately for deterrence, potential offenders think that the threat of capture and punishment applies to others but not to them.

> (Paul H. Robinson, "Moral Credibility and Crime," *The Atlantic Monthly*, emphasis added)

2 Using rhetorical questions

Rhetorical questions, assertions phrased as questions, vary the expression of your ideas and opinions.

> We need to recognize that ideas have consequences. By granting a special status to children, we go far toward ensuring that they will be self-occupied and all too often, irresponsible. *If children are fundamentally different from you and me, how could we possibly expect them even to begin to measure up to the same standards? How can you discipline them when, by definition, they are supposed to be creative, natural, and free?*

> (R. Keith Miller, "The Idea of Children," *Newsweek*, emphasis added)

22 Avoiding Mixed and Incomplete Messages

No matter how vivid, insightful, or stylish your writing, if your sentences don't make sense or say what you intend, the virtues of your writing will be lost on readers. The following guidelines will help you express your meaning accurately.

22a Write subjects and predicates that make sense together

Subjects must fit logically with their predicates, consisting of the main verb and any associated words. When they do not, the error is known as **faulty predication.** Subjects must be able to do what their verbs say they are doing. Subjects and subject complements must fit together naturally and appropriately.

has been neglected by
The ideal of national service ~~has dwindled among~~ many young Americans.

[Logically, an ideal cannot dwindle, which means "to become smaller." The problem is not the size of the ideal but people's awareness of or opposition to it.]

How to . . . Edit to Say What You Mean

As you reread your sentences, ask, "What's happening here?" Rewrite so that actions and events make sense.

- Identify actors and their actions, subjects and their verbs. Do they go together logically? As you rewrite, try to keep subjects and verbs as close together as possible. Your meaning will be clearer. (See 22a and b. To learn to identify subjects and verbs, see 8c and 9a.)

Study your sentences, asking, "What goes with what?" Rewrite to create logical relationships.

1. Be sure comparisons are logical and complete. (See 22c.)
2. Study your sentences to see whether they have all the words necessary to express your meaning accurately. (See 22d.)
3. Consider words that precede and follow commas. If one word group modifies the other, be sure the relation is logical. (See 23a and b.)
4. Check to see that pronouns are consistent in their reference and verbs are consistent in their forms. (See 24a–e.)

1 Using a subject that does not fit part of a compound predicate

A subject must make sense with all of its verbs.

Hot air ballooning experienced a renaissance
~~The renaissance of hot air ballooning came~~ in the early 1960s and since

then has grown increasingly popular.

[The original version says that a *renaissance* [. . .] *came* [. . .] *and has grown* [. . .] *popular*. But the renaissance did not grow popular. The writer means to say that hot air ballooning has grown popular.]

2 Using an illogical subject complement

An adjective or noun that follows a verb must logically describe or rename the subject of the sentence.

A   is an organization
~~The hospice concept is a program~~ that provides skilled and

compassionate care to dying patients.

[The original says that a concept is a program. The assertion is illogical, and neither word accurately describes a hospice.]

3 Using *is when, is where*

These phrases are common in casual speech, but often, especially in definitions, they create statements that are not grammatical or logical.

the
Algophobia is ~~when a person has~~ excessive fear of pain.

[*When* is an adverb of time, but *algophobia* is a condition. The revision connects the term to its definition.]

in which
Cubism was an early twentieth-century artistic style ~~where~~ painters

presented multiple perspectives of three-dimensional objects.

[*Where* is an adverb of place, but Cubism was an artistic movement.]

22b Avoid mixed constructions that say one thing in two ways

Many ideas can be expressed in more than one way. A **mixed construction** occurs when two ways of saying the same thing are combined in one sentence. To rewrite a mixed construction, identify the two patterns of expression and choose the one that best fits the surrounding sentences and most clearly expresses your ideas.

The *has*
~~According to a report by the~~ Center for U.S.-Mexican Studies uncovered

changed immigration patterns in California.

[In the original, a prepositional phrase, *according to a report,* seems to be the subject of the sentence—a grammatical impossibility. The revision uses a noun phrase, *the Center for U.S.-Mexican Studies,* as the subject. Another revision might follow the pattern begun by the original opening: *According to a report by the Center for U.S.-Mexican Studies, immigration patterns in California have changed.*]

22c Make comparisons logical and complete

1 Comparing noncomparable items

To write logically, compare subjects that are genuinely comparable.

Cosmetic manufacturers have experimented with rabbits because they
eyes.
have eyes similar to ~~the membrane of the~~ human ~~eye.~~

[The original sentence compares eyes to a membrane: *eyes similar to the membrane of the human eye.* The revision compares eyes with eyes.]

2 Using incomplete formulas

Comparisons are made with certain verbal formulas that bring the terms being compared into relationship with each other. To be logical, supply all words necessary to complete the formula. (See also 19d.)

Alcoholics often spend more time drinking with friends than *they spend with* their

families.

[The original seems to say that alcoholics drink with friends and families alike. Inserting *they spend with* distinguishes time spent with friends from time spent with families.]

3 Making incomplete comparisons

To be complete, comparisons must mention all items being compared.

The Miami Dolphins are not only a bigger and faster football team. *than the Chicago Bears* Man

for man, they are also more experienced.

4 Mixing comparative and superlative forms

Use the comparative *-er/more* form to compare two items, the superlative *-est/most* form to compare three or more items. (See also 18d2.)

The United States has ~~the highest~~ *a higher* divorce rate than any other country.

[The original sentence uses the superlative form to compare the United States to any other country. The revision uses the correct form for comparing two items.]

22d Include all necessary key words and function words

1 Checking for omitted key words

The omission of key words may produce illogical statements. As you rewrite, be sure your sentences have all the words necessary to express your ideas completely.

When we reached a clearing in the forest, we found ourselves knee-deep in green slime, *lost in six-foot* weeds ~~six feet tall~~, and *blinded by* clouds of flying insects.

[In the original, the hikers improbably appear to be knee-deep in six-foot weeds and clouds of insects, as well as slime. The added verb phrases describe their situation accurately.]

2 Checking for omitted function words

Function words help to identify the grammatical functions performed by the key words of sentences. Include all the function words necessary to signal the direction your sentences are taking.

- *The articles* a, an, *and* the. Include articles before nouns to make series or compounds grammatically complete.

Onto the stage walked a doctor, _{an} astronaut, and _{the} president of the

university.

[It is necessary to add *an* before a word beginning with a vowel and the definite article *the* before the title of a specific person.]

- *The subordinating conjunction* that. You may often omit *that* from your sentences: *Leslie stuffed her backpack with all [that] she would need for two weeks.* But include *that* if readers may not see that a clause follows a verb instead of a direct object.

Kevin found _{that} the historic house he wanted to photograph had been

demolished.

[Adding *that* indicates that the historic house is the subject of a clause, not the direct object of *found*.]

- *Verbs in compound structures.* Even though a verb may be common to both parts of a compound structure, you must repeat the verb to signal tense changes.

Without generous scholarships, our university has not _{recruited} and never will

recruit the best students.

[The original is ungrammatical: *has not* [. . .] *recruit*. *Recruited* is necessary to signal that the tense of the first verb differs from that of the second.]

- *The relative pronouns* who *and* whom. If a relative pronoun changes case from one part of a compound structure to another, use both case forms. (See 17e.)

Arthur Ashe was a man _{whom} many thought the greatest male tennis player of

his generation but who should be remembered as a social activist.

[*Whom* must be added to the first half of the compound to signal that it is in the object case as the direct object of the verb *thought*. In the second half, *who* is in the subject case as the subject of the verb *should be remembered*.]

23 Placing Modifiers

23a Move misplaced modifiers near the words they modify

A **misplaced modifier** is a word or phrase that is located incorrectly in relation to the words it modifies. The result may be an illogical sentence that is difficult to follow. If you spot a misplaced modifier, rearrange the sentence to make sense and make reading easier.

, which hummed quietly,
A small fan stood on the desk ~~which hummed quietly.~~

[In the original, the desk appears to hum quietly. The revision moves the modifier next to the word it modifies, *fan*.]

, driving through eastern Pennsylvania,
I knew I was near my destination when I tuned in a New York radio

station ~~driving through eastern Pennsylvania.~~

[In the original, the New York radio station appears to be driving through Pennsylvania. Locating the modifier next to *I* makes clear who is driving.]

1 Using limiting modifiers correctly

Limiting modifiers restrict or limit the meaning of the words they modify: *almost, even, exactly, hardly, just, merely, nearly, only, scarcely, simply*. To make your meaning clear and unambiguous, place these modifiers before the words they modify.

only
Barry ~~only~~ chose the chocolate-covered caramels.

almost
On average, Americans ~~almost~~ work as many hours per week as the

Japanese.

2 Avoiding squinting modifiers

Squinting modifiers appear to modify both preceding and following words, creating ambiguous meaning. Move the modifier before the word it modifies or rewrite to eliminate ambiguity.

Because she wanted to work for the National Park Service, Nancy
seriously
considered ~~seriously~~ studying for a degree in botany.

[The original seems to say that Nancy considered doing some serious studying. The revision says that the way she considered was serious.]

in the evening

The owner required his tenants ~~in the evening~~ to play their music quietly. ^

[The original seems to say that the landlord made his requirement in the evening. The revision says that the tenants must be quiet in the evening.]

3 Avoiding split infinitives

An infinitive is the *to* form of a verb: *to run*. **Split infinitives** occur when a modifier comes between *to* and the verb: *to quickly run*. Avoid split infinitives when they sound awkward or may confuse readers.

quickly

Dean's mother told him to ~~quickly~~ run to the store and buy a newspaper. ^

without much preparation

Sheri hoped to~~, without much preparation,~~ pass her French final exam. ^

It is, however, appropriate to write split infinitives in some circumstances:

- *To avoid ambiguity.* Consider the difference between these two sentences, the first containing a split infinitive: *The President proposed to further delay agricultural reforms. The President proposed to delay further agricultural reforms.* In the first sentence, the President proposed to increase the delay. In the second, the President proposed to delay more reforms.

- *To avoid awkwardness.* Consider this sentence containing a split infinitive: *With more practice, the relay team was able to nearly equal their best time.* This version is clearer and more natural than *With more practice, the relay team was able nearly to equal their best time.*

23b To connect dangling modifiers, rewrite or add missing words

A **dangling modifier** has no words to modify. It "dangles" disconnected or appears to make an illogical connection.

1 Rewriting dangling participles

A participle is the *-ing* or *-ed* verb form acting as an adjective. A **dangling participle** "dangles" because it has no logical actor to perform the action that it names. Rewrite to identify the actor; you also will have to change the form of the verb.

As I pedaled

~~Pedaling~~ around a sharp curve on the steep mountain road, the warning

of other bicyclists echoed in my head.

[In the original, the warning itself seems to be pedaling around a curve. The revision adds a subject and changes the verb to turn a phrase into a dependent clause.]

we had drifted
After ~~drifting~~ down the river for an hour, the bridge came into view.

[In the original, the opening phrase seems to modify *bridge*. Adding a subject, *we*, and turning the opening phrase into a dependent clause clarifies the meaning of the sentence.]

2 Rewriting a modifier that appears to modify a possessive

Modifiers that provide information about nouns or pronouns cannot modify possessive -'s words, which act as adjectives rather than nouns. Rewrite to omit the possessive or to supply a noun or pronoun.

Although recognized by many for her fundraising, Lucille Allen~~'s name~~

didn't become well known until she married the mayor.

[In the original, the opening phrase seems illogically to modify *Lucille Allen's name*. Dropping the possessive -'s and *name* makes all parts of the sentence fit together.]

3 Rewriting dangling appositives

A noun or noun phrase functioning as an appositive must stand near the noun or equivalent form that it can logically modify. Rewrite to create logical relations.

to be
The actress's sensitive performance revealed the mother~~'s character~~, a

strong, courageous person.

[In the original, the appositive *a strong, courageous person* illogically modifies *character*. Adding *to be* turns the appositive into a complement describing *mother*.]

24 Avoiding Faulty Shifts

24*a* | Maintain a consistent point of view

Point of view is the perspective of a piece of writing: **first person** (*I* or *we*), **second person** (*you*), or **third person** (*he, she, it, one,* or *they*). A faulty shift in point of view frequently involves a shift from first or third person to second person—from *I* or *they* to *you*. As you write, settle on a point of view appropriate to the subject and occasion. For informal writing, first-person point of view is usually appropriate; for formal writing, third person is often appropriate. Once you decide on your point of view, maintain it consistently.

My job washing dishes may be damp and dirty, but at least no one ever
me *I am*
bothers ~~you~~ while ~~you are~~ working.

Pedestrians stared suspiciously as the Jeffreys searched for the right
address. Wherever ~~you~~ *they* turned, ~~you~~ *they* were inspected from head to foot.

A note on direct address: Write *you* only when you mean to address
readers directly, as in instructions or advice: *When you finish a rough draft,
let it sit for a while before you begin revising.* (See 16a3.)

24*b* | Avoid inconsistent shifts in number

If you begin using the plural to write about a subject, stick to the
plural; if you begin using the singular, stick to the singular.

Televised violence makes many viewers afraid to leave their ~~home~~ *homes*.

24*c* | Stay in one tense unless the time of the action changes

When you use more than one verb to describe an action, put all verbs
in the same tense. A faulty tense shift between past and present sometimes
occurs in narratives about past events.

When General Picket was ordered to prepare his men to charge, the
young officer ~~cannot~~ *could not* contain his anticipation.

[The original version shifts from the past tense, *was ordered,* to the present, *cannot
contain.* The revision makes both verbs past tense.]

At the beginning of Shirley Jackson's short story, Mr. Johnson is in love
with the world. He ~~wanted~~ *wants* to make others feel as good as he ~~did~~ *does*.

[The original, from a student paper about a short story, shifts from present to past
tense. The revision makes all the verbs present tense, the appropriate tense for writing about literature and the events that take place in individual stories, novels, and
plays. (See also 13b1.)]

24*d* | Maintain a consistent mood and voice

1 Avoiding shifts in mood

Mood identifies the kind of statement a verb makes: an expression of
fact (**indicative mood**), a command or advice (**imperative mood**), and
wishes or speculation (**subjunctive mood**). Stick to one mood unless you
have reason to change. (See also 13f.)

plant marigolds
For best growth and color, ~~it is important that marigolds be planted~~ in

full sun. Water them often and pinch back the blooms.

[The original shifts from the subjunctive mood in the first sentence, *be planted,* to the imperative mood in the second, *water [. . .] and pinch back.* The revision puts both sentences in the imperative mood appropriate for instructions.]

2 Avoiding shifts in voice

Voice refers to the relationship between a subject and verb. (See 20a.) In active voice expressions, an active subject performs the action of the verb: *The child hit the ball.* In passive voice expressions, a passive subject is acted on: *The ball was hit.* Maintain a consistent voice unless you have reason to change.

she had achieved
Jane congratulated herself because all of her goals ~~had been achieved,~~

[The original shifts from the active voice, *congratulated,* to the passive, *had been achieved.* The revision maintains the active voice throughout.]

24e | Avoid inconsistent shifts from indirect to direct discourse

Direct discourse consists of word-for-word quotations and questions addressed directly to listeners or readers. **Indirect discourse** summarizes quotations and questions. Be consistent in the form of discourse you use. (For ESL, see 32c.)

Last week Dr. Lambert told us that we were behind schedule, ~~and~~
and would *our*
~~"You'll~~ have to finish ~~your~~ report by the end of the month.~~"~~

[The original shifts from summary to direct quotation. The revision maintains indirect discourse throughout. An alternative revision would quote all of Dr. Lambert's remarks: *Last week Dr. Lambert told us, "You're behind schedule. You'll have to finish your report by the end of the month."*]

Doctors in the nineteenth century were uncertain whether the causes of
whether they should
mental illness differed for men and women and ~~, if so, should they~~ be

treated differently~~?~~

[The original opens with an indirect question and shifts to a direct question. The revision maintains indirect discourse throughout.]

Choosing Words

How to . . . Choose the Right Words

Follow these guidelines as you write and edit.

1. Experiment as you write. When you come to a word that doesn't seem exact, try several alternatives. If you don't find the exact word, put a checkmark (✓) in the margin as a reminder to reconsider your choice as you revise. (See Chapter 25.)
2. Whenever possible, choose words you know well. Look up words outside your everyday vocabulary. To decide which word best fits the context of your writing, use the list of synonyms appearing after many dictionary entries, a thesaurus, or the guide to troublesome words and phrases in Chapter 29.
3. When possible, use concrete and specific "pictorial" words. (See 26a and b.)
4. Create metaphors and similes to describe your subject, make judgments, or express your feelings. Use the figurative language formula in the "How to Create Similes and Metaphors" box on p. 164 to get started: If _____ were a _____, it would/would not be a _____. (See 26c.)
5. Choose words that fit the seriousness of your subject. The more serious the subject, the more formal your vocabulary should be. (See 27a.)

25 Choosing Exact Words

25a Denotation: Choose words that say exactly what you mean

The **denotation** of a word is its literal, dictionary definition. Although writers don't intend to choose the wrong word, even the best occasionally choose a word that is not quite right. As you write and revise, look for mismatches between what you mean to say and what your words actually mean.

1 Checking for ambiguous words

Writers sometimes choose words that, in the context of their writing, have multiple, or ambiguous, meanings. To write unambiguously, choose specific words that express only the meaning you intend. (See 26a.)

Although many were dissatisfied with Judge Tanaka's decision, they did
agree that it was ~~fair~~.
impartial

[*Fair* may mean that the judge ruled without favoritism, the meaning of *impartial*. But *fair* may also mean in the best interests of each person involved or without self-interest. The exact meaning of *fair* is unclear in the original sentence.]

2 Checking for approximate words

Some words are near synonyms of other words. But, as Mark Twain observed, the difference between the right word and the almost-right word is the difference between lightning and a lightning bug. To distinguish between words with similar meanings, use the synonym section of dictionary entries or a thesaurus. (See 25c and d.)

At dawn, the cardinal's song echoed ~~quietly weakly feebly~~ over the roof tops.
faintly

25b Connotation: Choose words that convey appropriate feelings and attitudes

The **connotation** of a word is the emotional associations and attitudes that the word calls up. Words similar in dictionary definition often differ widely in connotative meaning. Consider the connotations of the word pairs in the following sentences. The words in each pair are similar in denotation but differ in connotation. Is the connotation of each word positive, negative, or neutral?

On the dining room table was a vase filled with *artificial/fake* flowers.

The old *cabin/shack* stood near the edge of a forest.

Political parties aim to *educate/indoctrinate* voters.

1 Matching connotation and the writer's attitude

Choose words whose positive, neutral, or negative connotation matches your attitude toward your subject. Find the right word in the synonym section of a dictionary entry or in a thesaurus. (See 25c and d.)

The ~~odor~~ of burning leaves reminds me of childhood.
scent

[*Odor* generally has negative, unpleasant associations. If the writer's memories are positive, *scent*, associated as it is with perfume, is the better choice.]

2 Expressing connotation in public writing

Decide whether words with strong connotations are suitable. Not all situations permit such expressions of feeling or attitude, either positive or negative. Informative writing in school and on the job usually requires neutral or subdued words.

A ~~mob~~ *crowd* of reporters ~~stormed~~ *rushed to* the rooming house where President Lincoln

lay dying.

[The strong negative connotations of the original words are inappropriate for writing from an objective perspective.]

25c | Learn to use all parts of a dictionary entry

A good college desk dictionary does more than give spelling, pronunciation, and basic definitions. To choose the exact words for your meaning, you need to know—and use—all that a dictionary entry contains. Here is an entry from *The American Heritage Dictionary.*

| | Pronunciation | Grammatical labels | Word endings |

Spelling and word division — **af·fect**[1] (-ə-fĕkt´) *tr.v.* **-fect·ed, -fect·ing, -fects. 1.** To have an influence on or effect a change in: *Inflation affects the buying power of the dollar.* **2.** To act on the emotions of; touch or move. **3.** To attack or infect, as a disease: *Rheumatic fever can affect the heart.* —**affect** (ăf´ĕkt´) *n.* **1.** *Psychology.* **a.** A feeling or emotion as distinguished from cognition, thought, or action. **b.** A strong feeling having active consequences. **2.** *Obsolete.* A disposition, feeling, or tendency. [Latin *affi-cere, affect-* : *ad-* + *facere,* to do; see **dhē-** in Appendix.]

— Usage label

— Etymologies (word origins)

SYNONYMS: affect, influence, impress, touch, move, strike. These verbs are compared as they mean to produce a mental or emotional effect. To *affect* is to act upon a person's emotions: *The adverse criticism the book received didn't affect the author one way or another. Influence* implies a degree of control or sway over the thinking and actions, as well as the emotions, of another: *"Humanity is profoundly influenced by what you do"* (John Paul II). To *impress* is to produce a marked, deep, often enduring effect: *"The Tibetan landscape particularly impressed him."* (Doris Kerns Quinn). *Touch* usually means to arouse a tender response, such as love, gratitude, or compassion: *"The tributes* [to the two deceased musicians] *were fitting and touching"* (Daniel Cariaga). *Move* suggests profound emotional effect that sometimes leads to action or has a further consequence: *The account of her experiences as a refugee moved us to tears. Strike* implies keenness or force of mental response to a stimulus: *I was struck by the sudden change in his behavior.*

— Examples illustrating the contexts appropriate for each synonym

— Synonyms (related words)

USAGE NOTE: Affect[1] and *effect* have no senses in common. As a verb *affect*[1] is most commonly used in the sense of "to influence" (*how smoking affects health*). *Effect* means "to bring about or execute": *layoffs designed to effect savings.* Thus the sentence *These measures may affect savings* could imply that the measures may reduce savings that have already been realized, whereas *These measures may effect savings* implies that the measures will cause new savings to come about.

Usage —

An example of appropriate usage —

1 Locating spelling, word division, and pronunciation

Words are divided by syllables: **af·fect.** Two words with the same spelling but different meanings are numbered to signal their difference. Compounds are written as one word (*multimedia*), with a hyphen (*multiple-choice*), or as two words (*multiple sclerosis*). When two or more spellings or pronunciations are correct, the preferred appears first. The phonetic alphabet (as in ə-fĕkt´) is explained in the dictionary's introduction and in the pronunciation key, usually found at the bottom of the page. Accent marks (´) indicate the most heavily stressed character or syllable.

2 Locating grammatical labels and word endings

Labels indicate the grammatical function (part of speech) of a word and its various endings: *tr.v.* **-fect·ed, -fect·ing, -fects.**

adj. adjective	*interj.* interjection	*prep.* preposition
adv. adverb	*n.* noun	*pron.* pronoun
aux. auxiliary	*pl.* plural	*sing.* singular
conj. conjunction	*pl. n.* plural noun	*tr.* transitive
def. art. definite article	*pref.* prefix	*intr.* intransitive
indef. art. indefinite article	*suff.* suffix	*v.* verb

Whenever a word changes grammatical function, alternatives are listed in boldface accompanied by a grammatical label:—**affect** (ăf´ ĕkt´) *n.* All abbreviations are defined in the dictionary's introduction (see the table of contents after the title page).

3 Locating definitions and etymologies

Definitions are numbered and arranged by frequency of use or according to meaning clusters. Letters following numbers identify closely related definitions. Examples occasionally illustrate a word's use. The **etymology** of a word (its origin or history) is often an important guide to its meanings and associations. **Affect,** for example, comes from Latin words (Latin *afficere, affect-* : *ad-, ad-* + *facere,* to do).

4 Locating usage labels

Labels preceding a definition tell under what conditions that definition is appropriate: *Informal, Slang, Nonstandard, Offensive, Archaic, Obsolete, Chiefly British.* Field labels identify special areas such as music, art, computer science, and medicine where specific definitions apply (see *Psychology* in the sample entry).

5 Locating synonyms and usage

Following the main entries of many words are notes that distinguish among related words (see the synonyms of *affect*) or that compare actual uses of words with what experts consider correct uses (see the Usage Note on *affect* and *effect*).

25d Use a thesaurus to find the exact word, not necessarily the biggest or fanciest

A **thesaurus** (from the Latin word for "treasure") lists words together with their synonyms, antonyms, and related words. A thesaurus may be a printed reference work such as *Roget's II; The New Thesaurus,* or *Webster's Collegiate Thesaurus,* or a data file accompanying a computer word processor. Here is an entry from *Webster's Collegiate Thesaurus.**

Headword — Grammatical label — Numbers identifying different senses of the headword

believe *vb* **1** to have a firm conviction in the reality of something — Illustration of the core meaning of the headword

Synonyms listed — < *believes* in ghosts >

syn accept, ‖ buy, swallow

Related words that are not synonyms — *rel* accredit, credit, trust; admit

idiom have no doubts about, hold the belief that, take (or accept) as gospel, take at one's word, take one's word for

Idiomatic equivalents — *con* discredit, distrust, doubt, mistrust, question, suspect; challenge, dispute; reject, turn down — Cross reference number

Contrasting words that are not antonyms — *ant* disbelieve, misbelieve

2 *syn* FEEL **3.** consider, credit, deem, hold, sense, think — A signal to check usage labels in a dictionary

3 *syn* UNDERSTAND **3.** assume, expect, gather, imagine,

Antonyms — ‖ reckon, suppose, suspect, take, think

1 Matching words to contexts

Although a thesaurus groups words having related meanings, it cannot identify the specific contexts in which each word is appropriate. As you decide between synonyms or related words, consider the denotation and connotation of each word, your readers' vocabulary, and the formality of the occasion. (See 27a and b.) In most contexts, synonyms are not interchangeable with one another.

~~anxious desirous~~ *eager*
We were ~~dying~~ to share our experiences from our vacation in Egypt.
                   ^

[*Dying* is too informal for academic and most public writing. *Desirous* sounds too stuffy. And *anxious* suggests apprehension. *Eager* combines the senses of anticipation and desire in a word appropriate for public writing.]

2 Choosing exact words instead of impressive words

Many writers use a thesaurus because they doubt that their words sound polished or impressive enough. But consider how you respond to people who try to impress you with their vocabularies. Use a thesaurus to help you find exact but familiar words. (See 27a and 27d1.)

*By permission. From Merriam-Webster's Collegiate® Theraurus © 1988 by Merriam-Webster, Incorporated.

$\overset{\textit{interest}}{}$ $\overset{\textit{began}}{}$ $\overset{\textit{a vacation}}{}$
My ~~absorption~~ in archaeology ~~commenced~~ with ~~an excursion~~ in Egypt.

25e | Distinguish between frequently confused words

Writers confuse one word with another for several reasons.

- **Homophones** sound alike but are spelled differently and have different meanings: *there, their, they're; affect, effect; complement, compliment.*

- **Near homophones** sound enough alike to be confused with each other: *adapt, adopt; allusion, illusion, delusion; ambiguous, ambivalent; lie, lay.*

- **False synonyms** are related but different words often used in similar contexts: *imply, infer; fewer, less; contagious, infectious; number, amount.*

- Some words have similar roots but different prefixes or suffixes: *disinterested, uninterested; empathize, sympathize; incredulous, incredible; assume, presume; nauseous, nauseate; sensuous, sensual.*

To avoid confusion, look up words outside your everyday vocabulary and memorize differences between words that you have confused. (For a list of frequently confused words, see the guide to usage in Chapter 29.)

$\overset{\textit{integral}}{}$
Movies have become an ~~intricate~~ part of American culture.

[*Intricate,* meaning complex or elaborate, and *integral,* meaning essential or necessary, are near homophones differing greatly in their denotations.]

25f | Use words idiomatically

An **idiom** is a word or expression given special meaning by native speakers of a language. It cannot be understood by knowing the meanings of the individual words alone. For example, native speakers of English say "Good evening" as a greeting but "Good night" as a farewell. Although they appear synonymous, these phrases are idiomatic expressions, each with its own meaning. Generally, idioms take three forms.

1 Misusing individual words

Some words are frequently used in some situations but not in others that may appear similar.

$\overset{\textit{buried}}{}$
The murderer ~~lodged~~ his victims in the crawl space beneath his house.

[*To lodge* may mean "to place, leave, or deposit an item," as in *The bone lodged in his throat.* Living persons may be "lodged," as in *We lodged our uncle at our neighbor's house.* But in idiomatic English, people are not "lodged" in anything but a residence.]

26 exact/d

2 Using stock phrases

Stock phrases are tired expressions, such as *sitting pretty, comes in handy, travel light, take your time, as good as, heavy-handed, make do, take stock, keep company,* and *change of heart,* which are overused. (See also 26d1.)

3 Misusing prepositions

Prepositions (*in, by, on,* and so forth) and preposition-like words called **particles** following verbs (*agree with/to, abide by, according to, argue with/about*) are idiomatic, appearing only in specific situations and with certain words.

A quiet walk through autumn leaves is always preferable ~~than~~ *to* weaving

through
~~in~~ the crowded aisles of some department store.

[Idiomatic English uses *better than* but *preferable to. Weaving through* is necessary to describe a person's path through a crowd.]

An ESL note: Native speakers of a language seldom use words unidiomatically, but nonnative speakers and native writers who choose words outside their everyday vocabularies may have difficulties.

- If you're uncertain of a word or phrase, check usage notes in Chapter 29 and in dictionary entries.

- For stock phrases not listed in dictionaries, check special dictionaries of idioms or phrase books in libraries or bookstores where English as a Second Language books are sold. (See the introduction to the ESL editing guide in Part IV.)

- For prepositions, look up the word preceding the preposition (*preferable* and *weaving* in the example earlier) in a dictionary. (See also 31g and 32f.)

26 Choosing Vivid Words

As a writer you want words that say what you mean, and you want powerful words that will focus readers' attention on your ideas. Such words transform writing into what the English poet Sir Philip Sidney called "a speaking picture." They are vivid and descriptive and bring ideas to life.

26a When possible, choose specific rather than general words

Words can be classified as specific, general, or somewhere in between. **General words** are umbrella terms that refer to many things. **Specific words** refer to individual persons, places, things, actions, or qualities.

GENERAL WORDS ⟵				⟶ SPECIFIC WORDS
artist		painter		Mary Cassatt
urban area		city		Calcutta
vegetation	tree	evergreen	fir	spruce
observe		look		stare
textured	uneven	rough	coarse	scratchy

Because they are precise in meaning and feeling, specific words tend to be more pictorial than general words and to make a subject clearer and easier to grasp. Choose them for these reasons.

Consider the italicized specific words in this passage from a memoir of childhood.

> The bodies of the men I knew were twisted and maimed in ways visible and invisible. The *nails* of their *hands* were *black* and *split,* the *hands tattooed* with *scars.* Some had lost *fingers.* Heavy lifting had given many of them *finicky backs* and *guts* weak from *hernias.* Racing against *conveyor belts* had given them *ulcers.* Their *ankles* and *knees* ached from years of *standing on concrete.* Anyone who had worked for long around machines was *hard of hearing.* They *squinted,* and the *skin of their faces* was *creased like the leather of old work gloves.* There were times, studying them, when I dreaded growing up.
>
> (Scott Russell Sanders, from *The Paradise of Bombs*)

As you write, create the rhythm of general and specific language illustrated by the preceding passage. Use general words to identify a subject, make assertions, and provide background. Use specific words to support assertions and bring ideas to life.

> Drivers are becoming increasingly ~~dangerous.~~ *hostile. They tailgate at seventy miles an hour, drag race from stop signs, curse, and honk at whatever they think threatens their sacred right to the road.*

> [*Dangerous* is a general word that may refer to unskilled drivers or, as the writer intended, to driver hostility. The added specific examples prove the point and dramatize it.]

26b When possible, choose concrete rather than abstract words

Concrete words refer to things you see, hear, taste, touch, and smell: *rock, trumpet, tomato, fur, rose.* **Abstract words** refer to conditions, qualities, and ideas: *democracy, justice, mercy, misery, hope, independence.* Use concrete words to bring abstractions to life. In the following passage, the emphasized concrete words explain and illustrate *entropy,* the principle of disorder.

> Because of its unnerving irreversibility, entropy has been called the *arrow of time.* We all understand this instinctively. *Children's rooms,* left on their own, tend to get messy, not neat. *Wood rots, metal rusts, people wrinkle* and *flowers wither.* Even *mountains wear down;* even the *nuclei of atoms decay.* In the *city* we see entropy in the *rundown subways* and *worn-out sidewalks* and *torn-down buildings,* in the increasing disorder of our lives. We know, without asking, what is old.
>
> (K. C. Cole, "Entropy," *The New York Times*)

1 Using concrete words for description

As you write and revise, think of concrete nouns to describe your subject and concrete verbs to dramatize its actions.

An autumn bicycle tour in western Wisconsin ~~is a wondrous sensory~~ *offers a sensory feast:* ^

~~journey.~~ *the intense red and yellow of maples, musty aromas of just-harvested corn and beans, sounds of cattle and roosters, and the texture and taste of apples mounded in baskets at roadside stands.*

2 Avoiding the seven deadly nouns

When possible avoid *area, experience, factor, field, situation, thing,* and *type*—words so abstract and vague that they deaden almost any idea.

the unequal distribution of local property taxes.
Urban public schools suffer from ~~a lack of funds, a situation caused by~~ ^

~~unfortunate property tax factors.~~

3 Choosing alternatives to forms of the verb *be*

When you can find alternatives to *is, was, were,* and so forth, your writing will become more vivid and pictorial.

protest
Americans ~~are concerned about~~ dwindling natural resources only when ^
lines of autos jam $\qquad$ *soar*
~~there are long lines at~~ gas stations, home construction costs ~~are high,~~ and
run into the hundreds of dollars.
monthly utility bills ~~are also high.~~ ^

26c │ Use figurative language to dramatize ideas, opinions, and feelings

Figurative language (also called **figures of speech**) uses words imaginatively and nonliterally to describe, evaluate, and express feelings. The most frequently used figure of speech is **figurative comparison,** which reveals hidden similarities between dissimilar subjects by transferring the features of one subject, called the **vehicle,** to the writer's true subject, called the **tenor.** Consider these lines from Robert Burns's famous love poem:

> O, My Luve's [love's] like a red, red rose
> That's newly sprung in June.

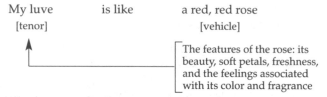

My luve   is like   a red, red rose
[tenor]   [vehicle]

The features of the rose: its beauty, soft petals, freshness, and the feelings associated with its color and fragrance

In two short lines, the poet describes his beloved, praises her beauty, and expresses his feeling for her. Because figurative comparisons say so much in so few words, they are an especially vivid use of language, one that can make your writing colorful and powerful, a pleasure for you and your readers.

1 Using similes

As in the preceding example, a **simile** explicitly compares two unlike subjects using *like, as, as if,* or *as though.* Describing an early morning walk on an ocean beach, essayist David Black tells how "the waves, as they slid up the sand, foamed and hissed like butter sizzling in a frying pan" (waves = sizzling butter). Along the way, he fills his pockets with water-polished rocks "shaped as perfectly as eggs" (rocks = eggs) and pauses to watch seagulls that "stood in crowds, each gazing over the heads of the others, like guests at a chic party on the lookout for celebrities" (gulls = guests). Here similes describe concrete subjects by adding details of sound, shape, texture, appearance, and action. But they may also describe less tangible subjects, as in this description of how Pueblo people speak:

> The structure of Pueblo expression resembles something like a spider's web—with many little threads radiating from a center, crisscrossing each other. As with the web, the structure will emerge as it is made and you must simply listen and trust, as the Pueblo people do, that meaning will be made.

> (Leslie Marmon Silko, "Language and Literature from a Pueblo Indian Perspective," in Leslie A. Fiedler and Houston A. Baker, Jr., eds., *English Literature: Opening Up the Canon*)

[Comparing the structure of Pueblo speech (tenor) to a spider web (vehicle) dramatizes the organization of the language but also suggests something of its delicacy and sensitivity.]

2 Using metaphor

A **metaphor** compares implicitly: not *X is like Y*, but *X is Y*. Tenor and vehicle are fused; one becomes the other.

> Superstition seems to run, a submerged river of crude religion, below the surface of human consciousness.
>
> (Robertson Davies, "A Few Kind Words for Superstition," *Newsweek*)

[*Superstition* (tenor) becomes *a submerged river* (vehicle) and acquires the river's traits: depth, darkness, cold, and power.]

> The bristlecone pine of American Indians, Hopis live where almost nothing else will, thriving long in adverse conditions: poor soil, drought, temperature extremes, high winds. Those give life to the bristlecone and the Hopi.
>
> (William Least Heat-Moon, *Blue Highways*, 1982)

[The *Hopis* (tenor), described as *bristlecone pine* (vehicle), acquire the bristlecone's traits of hardiness, longevity, and the ability to thrive in adverse conditions.]

26d Avoid clichés and mixed metaphors

1 Avoiding clichés

Clichés are overused, worn-out figures of speech or other expressions that have lost their power to communicate. How many of these clichés do you recognize?

avoid it like the plague	the ladder of success	since the dawn of time
beat around the bush	the last straw	stop and smell the roses
blind as a bat	light as a feather	water over the dam
the bottom line	off the beaten path	without a shadow of a doubt
crystal clear	on the brink	white as a ghost
fresh as a daisy	playing with fire	
	sadder but wiser	

If you write a catchy metaphor or simile that you've heard others use, chances are it is already a cliché. Create your own fresh, original figurative language. The figurative language formula in the "How to Create Similes and Metaphors" box (p. 164) will help.

2 Avoiding mixed metaphors

A **mixed metaphor** brings together two or more comparisons that don't make sense together and is often unintentionally humorous. To write effective metaphors and similes, make a single figurative comparison.

The Abbey Road album ~~was the springboard that~~ reignited the Beatles' musical career.

[According to the original, the album is compared to a springboard and, through the verb *reignited*, to something that could start a fire. But a springboard cannot start a fire. The revision omits the illogical metaphor.]

How to . . . Create Similes and Metaphors

If you're unsure how to create a metaphor or simile, use the following figurative language formula. Try several alternatives until you find one that is accurate, original, and appropriate. Then, as you write and revise, omit the formula and work the figure of speech into your sentences.

If ___*(my subject)*___ were ___*(choose from one of the following categories)*___ ,
it would/would not be ___*(make up a term to complete the formula)*___ .

a movement	a road	a piece of furniture
a place	a shape	an article of clothing
a toy	a sound	a means of
a person	a work of art	transportation
a smell	a beverage	an animal
a color	a building	the weather
an object	a musical	vegetation
a food	instrument	music

If *skydiving* were a *movement*, it would be a *dandelion seed drifting in the wind.*

When the parachute opened above me, I lost my prejump jitters, relaxed, and felt how graceful I was, floating as gently as a dandelion seed drifting in the wind. [a simile]

(Nancy Lee, student)

If *grammar* were *a musical instrument*, it would be *a piano played by ear.*

Grammar is a piano I play by ear, since I seem to have been out of school the year the rules were mentioned. All I know about grammar is its infinite power. [a metaphor]

(Joan Didion, "Why I Write," *New York Times Book Review*)

As you edit figurative language, avoid clichés (unoriginal figures of speech) and mixed metaphors (two or more figures of speech about the same subject that clash with each other). (See 26d.)

27 Choosing Appropriate Words

27a Choose words that fit the occasion

Choose an informal or a formal vocabulary appropriate for your subject and the occasion. An **informal vocabulary** will make your writing personal and give it a conversational style. A **formal vocabulary** will convey a serious and more objective attitude. Once you decide what vocabulary is appropriate, use these lists to guide your writing and editing:

FEATURES OF INFORMAL VOCABULARIES	FEATURES OF FORMAL VOCABULARIES
Contractions: *can't, shouldn't, won't,* and so forth	No contractions
Slang and regional expressions: *broke, strapped, dirt poor, beat my brains, brainy,* and so forth	No slang, few regional expressions: *poor, destitute, concentrate, study, intelligent,* and so forth
Frequent use of *I, we, us,* and *you* to express the writer's closeness to the reader	*I, we, us,* and *you* seldom used; emphasis on the subject rather than the writer or audience
Familiar words used in conversation: *poor, smart, my place, my house, think,* and so forth	Words that appear more frequently in writing; words with Latin roots: *impoverished, intelligent, residence, speculate,* and so forth
Words with obvious connotative meaning: *fake, phony, bright,* and so forth	Words with subtle connotations: *artificial, clever,* and so forth

1 Choosing words in academic writing

Generally use a formal vocabulary for informative or persuasive writing about serious subjects. You shouldn't sound stuffy or use words you're uncomfortable with, but choose words that convey the importance of the occasion. Refer to yourself as *I* if you are involved with your subject, but focus on your subject rather than yourself. Avoid slang and most contractions. Use an informal vocabulary for personal narratives, nonserious informative writing, and humorous writing.

2 Choosing words in job-related writing

For business letters, memos, and reports addressed to strangers or superiors, write with some formality. Choose familiar words to avoid sounding stuffy or pretentious, but consider words subdued in connotation that fit the seriousness of the occasion. In memos and reports addressed to co-workers, less formal words will convey your close professional relationship. Aim to sound as if you're talking to them about a subject of mutual concern. (See also 61a–d.)

3 Maintaining consistent formality

Maintain a consistent attitude toward your subject and a consistent relationship with readers. As you edit, look for shifts from one vocabulary to another. Because you talk more than you write, take special care in serious writing to look for shifts from formal to informal words.

Contemporary religious philosophers have ~~come down hard on~~ *severely criticized*

American society as selfish and materialistic.

[*Come down hard on* is slang. Its conversational tone makes this expression inappropriate for academic writing on serious subjects.]

~~Right now, though,~~ compressed natural gas has several ~~bugs~~ *problems* in its *Currently, however,*

storage that prevent its wide use as an alternative to gasoline.

[*Right now, though,* is too conversational and imprecise for serious academic writing. *Bugs* is slang and a cliché, inappropriate in objective writing.]

27b In most academic and public writing, avoid slang, regionalisms, and nonstandard words

The larger or more diverse your audience, the more careful you should be to choose words that all your readers will understand and feel comfortable with. You may speak a social or regional dialect of English rich with its own vocabulary, but for diverse readers, such words are inappropriate. Use a widely understood vocabulary instead.

1 Avoiding slang

Slang is the informal vocabulary of a group or subculture. It is colorful, rapidly changing, strong in feeling, and often not understood by outsiders. Consider the slang popular among young Americans during the last fifty years; note how dated some words sound: *cool, hot, downer* (to describe bad news), *dank, schwag, geek, groovy, gizmo, heavy* (meaning "serious"), *later* (for "goodbye"), *out of sight, razzle-dazzle, I read you.*

Some slang becomes widely accepted and proves so durable that it becomes part of the language: *movie, muckraker, handout.* More often slang is incomprehensible to outsiders, has a life of only a few months or years, and is more often spoken than written. For these reasons it is appropriate only for informal writing to readers you know well.

2 Avoiding regionalisms

A note on dialect: **Regionalisms** are words and expressions used by speakers from a specific geographic region. For example, in the south-central Midwest *considerable* means a large amount. In the upper Midwest *eat razor soup* means to make a wisecrack. In the eastern United States, cottage cheese is frequently called *smearcase*. In some parts of Texas, *borrego* (borrowed from Spanish, "a young lamb") refers to sheep and to fleecy-looking clouds. Like slang, regional expressions are often colorful and strong in feeling. But because their use is restricted, they may be misunderstood, and you should avoid them in serious writing for diverse audiences.

3 Avoiding nonstandard words

A note on dialect: **Nonstandard words** such as *nowheres, done told, theirselves,* and *don't never* appear in English dialects spoken by certain ethnic or social groups. Each dialect has its own grammar and vocabulary, and both are correct for speakers of that dialect. However, because these nonstandard words tend to be spoken rather than written and because they are not shared by speakers of other dialects, they are inappropriate for academic writing and other writing for diverse audiences. Use standard English words. (See Chapter 29. See also 13c–e, 17g, and 18e.)

27c Use jargon and neologisms only with specialized audiences

Jargon is the technical language of a profession, craft, trade, or activity. Computer operators, for example, use acronyms like *VGA;* metaphors like *motherboard* and *parking a hard drive;* words derived from people's names, like *baud;* compounds like *online* and *login;* shortened words like *e-mail* and *modem;* and old words with new meaning, like *server.*

A **neologism** is a newly invented word. Many neologisms begin their lives as jargon, slang, or media expressions: *vaporware, cyberspace, CAT scan, morphing, disco.* Many neologisms, such as *radar* and *scuba,* prove useful and eventually become part of standard English; the rest disappear.

Jargon and neologisms enable members of special-interest groups to communicate with one another clearly, economically, and efficiently. They cause problems, however, when addressed to outsiders. Therefore, follow these guidelines.

1 Writing for a nontechnical audience

When writing for a nontechnical audience, avoid jargon and neologisms. Choose accurate, widely understood words. If only jargon will say what you mean, provide definitions.

With new computer-imaging technology, movie makers are now able to
transform
~~morph~~ one image into another, for example, fading the head of a man
^

into that of a lion.

2 Academic writing

In academic writing for readers who understand your subject, choose
words appropriate to the field or discipline. Demonstrate your knowledge of
technical language, but avoid technical words merely to impress. If in doubt
about the proper vocabulary, check with your instructor.

3 Technical writing

In technical writing for knowledgeable readers—for example, in on-
the-job memos and reports—a technical vocabulary is appropriate. But carefully consider your audience's knowledge. (See also Chapter 61.)

A note on jargon: The term *jargon* is sometimes used broadly to refer to
difficult or flowery words used to impress readers. These words are never
appropriate. See the following section.

27d Avoid pretentious words, doublespeak, and most euphemisms

1 Avoiding pretentious words

Pretentious writing aims to impress more than communicate. Most
readers are annoyed by it. Therefore, avoid the following kinds of words:

- Unfamiliar "big" words, often with Latin roots

     teachers   slow to recognize how
Some ~~educators in the~~ humanities have been ~~dilatory in their cognizance~~
     ^   ^   *can improve their teaching*
~~of the pedagogical ramifications of~~ new instructional technologies.
                                                                      ^

- Flowery words

The warm sunrise promised
 ~~Rising into azure heavens flecked with billowy clouds, the warm sun~~
 ^   *a fine autumn*
~~foretold a wondrous autumnal~~ day.
                              ^

2 Avoiding doublespeak

Doublespeak, a term invented by George Orwell in his novel *1984,* is
words and expressions that deliberately mislead. Doublespeak aims to cre-

ate a favorable impression opposite that of the truth. It is an essential feature of political propaganda, but you can find it wherever writers disguise the truth: in advertisements; in government, military, and business writing; even, occasionally, in academic writing. Some examples of doublespeak:

downsizing = layoffs	revenue enhancements = tax increases
terminated = fired	sanitize = censor
final solution = kill	substandard housing = slum
preowned = used	

Remember Abraham Lincoln's axiom that you can't fool all the people all the time. Avoid misleading language.

3 Avoiding euphemisms

Like doublespeak, euphemisms hide the truth. But a **euphemism,** from Greek words meaning "good speech," is a pleasant-sounding word or expression that aims to soften a topic that some readers may consider distasteful, ugly, or difficult to speak of. Euphemisms usually appear in discussions of emotionally charged subjects like death (*to pass away, expire*), bodily functions (*go to the bathroom*), and sex (*make love, sleep together, adult entertainment*). Unless your audience will be offended or hurt by direct language, avoid euphemisms. They will make you seem prudish or mealy mouthed.

27e Avoid sexist and other offensive words

Ethical writing recognizes the dignity and individuality of all people, regardless of background, race, gender, or physical capacities. Choose words that respect the equality of men and women, nationalities, and regional and ethnic groups. Avoid words that belittle, abuse, or deny individual traits.

1 Avoiding sexist and racist words

Sexist words describe men or women, but more often women, in demeaning, often physical terms (*chick, stud, bitch*) or deny men and women equal status (*gals, the girls in the office, lady astronaut*). **Racist words** and **ethnic slurs** belittle or abuse members of races, nationalities, or ethnic groups (*dago, spic, polack, chink, gook, mick, kike, nigger,* and so forth). Every group has the right to decide what it wants to be called. Some Americans refer to themselves as *African-American,* others as *persons of color,* and still others as *Black;* most reject *Negro* or *colored*. Fairness obliges you to adopt the words each group uses to describe itself.

2 Avoiding stereotypes

Stereotypes are occupational titles, generic terms, or common expressions that exclude women or men, refer to a person's gender where it is irrelevant, deny equality, or describe restrictively. Omit biased language or replace stereotypes with nonrestrictive substitutes.

STEREOTYPE	ACCEPTABLE SUBSTITUTE
businessman	businessperson, executive
chairman	chair, head, moderator, chairperson
congressman	representative, legislator
fireman	firefighter
foreman	supervisor
handicapped	physically disabled
landlord/landlady	owner, manager
mailman	letter carrier, postal worker
mankind	humankind
policeman	police officer
salesman	salesclerk, salesperson
steward/stewardess	flight attendant
workman	worker

Two special problems:

1. Writers may unintentionally stereotype audiences. As you write, keep in mind the differences in your readers' gender and background.

    Employees are invited to bring their ~~wives~~ *spouse or a friend* to the company picnic.

    [Not all employees may be men; not all may be married. The revision recognizes the diversity of the audience.]

2. The use of *he, him,* and *his* to refer collectively to men and women may seem to exclude women. Instead of using these pronouns to imply *he and she, him and her, his and hers,* use masculine and feminine pronouns or, when possible, change the sentence from singular to plural. (See also 15d.)

    Each candidate must write an essay explaining ~~his~~ *his or her* qualifications for

    admission.

    When ~~a teenager~~ *teenagers* first ~~receives his~~ *receive their* driver's license, ~~he wants~~ *they want* to drive

    everywhere.

28 Editing Wordiness

Except for those who like to hear themselves talk, most people aren't wordy on purpose. But for writers, finding what to say and choosing the best words are often roundabout, messy processes of trial and error. They often end up with more words than readers need to get their message. And so they have to rewrite, cutting unnecessary words that in a final draft might cloud meaning or waste readers' time. To make your writing clear, forceful, and direct—and to earn readers' gratitude—say all that you have to say in as few words as possible.

How to . . . Edit Wordiness

Follow these guidelines.

1. Don't be concerned about wordiness as you plan and write a first draft. But if you're having trouble saying what you mean, look for words that get in the way of your message. Cutting extra words often clarifies meaning.

2. As you edit, look for these clues to wordiness and begin cutting where they occur.

   ■ Needless words, sentences, or extra paragraphs at the beginning or end of your writing
   ■ Needlessly repeated words or ideas (*the reason why is because*) (See 28a.)
   ■ Empty sentence openers (*In my opinion . . .*), needless intensifiers (*really, very*) or qualifiers (*somewhat, seems*), and unnecessary impersonal constructions (*there is, there are, it is*) (See 28b.)
   ■ Padded transitions that link sentences or sentence parts (*because of the fact that*), unnecessary clause openers (*which is/are, who is/are*), and nouns ending in *-ence, -ance, -ment,* and *-tion* that could be transformed into the main verb of the sentence (See 28c.)

3. If a wordy passage contains essential words, replace inflated expressions with concise synonyms, rewrite indirect expressions to make them direct, or combine two wordy passages into one. (See 28c3.)

28*a* Eliminate redundancy

Redundancy is unnecessary repetition, as in *first and foremost* or *crisis situation.* One word in each of these examples implies the meaning of the other. Eliminate redundancy from your writing, but remember that sometimes you need to repeat for emphasis or clarity. (See 20d and 22d.) Here are some repetitions to avoid.

1 Needlessly repeated words

As I watched her skate, ~~the impression that was most impressed on~~ me

what most impressed

was her athletic grace.

The man turned the pages of the magazine for a moment or two, then

laid ~~the magazine~~ on the end table.

it

[Use pronouns to avoid unnecessary repetition of nouns and to create variety.]

2 Needlessly repeated ideas

Cut unemphatic words that merely repeat the meaning implied by other, more important words.

~~The reason why airline~~ hijackings seldom occur in the United States ~~is~~

Airline

because the federal government has improved passenger screening

~~procedures~~.

[*Reason, why,* and *because* mean the same thing in this sentence; two of the three words can be cut. *Passenger screening* implies *procedures;* this word can be omitted.]

3 Redundant pairs

Writers sometimes pair words with the same meaning: *first and foremost, hopes and aspirations, hopes and desires, goals and objectives, honest and true,* and so forth. If you pair redundant words, cut one.

The ~~basic and~~ fundamental right to free speech is guaranteed by the U.S.

Constitution.

4 Redundant modifiers

Some modifiers are unnecessary because their meaning is contained in the words they modify: *basic fundamentals, the color blue, crisis situation, end result, past memories, period of time, personal opinion, shiny appearance, square in shape, true facts,* and so forth.

If the supplier expedites our order ~~as quickly as possible~~, we will

~~completely~~ finish the project before the deadline.

[*To expedite* means "to speed a process," and to finish something is to complete it; *as quickly as possible* and *completely* are redundant.]

28*b* | Cut empty words and phrases

1 Cutting empty sentence openers

The meaning of an opening phrase may be implied by the rest of the sentence. Generally cut openers such as *I think that, in some ways, needless to say, in some respects, for the most part, as everyone knows, the fact is, obviously,* and *as we see.*

The meeting will
~~The purpose of the meeting is to~~ inform employees about changes in

their benefits.

[Information about the subject of the meeting identifies its purpose.]

2 Cutting empty qualifiers and intensifiers

Intensifiers and **qualifiers** are modifiers that express degree: *very, definitely, really, truly, uniquely, wonderfully, apparently, may, seems, perhaps, probably, somewhat, quite,* and so forth. You may need them to indicate the strength of a statement or shade your meaning. More often, they suggest that writers doubt the force of their ideas. Prefer the plain truth.

After two semesters, ~~it seems~~ I ~~truly~~ feel like ~~something of~~ a veteran

college student.

3 Cutting unnecessary impersonal constructions

Impersonal constructions begin with *there is/are* or *it is.* They enable writers to move ideas to the end of a sentence or to emphasize actions that lack actors: *There are four reasons that General Lee lost the Battle of Gettysburg,* or *It is raining.* But when impersonal constructions are unnecessary, cut them and rewrite.

Some
~~There is some~~ urban land ~~that~~ is set aside each year for new parks but

not enough to equal the acres buried under new subdivisions and

shopping centers.

Businesses
~~It is clear that businesses~~ have a social obligation to support nonprofit
                                   ^

organizations in their communities.

28c | Compress padded writing

Wordiness sometimes results not only from extra words but from
padding, the use of inflated or indirect expressions. Look for and eliminate
the following wordy expressions in your writing.

1 Cutting padded phrases

Compress inflated phrases to one or two words.

INFLATED	CONCISE	INFLATED	CONCISE
as a matter of fact	in fact	for the reason that	because
at the present time	now, currently	in order to	to
because of the fact that	because	in spite of the fact that	although, even though
by means of	by	in the event that	if
due to the fact that	because	in the neighborhood	approximately, about
for the purpose of	for, to	in today's world	now, today
		prior to	before
		with regard to	about

We were impressed ~~by the fact~~ that the courthouse had been renovated

so quickly.

2 Cutting padded clauses

Compress padded dependent clauses to a phrase or word. (To learn to
recognize clauses, see 10b.)

In front of the troops stood their duffle bags, ~~which had been~~ packed

with all their gear for the next twelve months.

Unable
~~Because they don't know how~~ to handle their new freedom, some recent
                               ^

high school graduates have difficulty adjusting to college life.

3 Cutting padded sentences

Combine two padded sentences. (For sentence-combining strategies, see 21b.)

The most scenic tour of Mammoth Cave is a four-mile *, four-hour* walk that ~~lasts~~

~~about four hours. This tour~~ includes lunch in the Snowball Room and

ends at Frozen Niagara.

4 Avoiding indirect use of the passive voice verb form

As a grammatical term, *voice* refers to the relation between a subject and verb. The passive voice often requires more words than the active. Use the active voice to make your writing concise and direct. (To learn when the passive voice is appropriate, see 20a2.)

The judges
~~First prize was~~ awarded ~~by the judges~~ *first prize* to a poem, "Violet Voices."

5 Avoiding indirect use of nominals

A **nominal** is a noun derived from a verb, often ending *-ence, -ance, -ment, -tion: dependence/depend, guidance/guide, argument/argue, adaptation/ adapt.* Nominals often appear in wordy, indirect writing. When you can do so, transform a nominal into its verb form, eliminate empty words, and rewrite.

The   can be repaired only after it is removed
~~Repairs to the~~ compressor ~~are possible only after its removal~~ from the

refrigerator.

[Turning two nominals, *repairs* and *removal,* into verbs eliminates the empty verb *are,* and the sentence becomes direct and emphatic.]

29 A Guide to Usage: Troublesome Words and Phrases

This glossary contains commonly confused words (such as *less* and *fewer*); words frequently misused (such as *aggravate*); nonstandard words (such as *hisself*); pretentious or needlessly technical words, often referred to as jargon (such as *finalize*); wordy phrases (such as *reason why*); and colloquialisms inappropriate for formal writing (such as *okay*).

a, an. Use *a* before words beginning with a consonant sound or an *h* that is pronounced: *a student, a sparrow, a happy man, a hospital*. Use *an* before words beginning with a vowel sound (*a, e, i, o, u*) or silent *h*: *an apple, an investment, an honor, an honorable person*.

a lot (*not* alot). *A lot* is two words, not one. *We have had a lot of rain this spring.*

a while, awhile. *A while* is an article and a noun that mean "a period of time": *Stay with us for a while*. *Awhile* is an adverb and means "a short time": *He visited awhile and then left*. *Awhile* is never preceded by a preposition such as *after, for, in*.

accept, except. *Accept*, a verb, means "to receive, agree, or believe": *The singer accepted the bouquet from an admirer*. As a preposition, *except* means "but" or "other than": *Everyone is here except James*. As a verb, *except* means "to leave out, exclude": *The last three names were excepted from the list*.

adapt, adopt. *Adapt*, a verb, means "to adjust or to become accustomed": *Some wild animals have adapted to urban environments*. *Adopt*, also a verb, means "to take up and make one's own": *Many childless parents wish to adopt children*.

advice, advise. *Advice* is a noun, *advise*, a verb: *The lawyer advised her client to accept her advice*.

affect, effect. *Affect* is usually a verb meaning "to influence or act on." *Effect* is usually a noun meaning "a result"; occasionally it is a verb meaning "to bring about." *Smoking affects the body in many ways. Smoking has many harmful effects. Negative advertising may effect a decrease in tobacco use.*

aggravate. *Aggravate* means "to make worse or more troublesome": *High-sugar diets often aggravate childhood misbehavior*. In formal writing, avoid the colloquial use of *aggravate*, "to annoy or irritate." *The traffic was irritating* [not *aggravating*].

agree to, agree with. *Agree to* means "to consent": *The lawyers agreed to the proposed settlement*. *Agree with* means "to be in accord or to match": *She didn't agree with him about the causes of the problem*.

ain't. *Ain't* is nonstandard. Use *am not, is not, has not, have not,* and so forth: *They have not* [not *ain't*] *repaired the motor yet*.

all ready, already. *All ready* means "fully prepared." *Already* means "before or by this time." *By the time everyone was all ready to leave, it was already too late.*

all right (*not* alright). *All right* is two words; *alright* is nonstandard.

all together, altogether. *All together* means "in a group": *They stood all together near the doorway*. *Altogether* means "entirely, completely, totally": *They were altogether drenched by the sudden rain*.

allusion, illusion. An *allusion* is an indirect reference: *Writers and speakers make frequent allusions to Shakespeare*. An *illusion* is a false perception of reality: *A mirage is an optical illusion created by alternate layers of hot and cool air.*

among, between. Use *among* to refer to three or more things, *between* to refer to two: *There was little agreement among the members of the jury. It is so difficult to choose between strawberry and butter pecan ice cream.*

amount, number. Use *amount* with things that cannot be counted; use *number* with things that can: *The amount of happiness people enjoy is often related to the number of their friends.*

and etc. *Et cetera (etc.)* means "and so forth"; *and etc.* is wordy. (See also *etc.*)

and/or. Avoid *and/or* except in technical writing, where it may be necessary for precision.

angry at, angry with. *Angry at* is nonstandard; use *angry with: I was angry with* [not *at*] *him because he had cheated.*

anxious, eager. *Anxious* means "uneasy or worried." In formal writing, avoid using *anxious* to mean "eager." *We are eager* [not *anxious*] *to meet our new president.*

any one, anybody, anyone. *Any one* refers to a specific person or thing in a group: *Any one of our staff will help you. Anybody* and *anyone* mean "any person at all": *I have not found anyone who knows the answer. Anybody* and *anyone* are singular.

anyplace. *Anyplace* is appropriate for informal writing. For formal writing, use *anywhere.*

any way, anyway. *Any way* means "by whatever means or manner." *Any way you choose to travel will bring you unimagined adventures. Anyway* means "nevertheless, at least": *We asked them not to bother us, but they did anyway.*

anyways, anywheres. *Anyways* and *anywheres* are nonstandard forms of *anyway* and *anywhere.*

as, as if, like. *As if* is a subordinating conjunction that joins a subordinate clause to a main clause: *The last runners to finish looked as if they were in a trance. Like* is a preposition that should be followed only by a noun or noun phrase: *The last runner looked like a zombie.* In informal speech, *like* is often substituted for *as* or *as if,* but in formal writing, use *as: As* [not *like*] *the Bible says, it is easier for a camel to pass through a needle's eye than for a rich man to enter heaven.*

awful, awfully. The precise meaning of the adjective *awful* is "inspiring awe," but it also has the colloquial meaning of "extremely bad or terrible": *Modern technology has increased the awful power of military weapons. Julia was involved in an awful accident.* As an adverb, *awfully* has the colloquial meaning of "very"; avoid this sense of the word in formal writing: *Most unwed teenage mothers are very* [not *awfully*] *poor.*

awhile, a while. See *a while.*

bad, badly. *Bad* is an adjective that often follows linking verbs: *A bad storm is approaching. I feel bad today. Badly* is an adverb that modifies verbs, adjectives, and other adverbs: *He played badly.* (See 18c.)

basis, bases. *Basis* is singular, *bases,* plural.

being as, being that. *Being as* and *being that* are nonstandard; use *because* or *since*: *Because* [not *being that*] *I work overtime every day, I have almost no social life.*

beside, besides. *Beside* is a preposition meaning "at the side of or next to": *They walked beside the river. Besides* is a preposition meaning "in addition to or except for": *Besides jazz, I also enjoy bluegrass and gospel music. Besides* is also an adverb meaning "also or furthermore": *My pen has run out of ink; besides, my mind has run out of ideas.*

between, among. See *among.*

breath, breathe. *Breath* is a noun, *breathe* a verb: *Relax; take a breath; now breathe again.*

bring, take. Use *bring* when the action is toward the speaker: *Please bring me a cup of coffee.* Use *take* when the action moves away from the speaker: *Be sure to take traveler's checks on your vacation.*

but what, but that. *But what* and *but that* are colloquial phrases following expressions of doubt; use *that* instead: *I do not doubt that* [not *but what*] *they intend to do the right thing.*

can, may. *Can* expresses ability, knowledge, or capacity: *I can speak. May* expresses possibility or permission: *It may snow tomorrow. You may borrow my calculator.* In formal writing, avoid using *can* to mean permission: *May* [not *can*] *we send you a brochure?*

capital, capitol. *Capital* refers to a city, *capitol* to a building.

cite, site. The verb *cite* means "to mention as proof or to quote as an authority": *If you wish to be believed, cite your sources.* As a noun, *site* means "a place or setting for something": *They visited famous battlefield sites.*

cloth, clothe. *Cloth* is a noun, *clothe,* a verb: *The best cloth for sportswear pulls perspiration away from the skin. A compassionate government will feed, clothe, and house citizens who cannot care for themselves.*

coarse, course. *Coarse* means "rough in texture or unrefined": *The coarse fabric of his jacket scratched his skin. Course* usually refers to a unit of study, a direction of movement, a playing field, or part of a meal. *Of course* means "naturally or certainly." *Next semester I plan to take a course in Asian art. Of course, we are coming to the party.*

compare to, compare with. Use *compare to* when showing that two things are similar or belong in the same category: *In height, the Alps compare to the Rocky Mountains.* Use *compare with* when you intend to examine things side by side to discover similarities and differences: *Compared with the defense budget, the United States foreign aid budget is quite small.*

complement, compliment, complementary, complimentary. *Complement* means "to go with or complete" or "something that makes up a whole": *His artistic skill complements his creativity. A complement of marines led the attack. Compliment* means "to praise or flatter": *She complimented him for his tact. Complementary* means "completing or offsetting": *She chose complementary colors for the design. Complimentary* means "expressing a compliment or given freely, as an act of courtesy": *He received complimentary software with his new computer.*

conscience, conscious. *Conscience* refers to "moral awareness or the source of moral judgment": *Lying gave him a guilty conscience. Conscious* means "mentally aware or alert": *Before my morning coffee, I am barely conscious.*

continual, continuous. *Continual* means "recurring regularly or frequently": *The dog's continual bark kept him awake. Continuous* means "uninterrupted in time or sequence": *The siren rose and fell in a continuous wail.*

could care less. People generally use *could care less* when they really mean *couldn't care less.* The latter expression is logical and correct: *She couldn't care less* [not *could care less*] *about the lives and loves of Hollywood celebrities.*

could of. Nonstandard for *could have* or *could've*: *With his talent, John could have* [not *could of*] *been very successful.*

criteria. *Criteria* is the plural of *criterion,* which refers to a standard or rule for a decision or judgment. *One criterion for success is hard work. Two other important criteria are preparation and imagination.*

data. *Data* is the plural of *datum,* meaning "a fact or piece of information used to make a decision." Some readers object when *data* is used with singular verbs and modifiers; use plural verbs and modifiers instead: *These* [not *this*] *data show* [not *shows*] *that soil erosion is increasing.*

different from, different than. *Different from* is always correct: *Is a man's thinking process different from a woman's?* You may use *different than* when it is followed by a clause: *Television has made our thinking process different than it was fifty years ago.*

differ with, differ from. To *differ with* is to disagree with someone: *The student differed with her professor about the meaning of the poem.* To *differ from* is to contrast or be unlike: *The student's interpretation differed from her professor's.*

disinterested, uninterested. *Disinterested* means "unbiased, impartial, objective": *An umpire is supposed to be a disinterested observer. Uninterested* means "without interest": *He was uninterested in their opinion.*

done. In formal writing, avoid the imprecise use of *done* to mean "finished or complete": *By 1914, work on the Panama Canal was nearly complete* [not *done*].

don't. *Don't* is the contraction for *do not.* Avoid using *don't* as a contraction for *does not,* which is *doesn't*: *She doesn't* [not *don't*] *waste any time.*

due to. *Due to* means "because of." It is correct when used to introduce a subject complement following a linking verb: *The airplane's crash was due to icy weather.* Some readers object to the use of *due to* as a preposition: *The airplane crashed because of* [not *due to*] *icy weather.*

each. *Each* is singular. (See 14f and 15d.)

easy, easily. *Easy* is an adjective: *She makes a mile run look easy.* Do not use *easy* as an adverb modifying a verb; use *easily*: *She won the race easily* [not *easy*].

effect, affect. See *affect.*

elicit, illicit. *Elicit* means "to draw out or bring out": *With a little coaxing, she was able to elicit the right answer. Illicit* means "unlawful": *He was convicted of the illicit use of drugs.*

emigrate from, immigrate to. *To emigrate from* means "to leave one country or area for another: *During the 1840s many people emigrated from Ireland because of famine. To immigrate to* means "to enter and settle in another country or region": *During the 1840s many Irish immigrated to the United States.*

enthused, enthusiastic. Some readers object to the use of the informal *enthused* as an adjective. In formal writing, use *enthusiastic: I am an enthusiastic* [not *enthused*] *collector of 1950s movie posters.*

etc. Avoid *etc.* (*et cetera,* "and so forth") in formal writing; end a list with a specific example or *and so forth.* (Also see *and etc.*)

every body, everybody. See *every one.*

every day, everyday. *Every day* is the noun *day* preceded by the adjective *every: I try to exercise every day. Everyday* is an adjective meaning "appropriate for ordinary days or routine occasions": *Wear your everyday clothes to the party.*

every one, everyone. *Every one* is the pronoun *one* preceded by the adjective *every,* meaning "each individual or thing in a particular group": *Every one of the students was prepared for the exam. Everyone* is an indefinite pronoun meaning "every person": *Everyone was prepared for the exam.* Both are singular. (See 14f and 15d.)

except, accept. See *accept.*

explicit, implicit. *Explicit* means "fully and clearly expressed, with nothing implied": *I was given explicit instructions. Implicit* means "not directly expressed but understood": *We made an implicit agreement to avoid the issue.*

farther, further. *Farther* refers to physical distance: *I can run farther now than I could six weeks ago. Further* refers to quantities or degree and means "more or to a greater extent": *When we inquired further, we found he had changed jobs twice within a year.*

fewer, less. Disregard the supermarket signs that say "Ten items or less." Use *fewer* with items that can be counted, *less* with things that are not counted: *Fewer* [not *less*] *students now major in business. We had less snow this winter than last.*

finalize. Many readers object to *finalize,* meaning "to put into final form, complete or conclude," as jargon. Find more precise alternatives: *The baseball players' union completed* [not *finalized*] *negotiations for a new contract.*

firstly. *Firstly* sounds pretentious, as do *secondly, thirdly,* and so forth; use *first, second, third.*

further, farther. See *farther.*

goes. *Goes* is nonstandard for *says: When he says* [not *goes*], *"Folks, I'm not making this up," I know that he is making it up.*

good, well. *Good* is an adjective: *This salsa tastes good. Well* is an adverb: *This old watch still runs well.* Use *well* to refer to someone's health: *After a long rest, he is well again.* (See 18c.)

got, have. *Got* is the past tense of *get*. Do not use the colloquial *got* in place of *have*: *They have* [not *got*] *the best reputation for reliability*. Do not use *got, got to, has got to,* or *have got to* in place of *must*: *They must* [not *have got to*] *change their priorities*.

hardly, scarcely. Avoid the colloquial double negatives *can't hardly, not hardly, can't scarcely, not scarcely*: *I can hardly* [not *can't hardly*] *explain what it felt like*. (See 18e.)

have, got. See *got*.

have, of. Use *have* following the modal verbs *could, should, may, might, must,* and *would*: *They should have* [not *of*] *received an invitation*. (See 13e3.)

he/she, his/her. Many readers object to the awkward expressions *he/she, his/her*; use *he or she* or one of the alternatives in 15d.

hisself. *Hisself* is nonstandard; use *himself*.

hopefully. *Hopefully* means "in a hopeful manner": *He looked hopefully toward the clock.* Many readers object to its use, especially at the beginning of a sentence, to mean "it is to be hoped": *Hopefully, job opportunities for graduates will soon improve.* Indicate instead who is doing the hoping: *We hope job opportunities for graduates will soon improve.*

if, whether. Use *if* to introduce statements of condition and *whether* to introduce alternatives: *If we have enough volunteers, we can finish; it makes no difference whether they are young or old.*

impact. Many readers object to the use of *impact* as a verb: *The recent election will have an impact on* [not *will impact*] *proposed antipollution laws.*

implicit, explicit. See *explicit*.

imply, infer. *Imply* means "to express indirectly": *She glanced at her watch to imply that it was time to leave. Infer* means "to draw a conclusion": *After studying the evidence, we inferred that the fire was caused by lightning.*

infer, imply. See *imply*.

irregardless. Nonstandard for *regardless*.

is when, is where, is why, is because. Avoid these imprecise and illogical expressions in writing definitions and explanations: *A paceline is a line of cyclists tightly grouped* [not *A paceline is when cyclists group together tightly*] *to reduce wind resistance.*

its, it's. *Its* is a possessive pronoun: *The dog twitched its tail. It's* is the contraction of *it is*: *It's good to hear that they arrived safely.*

kind(s), sort(s), type(s). *Kind, sort,* and *type* are singular: *This kind of words is* [not *these kind of words are*] *known as "fighting words." Kinds, sorts,* and *types* are plural, referring to more than one kind or sort: *These kinds of flowers grow well in the shade.*

kind of, sort of. Avoid using *kind of* and *sort of* to mean "somewhat": *I was somewhat* [not *kind of*] *disappointed by the novel's conclusion.* Do not use *a* following either phrase: *It was the same sort of* [not *sort of a*] *speech politicians always make.*

lay, lie. *Lay,* a transitive verb meaning "to put or set down," always takes a direct object: *Lay the pencil on the table.* Its other forms are *laying, laid, laid.*

Lie, an intransitive verb meaning "to rest on a surface or occupy a position," does not take a direct object: *The pencil lies on the table.* Its other forms are *lying, lay, lain.* (See 13a5.)

lead, led. *Lead* (the metal) sounds like *led* (the past tense of the verb *to lead*); do not confuse them: *The officer led* [not *lead*] *his men into battle.*

leave, let. *Leave* means "to go away"; *let* means "to give permission or allow." Do not use *leave* when you mean *let*: *Let* [not *leave*] *him clean up the mess he has made.*

less, fewer. See *fewer.*

like, as. See *as.*

loose, lose, losing. *Loose* is an adjective meaning "not fastened or contained"; *lose* is a verb meaning "to misplace." Do not use one word when you mean the other, and do not write "loosing," which is not a word, when you mean *losing.* (See 13a6.)

lots, lots of. In formal writing, avoid the colloquial expressions *lots* and *lots of,* meaning "many, much, or a lot": *Many* [not *lots of*] *medicines are produced from rain forest plants.*

mankind. Many readers object that *mankind* excludes women. Use *humankind, humanity, humans,* or *the human race* instead.

may be, maybe. *May be* is a verb phrase: *The computer may be unplugged.* *Maybe* is an adverb meaning "possibly": *Maybe the computer is unplugged.*

may, can. See *can.*

media, medium. *Media* is the plural of *medium*: *Among the news media, television is the most popular medium but the least informative.*

most. In formal writing, avoid using *most* as a substitute for *almost: Almost* [not *Most*] *everyone arrived on time.*

must of. See *have, of.*

nauseous, nauseated. *Nauseous* means "sickening": *A nauseous gas filled the room.* *Nauseated* means "to feel nausea, loathing, or disgust": *I felt nauseated as soon as I smelled the gas.*

number, amount. See *amount.*

of, have. See *have, of.*

off of, off from. *Off of* and *off from* are redundant; write *off: The cat jumped off* [not *off of*] *the table.*

ok, O.K., okay. All three spellings are acceptable, but avoid these colloquial expressions in formal writing. Use the adjectives *acceptable, satisfactory,* or *all right* or the verbs *approve of, agree to,* or *authorize: If my application is satisfactory* [not *okay*], *will you authorize* [not *okay*] *my loan?*

passed, past. *Passed* is the past tense of the verb *pass: The sports car passed the truck.* *Past* refers to a time before the present or a place farther than another: *The old man spoke nostalgically of his past. He lives two houses past the grocery store.*

plus. In formal writing, avoid using *plus* to mean "and," "in addition," or "as well as": *Culture consists of the shared knowledge and beliefs of a human community, as well as* [not *plus*] *the tools that use and express culture.*

precede, proceed. *Precede* means "to come before"; *proceed* means "to go forward": *Preceded by her parents, the bride proceeded down the aisle.*

presently. *Presently* means "in a short time, soon"; do not use it to mean "now": *Currently* [not *presently*], *factory output is ninety percent of capacity. We will arrive presently.*

principal, principle. As a noun, *principal* means "the head of a school or organization" or "a sum of money"; as an adjective it means "first or most important." *Principle* is a noun meaning "a basic truth or law": *My principal taught me the principle known as the Golden Rule.*

proceed, precede. See *precede.*

quote, quotation. *Quote* is a verb, *quotation* a noun. Do not use *quote* as a substitute for *quotation*: *I have several good quotations* [not *quotes*] *supporting my opinion.*

real, really. *Real* is an adjective, *really* an adverb. In formal writing, do not use *real* as a substitute for *really*: *He was really* [not *real*] *pleased to receive the award.*

reason is because, reason why. *Reason is because* is illogical; use *that* instead of *because*: *The reason they lost was that* [not *because*] *they rarely ever practiced. Reason why* is redundant: *The reason* [not *reason why*] *the economy has improved is technological advance.*

scarcely, hardly. See *hardly.*

set, sit. *Set*, meaning "to put or place," has the principal parts *set, set, set*. It is a transitive verb that takes a direct object: *Set the computer on this desk. Sit*, an intransitive verb meaning "to be seated or to rest," has the principal parts *sit, sat, sat: Sit here next to me.*

shall, will. *Shall* has nearly disappeared as a helping verb used with *I* or *we* to signal action in the future. It now appears mainly in polite requests, legal documents, and emphatic statements: *Shall we go? Both parties shall agree. I shall return. Will* is appropriate for most future statements.

should of. See *have, of.*

since. Some readers object to *since* as a substitute for *because*. Use *since* to mean "from then until now" or "between then and now": *Because* [not *since*] *it rained so hard last night, the game has been postponed. We have been waiting since six o'clock.*

sit, set. See *set.*

site, cite. See *cite.*

so. In formal writing, avoid using *so* as a substitute for the intensifier *very*: *Lake Constance is very* [not *so*] *beautiful.*

someone, somebody, something. *Someone, somebody,* and *something* are singular. (See 14f and 15d.)

some time, sometime, sometimes. *Some time* is the adjective *some* modifying the noun *time: She wants to spend some time with her grandparents. Sometime* is an adverb meaning "at an indefinite or unstated time": *We'll be there sometime soon. Sometimes* is an adverb meaning "at times, now and then": *Sometimes we don't understand each other.*

sort, kind. See *kind(s), sort(s), types(s)*.

suppose to, use to. Write *supposed to* and *used to*. (See 13e1.)

sure. In formal writing, avoid using *sure* as an adverb; use *surely* instead: *We were surely* [not *sure*] *pleased by the news.*

take, bring. See *bring*.

than, then. *Than* is a conjunction that links unequal comparisons: *Harry types faster than Kevin.* *Then* is an adverb meaning "at that time or next in time": *He turned first one way and then another.*

that. See *who, which, that*.

that, which. Many writers use *that* to introduce essential or restrictive clauses, *which* to introduce nonessential or nonrestrictive clauses. (See 34e.)

theirself, theirselves, themself. *Theirself, theirselves,* and *themself* are nonstandard for *themselves*: *They decided to go by themselves* [not *theirselves*].

then, than. See *than*.

this kind. See *kind(s), sort(s), type(s)*.

to, too, two. *To* is a preposition; *too* means "very" or "also"; *two* is a number.

try and. *Try and* is nonstandard for *try to*: *Try to* [not *try and*] *remember where you last saw your keys.*

unique. *Unique* is an absolute meaning "one of a kind"; do not use *unique* with qualifiers such as *more* and *most*: *She is a unique* [not *the most unique*] *writer.* (See also 18d4.)

use to, suppose to. See *suppose to*.

ways. In formal writing, avoid the use of *ways* to mean "distance": *They have come a long way* [not *ways*] *to get where they are today.*

well, good. See *good*.

where. In formal writing, avoid using *where* to substitute for *that* or *when*: *I recently read that* [not *where*] *the news media are more balanced than critics claim. Surprisingly, Christmas is a time when* [not *where*] *many people are most unhappy.*

where . . . at/to. Redundant; omit *at/to*: *Where did they say we would find them* [not *find them at*]?

which. See *that, which,* and *who, which, that*.

who, which, that. Use *who* to refer to people, *which* to things, and *that* to groups of people or to things: *The man who just left carried a heavy suitcase, which he shifted from one hand to the other. I want a book that tells me something new.* (See 16d; see also *that, which*.)

who, whom. *Who* is used with subjects and subject complements, *whom* with objects. (See 17e.)

whose, who's. *Whose* is a possessive pronoun; *who's* is a contraction of *who is*: *Whose essay is this? Who's ready for dessert?*

will, shall. See *shall*.

would of. See *have, of*.

your, you're. *Your* is a possessive pronoun: *Your time is up. You're* is a contraction of *you are*: *You're our first choice.*

PART **IV.**

*ESL
Editing*

ESL Editing Guide

ESL Editing Guide

The complex features of English grammar and idiomatic expression sometimes puzzle even advanced speakers of English as a second language. For immediate answers to your questions about English, see Chapters 30–32. For detailed answers, see these and other widely available reference books:

- Dictionaries: *Longman Dictionary of American English* (White Plains, NY: Longman, 1983); *New Horizon Ladder Dictionary of the English Language* (New York: Signet, 1990); or *Oxford Advanced Learner's Dictionary*, 4th ed. (New York: Oxford, 1995).

- Phrase books and idiomatic dictionaries: NTC's *American Idioms Dictionary* (Lincolnwood, IL: National Textbook Company, 1994) or NTC's *Dictionary of American English Phrases* (Lincolnwood, IL: National Textbook Company, 1995).

- Practice for advanced ESL speakers and writers: Betty Schrampfer Azur, *Understanding and Using English Grammar*, 2nd ed. (Englewood Cliffs, NJ: Prentice-Hall, 1990), or Len Fox, *Focus on Editing* (White Plains, NY: Longman, 1992).

 ## Articles and Quantifiers

Articles (*a, an, the*) and quantifiers (*a few, many, some,* and so forth) introduce nouns, which may follow immediately or be preceded by other words.

article + noun
The snow lay in gentle drifts.

article + adjective + noun
A wet snow bent the boughs of the tree.

quantifier + noun
Some snow fell last night.

30*a* | Use *a/an* with nonspecific singular count nouns

Count nouns name persons, places, or things that can be counted; they may be singular or plural: *student/students, forest/forests, computer/computers.*

Nonspecific count nouns name a class of things or something not specifically identified: *A computer makes writing easier.* The indefinite articles *a* and *an* are used to introduce nonspecific singular count nouns.

How to . . . Edit English Sentences When English Is Your Second Language

1. Subjects and verbs form the core meaning of a sentence. Reread to be sure subjects and verbs make sense together in each sentence. (See 22a–c.) Use a dictionary or phrase book to check idioms.
2. As you revise, be sure that you've used all the words that English sentences require: subject pronouns, expletives like *there* to begin a sentence, and linking verbs like *was*. But avoid unnecessary repetition of subject pronouns, direct objects, adverbs like *there*, and conjunctions like *although* or *but*. (See 32a and b.)
3. Reconsider clause, phrase, and single-word modifiers to be sure they are placed properly and make sense with the words they modify. (See 23a and b, 32e3 and 4.)
4. Reconsider word endings to be sure words show the correct part of speech for their roles as nouns (for example, *response*), verbs (*respond*), adjectives (*responsive*), and adverbs (*responsively*). Use your dictionary to make decisions.
5. Reconsider word endings to be sure words show the appropriate number (singular or plural), person (first, second, or third), tense, or other verb marker.
6. Reconsider nouns to be sure they are preceded by an appropriate article, if necessary (see 30a–d).
7. Reconsider prepositions to be sure they are used idiomatically and at the beginning of prepositional phrases. Use your dictionary or an English phrase book. (For phrases expressing place and time, see 32f.)

1 Matching *a* with consonant sounds, *an* with vowel sounds

- Use *a* before words beginning with a consonant sound: *a book, a happy man, a pen*.

- Use *an* before words beginning with a vowel sound (*a, e, i, o, u*, or silent *h*, as in *hour*): *an apple, an episode, an impossible task, an operator, an understanding, an honor*.

2 Knowing when to use *a* or *an*

Use *a* or *an* in these following situations:

- To mean "one of a certain type": *A banana will give you more energy than an apple*.

Most moral issues have ^*a* gray area where right and wrong become cloudy.

30*b*

- To refer to something not specifically identified: *Choose an apple from this bowl.*

            an
  I have just received exciting job offer.
             ^

- To mention something for the first time: *A dish* [first mention] *fell from the shelf and broke. The dish* [second mention] *belonged to my grand-mother.*

A note on exceptions requiring the: The article *the* is used in a generic sense with certain nonspecific singular count nouns to mean "one of a certain type of thing":

- Species of animals: *The woolly mammoth lived in Siberia 6,000 years ago.*

- Inventions: *The computer is indispensable for most students.*

- Musical instruments: *The koto, a stringed instrument similar to the zither, is important to Japanese sacred music.*

30*b* | Never use *a/an* with noncount nouns

Noncount nouns name things that are not countable in English. Noncount nouns cannot be made plural and are never preceded by *a* or *an*.

- **Whole groups of similar items:** *baggage, clothing, equipment, furniture, garbage, hardware, jewelry, junk, luggage, machinery, mail, makeup, money/cash/change, postage, scenery, traffic,* and so forth

                                      one piece of
  When I return home next time, I will take only a luggage.
                                           ^
  [To refer to countable units of otherwise noncount nouns, use quantifiers like *one piece* or *a little.* See 30e3.]

- **Abstractions:** *advice, beauty, courage, education, grammar, happiness, health, homework, honesty, importance, information, knowledge, laughter, music, news, peace, progress, sleep, time, violence, wealth, work, vocabulary,* and so forth

  On American television, a violence is presented as attractive and

  exciting.

- **Liquids:** *water, coffee, tea, milk, oil, soup, gasoline, blood,* and so forth
- **Solids:** *ice, bread, butter, cheese, meat, gold, iron, silver, glass, paper, wood, cotton, wool,* and so forth
- **Gases:** *steam, air, oxygen, hydrogen, smoke, smog, pollution,* and so forth

- **Particles and powders:** *rice, chalk, corn, dirt, dust, flour, grass, hair, pepper, salt, sand, sugar, wheat,* and so forth

- **Languages:** *Arabic, Chinese, English, Polish, Sanskrit, Spanish, Urdu,* and so forth

- **Fields of study:** *chemistry, engineering, history, mathematics, psychology,* and so forth

- **Recreation:** *baseball, bridge, chess, soccer, tennis,* and so forth

- **General activities:** *driving, studying, traveling,* and other gerunds (*-ing* nouns)

- **Natural phenomena:** *darkness, dew, electricity, fire, fog, gravity, hail, heat, humidity, lightning, rain, sleet, snow, thunder, weather, wind,* and so forth

A note: Some nouns can be either count or noncount nouns: *Please bring us two coffees* [count noun]. *African coffee* [noncount noun] *is especially dark and strong.* Nouns of this kind must be learned; see an ESL dictionary.

30*c* | Use *the* with nouns whose specific identity your readers know

The definite article *the,* indicating "this" or "that," introduces a specific person, place, or thing singled out from others. Use *the* in these situations:

- When readers know the identity of the noun: *I enjoy going to the bank on payday.*

  Many societies have abandoned ⌃*the* death penalty.

- When the noun refers to a unique person, place, or thing: *Last year, the Pope visited my country.*

  In this poem, ⌃*the* poet asks us to praise God for His creation.

- When the noun is mentioned for the second time: *Last night I went to a new restaurant* [first mention]. *The restaurant* [second mention] *is called La Chosa.*

- When the words following the noun specify its identity:

  The notes on your experiment are detailed and complete.

  The student who won the chess championship was David Wu.

- When the noun is modified by a superlative adjective (see 18d):

  The tallest player on the team is Nestor Wozny.

  When I finally got married, **the most relieved person** in the room was my mother.

30d Do not use *the* with most proper nouns and with statements meaning "all" or "in general"

1 Proper nouns

Do not use *the* before most singular proper nouns, including languages (*Arabic, English*), a person's name (*Juan Ramirez*), organizations (*Environmental Technologies*), holidays (*New Year's*), continents (*South America*), countries (*Mexico*), states (*New Jersey*), cities and towns (*Dallas*), streets and roads (*42nd Street, Fifth Avenue*), squares (*Herald Square*), parks (*Central Park*), single lakes (*Lake Geneva*), bays (*Tampa Bay*), islands (*Easter Island*), and specific mountains (*Mount Kilimanjaro*).

In ~~the~~ Japanese, the saying "Look up into the sky" means "Stop and smell the roses."

Some singular proper nouns are exceptions and require *the*:

- Use *the* before phrases identifying a specific language: *the Chinese language, the language spoken by newcomers,* and so forth.
- Use *the* before the names of certain countries and organizations: *the United Nations, the Netherlands, the United States, the Philippines, the Ukraine, the People's Republic of China, the Commonwealth of Independent States.*
- Use *the* before the names of regions (*the East Coast*), deserts (*the Sahara*), peninsulas (*the Malay Peninsula*), and bodies of water other than lakes (*the Pacific Ocean, the Mediterranean Sea, the Mekong River*).

Use *the* before plural proper nouns, such as *the Himalaya Mountains, the Great Lakes, the Sunda Islands.*

2 General statements

Do not use *the* before plural or noncount nouns used in a general sense.

Students
~~The students~~ today are drinking less but smoking more.

In dangerous situations, ~~the~~ courage may not be as important as ~~the~~ patience.

3 Certain place expressions

Do not use *the* before general uses of the words *school, class, work, church, town,* and *bed.*

This semester I go to ~~the~~ school three days each week.

4 Games

Do not use *the* before the names of games: *chess* [not *the chess*], *baseball, soccer.*

5 Subjects of study

Do not use *the* before subjects of study: *economics* [not *the economics*], *history, mathematics, political science, sociology,* and so forth.

When I took ~~the~~ art history, I studied both Western and Asian painters.

30*e* Match quantifiers with appropriate count or noncount nouns

Quantifiers are words or phrases that tell *how much* or *how many: two inches of rain, a few students.* Use certain quantifiers with certain kinds of nouns.

1 Using quantifiers with singular count nouns

Use *one, each,* and *every* with singular count nouns: *one apple, each student, every computer.*

2 Using quantifiers with plural nouns

Use the following quantifiers with plural nouns to tell *how many:* numbers of two or more, *both, a couple of, a few, many, a number of* (*the*), *a percentage of* (*the*), *quite a few, several, too many.* For example: *two apples, many apples, a majority of the students, a number of computers.*

3 Using quantifiers with noncount nouns

Use *a little, much,* and *a great deal of* with noncount nouns to tell *how much: a little baggage, much snow, a great deal of progress.*

4 Using quantifiers with plural and noncount nouns

Use the following quantifiers with plural and noncount nouns to tell *how many* or *how much: all, almost all, almost no, a lot of, enough, hardly any, lots of, a majority/minority of* (*the*), *most, not any/no, plenty of, some.* For example: *all the apples, all the snow, hardly any students, hardly any progress, some computers, some fog.* When count nouns follow these quantifiers, be sure to make them plural.

Some ~~university~~ ^{universities} make an extra effort to help international students feel

at home.

A note on articles plus quantifiers: In general, do not use an article before a quantifier.

The zoo in my hometown had ~~a~~ one large animal, an old bear.

A favorite pastime of ~~the~~ many older people is going out to eat and talk.

Exceptions include *a few, a little, the most, all the, a number of, a majority of,* and so forth: *a few days ago, the most important discovery, all the time, a number of students, a majority of women.*

 Verbs

This chapter focuses on features of English verbs frequently troublesome to nonnative speakers of English. Features that may be troublesome to native and nonnative speakers alike are treated elsewhere:

- Irregular English verbs: see 13a.
- Specific uses of English verb tenses: see 13b.
- Subject-verb agreement: see 13c and Chapter 14.
- The helping verbs *be, have,* and *do*: see 13d.
- *-d, -ed,* and *-ve* verb endings: see 13e.
- The subjunctive mood for wishes and nonfactual statements: see 13f and 24d1.
- Voice: see 20a, 24d2, 28c4.

31a To express tense correctly, match appropriate helping and main verb forms

1 Forming tenses

Tense is the time of the action expressed by the verb: past, present, and so forth. Standard English has six tenses, and each of these tenses has a progressive form (a form of *be* + *ing*) to indicate continuous or ongoing action. To form each tense correctly, use the following combinations of helping verbs and main verbs.

- **Present tense:** action that takes place now. Use the base or *-s/-es* form of the main verb: *I sigh. He speaks. She confesses. I am working. He is working. You/we/they are working.*

- **Past tense:** past action. Use the past tense form of the main verb: *I sighed. He spoke. I/he/she was working. You/we/they were working.*

- **Future tense:** action that will take place. Use *will* plus the base form of the main verb: *I will sigh. He will speak. You/we/they will be working.*

- **Present perfect tense:** past action continuing or completed in the present. Use *has/have* plus the past participle form of the main verb: *I have sighed. He has spoken. He/she has been working. I/you/we/they have been working.* For information on past participles of irregular verbs, see 13a.

- **Past perfect tense:** past action completed before another past action. Use *had* plus the past participle form of the main verb: *I had sighed. He had spoken. I/he/you/we/they had been working.* (See 13a.)

- **Future perfect tense:** action that will begin and end in the future. Use *will* plus *have* plus the *-d/-ed/-n/-en/-t* past participle form of the main verb: *I will have sighed. He will have spoken. I/he/you/we/they will have been working.* (See 13a.)

As you revise, be sure to use the correct combination of helping and main verbs to express tense.

She is ~~change~~ *changing* her major from biology to botany.

[The progressive *-ing* verb form is necessary to form the present progressive tense, indicating present ongoing action.]

Scientists ~~had~~ *have* now demonstrated that some animals are capable of reason.

[*Has* or *have* is necessary to form the present perfect, indicating past action completed in the present.]

A note on tense consistency: Two or more verbs that refer to the same action must be in the same tense. (See 24c.)

2 Including helping verbs

Always include helping verbs even when the meaning or verb tense seems clear without them.

So far, they *are* the friendliest students in my dorm.

[The helping verbs *be, have,* and *do* may stand alone as main verbs. Here *are* is necessary to connect the subject *they* to its modifier, *the friendliest students.*]

She *has* been a member of Amnesty International for five years.

[*Has* is necessary to create the present perfect tense.]

3 Identifying verbs that lack progressive forms

The following types of verbs do not generally appear in the progressive -*ing* form.

- **Verbs referring to mental states:** *believe, doubt, feel, forget, imagine, intend, know, mean, need, prefer, realize, recognize, remember, suppose, understand, wish:*

  have known
  I ~~am knowing~~ the Patel family for seven years.
  　　　　^

- **Verbs referring to emotional states:** *appreciate, care, dislike, envy, fear, hate, like, love, mind.*

- **Verbs referring to the act of possessing:** *belong, have, own, possess.* *Have,* an exception, is sometimes used in an active sense: *She is having a baby.*

- **Verbs referring to sense perceptions:** *feel, hear, see, smell, taste.* Exceptions: These verbs may appear in progressive tenses with a change of meaning. For example, in *I can feel the soft ground beneath my sleeping bag, feel* refers to tactile experience. But in *I'm feeling good this morning, feeling* refers to the speaker's mood.

31b After the helping verbs *do, does,* and *did,* use only the base form of the verb

The helping verb *do* appears in questions, in negatives with *not* or *never,* and in emphatic statements. Use the appropriate form to signal tense and number (singular or plural): *do* is the base form, *does* is the -*s* form (third-person singular), and *did* signals the past tense. After *do, does,* or *did,* use the base form of the main verb. Do not omit these helping verbs even if the meaning is clear without them.

- A question: *Do you have the videotape I requested?*
- A negative statement: *He doesn't* [present tense: *does not*] *know what he wants for dinner.*
- An emphatic statement: *We did* [past tense] *offer to help whenever we could.*

31c Use modal verbs to indicate your attitude toward the action of a main verb

The modal helping verbs *can, could, may, might, must, shall, should, will, would, ought to, had better,* and *had to* express the writer's attitude toward an action.

- Capability: *I can help you with your calculus.*
- Intention: *I will finish by tomorrow.*
- Possibility: *They might go to the party.*
- Probability: *She must have gone home already.*
- Permission: *You may leave when you finish the exam.*
- Advisability: *He should edit his writing more carefully.*
- Necessity: *We must finish the book by this weekend.*

Use only one modal before a main verb.

They might ~~could~~ take a Spanish class next semester.

1 Using present/future modals

For action in the present or future, use *can, may, might, must, should, had better, ought to, will* plus the base form of the main verb: *Next semester I had better take fewer classes.* Do not add an *-s* to the modal even when the subject is *he, she,* or *it.*

will
Natasha says she come to the party this evening.
^

[The modal verb *will* is required to express future action even though the closing phrase, *this evening,* indicates future time.]

can
Tamiko assured her supervisor that she ~~cans~~ finish the project by
^

Tuesday.

[Modal verbs never take the *-s* verb ending.]

volunteer
With a little encouragement, Henry might ~~volunteers~~.
^

[To signal future action, the modal *might* is followed by the base form *volunteer.*]

play
Lucia might ~~to play~~ a Chopin sonata at her next recital.
^

[Following the future tense modal *might,* the base form of the main verb *play* is required rather than the infinitive *to play.* (For uses of the infinitive, see 31f.)]

2 Using past modals

For past action, use *would, could, might, had to* plus the base form of the main verb: *Carlos had to leave early in order to be home by midnight.* Do not use the past tense of the main verb.

could
As she listened to their explanation, she ~~can~~ understand their motives.
^

be
When I saw how pale she was, I thought she might ~~been~~ sick.
^

3 Using past perfect modals for potential past action

For past action that did not actually occur, use *could* (*not*) *have, should* (*not*) *have, would* (*not*) *have* plus the past participle of the main verb: *Edgardo should have covered his roses to protect them from frost.* (See also 31e.)

With regular feeding, the fish would not have ~~die.~~
died

They should ~~have~~ waited a week or two before planting the flowers.
have

31*d* Use the passive voice when a subject receives the action of a transitive verb

In passive voice expressions, a passive subject receives the action of a transitive verb. The subject is acted on instead of performing an action.

a subject being acted on

In ancient Ethiopia, coffee was consumed as a food rather than a beverage.

1 Confusing voice and tense

Do not confuse the passive voice with the past tense. A passive voice verb may appear in the past, present, or future tense. To form the passive, use the appropriate form of *be* to signal number and tense plus the past participle of the main verb. Note that *be, being,* and *been* must be preceded by another helping verb.

Present passive: *The music is played.*
Present progressive passive: *The music is being played.*
Present perfect passive: *The music has been played.*
Past passive: *The music was played.*
Past progressive passive: *The music was being played.*
Past perfect passive: *The music had been played.*
Future passive: *The music will be played.*
Future perfect passive: *The music will have been played.*

2 Misusing the passive voice

■ To form the passive voice, use the past participle form of the main verb, not the base or past tense form.

released
The movie will be ~~release~~ in China early next year.

driven
The emigrants who left Ireland in the 1840s were ~~drove~~ by famine.

- Include the appropriate form of *be* in all passive voice expressions.

In our culture today, too much emphasis $\overset{is}{\wedge}$ placed on material goals.

- Use the passive voice sparingly. (See 20a and 28c4.)

31*e* Use correct verb tenses in conditional (*if . . .*) sentences

Conditional sentences usually consist of two parts: (1) an *if* dependent clause stating conditions and (2) a main clause stating results.

┌── conditions ──┐┌──── results ────┐
If we have time, we'll go bicycling this weekend.

┌──── results ────┐┌── conditions ──┐
We used to go bicycling when we had the time.

┌────── results ──────┐┌── conditions ──┐
We would go bicycling this weekend if we had enough time.

┌──── conditions ────┐┌────── results ──────┐
If we had had enough time, we would have gone bicycling last weekend.

These examples illustrate three features of conditional sentences: (1) the *if* clause may appear before or after the main clause stating results; (2) not every conditional sentence contains *if*; and, most important, (3) the kind of conditional statement determines the tenses of the verbs.

1 Describing habitual past and present conditions

For conditions that occur again and again in the past or present, use the same tense in the *if* clause and the "results" main clause.

┌── present tense (*if* clause) ──┐┌── present tense (*results* clause) ──┐
If we have enough time, we go bicycling on weekends.

┌──── past tense (*if* clause) ────┐┌── past tense (*results* clause) ──┐
When we had enough time, we went bicycling on weekends.

2 Describing possible future conditions

To predict future conditions and results:

- In the *if* clause, use *if* or *unless* plus the present tense (not the future tense).

- In the "results" clause, use *can, may, might, should,* or *will* plus the base form of the verb.

┌─ present tense (*if* clause) ─┐ ┌─ *may* + base form (*results* clause) ─┐
If we have enough time, we may go bicycling this weekend.

┌─ *will* + base form (*results* clause) ─┐ ┌─ present tense (*if* clause) ─┐
We will go bicycling this weekend unless it rains.

3 Speculating about present or future conditions

To speculate about imagined conditions in the present or future:

- In the *if* clause, use *if* plus the past tense (not the present tense). *A note on* be: If you use a form of the verb *be* in the *if* clause, use *were* instead of *was*, whether the subject is singular or plural. (See also 13f.)

- In the "results" clause, use *could, might,* or *would* plus the base form of the verb.

┌─ past tense (*if* clause) ─┐ ┌─ *would* + base form (*results* clause) ─┐
If the weather were better today, we would go bicycling.

┌─ *might* + base form (*results* clause) ─┐ ┌─ past tense (*if* clause) ─┐
We might go bicycling if it stopped raining.

4 Speculating about past conditions

To speculate about what might, could, or should have happened in the past:

- In the *if* clause, use *if* plus the past perfect tense (*had* + the past participle).

- In the "results" clause, use *could have, might have,* or *would have* plus the past participle.

┌─ past perfect tense (*if* clause) ─┐ ┌─ *would have* + past participle ─┐
If it had stopped raining, we would have gone bicycling.

┌─ *could have* + past participle (*results* clause) ─┐ ┌─ past perfect tense (*if* clause) ─┐
We could have gone bicycling if the weather had been better.

31*f* Learn which verbs may be followed by an infinitive, gerund, or either verb form

An infinitive is the base form of a verb preceded by *to: to study.* A gerund is the *-ing* form of a verb used as a noun: *Studying is difficult after a full day's work.* Following certain verbs, infinitives and gerunds may appear as objects.

1 Verb + infinitive

- Some verbs are followed by an infinitive (*to* + base form) but not by a gerund:

agree	claim	deserve	offer	refuse
appear	come	hope	plan	seem
arrange	decide	intend	pretend	wish

The group agreed **to study** [not *studying*] in the library after dinner.

- When used in the active voice, a related group of verbs follows this pattern: verb plus noun or pronoun plus infinitive:

advise	convince	force	permit	tell
allow	encourage	instruct	persuade	urge
ask	expect	invite	remind	want
cause	forbid	order	require	warn

verb + noun + infinitive

We have invited Gary to join us for dinner.

verb + pronoun + infinitive

Brigit advised me to apply for a scholarship.

- A small group of verbs may be followed either by an infinitive or by a noun or pronoun plus an infinitive:

allow	cause	get	promise
ask	expect	help	want
beg	force	need	would like

verb + infinitive

The lawyer asked to address the court.

verb + noun + infinitive

Mercedes asked Luis to bring his laptop computer to class.

- When the verbs *have* ("cause"), *let* ("allow"), and *make* ("force") are followed by a noun or pronoun plus an infinitive, the *to* is omitted:

Please have the carpenters finish [not *to finish*] their work by Thursday.

2 Verb + gerund

- These verbs may be followed by a gerund but not by an infinitive:

admit	deny	imagine	postpone	resist
appreciate	discuss	keep	practice	risk
avoid	enjoy	mention	put off	suggest
consider	escape	mind	quit	tolerate
delay	finish	miss	recall	

Keiko recalled **leaving** [not *to leave*] her gloves in the car.

- The following expressions with prepositions often take a gerund or a possessive noun or pronoun plus a gerund:

accuse someone of	approve of	be capable of
apologize for	be accustomed to	be excited about
be fond of	dream of	look forward to
be interested in	feel like	object to
be responsible for	forgive someone for	prevent someone from
be tired of	get around to	stop someone from
be used to	have an influence on	succeed in
believe in	help in	talk about
concentrate on	insist on	think about
depend on	keep someone from	

verb + preposition + gerund

For more than a year Anne and Judy have dreamed of traveling to Italy.

verb + preposition + pronoun + gerund

I depend on his arriving on time.

3 Verb + infinitive or gerund

- Certain verbs may be followed by infinitives or gerunds with little or no change of meaning: *begin, continue, hate, like, love, prefer, start.*

  Ali **loves playing** the guitar.

  Ali **loves to play** the guitar.

- After the verbs *forget, remember, stop,* and *try,* the infinitive and gerund have different meanings:

  A Good Samaritan is someone who **stops to help** those in need. [provides assistance]

  Concerned with his own problems, Felix **has stopped helping** those in need. [no longer provides assistance]

31g Use two-word verbs correctly

Two-word verbs (also called **phrasal verbs**) consist of a verb and a preposition that together mean something different from the meanings of their individual words. Consider two-word verbs using *call*:

I promise to **call up** my parents this weekend. [to telephone]

When I get the information, I'll **call** you **back.** [to return a telephone call]

The Army **is calling up** its reserves. [to report for service]

The instructor **called** the student **in** for a conference. [to ask to come to a specific place for a specific purpose]

I'm going to **call on** you tomorrow. [to ask to speak, to visit]

The umpire **called off** the game because of darkness. [to cancel]

1 Using a dictionary or phrase book

Because English two-word verbs are so numerous and their meanings are almost always idiomatic, use a dictionary or phrase book of idioms as you write and edit. Check to see that you've used the correct verb and preposition combination for the meaning you intend.

2 Placing objects and prepositions after the verb

The preposition in a two-word verb, called a **particle**, is either inseparable or separable from the verb:

- An **inseparable particle** follows the verb immediately.

  The instructor **called on** Jigna to answer the question.

  Today's college students often **drop out** of school for a few years and then return.

  Rosendo **goes out** to dinner tonight to celebrate his promotion.

- A **separable particle** may be separated from a transitive verb in either of two ways:

  Noun objects. If the object of a two-word verb is a noun, place the noun after the particle or between the verb and particle: *The umpire called off the game* (verb + particle + noun). *The umpire called the game off* (verb + noun + particle).

  Pronoun objects. If the object of a two-word verb is a pronoun, place the pronoun between the verb and particle: *The umpire called it off* (verb + pronoun + particle).

32 More Grammar

32*a* Include all necessary words

1 Including subjects

Except for imperatives, all English sentences must have a subject. Be especially careful to include personal pronoun subjects that refer to antecedents in preceding clauses or sentences. Compare these examples:

The Hindu god Brahma is considered equal to Vishnu and Siva. However, **he** has had only one temple dedicated to him, at Pushkar in India.

Because Carlos practices speaking into a tape recorder, *he* has excellent

pronunciation.

Takao is such an optimist. ~~Says~~ *She says* that problems are only clouds hiding the

sun.

2 Including the expletives *it, here,* and *there*

Expletives are words used primarily to provide a subject for a sentence that doesn't logically have one or to introduce a subject following the verb. Usually an expletive is followed by a form of *be:*

It *is* raining again.

delayed subject
There *are* many Andean mountains higher than 6,700 meters.

Do not omit *it, here,* and *there* even though they contribute little meaning to your sentences, and be sure the verb agrees with its actual subject. (See also 14b.)

It is
~~Is~~ necessary to take health precautions before traveling in tropical

countries.

[*It* is required to introduce the subject of the sentence, *to take health precautions.*]

, there
Ten years ago was a severe drought in my country.

[The subject of the sentence is not *ten years ago* but *a severe drought* following the verb *was. There* is required to introduce it.]

Here are
~~Is~~ two solutions to the problems created by illegal immigration.

[The subject of the sentence, *two solutions,* requires the plural verb *are.*]

32b Avoid unnecessary repetition

1 Avoiding unnecessary repetition of a subject

Do not repeat a subject within its own clause, even when the subject and verb are separated.

American cigarette manufacturers ~~they~~ now advertise heavily
throughout Asia.

The Wei River, at flood stage for nearly three weeks, ~~it~~ began to recede
at last.

2 Avoiding unnecessary repetition of objects or adverbs

Do not repeat an object or adverb in an adjective clause beginning
with a relative pronoun (*who, which, whom, whose, that*) or relative adverb
(*where, when*).

Ahmed is the one person whom I can always trust ~~him~~ to tell the truth.

[The relative pronoun *whom* is also the object of the verb *trust*; the objective pronoun *him* is unnecessary. Even if *whom* were omitted, *him* would be unnecessary:
Ahmed is the one person I can always trust to tell the truth.]

Marrakech sits on a high plain where the air is thin and the sun is

brilliant ~~there~~.

[*There* repeats the meaning of the relative adverb *where* and is therefore unnecessary.]

3 Avoiding unnecessary repetition of conjunctions

Conjunctions link words, phrases, and clauses. Coordinating conjunctions (*and, or, but,* and so forth) link words of equal value. Subordinating
conjunctions (*although, because, if, when,* and so forth) link dependent clauses
to main clauses. To link clauses, use only one conjunction. (See also 8g.)

Although I'm happy here, ~~but~~ I miss the sweet sounds and smells of

home.

[The subordinating conjunction *although* links the first clause, *I'm happy here*, to the
main clause; *but* is unnecessary. To emphasize the clauses equally, the writer would
omit *although* and retain *but*: *I am happy here, but I miss the sweet sounds and smells of
home.*]

32c Follow these guidelines to summarize questions and speech

1 Summarizing questions

Summarized questions (also called **indirect questions**) are usually
part of a longer statement of fact; therefore, they follow the word order
and punctuation of declarative sentences (see 10c2).

- *Subject plus verb.* After the question word (*who, which, when, why, where, how,* and so forth) that introduces the summarized question, place the subject before the verb.

  The panel considered where ~~is~~ air pollution ^*is*^ the most severe.

- *Using* whether *for* yes/no *and* or *questions.* Use *whether* to introduce summarized *yes/no* questions and *or* questions that pose alternatives.

  I have not decided ^*whether I will*^ ~~will I~~ go home for the summer or attend summer

  school.

- *Omitting* do, does, did. Omit *do, does, did* from summarized questions; signal tense (the time of the action) with the correct form of the main verb.

  He asked me ^*whether*^ ~~did~~ I ^*needed*^ ~~need~~ help with my experiment.

  [*Needed* matches the past tense form of the main verb *asked.*]

- *Punctuation.* Punctuate summarized questions in a way appropriate to the complete sentence.

  The judge asked the jury whether it had reached a verdict?. ^.^

2 Summarizing speech

In **summarized speech** (also called **reported speech** or **indirect quotation**), a writer restates a direct quotation in his or her own words, without quotation marks.

- *Summarizing in a noun clause.* Write the summarized speech as a noun clause within your own sentence.

DIRECT QUOTATION	SUMMARIZED SPEECH
She said, "A monsoon is a strong seasonal wind."	She said that a monsoon is a strong seasonal wind.

  [*That* may be omitted from certain noun clauses. (See 22d2.)]

- *Changing present tense to past tense and present progressive to past progressive.* Change the present tense or present progressive of a direct quotation to the past tense or past progressive in summarized speech. *An exception:* Use the present tense if the summarized speech is a general truth or habitual action, as in the preceding example.

DIRECT QUOTATION	SUMMARIZED SPEECH
She said, "My report is finished."	She said that her report was finished.
She said, "I am finishing my report."	She said that she was finishing her report.

- *Changing past tense or present perfect to past perfect.* Change the past tense or present perfect of a direct quotation to the past perfect of summarized speech.

DIRECT QUOTATION	SUMMARIZED SPEECH
She said, "They arrived an hour ago."	She said that they had arrived an hour ago.
She said, "I have tried to help him."	She said that she had tried to help him.

- *Changing modal verbs.* When summarizing speech, change *can* to *could, will* to *would, may* to *might, must* to *had to.*

DIRECT QUOTATION	SUMMARIZED SPEECH
She said, "I will call him next week."	She said that she would call him next week.

- *Summarizing commands.* To summarize commands, use *to* plus the base form of the verb (the infinitive).

DIRECT QUOTATION	SUMMARIZED SPEECH
She told her students, "Go to the lab."	She told her students to go to the lab.

32d Show possession with an apostrophe or an *of* phrase

English signals a possessive noun with an apostrophe or a phrase beginning with *of*: *India's president, the president of India.* In some cases, as in the preceding examples, the forms are interchangeable; often they are not.

1 Indicating possession with an apostrophe

To make a singular noun or an indefinite pronoun possessive, usually add an apostrophe followed by s (-*'s*): *the student's book, someone's book.* To make a plural noun ending in -*s* possessive, usually add only an apostrophe: *the students' request.* An apostrophe is generally used with nouns referring to persons and other living beings: *the president's address, the lions' roar.* (For more on the possessive form and the apostrophe, see 17d and 37a.)

2 Indicating possession with *of*

To signal possession when referring to things, you would typically use an *of* phrase: *the body of the car, the soles of my feet.* An *of* phrase may also be used to emphasize what is possessed: *the novels of Chinua Achebe.* Do not use possessive *of* phrases with personal pronouns: *her book,* not *the book of her.*

effect of

Many parents do not consider the TV violence ~~effect~~ on their children.

his

Without ~~the~~ help ~~of him~~, we could not have afforded the trip.

Exceptions: The apostrophe form of the possessive appears frequently in references to time (*an hour's drive, a month's time*), natural phenomena (*the sun's rays, Earth's atmosphere*), political organizations (*the city's parks, the nation's tax system*), and groups of people working together (*the ship's crew, the company's employees*).

32e | Use adjectives and adverbs with care

1 Forming adjectives

Adjectives modify nouns by telling *which one, what kind, how many: the tall man, a new student, four flowers.* (See 8d and 18a.) Some languages add singular and plural endings to adjectives so that they match the nouns they modify, but in English adjectives are neither singular nor plural. Do not add *-s* to adjectives even when they precede plural nouns:

After only four full~~s~~ days of work, Zahid knew this job was the one he

wanted.

2 Using participles (*-ing* and *-ed* verb forms) as adjectives

To form some adjectives, English uses the present participle (*-ing*) and past participle (*-ed, -en, -n,* or *-t*) of verbs: *a terrifying story, a crowded street.* Both kinds of participles may appear before a noun or after a linking verb: *The terrifying story is true. The story is terrifying. The terrified child could not speak. The child seemed terrified.* But present and past participles may not be used interchangeably.

- Use **present participle adjectives** (ending in *-ing*) to describe something causing or stimulating an experience: *The survivors told a terrifying story to their fearful listeners* [the story caused terror in the listeners].

  breaking

  They jumped in surprise at the sound of ~~broken~~ glass.

- Use **past participle adjectives** (ending in *-ed, -d, -en, -t*) to describe a person or thing undergoing an experience: *The listeners shuddered, terrified by the survivors' story* [the listeners experienced terror].

  embarrassed

  I felt ~~embarrassing~~ when my instructor read my paper aloud.

3 Arranging cumulative adjectives

Cumulative adjectives are two or more adjectives that are not separated by commas and that modify the whole phrase following them: *the large round Persian rug.* To use cumulative adjectives correctly, arrange them in this order:

1. Article, possessive, or quantifier: *the, my, Teresa's, some, four,* and so forth
2. Comparative and superlative: *younger, older, best, worst, least*
3. Evaluator (a word that can be preceded by *very*): *beautiful, courageous, responsible*
4. Size: *large, small, gigantic, tall*
5. Length or shape: *long, round, oval, square, triangular*
6. Age: *young, old, new, antique, modern, twentieth-century*
7. Color: *green, yellow, violet*
8. Nationality: *Peruvian, Iranian, Polish, Canadian*
9. Religion: *Baptist, Buddhist, Christian, Hindu, Muslim, Protestant*
10. Material: *wood, walnut, metal, gold, wool*
11. Noun used as an adjective: *guest* (as in *guest room*), *history* (as in *history class*)
12. Noun modified: *room, class, truck, table*

Compare these examples:

Four old wooden clocks will be sold at the auction.

The baby was being entertained by her older ~~two~~ sisters.
_{two}

A note on adjective series: Avoid long series of cumulative adjectives. Generally use no more than two or three between an article, possessive, or quantifier and the noun they modify: *an old Hindu temple, Kevin's famous buttermilk pancakes, several well-known European scientists.*

4 Placing adverbs

Adverbs that modify verbs may appear at the beginning, end, or in the middle of a sentence. However, do not place an adverb between a verb and a direct object. (See also 23a.) Compare these examples:

Carefully, she took her daughter's hand.

He turned the dial **carefully.**

He walked **carefully** along the ledge.

To complete my art history project, I examined ~~carefully~~ Mayan architecture.
_{carefully}

32f Choose the appropriate preposition for expressions of place and time

English expressions of place and time beginning with *at, in,* and *on* can be troublesome. Here are guidelines to their use. Note, however, that exceptions do exist. Consult an ESL dictionary, such as the *Longman Dictionary of Contemporary English* or the *Oxford Advanced Learner's Dictionary.*

1 Indicating place

- Use *at* before a location, meeting place, the edge of something, the corner of something, or a target: *arriving at school, seated at the table, turning at the corner of Fifth and Maple streets, aiming at the bull's eye.*

- Use *in* before an enclosed space or geographic location: *growing in the garden, standing in the phone booth, hiking in the desert, living in Mexico City.*

- Use *on* before a surface or street: *lying on the table, hanging on the wall, walking on Fifth Avenue.*

2 Indicating time

- Use *at* before specific expressions of time: *She arrived at 2:30. They left at dawn.*

- Use *in* before a month, year, century, period of time, or part of a twenty-four-hour period: *in May, in 1865, in the twentieth century, in an hour, in the morning.*

- Use *on* before a day or date: *on July 20, on Thursday.*

3 Arranging place and time phrases

In most English expressions, *place* comes before *time: My relatives arrived at my house in the early morning.* However, a prepositional phrase indicating time may appear at the beginning of a sentence: *In the early morning, my relatives arrived at my house.*

PART **V.**

Punctuation

Punctuating

Punctuating

How to . . . **Edit Common Punctuation Errors**

Read your writing aloud to hear punctuation errors. Then follow these guidelines.

Periods. Remove unnecessary periods following (1) the titles of your papers, (2) abbreviations that end a sentence, (3) question marks and exclamation points, (4) all-capital abbreviations. (See 33a4.)

Commas. Add required commas (1) before a coordinating conjunction like *and* or *but* joining independent clauses, (2) after introductory words, (3) between items in a series, (4) between coordinate adjectives, (5) before and after word groups that interrupt the flow of a sentence. (See 34a–g.)

Omit unnecessary commas (1) between subjects and predicates, (2) between verbs and the remainder of the predicate, (3) before indirect quotations, (4) before the comparative *than,* (5) after subordinating conjunctions like *although* and phrases like *such as* to introduce a list, (6) before and after essential modifiers, (7) before parentheses or brackets, (8) after question marks or exclamation points. (See 34k.)

Look for comma splices—the error that results when independent clauses are joined by only a comma (see 12b). Add a coordinating conjunction like *and* or *but,* or replace the comma with a period or semicolon.

Semicolons. Use a semicolon instead of a comma before a transition or conjunctive adverb (such as *for example* or *however*) that links independent clauses (see 12b3). To identify independent clauses, use the yes/no question test (see the "How to Edit Sentence Fragments" box, p. 82). If items in series contain internal commas, use semicolons between items (see 35c).

Do not use semicolons between (1) dependent and independent clauses, (2) modifiers and the words they modify, or (3) lists and the words that introduce them. (See 35d.)

Colons. After an independent clause, use colons to introduce lists, quotations, and explanations (see 36a). To identify independent clauses, use the yes/no question test (see the "How to Edit Sentence Fragments" box, p. 82).

Omit colons (1) after words like *such as, like,* or *including;* (2) between verbs and the remainder of the predicate; (3) between subordinating conjunctions and the clauses that follow; or between prepositions and their objects (see 36c).

(continued)

How to . . . **Edit Common Punctuation Errors** *(continued)*

Apostrophes. To decide whether a noun is possessive and requires an apostrophe, try to create an *of* phrase (*the lions roar = the roar of the lion*). If you can do this, the original word takes an apostrophe: *the lion's roar.* (See 37a.) Keep in mind that possessive and relative pronouns do not take apostrophes: *his, hers, its, your, yours, ours, theirs,* or *whose* (see 37d).

Quotation marks. Use double quotation marks around quotations, no matter how brief. Use single quotation marks only for quotations within quotations (see 38a and c).

Place periods and commas inside double and single quotation marks. Place semicolons and colons outside quotation marks. Place question marks and exclamation points inside if they are part of the quotation, otherwise outside (see 38b).

Use quotation marks around the titles of short works (see 38d). Use underlining or italics for the titles of long works (see 41a).

Omit unnecessary quotation marks around indented quotations, the titles of your own writing, slang, and indirect or summarized quotations (see 50d1 and 38f).

33   End Punctuation

33a   Use a period to mark sentences and abbreviations

1   Marking sentences

Use a period to end all sentences except direct questions and genuine exclamations. Use a period to end sentences that summarize questions, make polite requests not phrased as questions, and give commands that are not exclamations.

Edyta called the ticket office to ask whether the concert had been canceled.

Return the rental car by Friday at noon.

2   Marking abbreviations

The punctuation of abbreviations varies. When in doubt, consult a dictionary, style manual, or publication guide appropriate to your subject or audience. The Modern Language Association provides these guidelines.

- *Abbreviations ending in lower case.* Use a period after most abbreviations ending in lowercase letters. Do not put a space between lowercase letters that represent separate words.

Mr.	Dr.	Sept.	etc.	p.m.
Mrs.	Inc.	Capt.	introd.	e.g.
Ms.	Jan.	Maj.	a.m.	i.e.

- *Abbreviations that end sentences.* When an abbreviation ends a sentence, do not add a second period.
- *All-capital abbreviations.* Do not use a period in all-capital abbreviations or after US Postal Service abbreviations of state names.

ALL-CAPITAL ABBREVIATIONS				US POSTAL SERVICE ABBREVIATIONS
NATO	FBI	IQ	CAT scan	CA
UNESCO	USA	COD	BA	MA
NAACP	NRA	IOU	PhD	TX

3 Writing about literature

When citing a passage from a literary work, use a period with no intervening spaces between the divisions of the work.

Hamlet 3.2.16–23 or *Hamlet* III.ii.16–23 [act, scene, lines]

Paradise Lost 10.55–57 or *Paradise Lost* X.55–57 [book, lines]

4 Avoiding unnecessary periods

- *Paper titles.* Do not use a period after the titles of your papers, even if they are complete sentences.
- *Second periods.* When an abbreviation ends a sentence, do not add a second period.

The shipment will be delivered by 9 a.m./

- *Sentence within a sentence.* Do not use a period after a sentence within a sentence.

"Cure the disease and kill the patient" was a statement made by Francis Bacon, not Benjamin Franklin.

By 1893, fewer than a thousand buffalo remained in the United States (at the beginning of the century there had been 20 million).

33b Use a question mark to signal questions, requests, and doubts

1 Signaling questions

Use a question mark after direct questions.

How long did Henry David Thoreau live at Walden Pond?

A note on indirect or summarized quotations: Do not use a question mark after indirect or summarized questions. (See 38a; for ESL, see 32c1.)

She asked when the order would be delivered.

A note on questions in series: You may use question marks after questions in a series even when they are not complete sentences.

Will reducing income taxes stimulate savings? Encourage investment? Weaken social programs? Enlarge the federal budget deficit?

2 Signaling expressions of doubt

Use a question mark to signal doubt.

Professor Isaacs is not giving a final exam this semester?

3 Signaling polite requests

Use a question mark after a polite request phrased as a question.

Will you please send me an admissions application?

4 Punctuating a question within a sentence

When a question within a sentence is followed by other words, put a question mark after the question and a period at the end of the sentence.

"What time does the play begin?" he asked.

33c Use an exclamation point for an outcry, emphasis, and irony

1 An outcry

"A horse! A horse! My kingdom for a horse!" cried the desperate king.

2 An expression of emphasis

Alderman Paddy Bauler became famous for declaring, "Chicago ain't ready for reform!"

3 An expression of irony

Standing in the mud, shivering in the rain, she muttered, "I keep reminding myself that this is the vacation of a lifetime!"

34b ,

A note on unnecessary exclamations: Avoid overusing exclamation points. They rarely appear in academic writing, especially in serious informative writing. Even in personal or narrative writing, too many will create a melodramatic or false tone.

34 The Comma

34a Use a comma before a coordinating conjunction (*but, and*) that links independent clauses

When the coordinating conjunctions *and, but, or, nor, so, for,* and *yet* link independent clauses—word groups that can be punctuated as complete sentences—they are preceded by a comma. (To identify independent clauses, use the yes/no question test in the "How to Edit Sentence Fragments" box, p. 82.)

> Groups of sharks attack their prey ferociously, but they never bite one another.

A note on short independent clauses: If the meaning of a compound sentence is clear and the independent clauses are short, you may omit the comma before the conjunction.

> The whistle bellowed once and the boat left the dock.

A note on conjunctions that link phrases or dependent clauses: Do not use a comma before conjunctions that link phrases or dependent clauses. (To learn to identify phrases and dependent clauses, see 10a and b.)

> The musicians played sad songs marching to the funeral/but joyful
>
> songs on their return.
>
> [The *but* in this sentence joins two phrases, *sad songs* [. . .] *but joyful songs* [. . .], so the comma is unnecessary.]

34b Use a comma after introductory words

Use a comma to set off an introductory word, phrase, or dependent clause from the rest of the sentence. (To learn to identify phrases and clauses, see 10a and b.)

> Unfortunately, exotic species introduced to new habitats often threaten native species.

Growing up in Africa, she had been entertained by storytellers of all kinds.

After Harriet Tubman escaped the South, she became a "conductor" on the Underground Railroad that carried slaves north.

A note on brief phrases and clauses: You may omit the comma following a brief introductory phrase or clause.

By noon the storm had passed.

But be sure to use commas to prevent misreading.

When Carol returned, her baby's smile greeted her gaily.

34*c* | Use a comma between items in a series

Use a comma to separate three or more words, phrases, or clauses written as a series. The Modern Language Association and the American Psychological Association require a comma before the conjunction preceding the last item in the series.

Winter drivers should carry a scraper, shovel, sand, flares, extra washer fluid, and a blanket.

34*d* | Use a comma between coordinate adjectives but not between cumulative adjectives

1 Using a comma between coordinate adjectives

Two or more adjectives are **coordinate** if each one modifies the noun by itself. Use a comma after each adjective to signal its separate function.

Muhammad Ali was a **skilled, fierce, imaginative** boxer.
[Each adjective—*skilled, fierce, imaginative*—modifies *boxer* by itself.]

2 Avoiding a comma between cumulative adjectives

Two or more adjectives are **cumulative** if each one modifies all the words that follow it, adjectives and noun together. Because meaning accumulates as the phrase unfolds, do not separate the adjectives with commas.

Muhammad Ali was **the most famous war** protestor to refuse military service during the Vietnam War.
[*War* modifies *protestor, famous* modifies *war protestor,* and *most* modifies *famous war protestor.* Meaning accumulates as the phrase unfolds.]

3 Identifying coordinate and cumulative adjectives

Two tests will help you distinguish between coordinate adjectives and cumulative adjectives.

- **The *and* test.** If you can put *and* between the adjectives, they are coordinate and require a comma between them to signal their separate functions. Consider the two preceding examples: *A skilled and fierce and imaginative boxer* signals coordinate adjectives that require commas to separate them. But you would not write *most and famous and war protestor,* so these are cumulative adjectives not separated by commas.

- **The reversal test.** If you can reverse the order of the adjectives, they are coordinate and require a comma between them (*skilled, fierce, imaginative boxer* may become *fierce, skilled, imaginative boxer*). But you would not write *war famous most protestor.*

34e Use commas to set off nonessential modifiers; do not use commas to set off essential modifiers

1 Using commas with nonessential modifiers

Nonessential modifiers (also called **nonrestrictive modifiers**) are words, phrases, or clauses that add extra information but are not essential to the basic meaning of a sentence. Omitting nonessential modifiers does not drastically alter the meaning. Use commas to signal their nonessential nature.

Arthur Jensen, **my minister,** has volunteered to head the Heart Fund drive.

[Because it is nonessential, *my minister* is set off by commas.]

The Ferris wheel, **named for the man who invented it,** was first erected in 1892 at the Chicago World's Fair.

[Information about the inventor of the Ferris wheel is nonessential to a sentence about the wheel's first location and is set off by commas.]

Many nineteenth-century pioneers came first to Kansas City, **where one branch of the Oregon Trail began.**

[Information about the Oregon Trail is important but not essential to a sentence about Kansas City, so it is set off by a comma.]

2 Avoiding commas with essential modifiers

Essential modifiers (also called **restrictive modifiers**) restrict the meaning of the words they modify to a special sense. If they are omitted, the meaning of the sentence changes. To signal their essential nature, do not set off essential modifiers with commas. Consider how commas change the meaning of this sentence:

My brother **who lives in Little Rock** often comes to visit. [essential modifier]

[The modifier *who lives in Little Rock* identifies which of the writer's brothers often comes to visit. Because it is essential to the basic meaning of the sentence, it is not set off by commas.]

My brother, **who lives in Little Rock,** often comes to visit. [nonessential modifier]

[The writer's only brother, who happens to live in Little Rock, often comes to visit. The brother's location is not essential to the basic meaning of the sentence, so it is set off by commas.]

3 Identifying nonessential and essential modifiers

To tell whether a modifier is nonessential or essential, try reading the sentence without the modifier. If the basic meaning is unchanged, the modifier is nonessential and needs to be set off by commas. If the sentence changes or loses meaning, the modifier is essential and should not be set off. Compare:

Ernest Hemingway's story "Hills like White Elephants" portrays a couple debating the consequences of an abortion.

Ernest Hemingway's story [. . .] portrays a couple [. . .]

[Without the title of the story and *debating the consequences of an abortion,* the sentence has no meaning. These are both essential modifiers not set off by commas.]

If after rereading you're still not sure whether a modifier is nonessential or essential, use these clues.

- Modifiers of proper nouns (see 8a) are usually nonessential and set off by commas.

  Nimi speaks Hindi, **the official language of India.**

- Clauses beginning with *although, even though,* and *whereas* are usually nonessential and set off by commas.

  The burglar was captured within hours, **even though he was sure he had left no clues.**

- Modifiers of indefinite pronouns such as *anyone* and *something* are usually essential and are not set off by commas.

  Anyone **who studies the textbook** can pass this course.

  [The clause *who studies the textbook* is essential to identify *anyone* and is therefore not set off by commas.]

- Relative clauses beginning with *that* are essential modifiers and are not set off by commas.

  The cars **that require the fewest repairs** have the highest resale value.

Use Commas to Set Off Transitions

- If you can substitute *that* for *who*, *whom*, or *which*, the clause is an essential modifier and is not set off by commas. (For when to use *that*, see 16d.)

  The painter **whom/that** I admire most is Edward Hopper.

- If you can omit *who*, *whom*, or *that*, the clause is an essential modifier and is not set off by commas.

  The painter **[whom]** I admire most is Edward Hopper.

- Concluding adverb clauses beginning with *as soon as*, *before*, *because*, *if*, *since*, *unless*, *until*, and *when* are essential to the basic meaning of a sentence and are not set off by commas.

  Students should sign up for flu vaccinations **as soon as they arrive on campus.**

34f | Use commas to set off transitions, parenthetical expressions, and contrast statements

1 Commas with transitions

Set off conjunctive adverbs such as *however* and transitional phrases such as *for example* with commas. (For a complete list of conjunctive adverbs and transitional phrases, see 12b3.)

Most people refuse to think about pain. Some kinds of pain, **however**, are important to recognize and understand.

Some common painkillers have harmful side effects. **For example**, aspirin may cause internal bleeding.

A note on transitions that connect independent clauses: When you connect independent clauses with a transition, use a semicolon before the transition and, usually, a comma following it. (See 35b.)

Professional athletes must often play in pain; **consequently**, they turn to trainers for strong pain suppressants.

If little or no pause follows a transition, you may omit the comma.

We have never planned a long bicycle trip; **therefore** we're asking for your suggestions.

2 Commas with parenthetical expressions not enclosed in parentheses

Use commas to set off parenthetical expressions that add supplemental or explanatory information. Notice that a parenthetical expression is not necessarily enclosed in parentheses.

---

sen...ce.
yea...re g

C...
A...no.
The...lizz
In A...

3 Addre...es

Use cor...
fore a zip co...

The region...
Seneca, IL...

The Women...Chr.
Ohio, in 1874

4 Numbers

In numbers of n...
als into groups of thr... co
four-digit numbers.

1,466 *or* 1466

186,000

6,286,836

Exceptions: Do not use...mn
phone numbers, or years: 62...5 M.

A note on units of measure that are spelled out: When units of measure are written as words, use commas to separate feet and inches, pounds and ounces, and so forth.

My Labrador puppy stands **one foot, two inches** tall and weighs **twenty pounds, four ounces.**

34i Use commas to signal omissions and prevent misreading

The hikers took the right fork in the path; their rescuers, the left.

To Paul, Carlos remained a puzzle.

34j Follow these guidelines to use commas with quotation marks, parentheses, and brackets

1 Commas with quotation marks

Place commas inside closing quotation marks, single and double, whether the quotation is a word, phrase, sentence, or several sentences. (See 38b.)

It is "time to stop thinking of wild animals as 'resources' and 'game,'" claims Joy Williams in her argument against hunting.

2 Commas with parentheses and brackets

Place commas outside closing parentheses and brackets.

Caused by an extra number 21 chromosome (three instead of the usual two), Down's syndrome is characterized by mental retardation and a flattened facial profile.

34k Avoid unnecessary commas

1 Unnecessary comma dividers

- Do not use a comma between a subject and its predicate.

Taxes that communities receive from legalized gambling~~,~~ are often offset by the losses of local gamblers.

- Do not use a comma between a verb and its object or complement.

People in their thirties often protest/ their limited career choices.

- Do not use a comma before conjunctions joining phrases or dependent clauses. (To learn to identify phrases and dependent clauses, see 10a and b.)

  The coach warned her team that their next opponents were not only tall

  and fast/ but also very smart.

- Do not use a comma before the conjunction *than* in comparison statements.

  I'd rather visit the ancient ruins of Egypt and Greece/ than go to Disney

  World.

- Do not use commas between cumulative adjectives or between adjectives and nouns.

  Eddie fished all day but caught only one/ small/ red snapper.

  [*One* and *small* are cumulative adjectives and should not be separated by commas.]

  One wrong turn after another led him into difficult, nearly impassable/

  terrain.

  [*Impassable* is an adjective modifying the noun *terrain,* so no comma is needed.]

- Do not use a comma before a summarized or indirect quotation.

  A famous philosopher once wrote/ that anything worth saying can be

  said clearly.

2 Unnecessary introductory commas

- Do not use a comma after *such as* or *like* to introduce a list.

  Many people, such as/ Arabs, Indians, and southern Europeans, have

  personal space requirements different from those of northern Europeans.

- Do not use a comma after the subordinating conjunction *although.*

  The mayor continued the sprinkler ban, although/ rain had fallen weekly

  for a month.

- Do not use a comma after a phrase that opens an inverted sentence.

  On the highest hill/ stands a house designed by Frank Lloyd Wright.

- Do not use commas before the first or after the last item in a series (but do use commas between items in a series).

Laura's favorite flowers are/ hollyhocks, day lilies, and irises.

Someone who enjoys camping, hiking, and cycling/ shouldn't mind a little rain.

3 Unnecessary commas to set off essential modifiers

Do not use commas to set off modifiers essential to the basic meaning of a sentence.

The friends/ whom Lacy trusted the most/ repaid her faith in them.

[Readers need the modifier *whom Lacy trusted the most* to know which friends are referred to. It is essential and not set off by commas.]

The wagon train crossed the river/ where it was shallowest.

[Readers need the modifier *where it was shallowest* to know where the wagon train crossed the river. It is essential and not preceded by a comma.]

4 Unnecessary commas with other punctuation

- Do not use a comma before parentheses, only afterward.

Although critics of rock and roll often quote Plato/ (who favored the strict regulation of music), few have examined his argument carefully.

- Do not use a comma after a question mark or exclamation point.

"What's a thousand dollars?"/ asked Groucho Marx. "Mere chicken feed. A poultry matter."

35 The Semicolon

35a Use a semicolon to join closely related independent clauses

A semicolon usually links grammatically equal word groups. Use it in place of a comma and coordinating conjunction (*and, but, so, or, nor, for, yet*) to link independent clauses closely related in subject or structure. To iden-

PART VI.

Mechanics, Spelling, *and* Document Formatting

Mechanics

VI mechanics/format

Mechanics

40 Capital Letters

40*a* Capitalize the first word of sentences, deliberate fragments, and lines of poetry

1 Sentences

The wind blew the snow in swirling circles.

A note on quotations: Do not capitalize the first word of a quoted sentence you have woven into your own sentence.

President Harry Truman's motto "the buck stops here" is a vow of personal responsibility many people admire but seldom practice.

A note on a sentence following a colon: If a complete sentence follows a colon, capitalize the first word.

Stars are not all that twinkle in the night sky: The brightest lights may be reflections from satellites or the space shuttle.

A note on parenthetical sentences: Do not capitalize the first word of a parenthetical sentence contained within another sentence.

Western ranchers claim that wolves reintroduced to the wild will kill their livestock (conservation groups, however, have pledged to repay them for losses).

2 Deliberate fragments

Capitalize the first words of deliberately written sentence fragments.

The Pueblo people believe that lightning strikes bring death to evildoers. And magical powers to persons of good will.

3 Poetry

When you quote poetry, capitalize the first word of a line unless the original is not capitalized.

FIRST WORDS CAPITALIZED

Gather ye rosebuds while ye may,
Old time is still a-flying;
And this same flower that
   smiles today
Tomorrow will be dying.
               (Robert Herrick)

FIRST WORDS UNCAPITALIZED

Fiesta laughed with me in San Juan
many compas fired their rifles
   at the stars
music played on radios till dawn
where Venus danced the *cumbiá*
with Mars

               (Rex Burwell)

40*b* Capitalize proper nouns and words derived from them

Proper nouns name specific persons, places, and things (*Confucius, Grand Canyon, the US Constitution*). Proper nouns and their derivatives are capitalized. Common nouns name a general category of persons, places, and things (*a religious leader, a canyon, a government document*) and are not capitalized unless they are part of a specific name, as in *Grand Canyon*.

1 Capitalizing the names and titles of people

- *The names of people.* Capitalize the names, nicknames, and initials of real and imaginary persons, and words derived from names: *William Shakespeare, Shakespearean, Abraham Lincoln, Honest Abe, the Great Emancipator, Lincolnesque, Dwight D. Eisenhower, Ike, Mickey Mouse.*

- *Races and nationalities.* Capitalize races, nationalities, geographic groupings of people, languages, and words derived from them: *Asian, Spanish, Hispanic, African, English, Native American, Polish-American.*

- *Titles of persons.* Capitalize civil, military, religious, and professional titles immediately preceding a personal name: *President Lincoln, General Grant, Pope Paul, Queen Victoria, Senator Kassebaum.* Capitalize titles used in place of names in introductions, toasts, and direct address: *Dear Senator.* Do not capitalize titles following a name: *Abraham Lincoln, sixteenth president of the United States; Victoria, queen of England.*

- *Kinship names.* Capitalize kinship names followed by a given name or used in place of the name; otherwise, lowercase. Compare these examples:

This year **Aunt Jennifer** is helping to pay my tuition.

When she was first married, ~~mother~~ *Mother* worked in a furniture factory.

Rebecca's ~~Father~~ *father* has just been admitted to the hospital.

40b **cap**

■ *Abstractions.* Capitalize abstract words if they have been personified with the attributes of people; otherwise, lowercase.

All Nature wears one universal grin.
> (Henry Fielding, from *Tom Thumb the Great*)

In nature there are no rewards or punishments; there are consequences.
> (Horace Annesley Vachell, from *The Face of Clay*)

2 Capitalizing religious terms

Capitalize the names of religions, deities, holy persons, holy writings, religious groups and movements, religious events and services, and words derived from these terms.

Islam, Islamic	the Bible	the Crucifixion
the Lord, our Lord	the Ten	Holy Communion
Christ, the Savior	Commandments	the Sermon on
Buddha, Buddhism	Catholicism	the Mount

A note: The adjective *biblical* is usually not capitalized, and the word *bible* is not capitalized when it refers to a book considered authoritative: *When Judy is in the kitchen,* The Joy of Cooking *is her bible.*

3 Capitalizing cultural and historical terms

Capitalization of cultural and historical terms varies; check your dictionary. In general, capitalize the names of historical, political, and cultural events and documents; capitalize historical periods only when proper nouns or to avoid ambiguity.

Boston Tea Party	the Fall of Rome	*but:* ancient Rome
Reconstruction	the Renaissance	*but:* the sixteenth century
Prohibition	the Roaring Twenties	*but:* the twenties

A note on archaeological periods: Capitalize time periods recognized by archaeologists and anthropologists: *Bronze Age, Neolithic era, Paleolithic times.* Lowercase recent periods: *the space age, the cold war, the civil rights era.*

A note on philosophical and artistic terms: Capitalize philosophical, literary, and artistic terms derived from proper nouns; otherwise, lowercase: *Platonism* but *existentialism;* a *Gothic novel* but a *horror story.*

4 Capitalizing geographic regions, place names, and structures

■ *Countries, regions, continents.* Capitalize geographic names of countries, regions, and continents: *Spain, Europe, the Arctic, the Southern*

Hemisphere, the South, New England, North Pole, the Badlands of South Dakota, the Texas Panhandle, the New World. Do not capitalize terms that indicate direction:

When they retire, Peter and Becky plan to move ~~South~~. *south*

- *Place names.* Capitalize the names of cities, counties, states, empires, colonies, locales, and popular place names: *New York's Lower East Side, the City of Brotherly Love, the Loop (Chicago), Cook County, Louisiana, the Buckeye State, Soweto Township, Land of the Rising Sun.*

- *Geographic names.* Capitalize the names of rivers, lakes, oceans, islands, and other specific geographic places: *the Fox River, Lake Itasca, the Indian Ocean, Long Island, the San Juan Mountains, the Nile Delta.*

- *Structures:* Capitalize the names of buildings, streets, highways, bridges, and monuments: *the White House, the Capitol, the Pyramids, New York Thruway, Fifth Avenue, Forty-Second Street, Woodfield Mall.*

A note on generic place names: Generic place names that precede a name or stand alone are usually lowercase: *the city of New York.*

5 Capitalizing the names of objects

- *Celestial bodies.* Capitalize the names of celestial bodies: *Earth, the North Star, Halley's Comet, the constellation of Orion, the Big Dipper.*

- *Means of transportation.* Capitalize the names of ships, trains, aircraft, and spacecraft: USS *Constitution, Voyager 2.*

- *Trademarks and brand names.* Capitalize trademarks and brand names but not the generic products associated with them: *Coca-Cola, Coke,* but *cola; Levi's jeans; Kleenex tissue; Tylenol,* but *aspirin.*

6 Capitalizing dates and time designations

Capitalize days of the week, months, and holidays: *Tuesday, July, Halloween, Lent, Ramadan.* Lowercase seasons, decades, centuries, and time zones that are spelled out: *spring, the nineties, the nineteenth century, central daylight time.*

7 Capitalizing the names of organizations

Capitalize the names of companies, civic organizations, institutions, and government agencies: *Hudson's Bay Company, La Chosa Restaurant, United States Congress.* Lowercase generic organization names and plural generic names that follow organization names: *adoption court, the president's cabinet, the legislative branch, Barnes & Noble, Borders bookstore.*

8 Capitalizing academic terms

Capitalize the names of specific courses: *I'm taking two literature courses, Literature of the Nonwestern World and Fiction 115.* Lowercase school terms (*spring semester*), generic degrees, and the names of academic subjects except foreign languages: *bachelor's degree, political science,* but *Spanish.*

9 Capitalizing plants and animals and medical terms

Capitalization of the names of plants and animals and of medical terms is varied; see your dictionary. Generally capitalize only a proper noun that is part of the name and lowercase the common noun: *Canada thistle, Virginia creeper, an Irish setter, a Dalmatian puppy, Down's syndrome;* but *cocker spaniel, rheumatic fever.*

10 Capitalizing acronyms

Acronyms are all-capitals abbreviations formed from the first letters of words, such as names of organizations, government agencies, companies, and institutions (*OPEC, IBM*) and technical, scientific, and military terms (*CD-ROM, HIV*).

40*c* Capitalize the first, last, and all major words in the titles of works

1 General guidelines

- *Titles and subtitles.* Capitalize the titles and subtitles of written works such as books and essays, performances such as plays, visual works such as painting and sculpture, and media productions such as television and radio programs: *Moby Dick, Adam's Task: Calling Animals by Name,* "The Murders in the Rue Morgue," *Hamlet,* the *Mona Lisa.*

- *First, last, and major words.* Capitalize first, last, and major words. Do not capitalize articles (*a, an, the*), prepositions (*in, from, on,* and so forth), coordinating conjunctions (*and, but, for, yet, so, or, nor*), and the *to* in infinitives (*How to Repair Almost Anything*).

- *Compounds.* Always capitalize the first word of a compound in a title (*The Modern City-State*); capitalize the second word only if it is important. Compare *Twenty-First Century, A-Bomb,* and *Citizen-Soldier* with *Medium-sized.*

- *Newspapers and news stories.* Do not capitalize, italicize, or underline *the* before a newspaper name.
  the
  When I can afford it, I buy ~~The~~ *New York Times.*

In newspapers usually only the first word and proper nouns are capitalized in a headline: *"Destruction of the last smallpox virus delayed."* But when you give the title of a newspaper article in your writing, capitalize according to the preceding guidelines: *"Destruction of the Last Smallpox Virus Delayed."*

2 APA guidelines

These are the American Psychological Association guidelines for writing in the social sciences.

- *Titles in the text of your writing.* Capitalize the first and last words. Also capitalize all words of four letters or more and both words of a hyphenated compound: *Landscape, History, and the Pueblo Imagination.* Lowercase articles (*a, an, the*). Also lowercase prepositions and conjunctions of one to three letters (e.g., lowercase *to, in,* and *why,* but capitalize *Toward, Into,* and *When*).

- *Titles in a list of references.* Capitalize only the first word of a title, the first word of a hyphenated compound, the first word after a colon, and proper nouns: *Landscape, history, and the Pueblo imagination; Modern media: The electronic transformation of America.*

40*d* | Avoid unnecessary capital letters

1 Avoiding capitals with *a, an,* and *the*

Do not capitalize the articles *a, an,* and *the* before proper nouns unless they are the first or last words of a title. Compare these examples:

Gene Kelly did his best dancing in *An American in Paris.*

Today there are few genuine luxury liners like ~~The~~ *the* *Queen Elizabeth II.*

2 Avoiding capitals for emphasis

Do not capitalize words for emphasis.

Fantasia is the ~~GREATEST~~ *greatest* cartoon ever produced by the Disney studio.

[Create emphatic sentences by rewording and rearranging: *The greatest cartoon ever produced by the Disney studio is* Fantasia.]

The fairest system of taxation is the ~~Graduated Income Tax~~ *graduated income tax.*

3 Avoiding capitals with common nouns derived from proper names

Do not capitalize personal, national, or geographic names when used with special meanings. Common nouns derived from proper nouns are often not capitalized: french fries, diesel engine, and venetian blinds. But other such common nouns are capitalized: Arabic numerals, Homeric poetry, and Russian dressing. See your dictionary for correct capitalization.

41 Italics/Underlining

In typed or handwritten papers, use underlining whenever italics would appear in printed works. If your computer has the capability to italicize and its italic type is easily recognizable, italicize. But note that the Modern Language Association and American Psychological Association recommend underlining. In academic writing, use the following guidelines.

Computer Tip: **Italics and Underlining in Online Writing**

For guidelines on underlining online writing, see 48e5.

41a | Italicize or underline the titles of separately produced works

1 Italicizing written works

Italicize or underline the titles and subtitles of books and pamphlets, the names of magazines and newspapers, and the titles of long poems: *The Invisible Man* or <u>The Invisible Man</u>, the *New York Times* or the <u>New York Times</u> (do not italicize or underline *the* before newspaper titles).

2 Italicizing visual and performing arts

Italicize or underline the titles and subtitles of movies and plays, television and radio programs, paintings, sculpture, and cartoons: *Hamlet* or <u>Hamlet</u>, Picasso's *The Bather* or <u>The Bather</u>, *Star Trek* or <u>Star Trek</u> (specific episodes of television and radio programs are enclosed by quotation marks and neither italicized nor underlined: "The Trouble with Tribbles").

3 Italicizing long musical compositions, recordings, and choreographic works

Italicize or underline the titles of long musical compositions, recordings (records, tapes, and compact discs), and choreographic works: _Sgt. Pepper's Lonely Hearts Club Band_ or <u>Sgt. Pepper's Lonely Hearts Club Band</u>, _Swan Lake_ or <u>Swan Lake</u>.

A note: Individual song titles are enclosed in quotations marks: "Heartbreak Hotel." Do not italicize, underline, or use quotation marks around musical compositions identified by form, number, or key: Beethoven's Symphony no. 5 in C minor.

4 Exceptions

Do not italicize or underline the titles of sacred writings (including all books and versions of the Bible), the titles of legal documents, descriptive titles, or the titles of your own writing.

the King James Version of the Bible	the Constitution
Genesis	the Declaration of Independence
the Talmud	Lincoln's Gettysburg address
the Koran	Kennedy's inaugural address

41_b_ Italicize or underline the names of ships, trains, aircraft, and spacecraft

Mayflower or <u>Mayflower</u>	_Spirit of St. Louis_ or <u>Spirit of St. Louis</u>
Dixie Flyer or <u>Dixie Flyer</u>	_Apollo 8_ or <u>Apollo 8</u>

41_c_ Italicize or underline foreign words and phrases

Italicize or underline foreign words or phrases, whether part of a quotation or your own words. Translate or explain foreign words if readers may not understand them.

Special effects in the ancient Greek theater included the _deus ex machina_ ("the god from the machine"), an actor suspended above the stage.

Exceptions: (1) Do not italicize or underline foreign words used frequently in English: ad hoc, cliché, laissez-faire, per diem, sauerkraut, status quo, versus, and so forth. (2) Do not italicize or underline quotations entirely in another language and non-English titles enclosed in quotation marks.

41d Italicize or underline letters, words, and numbers used as nouns

With grade inflation, *A*'s have become as common as *B*'s and *C*'s.

Freud's term *narcissism* has nothing to do with the flower; it refers to the myth of the Greek youth Narcissus who fell in love with his reflected image.

The number *3* has symbolic meaning in many religions.

A note on quotation marks in place of italics or underlining: Quotation marks are sometimes used to set off words used as words: "narcissism." (See 38e.)

A note on italics, underlining, and the plurals of letters, words, and numbers: Do not italicize or underline the apostrophe or s following letters, words, and numbers used as nouns: *p*'s and *q*'s or p's and q's; *7*'s or 7's; *yea*'s or *nay*'s, yea's or nay's. (See 37c.)

41e Occasionally italicize or underline for emphasis

Many travelers are uncomfortable when foreign countries feel like *foreign* countries.

Too many italics or too much underlining will make your writing sound strained or false. Find emphatic words and sentence patterns that emphasize important ideas. (See Chapter 20.)

most offensive
The TV announcers ~~I can't stand most~~ are the gushing, friendly types.

42 Abbreviations

🖳 *Computer Tip:* Abbreviations in Online Writing

For guidelines to abbreviations commonly used in informal e-mail messages, see 48e5.

42a | General guidelines

1 Using abbreviations correctly

- *Parenthetical statements.* In the text of most formal writing, use abbreviations only in parenthetical statements. Compare:

  The first insecticides were naturally occurring plant products, **for example,** pyrethrum from dried chrysanthemum flowers.

  The first insecticides were naturally occurring plant products (**e.g.,** pyrethrum from dried chrysanthemum flowers).

- *Familiar abbreviations.* You may use familiar abbreviations in the text of your writing: *MTV, HIV, CAT scan,* and so forth.

- *Repeated terms.* Use abbreviations for repeated names and technical terms. For the first use, write out the term completely and include the abbreviation in parentheses. From then on, use the abbreviation alone.

  The **Race Across America (RAAM)** is sponsored annually by the **Ultra-Marathon Cycling Association (UMCA).** The **UMCA** sponsors other races as well.

- *Visual aids and documentation.* Use abbreviations in tables, graphics, notes, and documentation. (See 46b3 and 4. For MLA documentation, see 52a. For APA documentation, see 54b.)

2 Punctuating abbreviations and acronyms

- *Personal names.* Use a period and a space following initials: *H. L. Mencken.*

- *Acronyms.* Do not use periods or spaces between the letters of acronyms: *USA, NY, COD, IQ, NAACP, PhD, rpm.*

- *Abbreviations ending in lowercase letters.* Use a period after most abbreviations that end in lowercase letters: *intro., e.g., pp., assn.*

42b | Titles with personal names

Generally avoid titles in academic writing except to give the qualifications of people whose opinions or information you use. You may use titles frequently in other kinds of writing.

1 Abbreviated titles

- *Titles always abbreviated.* Always abbreviate *Mr.* and *Mrs.,* as in *Mr. Edward O'Connell* or *Mr. O'Connell, Mrs. Judy Chang* or *Mrs. Chang.*

42d | abbr

- *Titles before or after full names:* Abbreviate titles before or after a full name. *Prof. Elizabeth Hull, Gen. Colin Powell, William Wrigley, Sr.; Darlene Clark Hine, PhD.* Do not use abbreviations without names; avoid redundant titles.

My English ~~prof.~~ *professor* plans to travel the route of the European Grand Tour.

The speaker at this year's honors convocation will be Dr. Barbara

Hickey,~~Ph.D.~~

2 Unabbreviated titles

Spell out titles used with surnames (last names) alone: *Professor Hull, General Powell, Doctor Spock, Saint Joan, Senator Simon.* Do not abbreviate given names: not *Benj. Franklin* but *Benjamin Franklin.*

42c | Dates and time

1 Abbreviating date and time markers

Always abbreviate *a.m., p.m., AD, BC, BCE* ("Before the Common Era"), and *CE* ("Common Era"). Place *AD* (*anno Domini,* or "in the year of the Lord") before the date: *AD 1066.* Place *BC* ("before Christ") after the date: *461 BC.* Use date and time markers only with specific times and dates: *3:30 p.m., 1066 CE.*

I study best in the early ~~a.m.~~ *morning*, when everyone else is asleep.

2 Spelling out months, days, and other time designations

- *Months and days.* In the text of formal writing, spell out months and days: *Thursday, October 31. Exception:* In notes and documentation, abbreviate days and months except May, June, and July.
- *Other time designations.* Spell out other time designations in the text of your writing: not *hrs.* but *hours*; not *wks.* but *weeks*; not *Xmas* but *Christmas.*

42d | Geographic terms and place names

1 Spelling out place names and addresses in text

In the text of your writing, spell out place names such as the names of continents, countries, states, territories, and cities, as well as the names of streets, cities, and states in addresses: *South America; United States; Michigan; Virgin Islands; Fort Wayne; 150 State Street, Boston, Massachusetts; Herald Square.*

2 Abbreviating place names in notes and documentation

In notes and documentation, abbreviate the names of states, territories, countries, and continents: *MS* for *Mississippi, Ecua.* for *Ecuador, Gr.* for *Greece, No. Amer.* for *North America,* and so forth.

42e Organization names

1 Abbreviating familiar organizations

Use familiar organizational abbreviations in the text of your writing: *IBM, IRS, NBC, YMCA.* Spell out the names of organizations unfamiliar to your readers: *Littman Brothers, Chicago and North Western Railroad, Eastridge Neighborhood Organization,* and so forth. *Incorporated* is usually written *Inc.* or omitted.

2 Abbreviating in notes and documentation

In notes and documentation abbreviate consistently: *Assoc., &, Co., Corp., Bro., Bros., Inc., Ltd., RR,* and so forth: *Capstone Corp., Littman Bros.*

42f Units of measure

1 Spelling out the names of units of measure in text

Spell out most units of measure in the text of your writing: *inches, cubic foot, gallons, kilograms, meter, megabytes, square yards,* and so forth. Exceptions: *mph, mpg, rpm, Hz (Hertz).*

2 Abbreviating in technical writing and notes

Abbreviate in technical writing and notes: *in., kg, sq. yds., cu. ft., gal, MB,* and so forth.

3 Spelling out plural terms

Always spell out the plural terms *inches, feet, meters,* and *gallons: 25 inches, 540 square feet, 47 meters, 300 gallons.*

42g Latin and other scholarly abbreviations

Avoid Latin and other scholarly abbreviations in the text of your writing, unless they appear in material enclosed in parentheses. Such abbreviations are appropriate in tables, notes, and documentation. In text, use the English equivalents of the Latin terms and spell out ordinary English words. (See also 52b and 54b3.)

cf.	*confer,* "compare"	i.e.	*id est,* "that is"
e.g.	*exempli gratia,* "for example"	NB, n.b.	*nota bene,* "note well"
		n.d.	no date of publication
et al.	*et alii,* "and others"	p., pp.	page, pages
		UP	University Press
etc.	*et cetera,* "and so forth"	vs., v.	versus, "against"

43 Numbers

43a Write numbers as words or figures according to the following guidelines

1 Spelling out numbers that begin a sentence

Spell out numbers that begin a sentence. If the number is large, rewrite or rearrange the sentence. Compare these examples:

Three hundred students visited the state capitol on a field trip.

The strike involves
465 employees ~~are on strike.~~

2 Using Modern Language Association guidelines for numbers

- *Numbers expressible in one and two words.* Spell out whole numbers from one to ninety-nine, including zero if the figure "0" would be confusing; and spell out large whole numbers expressible in two words: *seven, eighteen, twenty-six, two hundred, fifteen thousand.* Use a hyphen for numbers from twenty-one to ninety-nine. *An exception:* When using numbers frequently in technical or business writing, use figures for all numbers except those beginning a sentence.

- *Numbers expressible in more than two words.* Use figures for numbers of more than two words: *340; 1,650; 2,989,000.* Counting from the right, use commas to separate groups of three digits, except in addresses, telephone numbers, dates, and page numbers: *22,560* but *7201 South Locust.*

3 Using American Psychological Association guidelines for numbers

- Spell out numbers from one to nine.
- Use figures for numbers over nine: *10; 68; 200; 3,462.*

4 Using numbers in addresses

Always use figures in addresses: *PO Box 14; 15 West Pine Street; 137 North Maplewood; Route 59.*

5 Using numbers for time, dates, and time periods

- *Time.* Spell out the time except when using *a.m.* or *p.m.*: *seven o'clock in the morning, twelve midnight, half past four, 6:30 a.m., 9:45 p.m.*
- *Decades.* Spell out decades or use figures: *the nineties, the 90s, the 1990s.*
- *Centuries.* Spell out centuries; hyphenate when used as adjectives.

  In the **twentieth century**, major wars were fought in nearly every decade.

  Next semester I'm taking a **twentieth-century** American history course.
- *Historical dates with abbreviations.* Use figures with *AD, BC, BCE* ("before the Common Era"), and *CE* ("Common Era"): *AD 1066, 461 BC, 32 BCE, 1456 CE.* Notice that *AD* (*anno Domini*) precedes the date, *BC* ("before Christ") follows the date.
- *Inclusive dates.* For inclusive dates, write both years in full unless they are in the same century: *1895–1910* but *1941–45.*

6 Writing fractions, ordinal numbers, and ratios

- Common fractions and ordinal numbers. Spell out common fractions (*one-half, two-thirds*) and the ordinal numbers *first* to *ninth.*

  Nearly **one-half** of our employees have been sick since the **first** of the year.
- Decimal fractions, numbers followed by fractions, and ratios. Use figures for decimal fractions, numbers followed by fractions, and ratios: *a 3.8 grade average, a hat size of 7 3/4, a ratio of 4:1* [or *four to one*].

7 Writing numbers with abbreviations and symbols

Use figures with abbreviations and symbols.

$29.00	4 MB	62 km
14 mi. (miles)	65 mph	4" × 6"
8 hrs.	9 V battery	32°–43°
18% or 18 percent	50 lbs.	35-mm film

An MLA note: If your writing contains few numbers, spell out one-, two-, and three-word percentages and amounts of money: *twenty-six per-cent, sixty-nine cents, fifteen dollars, three hundred dollars.*

8 Writing well-known phrases containing numbers

Generally spell out well-known phrases containing numbers: *the Ten Commandments, the Twelve Apostles, the Fourth of July.*

9 Writing page numbers and divisions of written works

Use figures for page numbers, book divisions, and acts, scenes, and lines of plays: *page 7, paragraph 47, volume 5, chapter 16; Hamlet 3.2.46* or *Hamlet III.ii.46.*

An MLA note: To cite inclusive page numbers, give the second page number in full, through *99: 7–23, 85–96.* For higher numbers, give only the last two digits of the second page number unless more are necessary to prevent confusion: *122–34, 200–05, 1220–32* but *98–103, 287–303, 1238–1342.*

An APA note: When citing inclusive numbers, give all the digits of both numbers: *23–32, 458–467, 1152–1158.*

43*b* | When one number modifies another, write one as a figure, the other as a word

1 Writing large rounded numbers

Write large rounded numbers as a combination of figures and words.

The population of China today is **1.25 billion.**

Congress proposes to cut **$375 million** from the national parks budget.

2 Writing back-to-back numbers

Write back-to-back numbers as a combination of figures and words.

Last year Maria taught a class with **34 ten-year-olds.**

The order requests **seventy-five 8 × 10 glossy prints.**

Each of the **first 10** customers was given a potted plant.

43*c* | Write related numbers alike, as words or figures

Related numbers that appear together in the same sentence or paragraph should be written alike, as words or figures. If, according to the guidelines in 43a, you write some numbers as figures, be consistent and write all the numbers in your series as figures.

Within two decades, the university has grown from ~~ten thousand~~ *10,000* to

25,550 students.

44 The Hyphen

Type a hyphen as one keystroke, with no space before or after: *student-athlete*. Do not confuse a hyphen (-) with a dash (—). (See 39a.) To use hyphens correctly, note how your dictionary lists words:

- Use a hyphen to join words listed with a hyphen (*half-life*).
- If you must divide a multisyllable word listed with dots between syllables, use a hyphen. The word **har•mo•nize** may be divided *har-monize* or *harmo-nize*.
- Compounds listed as two words (*half note*) are written without hyphens.

44*a* | Avoid word division at the end of a line

The Modern Language Association and American Psychological Association guidelines forbid word division at the end of a line, and this is good advice for most writing. If a whole word won't fit, leave the line a little short and begin the word on the next line. Most word-processing programs have automatic word wrap to do this for you.

- Divide already hyphenated words only at the hyphen.

Downhill skiing became more frightening than exciting for me after my ~~bro-in-law~~ *brother-in-law* ~~ther-in-law~~ broke his leg in a bad fall.

- Divide personal names (1) between first and last names: Mary / Cassatt; (2) after the middle initial: Susan B. / Anthony; (3) if necessary,

between initials and the last name: H. L. / Mencken. Never divide between initials.

 Computer Tip: **Dividing Internet Addresses**

To divide Internet addresses (URLs), see 48a5.

44b | Use a dictionary to hyphenate compounds

A **compound** is a word made up of two or more words. Compounds may be hyphenated (*cross-stitch, cross-reference, cross-examine*), written as separate words (*cross hair, cross section, cross matching*), or written as one word (*crossbow, crossroad, crossword*). Your dictionary will show you the correct forms. If you don't find a compound listed, write the word as two words.

44c | Hyphenate compound adjectives before a noun but not following a noun

Compare the following pairs of sentences.

I've written a **first-rate** essay. My essay is **first rate.**

Darrell uncorked a **seven-year-old** bottle of wine. Darrell uncorked a bottle of wine that was **seven years old.**

The film received **less-than-enthusiastic** reviews. The reviews were **less than enthusiastic.**

A note on -ly adverbs followed by an adjective: Do not hyphenate a compound modifier consisting of an *-ly* adverb and an adjective.

Heavily‖traveled mountain paths contribute to significant soil erosion.

A note on hyphenated adjectives in series: In a series of hyphenated adjectives, use the second word of the compound only with the last modifier: *We plan to rent a two-, three-, or four-bedroom cottage for our vacation.*

44d | Hyphenate after the prefixes *all-, ex-, great-,* and *self-* and before the suffix *-elect*

all-American athlete	great-grandson	self-respect
ex-mayor	great-great-grandmother	senator-elect

Spelling

44*e* | **Hyphenate spelled-out fractions, numbers from twenty-one to ninety-nine, and combinations of figures and words**

one-half   eighty-eight
two-thirds   100-yard dash
seven-eighths   mid-1800s
forty-seven   pre-1960
fifty-two   post-twentieth century

44*f* | **Hyphenate to prevent misreading**

Without hyphens, some words might be misread or confused with other words.

Until a fertilized ovum is implanted in the uterus, it exists in a
pre-embryonic
~~preembryonic~~ state.
            ^

[Without a hyphen, readers may pronounce one long *e* sound instead of a long *e* followed by a short *e*.]

                                    re-sign
The lawyer asked her client to ~~resign~~ the agreement.
                                    ^

[Without a hyphen, *re-sign*, "to sign again," could be confused with *resign*, "to relinquish."]

Spelling

45 Spelling

45*a* | **Use a word guide, electronic dictionary, or spell checker**

As you edit your writing, look up any words that are not part of your everyday writing vocabulary. Use one of the following aids.

How to . . . Edit Spelling Without a Dictionary or Spell Checker

If you don't have a dictionary, spell checker, or spelling guide available, use these tips to figure out the correct spelling of words.

1. Compare spellings. Write out alternate spellings to compare. Correctly spelled words often look and feel right.
2. Disassemble words. Divide them into syllables and sound them out. Try to see and hear the word as you've actually spelled it. Is it *tra-deg-y* or *tra-ged-y*? *lon-li-ness* or *lone-li-ness*? *nec-cess-ary* or *ne-cess-ary*? *di-satisfied* or *dis-satisfied*? *tom-morrow* or *to-morrow*?
3. Find related words to help you spell the unaccented vowels that often sound like *uh* no matter what their spelling.

comp ? tition + comPETE
  = competition
gramm ? r + gramMARian
  = grammar
infin ? te + fiNITE
  = infinite

prev ? lent + VALue
  = prevalent
rel ? tive + reLATE
  = relative
sep ? rate + PARE
  = separate

4. Use memory aids. Make up phrases or sentences to associate with the correct spelling of words—the sillier the better. Everyone knows "The princiPAL is my PAL." How about "I get all *A*'s in grAmmAr" or "A secretAry never tArries"? You can think of others.

1 Using word guides

Word guides such as *Webster's Instant Word Guide* are pocket-sized books that list words without definitions, pronunciations, or grammatical information. If you're sometimes so unsure of a spelling that you can't look up the word, consider a word guide like *Webster's Bad Spellers Dictionary*, which lists words by their correct spellings and by their most frequent misspellings.

2 Using electronic dictionaries

Pocket-sized electronic dictionaries such as the *Franklin Wordmaster* and the *American Heritage Dictionary* will confirm an accurate spelling, correct a misspelling, or provide alternatives for unrecognized words you've typed in. Look for one with a word list of at least eighty thousand words.

3 Using spell checkers

If you write with a computer, your word processing program probably has a spell checker. Use it. Many writers who seem to be poor spellers are, in fact, poor typists who forget to run their spell checkers. But even if you use yours faithfully, proofread carefully when you finish to guard against the limitations of these software programs.

🖥 *Computer Tip:* Using Spell Checkers

1. Spell checkers do not distinguish between sound-alike words. If you type *their* when you mean *there,* your spell checker will not correct you.
2. Spell checkers do not correct mistakes that produce correctly spelled words. If you mean to type *band* but type *hand* or *and,* your spell checker will not recognize your mistake.

45b | Make a checklist of your spelling errors

Make a personalized checklist of your spelling errors. Buy a small alphabetically arranged address book or a pocket notebook. Find out which words you misspell and list them there. Write the word down, first as you misspelled it (to help you spot errors as you proofread) and then correctly spelled. To help yourself see the error, underline it.

WRONG	RIGHT
for*fil*ling	fulfilling
gove*rm*ent	government
gramm*er*	grammar
rec*on*ize	recognize
thi*er*	their
w*er*e	where

45c | Learn the most important spelling rules

1 Putting *i* before *e*

Almost everyone knows the beginning of this rhyming rule: *i* before *e* except after *c*. Not many know the remainder.

> *i* before *e* except after *c*
> or when sounding like *a*
> as in *neighbor* and *weigh*

- *i* before *e* = *believe, chief, field, relief, siege, yield*
- *i* before *e* except after *c* = *ceiling, conceive, deceive, receive*
- *e* before *i* when pronounced like the letter *a* = *eight, freight, neighbor, weigh, vein*

- *i* before *e* exceptions: *conscience, financier, science, species, sufficient*
- *e* before *i* exceptions: *counterfeit, either, foreign, forfeit, height, leisure, neither, seize, sheik, sovereign, weird*

2 Adding silent e at the end of a word

English generally requires a silent *e* at the end of a word to keep a preceding vowel long in sound: *mat/mate, met/mete, kit/kite, hot/hotel, cut/cute.* To add a suffix to a word that ends with a silent *e*, follow these rules.

- Drop the silent *e* when the suffix begins with a vowel: *cute/cutest, desire/desiring, fame/famous, imagine/imaginary, love/lovable, prime/primal, retrieve/retrieving.* An exception: *mileage.*
- Keep the silent *e* when a suffix begins with a consonant: *achieve/achievement, care/careful, live/lively, lone/lonely, sincere/sincerely.* Exceptions: *argument, judgment, awful, truly, duly, wholly.*
- Keep the silent *e* when a word ends in -*ce* or -*ge* and the suffix begins with *a* or *o*: *service/serviceable, change/changeable, courage/courageous.*
- Exceptions to avoid confusion or mispronunciation: *dying/dyeing, hoeing, toeing, shoeing, singing/singeing.*

3 Changing y to i

- When a word ends with a consonant plus *y*, change *y* to *i* and add the suffix: *busy/business, community/communities, embody/embodiment, lonely/loneliness, modify/modifier, penny/penniless.* Exceptions: *babyish, cityless, fairylike.*
- When the suffix is -*ing* or -*ist*, do not change the *y* to *i*: *copy + ing = copying, essay + ist = essayist; lobby + ing = lobbying; study + ing = studying.*
- When a word ends in a vowel plus *y*, add the suffix: *boy/boyish, buy/buyer, obey/obeying, sway/swayed, valley/valleys.* Exceptions: *daily, gaily, laid, paid, said.*

4 Doubling consonants

Double the consonant at the end of a word when the word meets all three of these tests:

- The word ends in a vowel plus a consonant: *begin, cut, fog, glad, occur, prefer, regret.*
- The suffix begins with a vowel: -*ed*, -*en*, -*ing*, -*y*.
- The word has one syllable or is accented on the final syllable: *beginning, cutting, foggy, gladden, occúrrence, preférring, regrétted;* but *bénefited, concealed, gláddened, láboring, préference.*

5 Adding the suffix -*ly*

- When a word ends with one -*l*, add -*ly*. Do not drop the -*l* at the end of the word: *casual/casually, formal/formally, real/really, usual/usually.*

- When a word ends -*ll*, add only -*y*: *chill/chilly, hill/hilly.*

6 Adding suffixes to words ending in -*ic*

- When a word ends in -*ic* and the suffix begins with -*e*, -*i*, or -*y*, add -*k*. *Traffic + ed* = add -*k*: *trafficked; picnic + ing* = add -*k*: *picnicking. Panic + y* = add -*k*: *panicky.*

- Some words ending in -*ic* take the suffix -*ally*: *heroically, logically, tragically.*

7 Forming plurals

- To form the plural of most nouns, add -*s* to the singular: *boat + s = boats; glove + s = gloves; shoe + s = shoes; Johnson + s = Johnsons.*

- When a noun ends -*s*, -*sh*, -*ch*, -*x*, or -*z*, form the plural with -*es*: *Jones + es = Joneses; dish + es = dishes; church + es = churches; box + es = boxes; buzz + es = buzzes.*

- When a noun ends in a consonant plus *o*, the plural varies:

ADD -*S* ONLY	ADD -*ES* ONLY	ADD -*S* OR -*ES*
autos	echoes	zeros, zeroes
memos	heroes	cargos, cargoes
pianos	tomatoes	
	potatoes	

- When a noun ends in -*f* or -*fe*, add -*s* to some words: *roofs, safes, chiefs.* To form the plural of others, change the *f* to *v* and add -*es*: *hoof/hooves, thief/thieves, wharf/wharves, wife/wives.*

- Some words have irregular plurals: *child/children, ox/oxen, goose/geese, mouse/mice.*

- Some words have the same form for singular and plural: *deer, jeans, glasses* (for the eyes), *pliers, rice, sheep, swine, trousers, wheat.*

- To form the plural of letters, add an apostrophe plus *s*: *the three* R's, *dot your* i's *and cross your* t's.

- To form the plural of numbers and abbreviations, omit the apostrophe unless it is needed to prevent confusion: *1990s, BAs.*

- To form the plural of most compound nouns, add -*s* to the last word unless the first word is more important: *checkbooks, masterminds, student-athletes;* but *mothers-in-law, attorneys general, courts martial, editors-in-chief, passers-by.*

- To form the plural of most English nouns that originally were Latin, Greek, or French words, use the plural from the original language.

SINGULAR	PLURAL	SINGULAR	PLURAL
alumna (female)	alumnae	datum	data
alumnus (male)	alumni	medium	media
antenna	antennae	memorandum	memoranda
basis	bases	phenomenon	phenomena
chateau	chateaux	psychosis	psychoses
criterion	criteria	radius	radii
crisis	crises	thesis	theses

8 Recognizing differences in American, British, and Canadian spelling

American spelling varies slightly from the British and Canadian in the use of *a/ae*, *e/oe*, *o/ou*, silent *e*, *c/qu*, *ck/que*, *ct/x*, *l/ll*, *ter/tre*, and *z/s*. Consult your dictionary, and use American spelling in the United States.

AMERICAN SPELLING	BRITISH AND CANADIAN SPELLING	AMERICAN SPELLING	BRITISH AND CANADIAN SPELLING
anemia	anaemia	honor	honour
apologize	apologise	judgment	judgement
check	cheque	licorice	liquorice
connection	connexion	theater	theatre
fetus	foetus	traveled	travelled

Document Formatting

46 Formatting Your Writing

46a Give your writing a professional, easy-to-read appearance

To communicate effectively, your academic, business, and public writing must be neat, easy to read, and appropriately formatted. Two formats for academic writing, the Modern Language Association (MLA) style and the American Psychological Association (APA) style, are described later in this chapter (see 46c and d). Other formats are described in the style manuals listed in 56b. For business formats, see Chapter 61. To determine the appropriate manuscript form, check with your instructor.

1 Writing with computers

- *Paper.* Use high-quality, white, 8½ × 11-inch computer paper. If you use continuous-form paper, remove the perforated edges, separate the pages, and put them in order.

- *Printers.* Ink jet or laser printers are always acceptable. Some readers object to dot-matrix printers. Find out before you begin. If you use a dot-matrix or print-wheel printer, be sure your ribbon is fresh and the paper properly aligned to produce correct margins. If necessary, set your printer to letter-quality or near-letter-quality printing.

- *Fonts.* Use standard 10- or 12-point fonts: Times Roman, Courier, Geneva, or Helvetica. Avoid cursive and other fancy fonts.

- *Formatting.* Set automatic formatting commands in advance, including spacing, margins, line justification, automatic paging, word wrap, and headers (most word processing programs do this for you). Use italics, underlining, and boldface sparingly (see Chapter 41), and avoid stylistic flourishes that may distract readers.

- *Margins.* Leave 1-inch margins on the top, bottom, and both sides of the page. If you are required to submit your paper in a binder, leave a 1½-inch left margin.

- *Line justification.* Justify your left margin: make the lines of text align on the left but not on the right. Avoid both right justification and proportional spacing.

- *Punctuation.* Never begin a line with a comma, colon, semicolon, hyphen, dash, end punctuation, or one or two ellipsis points. Never end a line with opening quotation marks, parentheses, or brackets standing alone, not connected to a word.

- *Corrections.* Proofread your final draft carefully. Run your spell checker, correct, and reprint. Give your paper a last check to be sure everything has printed correctly.

- *Binding.* Paperclip the pages of your writing. Do not use staples, pins, or braids.

2 Writing with a typewriter

- *Paper.* Use high-quality, white, 20-pound, 8½ × 11-inch typing paper. Avoid erasable paper, because it smears easily. If you wish to use erasable paper to make corrections easier, turn in a clean, legible photocopy of your final draft. Type on one side of the paper only.

- *Ribbon.* Use a fresh ribbon, and be sure the typeface is clean.
- *Typing guidelines.* See 46a1 for general guidelines regarding font selection, margins, punctuation, and binding.
- *Corrections.* Use correction fluid. Insert corrections by hand or typewriter. If you make numerous or lengthy corrections, retype the page. (For a list of correction symbols, see 4d2.)

3 Writing by hand

If possible, avoid handwritten work. Your school or local library probably has typewriters or computers for your use. See your Writing Center head or a librarian for information. If you must do an out-of-class paper by hand, check with your instructor first; then follow these guidelines:

- *Paper.* Use high-quality, wide-ruled, white theme paper, 8½ × 11 inches. Do not use spiral notebook paper. Write on one side of the paper only.
- *Ink.* Write in blue or black ink. Form your letters carefully. Don't run words into each other, and guard against smudges. If your handwriting is difficult to read, print, but do not use all-capital letters.
- *Spacing and margins.* Write on every other line to the right of the ruled vertical margin. Leave 1-inch right and bottom margins.
- *Punctuation.* Never begin a line with a comma, colon, semicolon, hyphen, dash, end punctuation, or one or two ellipsis points. Never end a line with opening quotation marks, parentheses, or brackets standing alone, not connected to a word.
- *Corrections.* Make corrections neatly, using correction fluid produced for pen and ink. (For a list of correction symbols, see 4d2.)
- *Binding.* Paperclip the pages of your writing. Do not use staples, pins, or braids.

46b | Use headings, lists, tables, and graphics to clarify ideas

Computer word processing programs give writers powerful tools for enhancing ideas. Even without a computer, you can add headings, lists, tables, and graphics to your writing. But be aware that too many extra features will destroy continuity and distract readers. To be effective, visual aids should

- Add to rather than duplicate your text
- Convey essential information, not be merely decorative

- Be easy to understand
- Make your subject easier to understand

A note on format: Specific subject areas may have specific formats for visual aids. Ask your instructor.

1 Formatting in-text headings

Essays and many other kinds of writing do not require headings. However, reports and other technical documents such as proposals and grant requests are divided by headings that identify topics and guide readers. If headings are appropriate for your writing, use the following format based on American Psychological Association (APA) guidelines:

- *Heading levels.* Use from one to five levels of heading, depending on the complexity of your writing. The following headings are arranged from most to least important and show the position and capitalization style to use. The phrase *capital and lowercase letters* directs you to capitalize the first, last, and all major words in the heading (see 40c).

CENTERED ALL CAPITAL LETTERS

Centered Capital and Lowercase Letters

<u>Centered, Underlined, Capital and Lowercase Letters</u>

<u>Flush Left, Underlined, Capital and Lowercase Letters</u>

    <u>Paragraph indent, underlined, sentence-style capitalization and punctuation.</u> The text immediately follows the heading on the same line.

- *Numbering.* Headings are not numbered except in scientific writing.
- *Punctuation and capital letters.* Do not end centered and flush-left headings with a period. For run-in heads at the beginning of paragraphs, capitalize the first letter of the first word, lowercase the remaining words, and end with a period. Underline as in the preceding examples.
- *Spacing.* Double-space above and below headings that appear on a line by themselves. Double-space within multiline headings.
- *Length and consistency.* Keep headings brief and grammatically parallel (see Chapter 19). Headings at a particular level should have the same grammatical form: noun phrases, verb phrases, questions, and so forth.
- *Grammar.* Make the grammar of a heading suggest the content of the section. Use nouns or noun phrases to introduce information or explanation (e.g., *Exotic Species*); *-ing* verbs to introduce processes, actions, or events (e.g., *Preserving Native Species*); commands to introduce in-

structions (e.g., *Reintroduce Natural Predators*); questions to interest readers (e.g., *How May Endangered Songbirds Be Saved?*).

- *Format*. Do not put each heading on a new page. But if a heading comes at the bottom of a page, move it to the next page unless it is followed by at least two lines of text.

2 Formatting lists

Use lists to clarify steps in a process, materials, ingredients, parts, advice, or items to be covered. To make a list, follow these guidelines:

- Write a lead-in followed by a colon, as in the preceding sentence.
- Precede each item in the list with a marker: a number or letter plus a period and 2 spaces; or a dash or bullet (•) plus 1 space.
- Begin each item flush with the left margin. Indent runover lines one-half inch or 5 spaces to form a hanging paragraph. For greater emphasis, indent the first line of each item 5 spaces and runover lines 1 inch or 10 spaces.
- Make items grammatically parallel: a phrase, sentence, or other grammatical form.
- Do not use periods after items in a vertical list unless one or more items are complete sentences.

3 Formatting tables

Tables present information in a systematic way, usually in columns. Use tables sparingly to eliminate complex, number-filled text. Place each table close to the text to which it relates. Give each table a number: *Table 1*, *Table 2*, and so forth. Briefly introduce each table in a sentence or refer to it in parentheses: (*see Table 1*). Here are the Modern Language Association (MLA) guidelines for tables. (See Table 1, p. 270.)

- Double-space throughout each table. Do not use all capital letters.
- Position the table number (e.g., *Table 1*) flush left on a line by itself. Then double-space and provide a descriptive caption, also placed flush left. If the caption is long, indent each additional line a quarter-inch or 2 spaces from the left. Do not use all capital letters. Double-space the caption.
- Between ruled lines, write descriptive headings for each column.
- Arrange each column beneath its heading.
- Double-space below the last line of the table and make a ruled bottom line.

269

Table 1

1992 Recreational Visits to Selected Areas Administered by the National
   Park System

Classification	Recreational Visits
National Lakeshores	3,906,495
National Parks	58,729,193
National Parkways	30,652,974
National Recreation Areas	50,315,794
National Rivers	4,532,849
National Seashores	19,954,228
Wild and Scenic Rivers	895,945
Parks--Other [a]	15,346,962
National Total	211,906,380

Source: Adapted from United States Dept. of the Interior, National Park
   Service, <u>Statistical Abstract</u> (Denver: Dept. of the Interior, 1992) 2.

   [a] Parks without national designation include National Capital Park,
National Mall, and the White House.

- If the table needs a source note, double-space below the bottom line
  and type the word "Source" followed by a colon and 1 space and the
  source of the table. Indent additional lines (if any) a quarter-inch or 2
  spaces.
- Use raised lowercase letters (e.g., [a, b, c,] and so forth) for notes to the
  table.

An APA note: Underline the descriptive caption preceding the table
(e.g., <u>1992 Recreational Visits to Selected Areas Administered by the National Park System</u>). After the table, in place of the word *Source,* use *Note*
underlined and followed by a period also underlined (<u>Note.</u>) and then 2
spaces. Then type "From" and give the source of the table, using the appropriate APA citation format (see 54c).

4 Displaying graphics

Graphics, or figures, include charts, drawings, maps, graphs, and
photographs. Use them to reveal relationships among data, to draw at-

tention to details, and to dramatize important points. Draw them by hand, cut and paste reproductions, or use a computer graphics program. Introduce each graphic and place it appropriately on the page near related text.

Give appropriate documentation following the graphic. These are the Modern Language Association guidelines:

- Double-space below your graphic. Flush left, write the label "Fig." and an Arabic numeral followed by a period (see Figure 1 below).

- On the same line, write a caption using an initial capital and lowercase letters, followed by a comma and documentation of the source. Double-space throughout.

- See the examples of a drawing, pie chart, and line graph on page 272. See also the bar graph in the sample MLA research paper (p. 357).

An APA note: Below the graphic, write and underline the word *Figure,* the numeral, and a period (<u>Figure 1.</u>); then leave 2 spaces and write a caption, using sentence-style punctuation. If necessary, type "from" and document the source of the graphic, using the appropriate APA citation format (see 54c).

A drawing that dramatizes important relationships

Fig. 1. Maslow's Needs Hierarchy, from Abraham H. Maslow, <u>Motivation and Personality</u>, 2nd ed. (New York: Harper, 1970).

A pie chart that reveals proportions

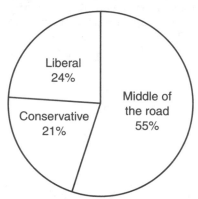

Fig. 2. Political identification of 1998 Harper College freshmen.

A line graph that reveals relationships among information and changes over time

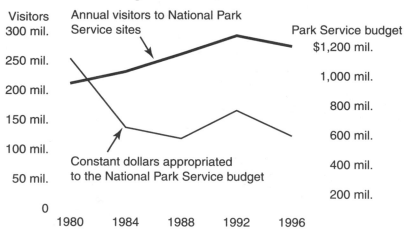

Fig. 3. National Parks annual visits and funding.

46c Use the Modern Language Association format for writing in the humanities

The following format, based on the *MLA Handbook for Writers of Research Papers,* 4th ed. (New York: MLA, 1995), is appropriate for writing in

46c MLA

English composition, literature, and foreign language courses; it is also used in the humanities, philosophy, religion, and history.

A note: See 46a for general information on computerized writing, typing, and handwritten work. To determine the appropriate format for your papers, check with your instructor.

1 Formatting the identification heading and title

Most college writing does not require a title page. Use an identification heading instead. On your first page, 1 inch from the top and left margins, list your name, your instructor's name, course title and section number, and date, double-spacing throughout. Double-space to reach the title line; center your title. If the title runs more than one line, double-space the lines; use a colon between a title and subtitle. Capitalize the first and last words and all words except articles, prepositions, conjunctions, and the *to* in infinitives (e.g., *to Write*). Do not use underlining, italics, and quotation marks unless your title contains another title or a direct quotation. Double-space between your title and the first line of text. (See 4f, Chapter 53, and 58d for sample papers in the MLA format.)

2 Formatting the title page

If your instructor requires a title page, center the title one-third of the way down the page. In the center of the page, write "by," double-space, and give your name. Two-thirds of the way down the page and centered on separate lines, write the course name, your instructor's name, and the date, double-spacing between lines. On the first page of text, repeat the title, centered on the first line. Double-space between the title and first line of text. (See the sample title page in Chapter 53.)

3 Indenting

- *Paragraphs.* Indent the first word of a paragraph one-half inch or 5 spaces from the left margin. If you write by hand, indent 1 inch.

- *Long quotations.* If a prose quotation runs more than four typed lines, indent it 1 inch or 10 spaces from the left margin. If an indented quotation runs longer than one paragraph, indent the first line of successive paragraphs an additional quarter-inch or 3 spaces. Indent more than three lines of poetry 1 inch or 10 spaces from the left margin, or center the poetry so that it looks balanced on the page. (See 50d.)

4 Spacing

Double-space between all lines, including titles, headings, indented quotations, and outlines. Space once after a colon and after end punctuation (periods, question marks, and so forth). Leave no space between end punctuation and closing quotation marks, parentheses, and brackets. Space once after periods following initials or abbreviations and after periods within bibliographic citations.

5 Paging

If your paper does not have a title page, begin numbering with Arabic numeral one (1) on the first page. In the upper right corner, one-half inch from the top of the page, put your last name followed by 1 space and the page number (e.g., *Lopez 1*). Do not use the word *page*, the abbreviation *p.*, parentheses, dashes, or other punctuation. Number consecutively to the end of your paper, including notes and documentation. Double-space beneath the page heading or position the first line of text 1 inch from the top of the page.

If your paper has a title page and other **preliminary pages** such as an outline, leave the title page unnumbered and use lowercase Roman numerals for the other preliminary pages. Count the title page as page i, but begin page-numbering on the following page, which is page ii. In the upper right corner, one-half inch from the top, put your name followed by 1 space and Roman numeral two (e.g., *Lopez ii*). Use lowercase Roman numerals for all of the preliminary pages: ii, iii, iv, and so forth. Then, on the first page of text, begin a new series of numbers; put your last name followed by 1 space and Arabic numeral one (e.g., *Lopez 1*). Double-space beneath the page heading or position the first line of text 1 inch from the top of the page.

🖥 *Computer Tip:* Using Headers

Create a page header to insert your name and page numbers automatically at the top of each page. If necessary, turn on the consecutive page numbering feature.

6 Headings

Identify the parts of your paper by appropriate section headings: *Outline,* the paper's title on the first page of text, *Notes,* and *Works Cited.* Center the heading 1 inch from the top of the page and capitalize it correctly. Double-space to the first line of text. (See the sample research paper in Chapter 53.)

In-text topic headings to divide the body of an essay are seldom necessary. However, headings may be useful or required for complex technical writing such as reports (see 46b1).

7 Order of pages

Arrange your paper in this order:

Title page, if required
Acknowledgments page, if required
Outline, if required
Body of the paper
Notes, if necessary
Works Cited, if necessary

46d Use the American Psychological Association format for writing in the social sciences

The following format, based on guidelines for student writing in Appendix A of the *Publication Manual of the American Psychological Association,* 4th ed. (Washington, DC: APA, 1994), is appropriate for writing in the social sciences, education, business, linguistics, biology, and earth sciences. Note that the APA format for student papers differs slightly from that of papers to be published in APA journals. See your instructor for the appropriate format for your writing.

A note: See 46a for general information on computerized writing, typing, and handwritten work.

1 Formatting the title page

Prepare a title page for your paper. (See the APA sample report in 54d.)

- *Page head.* In the top right corner, one-half inch from the top of the page, put a short form of your title (the page head) followed by one-half inch or 5 spaces and the page number. The page head and page number will appear at the top of all pages of your paper. If you use a computer, you can probably insert the heading and page numbers automatically.

- *Title.* Center the complete title in the middle of the page. Capitalize the first and last words and all words of four letters or more. If your title runs more than one line, double-space; use a colon between a title and subtitle.

- *Identifying information.* On separate, double-spaced lines beneath the title, put your name, the course title and section number, your instructor's name, and the date.

2 Formatting preliminary pages

In addition to the title page, you may be required to include some other **preliminary pages:** acknowledgments, a table of contents, a list of tables and figures, or an abstract. On each preliminary page, type your page header and page number at the top right. Type the heading for each page centered, in capital and lowercase letters: *Table of Contents, Abstract,* and so forth. Double-space beneath the heading.

3 Formatting an abstract

An **abstract** is a brief, comprehensive summary (100–120 words) of your paper. Write the abstract after you have written the paper itself. Report rather than evaluate or comment. Do not use *I* or *we.* Define all terms and abbreviations; write all numbers as figures. Type the abstract in one double-spaced paragraph beginning two spaces beneath the heading (*Abstract*). Do *not* indent the first line. (See the example in the sample APA report in 54d.)

4 Indenting

- *Paragraphs.* Indent the first word of a paragraph one-half inch or 5 spaces from the left margin.
- *Long quotations.* If a quotation runs more than 40 words, indent it one-half inch or 5 spaces from the left margin, none from the right. If an indented quotation runs longer than one paragraph, indent the first line of successive paragraphs an additional one-half inch or 5 spaces. Do not use quotation marks unless they appear in the original.

5 Spacing

Double-space throughout, including titles, headings, indented quotations, tables, graphics captions, notes, and references. Space once after commas, semicolons, colons, and punctuation at the end of a sentence. Leave no space between end punctuation (periods, question marks, and so forth) and closing quotation marks, parentheses, and brackets. Space once after periods following a person's initials and within reference citations.

A note: If your instructor permits, you may single-space within titles, headings, tables, and references to improve readability, and you may triple- or quadruple-space before major in-text headings and before and after in-text tables.

6 Placing tables and figures

Unless instructed otherwise, place tables and figures in the body of your paper, near the text they illustrate. (See also 46b3.)

7 Paging

Unless instructed otherwise, number the pages of your paper consecutively, beginning with the title page and continuing to the end, including notes, references, and appendices. Use Arabic numerals (1, 2, 3, and so forth). At the right margin, one-half inch from the top of the page, put the page header followed by one-half inch or 5 spaces and the page number. Double-space below the page number.

A note on preliminary pages: Your instructor may require you to use lowercase Roman numerals (i, ii, iii, and so forth) on preliminary pages such as the title page and abstract.

8 Formatting in-text headings

APA-style papers frequently contain in-text section and topic headings. See 46b1 for placement and capitalization information.

9 Arranging the order of parts

Arrange an APA paper in this order:

Title page
Acknowledgment page, if required
Table of Contents, if required
List of Tables and Figures, if required
Abstract, if required
Text of the paper
References
Appendices, if required

46*e* Create a Web site for academic or personal use

An increasingly popular assignment in writing classes is the composition of Web sites. As your Internet interests expand, you may even want to create a Web site for personal use. To begin with, a basic Web site consists of three parts: (1) text written by you, (2) links to other Web sites, and (3) interesting and appropriate graphics. Advanced pages may include animation, sound, movies, tables, and frames. However, you should try these only when you are comfortable with simpler pages.

The code needed to produce Web pages (called *HTML*, for *HyperText Markup Language*) is not difficult to learn, but it is easier to use a commercial Web site layout program to produce your page. Such programs enable you to make the page look the way you want it to, and the software writes the necessary HTML code for you. In fact, many modern word processing programs can turn a word-processed document into HTML.

1 Creating the site

Composing a Web site is similar in many ways to composing any other piece of writing. You need to plan your page beforehand, write a rough draft, and then revise until you have it the way you want it. To plan your site, follow these guidelines.

- Consider your purpose and audience. Be sure you actually have a purpose—that is, be sure that you're adding something of value to the Internet. Ask yourself, would anyone really want to see pictures of your bicycle?

- Sketch out the content of your entire Web site—that is, all the inter-linked screens or pages you'll be creating. What information needs to be on the opening page: the **home page**? What needs to be on other pages linked from the home page?

- Decide on the text you'll include. Research the Web for other sites to link to. Either create or find the graphical material you'll use. Now you're ready to work on creating the actual site.

- Begin composing the rough draft of your site. Text on a computer screen is more difficult to read than text on paper. For this reason, make your pages easy to understand at a single glance. Keep them short (one or two full screens at most), with lots of white space and carefully chosen graphics. Think of Web sites as interlinked pages (links to related pages—your own or others), not as long essays. Write in short paragraphs and relatively short sentences.

- Make effective use of the tools that HTML provides you: headings of various sizes, indented blocks of text, centered text and images, bul-leted and numbered lists, and horizontal rules to make the structure of your page immediately apparent to the reader. Treat your text with the same care you treat the text in other academic papers: carefully revise it until it reads the way you want it to for your audience. (For more formatting tips, see 46b.)

- Add your graphics. Use graphics sparingly but effectively. Try to keep them small, because in the split-second world of the Internet, readers will not wait minutes for images to appear, no matter how wonderful they are. Finally, avoid using images that move, flash, or blink. They may distract or even annoy your reader.

- Create links. A link is the *hot* text (usually shown in blue and underlined) that transports the reader to another Web site somewhere else on the Internet. A link to another Web site looks like this: **http://www.abacon.com**. Consider linking your site to other relevant Internet sites, to other pages within your own Web site, and to useful e-mail addresses. Be sure to make navigation easy; provide links back and forth to all other levels (pages) of your site.

- Use *mailto* tags. One variation on the link is the *mailto* tag. Instead of providing the user with an *http://*-type web address (called a *URL*, for *Uniform Resource Locator*), you provide an e-mail address, usually your own. Then, when a reader clicks on this link, a message is automatically preaddressed to that e-mail address. The reader only needs to compose his or her message and send it directly to you. A *mailto* link looks like this: **mailto:jrodriguez@stateuniversity.edu**.

- Add the date and your address. As a matter of etiquette, at the bottom of the first page provide the date the page was created or most recently changed, and include your own e-mail address.

- Keep revising and testing. Continuously test everything. Is the page attractive and simple to grasp? Is the writing clear and effective? Do all the links work? When you answer these questions affirmatively, you're ready to upload your complete Web site—all linked pages and graphics—onto your Web server.

2 Some final tips

Since pages will look slightly different when viewed in different browsers, test and refine your page on both Macintosh and Windows computers, using both Netscape Communicator and Microsoft Internet Explorer browsers.

The Web changes rapidly. You must maintain your Web site after creating it. Update it frequently; keep all content up-to-date; recheck all links.

For a complete discussion of writing for the Web, consult the *Yale HTML Style Guide*: <http://info.med.yale.edu/caim/manual/contents.html>. For a sample Web site illustrating the principles of Web design covered in this section, see the Allyn & Bacon Web site on p. 280.

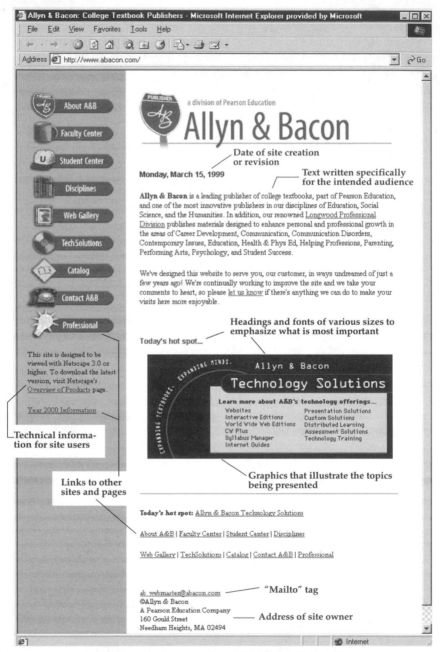

Site designed to move users from left to right and top to bottom
Sparing use of simple, easy-to-understand graphics

PART VII.

Research and *the* Internet

VII research/internet

The Research Project

VII research/internet

The Research Project

Choosing a Topic, Finding Sources, Preparing a Bibliography

47

The research project is such an efficient method for gathering and presenting reliable information that it is a frequent assignment in college and other environments where facts and ideas are important. The research papers you write will be similar to those written by professionals: reports, reviews of other researchers' findings (the "review of research"), thesis-support essays, and literary research papers. The following guidelines will help you meet the special challenges of these projects.

47a Choose a researchable topic

1 Identifying possible topics

In most respects, choosing a research paper topic is like choosing any topic. The topic you choose should interest you and stimulate your curiosity. (See the guidelines for choosing topics in 2a5.) Research projects, however, follow an additional guideline. Your topic must be genuinely researchable: reliable information and trustworthy opinions must be available to you. To identify appropriate topics, here's what to do:

- Ask the experts. If you don't already have a list of topics given to you as part of an assignment, ask your professor or other experts for recommendations.

- Check reference sources. Read about interesting topics in encyclopedias or other reference works. Look for problems, questions, or controversies that have stimulated the writing of scholars and others. A librarian will help you locate these sources.

- Check source lists. Skim bibliographies, indexes, and other source lists in your library. The titles of books and articles may suggest topics that have received the serious attention necessary for your research.

- Think critically about current popular topics. Before you choose a current popular topic like abortion, the legalization of marijuana, or same-sex marriages, ask yourself whether you have significant questions to answer or serious opinions to test. If you choose a topic only because everyone else is talking about it, your research project may end up boring your readers—and yourself. Also consider the sources of information available on popular topics. Newspapers, magazines, and the Internet may be filled with them, but their information may be unreliable. Look for topics that appear to have dependable information sources available. (See 1a3 and 49a and b for guidelines on evaluating information and information sources.)

💻 *Computer Tip:* Using Internet Subject Directories

Classified subject directories are Internet search tools that group information sources according to topics (see 48a1). Look up topics that interest you to find sources on your topic. The sources' titles alone may suggest problems, questions, or controversies worth investigating.

2 Narrowing and focusing your topic

Professional researchers rarely investigate a whole topic in one project. They choose a part, a single issue, or a key question to investigate in depth in the time available. Do the same. Once you have a topic, narrow it and draw the line of inquiry you'll follow in your research.

- *Writing baseline notes.* Before you begin research, write brief notes exploring your current thinking about your topic and establishing a baseline for investigation. Write down what you feel, believe, and know. Remind yourself where your ideas come from. Are your sources trustworthy? Your notes may raise research questions for you to answer. They may also reveal assumptions that influence your thinking. Knowing your biases will help you evaluate information more objectively.

- *Reading background materials.* If you haven't already read encyclopedias or other reference sources, do so now. Look for enduring issues, questions, or problems having to do with your topic. Your librarian will help you locate these sources.

- *Posing key questions or describing a problem.* Pose questions to answer. They may combine the reporter's six questions: *who, what, when, where, why,* and *how.* Or briefly describe a problem for your research to solve. For example:

  The exploding popularity of America's national parks is reducing the enjoyment of visitors and harming the environment. What can be done to protect park environments and at the same time increase the enjoyment of these beautiful attractions?

- *Stating your purposes.* Your purposes may change as you investigate a topic, perhaps transforming you from a reporter of information to an advocate for a position. But thinking about your purpose will reveal what you're looking for and why. Write a brief statement about why you're investigating your topic. For example:

> My purposes are to investigate interpretations of Charlotte Perkins Gilman's "The Yellow Wall-Paper" to discover the symbolism of the wallpaper and the causes of the narrator's insanity.

- *Writing a tentative thesis.* What do you expect to discover by your research? If you know little about your subject, you'll have little to say here, but if your purposes are critical or argumentative, you may already have opinions. Research may lead you to revise your thesis, even disprove it, but stating it now will point the direction of your investigation. Write your thesis as a declarative sentence:

> I expect to discover/prove/explain/demonstrate/show that ___[make an assertion about your subject]___.

> I expect to prove that the wallpaper in Charlotte Perkins Gilman's "The Yellow Wall-Paper" symbolizes the narrator's suffocating life and the causes of her deepening insanity.

How to . . . Focus a Research Project

At the beginning of a research project, many things about the project will seem unclear—especially if you've not written many research papers. Help yourself focus your project by writing the following exercise. Complete as many items as possible.

1. My general subject area:
2. My specific research topic:
3. My key question:
4. My purposes (to report, explain, evaluate, or persuade):
5. My tentative thesis (if possible):
6. What words in my topic, question, or thesis are vague or unclear? What opposing opinions or questions could be offered in response to my thesis? Do my stated purposes fit the language of my questions or thesis?
7. The date this project is due:
   a. Number of days for researching:
   b. Number of days for organizing:
   c. Number of days for writing:
   d. Number of days for revising and preparing the final draft:

47b Choose a variety of appropriate sources

Good research projects use a variety of sources that provide different kinds of information and differing viewpoints. As you begin a search for sources, consider what will meet your needs.

1 Locating primary and secondary sources

Primary sources provide the raw materials of a subject, unfiltered and unexplained. Charlotte Perkins Gilman's story "The Yellow Wall-Paper," like all literary works, is a primary source. So are statistics about visits to America's national parks. So, too, are interviews, eyewitness accounts, personal papers, court records, news stories, and the results of surveys and experiments. Part of your work as a researcher is to give raw materials the evaluation and explanation that will make them meaningful.

Secondary sources explain and interpret primary sources and present opinions. A scholar's essay interpreting "The Yellow Wall-Paper" is a secondary source, as is an essay proving the damage caused to national park environments by large numbers of park visitors. Secondary sources use primary source information to fulfill a purpose.

In your research, you'll use both kinds of sources, perhaps secondary more than primary. But whenever possible, use primary sources to form your own opinions.

2 Locating balanced sources

If you've chosen a controversial topic, such as federal funding of abortions for the poor or the genetic basis of intelligence, look for sources to represent all sides. The best correction for undue bias in one source—which you may not see if you read only one side of an issue—is a voice from the other side. Divide your research among competing opinions. Read those you disagree with as well as those you agree with. You'll end up with a fairer, clearer presentation of your topic and opinions.

3 Locating electronic sources

With the rapid development of computer technology, a vast number of sources are now available electronically. CD-ROM publications will, among other things, provide you with reference sources, indexes such as the *Academic Index*, and encyclopedias such as *Encarta*. Sources available through a computer network and the Internet include electronic books and periodicals, government documents and information services, scientific and meteorological databases, business documents, announcements by special-interest organizations, mailing lists, and personal communications. There are electronic sources for nearly every researcher. (For more on searching the Internet, see 48a–d.)

4 Using a checklist of sources

The following list indicates the range of sources available to you. Look it over at the beginning of a project, and check off appropriate sources. Return to the list later, in the middle of your research when you know more about your topic, to identify other sources.

_____ *Bibliographies, abstracts, indexes, and Internet subject directories.* These references provide the publication information necessary to locate books, articles, newspaper stories, and other sources on your topic. Examples: *MLA International Bibliography, Academic Abstracts, Social Science Index,* and *Yahoo!* Available in print or electronically.

_____ *Encyclopedias.* General encyclopedias such as the *Encyclopedia Britannica* provide background information. Specialized encyclopedias such as the *Encyclopedia of American History, Encyclopedia of Psychology,* and *Encyclopedia of Biological Sciences* provide more specific information. Available in print or electronically.

_____ *Other references.* Similar to encyclopedias are biographical guides such as the *Dictionary of American Biography;* abstracts, almanacs, and yearbooks such as *Facts on File* or *World Almanac and Book of Facts;* atlases such as the *National Geographic Atlas of the World;* and dictionaries.

_____ *Books.* Indispensable for most academic research, books give the long and broad views of a subject. Classic literary works are increasingly available electronically. On the Internet, see Project Gutenberg and Alex.

_____ *Essays in anthologies.* Scholars frequently compile the best essays on a particular topic and publish them together in book form. Such anthologies are frequently available on literary and controversial topics.

_____ *Book reviews.* Book reviews are available in periodicals, in electronic versions of periodicals, and in summarized form in *Book Review Digest, Book Review Index,* or *Current Book Review Citations.* Check these sources in print or on the Internet to evaluate a book's quality and coverage of a topic.

_____ *Articles.* Periodical articles are often more current and focused than books. When possible, rely on scholarly articles in academic journals, written by experts for experts, instead of articles in popular magazines, written for general audiences. Available in print and electronically.

_____ *Newspapers.* Complete editions of major newspapers such as the *New York Times* are available at your library on microfilm. Daily editions are available electronically. Individual news stories from local newspapers are available through *Newsbank,* available on CD-ROM.

_____ *Information services.* Professional and commercial services such as Dialogue, Nexis/Lexis, and ERIC provide publication information on a vast number of topics. They frequently provide abstracts or full texts of the documents they list. Available electronically, usually through computers in your library's reference section.

_____ *Government documents.* Government sources contain legislative and judicial information, scientific reports, statistics, cultural and historical information, recreational and health information, and practical how-to information. Available in print and electronically.

_____ *Archival materials.* Most libraries have special collections of letters, diaries, rare books, and local historical materials.

_____ *Audiovisual materials.* Maps, charts, photos of visual art, films, musical recordings, tapes, or recorded television and radio programs may be appropriate for your topic. Many are available both in print and electronically.

_____ *Special online sources.* E-mail, computer bulletin boards, news group subscription services, and discussion groups may provide you with expert or personal sources of information. Use these sources with care. (See 48e and 49b.)

_____ *Businesses, government agencies, and other organizations.* Businesses and other special-interest organizations may provide you with print or electronic sources of information related to your topic, or experts to interview.

_____ *Surveys and interviews.* You may develop your own sources of information by conducting interviews or surveys.

47c Follow a systematic search strategy to identify sources

1 General search guidelines

- Consult reference librarians. Whenever you have a research question you can't answer on your own, turn to reference librarians. They are experts on the library and research.

- List key words. List key words for your topic that you'll use to search for sources. For example, key words for research on Charlotte Perkins Gilman's "The Yellow Wall-Paper" might include her name and the title of the story, *mental illness* (one of the topics of the story), *nineteenth-century medicine* (another topic), and *feminism* (an intellectual movement that considers Gilman's work important).

- List synonyms and related terms. As you list key words, think of synonyms to expand or narrow your search. Research on overcrowding in national parks might use such related terms as *government lands, federal lands, national forests, national monuments, wilderness, conservation,* or *environmentalism.*

- Use the *Library of Congress Guide to Subject Headings.* This multivolume work, available in your library's reference section, identifies subject headings for the US Library of Congress classification system.

Your reference librarian will show you how to use it to identify key search words.

- Expand or narrow the search. If key words are not leading to sources, expand your search with more general words, or narrow it with more restrictive ones. A researcher getting nowhere using "The Yellow Wall-Paper" as a search term might expand his search with the author's name. Another researcher, not finding what she wants using the term *national parks,* might narrow her search to specific parks like Grand Canyon or Yellowstone.

- Learn the abbreviations for search terms. Nearly every search tool, print or electronic, uses abbreviations in its description of sources. Learn what these stand for by checking introductory glossaries or help screens.

- Take advantage of special library services. Many libraries will reserve sources for you on request or order them through interlibrary loan. See your reference librarian early in your research process.

2 Special guidelines for electronic searches

- *Finding help electronically.* Most electronic search tools come with instructions for their use. Look for introductory screens, welcome messages, help screens, or files with names like "?", "Readme," "About . . . ," "FAQ [frequently asked questions]," or "Formulating a search with . . . "

- *Using word variations.* In addition to key words and synonyms, try singular or plural word forms, different word combinations (*parks, national parks, government land,* and so forth), different disciplines (botany instead of biology, psychology instead of literature), and truncated words in which an asterisk (*) or a pound sign (#) replaces part of a word (*environ** will help you search for sources containing key words such as *environment, environmental, environmentalist, environmentalism,* and *environmental movement*).

- *Boolean searching.* A **Boolean search** (named after George Boole, a nineteenth-century mathematician and logician) uses the terms *AND, OR, NOT,* and *NEAR* (written in all capital letters) to expand or restrict a search.

  AND. If you tell an electronic search tool to look for *national parks* alone and *pollution* alone, it will list all works having to do with either subject. But if you tell it to search for *national parks AND pollution,* it will narrow your search to only those sources in which both terms appear.

  OR. If you wish to expand a search, use *or.* Telling a search tool to look for *preservation OR conservation* will lead to all sources that contain either term.

NOT. Using *not* will narrow a search. Telling a search tool to look for *national parks NOT Yosemite* will lead to all sources about national parks except those mentioning Yosemite National Park.

NEAR, ADJACENT, or **FOLLOWED BY.** In some electronic search tools, especially those used for searching the Internet, you can use *near, adjacent,* or *followed by* to narrow a search. Telling a search tool to look for *National Parks NEAR pollution* will lead you only to those sources in which these terms appear within a few words of each other.

- *Checking accuracy.* If you're not getting anywhere, check your typing for correct spelling and accurate search commands. Also note that not all electronic search tools recognize the Boolean operators described above. Some use symbols like plus or minus signs: + or – (see 48c3).

- *Checking abstracts.* Some search tools, especially on CD-ROM, include abstracts briefly summarizing sources. Check these to decide whether a source is worth reading.

- *Accessing sources.* Many electronic databases provide options for viewing all or part of a source, downloading it to your computer, or printing it out as hard copy.

47d Use library search tools to identify sources

1 Using card catalogs and microfilm files

If your library uses cards in drawers or files on microfilm to catalog its holdings, each source will be listed at least three times—according to subject, author, and title. Look for a heading at the top of each card. If yours is a literary topic, look up the author's name to find information about the work you're studying. Microfilm catalogs may permit you to print publication information.

2 Using computerized catalogs

If you use a computerized library catalog, you will be presented with a series of successively restricted screens: first an initial search screen, then lists of subject categories, then lists of sources, and finally a screen containing detailed publication and availability information about a single source. See the sample screen on p. 289 and notice the kinds of information it contains to help you find the source and evaluate its suitability for your research project. *A bibliography note:* When you list publication information for a library source that you intend to use in your paper, arrange it in the appropriate format. (See 52a and b for the MLA format and 54b and c for the APA format.)

COMPUTER CATALOG SCREEN: DETAILS FOR A BOOK

Main Author:	Sellars, Richard West, 1935-
Title:	Preserving nature in the national parks: a history / Richard West Sellars
Primary Material:	Book
Subjects:	United States. National Park Service--History.
	National parks and reserves--United States--Management--History.
	Nature conservation--United States--History.
	Natural resources--United States--Management--History.
Publisher:	New Haven: Yale University Press, c1997.
Description:	xiv, 380 p.: il.; 24 cm.
Notes:	Includes bibliographical references (p. 293-360) and index.
Location:	Mainstack
Call Number:	SB482.A4 S44 1997
Number of items:	1
Status:	Not Charged

- *Subject, author, and title searches.* Search electronic catalogs for sources as you would a print catalog, according to subject, author, or title.

- *Expanding or narrowing a search.* To expand or narrow your search, combine search terms and use the Boolean operators *and, or, not,* and *near.* (See 47c2.)

- *Partial title or author names.* You can search for sources even when you have only a partial title or name. Type in what you know, and the catalog will list all sources with titles or author names that contain what you've typed.

- *Checking availability.* After you've recorded or printed complete publication information for a likely source, use the computer to check for availability (whether it's on the shelf or checked out) and location (in the main stacks, on reserve, or at a branch library).

3 Using CD-ROM indexes

Indexes contain lists of sources arranged alphabetically. Some, like *The Reader's Guide to Periodical Literature,* list only periodical articles; others, like *The Academic Index,* include books, articles, and other sources. Some, like *NewsBank,* list sources on a broad range of topics; others, like the

Modern Language Association's *International Bibliography,* are devoted to one general subject area.

Many of these indexes are available on CD-ROM disks read by personal computers in your library's reference section. These electronic indexes contain publication information to help you locate the source and often an abstract or brief summary of it or even its full text. See the sample screen below for a source listed in a periodical index. *A bibliography note:* When you write publication information for a source listed in an index, arrange it in the appropriate format. (See 52a and b for the MLA format and 54b and c for the APA format.)

Forum for Applied Research and Public Policy
Spring 1997 v12 n1 p6(9)

Periodical title and publication information: date, volume, issue, page number, and length

Paradise lost in U.S. Parks? (problems of national parks) *William R. Lowry.*

Article title, subject, and author

Subjects Covered:
national parks
management
pollution
ecology
funding

Topics covered in the article

Abstract: Several problems have plagued the U.S. National Park Service in recent years. Water and air pollution and nearby developments could eventually threaten a park's ecology. The fate of National Park Service policies and programs is at the mercy of politicians while funding is another problem with the government's failure to increase funds to improve park services despite the 30% rise in total visitors since the 1980s.

Summary of the article

- *Years of coverage.* CD-ROM indexes usually cover several years of publication, making them more comprehensive than a single print volume of an index. If a CD-ROM index does not go back far enough for the sources you need (e.g., for literary or historical research), use the print versions of the index.

- *Search strategy.* Search for sources as you would in any electronic catalog, by key words, title, author, or combinations of these.

- *Viewing and recording information.* Generally, you can print publication information from CD-ROM indexes, and many will also permit you to view and print abstracts or complete copies of articles.

4 Using print indexes

Print versions of many of these indexes are located in the reference section of a library. Issued annually, they list publications for a single year. To investigate what has been published over a number of years, you would have to search several volumes. Search for sources as you would in any index—by subject, author, or title.

$47e$ Compile a bibliography of sources

A **bibliography** is a systematic list of sources. You'll use this list to locate sources and, as you write your paper, to document borrowed information.

🖳 *Computer Tip:* Using a Bibliography Generator

A computer program known as a bibliography generator, such as BiblioCite or EndNote, can arrange publication information for you in the appropriate bibliographic style.

1 Noting bibliographic information

As you identify a source on your topic, record publication and location information for it. At the beginning of your research, you may simply print this information from electronic catalogs and indexes. Later you'll turn it into individual bibliographic citations, each in a format appropriate to your discipline or subject area.

- *Writing note cards.* If you write bibliographic information by hand, use cards instead of lists on sheets of paper. Individual cards, each with its own source, will be easier to use as you search for titles, add and drop sources, and arrange these cards for documentation. *A shortcut:* Divide sheets of notebook paper into quarters, write a citation in each quarter, and cut the sheets into individual slips when you begin searching for the sources themselves.

- *Using a computer.* If you write with a computer, you may compile bibliographic information in a file that you alphabetize, update, and correct as you go along. You won't need note cards. At the end of your project, you can rework this file to become the list of works cited or list of references accompanying the final draft of your paper.

- *What to include.* Note the author's name, title of the individual work, other relevant identifying information such as editor and edition, publication information, page numbers, and call numbers for locating a source in the library. If it is an electronic source, note the medium—for example, *CD-ROM* or *online*—the computer service, the date of your search, and the URL, or electronic address.

 Computer Tip: **Copying and Pasting Information**

> If you use Internet search tools, you may be able to copy online bibliographic information and paste it into your bibliography file. Be aware, however, that you may have to reorganize this information to fit a required documentation style such as the MLA or APA format.

- *Incomplete information.* If a catalog or index does not provide complete information, leave blanks to be filled in later when you have the actual source.

- *Documentation styles.* As you write bibliography notes, follow the documentation style assigned by your instructor or preferred by the discipline in which you are writing. Use the Modern Language Association (MLA) style for papers in the humanities, including literature, history, religion, and the arts. (For sample MLA citations, see 52b.) Use the American Psychological Association (APA) style for writing in the social sciences. (For sample APA citations, see 54c. For a list of style manuals in other disciplines, see 56b.)

- *Comparing publication information.* When you actually locate a source, compare the publication information on its title page or in its preliminary pages with the publication information in your notes. Correct or complete your citation.

The following are bibliography notes for a book and an Internet source. The notes are written in the MLA documentation style.

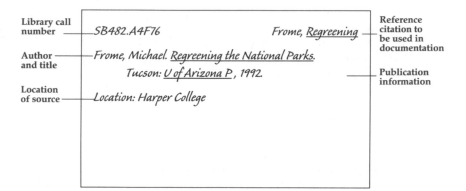

Library call number — SB482.A4F76   Frome, *Regreening* — Reference citation to be used in documentation

Author and title — Frome, Michael. *Regreening the National Parks.*
            Tucson: *U of Arizona P*, 1992.   Publication information

Location of source — Location: Harper College

Title ——————

"Effects of Visual Air Quality on Visitor Experience."

Internet site ——

NPS, "Effects" —— Reference citation

Protected Areas Air Resources Web. 24 Oct. 1996. —— Publication or revision date

Internet address ——

National Park Service. 11 Aug. 1998 ——

<http://www.aqd.nps.gov/ard/visitexp.htm>.

Date of user access to source

2 Writing a working bibliography

At the beginning of your research, your instructor may ask you to prepare a **working bibliography** listing all the sources you plan to read. When you finish your paper, you'll use an updated and corrected version to prepare the Works Cited or reference list accompanying your finished project.

To prepare a working bibliography, arrange your note cards in the order required by the documentation system you're using and copy your entries on a sheet of paper following the appropriate format. Or, if you've compiled a computerized bibliography file, format your citations appropriately and print them. See 52a for Modern Language Association guidelines and the sample MLA papers in Chapter 53 and 58d. See 54b for American Psychological Association reference list guidelines and 54d for a sample reference list.

3 Writing an annotated bibliography

Your instructor may assign an **annotated bibliography**, a list of sources in which each entry is followed by a brief descriptive and evaluative paragraph. Such a bibliography will inform readers of the content, relevance, and quality of the sources you cite. To prepare an annotated bibliography, do the following:

- Select sources that provide a variety of perspectives on your topic.
- Cite each work in the appropriate documentation style, such as MLA or APA style.
- After each citation, write a brief descriptive paragraph in which you evaluate the credentials of the writer, identify the intended audience, compare the work to similar works, and explain what it contributes to your topic.

48 Searching the Internet

If you use a computer for research, sooner or later you'll come to the **Internet,** an expanding global network of millions of computers. It contains many lists of sources and often the sources themselves, which you can read on screen, print, or, perhaps, transfer to your own computer. You can learn more about this vast electronic world of information by connecting to the Internet and reading the following sources:

- For introductions to the Internet, see *Links to Online Sources for Help Using the Internet,* at <http://www.mont.ib.md.us/tutor.html> or *Walt Howe's Internet Learning Center,* at <http://people.ne.mediaone.net/walthowe/index.html>.

- Two online electronic magazines (known as "e-zines") are aimed at new and developing Internet users: *Sherlock@* and *ZDNet Internet User.*

48a | Learn to navigate the Internet

1 Connecting to the Internet

To see Internet sources like those just listed, you need a computer with a telephone modem, an Internet service provider such as America Online or one made available by your college or university, and, for much of your Internet searching, browser software like Internet Explorer or Netscape Communicator. When you click with your mouse on the "Search the Internet" icon of your service provider's start screen (an image of a globe or flashlight), you'll bring up the **home page,** the first screen of your browser program, and see the following:

- An "Address" or "Go to" box: Type an Internet address to take you to a specific site.

- Back button: Back up to a previous site.

- Forward button: Move forward to return to the site you just moved back from.

- Print button: Print the current page.

- Refresh or reload button: Reload the current display on your monitor.

- Bookmark or Favorites menu: Set an electronic bookmark so that you can return to an interesting site without having to go through other sources or sites to get to it.

- History option: From the Go or Window menu, return to recent sites you have visited.
- Lots of advertisements or announcements: Don't let these distract you.

2 Visiting Internet sites

To read Internet sources like the ones listed at the beginning of this chapter, you will have to visit their individual sites at specific Internet addresses. In the "Address" or "Go to" box, you'll type the occasionally lengthy combination of letters and sometimes numbers that make up an address, then click "Enter" or "Return." Suppose you are searching for information about US national parks. You might visit the National Park Service's site at <http://www.nps.gov/parks.html>. Try typing this address in the "Address" box of your browser screen; omit the angle brackets (< . . . >), which are used only to enclose Internet addresses in printed text. When you press the "Enter" or "Return" key, you'll be carried to the Park Service's home page, a display of images, text, and options for visiting other sites.

3 Using hypertext links

On most Internet pages or screens, you'll see special images or highlighted or underlined text known as "links." You can tell whether something is a hypertext link by using your mouse to move the arrow across the screen. If a hand appears when you move across an image or text, that is a link. Click on it and you'll be taken from the site where you are now to another related site. (Click on the "Back" button to return to your original site.) Hypertext links are the most obvious way in which Internet sites form a network.

For example, if you are viewing the National Park Service's home page and move the arrow over the image of a park ranger's face and the words "Visit the Parks," you'll see the little hand appear, telling you that you are on a link. Click on that link and you'll be led to another site with further links to National Parks information, maps of specific parks, and other special features, one of which is titled "The National Parks: Lesser-Known Areas." Click on that link, and you'll be taken to an essay that you can read. Using the Internet in this way, clicking on hypertext links in one source to carry you to links in another containing links to still other sites, is what is known as "surfing the 'Net."

4 Managing Internet addresses

The addresses that enable you to navigate the Internet are also known as **URLs (Uniform Resource Locators).** They are composed of three parts: a "protocol" identifying the computer language used to gain access to a site, the "domain" identifying the owner of a site, and a "directory path" indicating where this address leads on the Internet. Here are the parts of the address for the National Park Service's home page:

protocol	domain	directory path

http://www.nps.gov/parks.html

Because these addresses are often difficult to locate and even harder to remember, it's important to keep track of them as you make your way from site to site. Happily, your computer will help you out in three ways:

- You can set an electronic bookmark. Select the "Add Bookmark" option from the Bookmark menu in Netscape Communicator or the "Add to Favorites" option from the Favorites menu in Internet Explorer. Communicator immediately adds the address to the Bookmark menu. Explorer pops up a window that allows you to edit the address and organize your bookmarks into folders.

- Go to the "history file," which you'll find via the "History" option of the Window menu in Netscape Communicator or via the "Open History Folder" option in the Internet Explorer's Go menu. Here you'll find recorded all the addresses of recently visited sites.

- When you print an Internet file, many browsers will automatically print the address of that file on each page. With Netscape and some others, you must choose this feature from the "Preferences" file. If your browser does not print the address, be sure to copy it accurately for later reference.

As you find interesting sites, add their addresses to your "Bookmarks" or "Favorites" file and make written notes of the other important information you'll need to document this source in your paper: (1) author's name, if available; (2) publication information for print and online versions of a source; (3) the Internet address (URL); (4) the date of publication; and (5) the date you gained access to the site. Because Internet sources frequently change content and location, this last date is important. If you go back to a site at a later date, it may be quite different from the site you visited on an earlier occasion—or it may no longer be there. (For more on documenting Internet sources, see 52b3 for MLA guidelines and 54c3 for APA guidelines.)

5 Writing Internet addresses

- *Using URLs in the text of your writing.* Enclose Internet and e-mail addresses in angle brackets. Do not leave internal spaces or drop internal punctuation or capitalization. For example:

  Further information about the increase in air pollution at the Grand Canyon is available at the Environment Defense Fund site, <http://www.edf.org>.

- *Using URLs in bibliographies.* Do not italicize or underline URLs or e-mail addresses in the list of Works Cited. Enclose them with angle brackets. For example: <http://www.edf.org>.

- *Breaking addresses.* If you must break a URL or e-mail address, follow these MLA guidelines: (1) Break only after a slashmark (/). (2) Never add a hyphen when you must break an address. (3) Do not break the protocol (*http://*). (4) Add a period after a URL at the end of a sentence. For example:

  The US Forest Service environmental impact statement is now available at <http://www.canyonforestvillage.com/eis.htm>.

6 Reading and saving Internet sources

When you find a site that looks promising, you have several options.

- Read the source on screen and take notes. Take computerized notes by creating a file in your word processor and splitting your computer screen between the Internet site and the notes file. Switch between them as you read. (See the computer tip in 2e.)

- Print the source and read it later, highlighting the text or taking notes. To save time (and printer ink or toner), turn off any images in the text by clicking the appropriate link.

- Copy the source; then cut and paste it into a file in your word processing program by using the commands in your Edit menu. Be aware that you'll probably have to reformat your borrowing when you make such a transfer. Even more important, to avoid plagiarism be sure to document your borrowing of this now-quoted material. (See 50e.)

- You can save many sources on your own computer by performing a download using your browser software. You'll use the Save or Save As commands in your File menu. Saving other sources is trickier, and you may need special FTP (File Transfer Protocol) software such as WSFTP for Windows (available for you to download at <ftp://ftp.tidbits.com/pub/tiskwin/ws_ftp.zip>) and Fetch for the Macintosh (available at <ftp://ftp.tidbits.com/pub/tidbits/tisk/tcp/fetch-301.hqx>). Remember to reformat text that you download.

7 Learning the basics of Internet research

Learning to use the Internet is a lot like learning to drive a car. What you learned in driver's ed. about skillful and safe driving was probably not as useful as what you learned behind the wheel. So, too, with the Internet. Reference librarians and computer lab personnel are ready to answer your questions, and you can consult books such as *Casting Your Net: A Student's Guide to Research on the Internet* (Allyn & Bacon, 1997). But you'll gain the most useful information and skills while actually searching the Internet.

Many Internet sites have help screens or answers to "Frequently Asked Questions" (FAQs). There are even a number of master sites to link you to introductions to the Internet, guides to research, and search tools for locating information sources. For a list of these sites, see pages 433–34. Try them out. Experiment; practice; be patient if you don't always find what you're looking for. The following pages will help you develop your searching skills.

48*b* | Search the World Wide Web

If the Internet is something like a virtual continent-size nation with a complex network of electronic highways connecting all parts of the country, then the World Wide Web is the largest state in this country, a vast region (Internet "space") of millions of computers and millions upon millions of Web sites containing text, graphics, or sound—whatever can be sent electronically. Because of its size, ease of use, and the kinds of information it pulls together, the Web is currently the most popular path to gain access to and utilize the Internet.

You can locate sources on the Web in two ways. If you know a site's URL (address) because it has been given to you, you can type it into your browser's "Address" box (Web addresses always begin "http://"). The other method, which you'll probably use more often, is to use one of the electronic search tools described in the following sections. The tool you choose will depend on how focused your research topic is and the kind of information you're looking for. To learn to use these tools and to see how they differ, try the same search on several different tools.

1 Using search engines for key word searches

If you have a clear idea of your research topic and have key terms to describe it, then you should do a key word search using a search engine like Excite!, AltaVista, Lycos, or HotBot. A **search engine** scans the texts of documents in its database looking for the key words you've told it to search for. (See Appendix A2, p. 434, for a list of search tools and the master sites that will connect you to them.)

If, for example, you tell a search engine to look for sources about *standardized testing* and *bias,* it will give a list of all sources containing these key words. The sources are arranged in order of their relevance to your topic: how many times a source uses your key words or how closely a source matches what you're looking for. When you first use a particular search engine, be sure to check its FAQs file ("Frequently Asked Questions") or help screens for guidance to its use. See pp. 300 and 301 for sample screens illustrating a key word search.

2 Using classified subject directories for browsing

If you're hazy about a topic or unsure of its key words, then you should browse the Internet with a subject directory like Yahoo!, World-Wide Web Virtual Library, or Magellan. A subject directory will carry you down through a series of menus from general to more narrow topics until you find the specific topic you want to investigate and a list of sources written about that topic. (See Appendix A2, p. 434, for sites to take you to these tools.)

If, for example, you are investigating the effects of visitors on US national parks but are unsure how to look for sources, you might turn to Yahoo! In your browser's address box you'll type its URL and be taken to its home page. There you will see a number of hypertext topic links: *Art &*

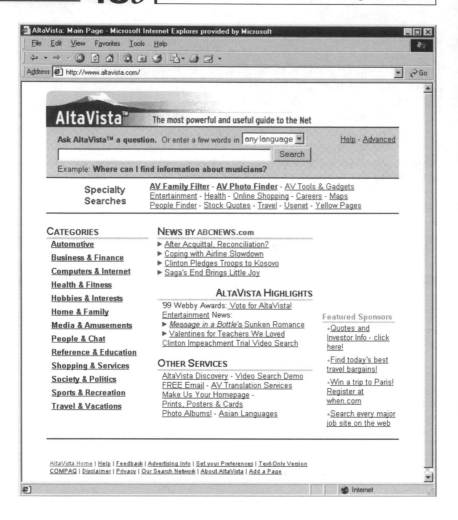

Humanities, Government, News & Media, Society & Culture, and so forth. Beneath each of these are more specific topic links. For example, under *Society & Culture* are *People, Environment, Religion.* Click on *Environment* and you'll be taken to a list of even more specific topic links, all having to do with the environment, among them, *Environmental Studies, Parks,* and *Pollution.*

Browsing through Yahoo! in this way, moving through successively restricted topic lists, you'll come eventually to individual Internet information sources, such as "Monitoring for Gaseous Pollutants in the Parks," which you can read on screen or download to your computer. See pp. 302 and 303 for sample screens illustrating a search using Yahoo!

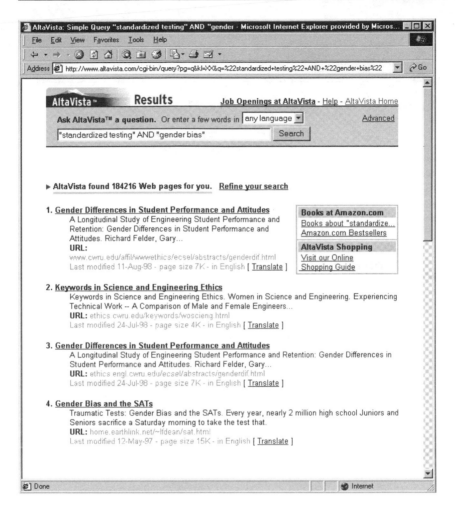

3 Using other search tools

- If you have the time, try **multi-tool searching.** Search for sources on your topic using both a search engine and a subject directory. Or choose a multi-engine (also called a "meta-search") tool like All-In-One or Mamma. (See Appendix A2.) *A note on multi-tool searching:* Because no search tool, not even a multi-search tool, lists all the sources on a topic and because no two search tools list the same sources, you should always use more than one search tool. The more search tools you use, the greater your chance of success in finding sources.

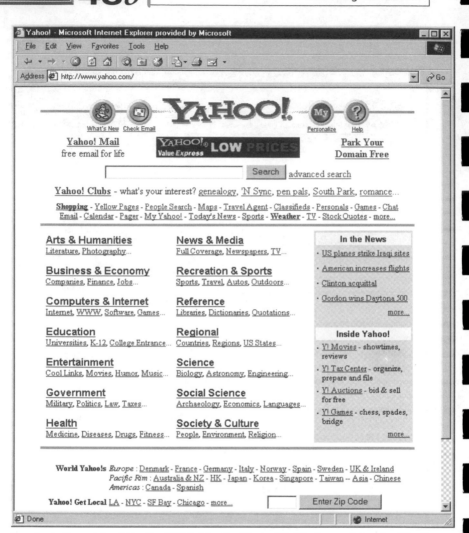

- Because finding quality online sources on a topic is often difficult, you may want to turn to **agent software** like Surfbot at <http://www.verity.com/>. Such a computer program will search any way you instruct it, investigating the databases you specify, filtering, classifying, and listing sources for you.

- Librarians have access to specialized databases and search tools that may provide the quality sources you need. Tell them your topic and ask whether they have special resources to help you.

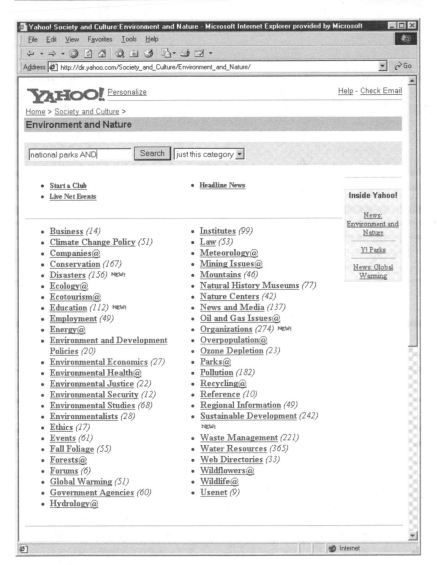

48c Use effective search techniques

The Internet is vast, constantly changing, and lacking an overall organization. Therefore, searching for sources is more challenging than looking for a book or magazine article in the library. You'll improve your online searches if you practice the following techniques.

How to . . . Search the World Wide Web

Use these tips and guidelines to search the Web successfully.

1. Click on the "Find" button or "Search the Internet" icon of your browser (NetFind, Netscape Navigator, or Internet Explorer) and you'll be taken to the home page of a default search engine like Excite! If you wish, type in the URL (address) of another search tool, like Yahoo!, in the "Address" or "Go to" window of your browser. Use the links to search tools listed in Appendix A2.
2. Create bookmarks for your favorite search tools or collect their addresses in a folder. See 48a4.
3. To make a key word search using a search engine like Excite! or Infoseek, do the following. Type your key words into the query box and then click on the "Find," "Search," or "Seek" button. Use the scroll bar to examine the list of sources. Read the brief descriptions that follow. Then click on the highlighted hypertext of an interesting title or address and be taken directly to the source. Examine the source to see whether it meets your needs. If it does, give it a bookmark (see 48a4); then read it, print it, or save it (see 48a6).
4. To browse a subject directory for specific topics and sources, do the following. Type the address of a subject directory like Yahoo! in your browser's address box, <http://www.yahoo.com>. Be sure to omit the angle brackets. From the list of topics displayed, choose one that interests you, click on it, and examine the list of subtopics that appear. Choose increasingly specific topics until you find a topic that suits you. Use the scroll bar to examine the list of references. Click on titles to see complete documents. Bookmark an interesting source (see 48a4); then read it, print it, or save it (see 48a6).
5. To make a multi-engine search for sources, try a tool such as Savvy-Search. In the "Address" window of your browser, type the following address without the angle brackets: <http://www.cs.colostate.edu/~dreiling/smartform.html>. Then follow the instructions for making a key word search (see item 3 above).
6. If your search is unsatisfactory, try another search tool. None lists all sources on the Internet, and each tool searches in a different way. Also, focus your search by choosing different or additional key words (see 48c).

1 Using help screens and FAQs

Develop an understanding of the search tools you use. Every search tool comes with guides to its use. Examine the home page or first screen for links to a help screen or a "Frequently Asked Questions" (FAQs) file.

Also, the Internet has many master sites to help you learn the tricks of on-line searching. (See Appendix A1.) As you experiment with a search tool, don't be intimidated by links called "advanced," "super search" or "expert searching." Try out the hints they provide.

2 Focusing and narrowing your search terms

Large Web search tools like Excite! and HotBot have so many documents in their databases that they are difficult to use unless you have unusual or specific key words to cue your search. At the beginning of a search spend a few minutes thinking about the best key words for your topic.

- Avoid general terms except when they are modified by more specific ones. Searching for *parks* will give you millions of sources. *National parks* will limit your sources somewhat, but you'll still get citations for parks in Canada, New Zealand, and Australia, as well as the United States. Limiting yourself to *US national parks* will focus your search further.

- Use Boolean search operators to link key words (see 47c2). Searching *Grand Canyon AND visitors AND air pollution* will lead to a focused search. Whenever possible, use a unique phrase as your search term; you'll see listed only those documents in which that phrase appears.

- Search for organizations associated with your topic. They will provide you with hypertext links to other sites containing additional information. If your topic is controversial, however, remember to search for organizations on all sides of an issue. For example, search for both the National Right to Life and the National Abortion and Reproductive Rights Action League sites. (To identify some of these sites, see Appendix A6.)

- Narrow the field of your search. When appropriate to your topic, click on the buttons that allow you to restrict your search by date or geographic location.

3 Using search operators with Internet search tools

In 47c2, you learned to use Boolean search operators to narrow a search for sources: *AND, OR, NOT, NEAR,* and so forth. Be sure to type these operators in all capital letters between the terms you're searching for. Be aware that not all search tools will accept these operators; some use punctuation marks or symbols instead. See the search tool help screens for further information. AltaVista gives you the most detailed assistance; Hotbot, the most concise.

- Use double quotation marks (" . . . ") to treat a group of words as a phrase—for example, *"automobile pollution in national parks."*

- If your search tool accepts them, use "+" (plus) as you would the Boolean *AND;* use "−" (minus) as you would the operator *NOT.* For example: *Yosemite + pollution − automobile.*

- Use an asterisk "*" to truncate a key word to its base, so you can search for variants of the word. For example, shorten *pollution* to *pollut** to search for variants like *pollution, pollute, polluter,* and *polluting.*

- Use capitalization to treat adjacent words as proper names; use a comma between proper names—for example, *Aldo Leopold, John Muir, Gifford Pinchot.*

4 Solving common search problems

Some search problems appear so often for so many researchers that you need to be aware of what they are and how to solve them.

- *Typing URLs correctly.* It's easy to mistype a computer address. If you're not finding the source you're looking for, check the address to be sure you've typed all the letters, numbers, and punctuation correctly. Look carefully for incorrect capital letters and unnecessary spaces.

- *Narrowing a topic that is too broad.* If your topic is too broad, begin by searching in a subject directory. When you find a more restricted topic, switch to a key word search. You'll limit yourself to the last topic category and produce a shorter list of sources to examine.

- *Coping with too many sources.* If your search is leading you to too many sources, concentrate on the top ten or so. Examine them to see whether their hypertext links will lead you to more relevant sources. America Online's "more like this" option is useful here.

- *Coping with too few sources.* If your search is not leading to enough sources, broaden it by omitting the least-required key word.

- *Coping with lengthy files.* If you want to print or download a lengthy file and if you can live without the graphics, click on the "text only" option if it exists at that site. You'll get only the text of the file, and you'll get it more quickly.

- *Guessing relevant sites with unknown addresses.* If you are unable to find relevant sources, try to guess the URL (address) of an organization associated with your topic. In the "Address" box of your browser, type in a basic Web template beginning *<http://www.* Then add the name or abbreviation of a relevant organization. Conclude with the appropriate domain suffix: *.com* (commercial); *.edu* (educa-

tional); *.gov* (government); *.mil* (military); *.net* (network management); *.org* (noncommercial; nonprofit organization). For example, if you are researching standardized tests, you might guess that the URL of the Educational Testing Service would look something like <http://www.ets.org>, and you'd be right.

- *Locating sites that have moved.* Not infrequently, Internet sources move from one host computer to another. When they do, their addresses change. To find a source that has moved, type a URL into a browser "Address" box, but then delete parts of it, beginning at the right and stopping at each slashmark. If, for example, you're searching without success for an article on pollution in US National Parks called "Effects of Visual Air Quality on Visitor Experience," which was originally located at <http://www.aqd.nps.gov/ard/visitexp.htm>, begin by omitting *visitexp.htm* to see whether you can locate the article at another site.

- *Locating publication information.* Sometimes it is difficult to locate all the publication information necessary to document Internet sources. For authors and publication dates, look in headers and footers. Also, authors may have included e-mail addresses containing their names (look for the @ symbol appearing in all e-mail addresses). For titles, look at the top of your browser screen window or in the upper corner of text. If a title seems incomplete, go to the Document or Source Information window. If a document is untitled, create an appropriate title enclosed in square brackets [. . .]. For information about publishers, see the "About this Site" or home page link. Or you may be able to reach a home page by shortening the URL to the domain name. For example, if you can't locate publication information at <http://www.mla.org/main_stl.htm>, shorten the address to <http://www.mla.org>.

48d Search other Internet spaces

As it rapidly expands, the World Wide Web is adding to its search capabilities and to the sites to which you can gain access. It is now possible to get to non-Web sites through Web "gateways," Web addresses that connect to non-Web sites. However, the Web has not yet colonized the whole Internet, and because many non-Web sites are potentially useful to researchers, you need to know about them.

1 Visiting Gopher sites

Developed at the University of Minnesota and named after its mascot, Gopher enables you to "go for" text-based Internet sources by burrowing through a series of hierarchically arranged menus leading ever more deeply into a topic.

- *Direct visits using Gopher addresses.* To visit a Gopher site directly, type its address into your Internet browser. Note that Gopher addresses begin "gopher://." The search engine for Gopher files is Veronica. Reach it at <gopher://veronica.scs.unr.educ/11/veronica>.

- *Indirect visits using Web gateways.* To gain access to Gopher files through the World Wide Web, type in the following Web address for the Veronica search engine: <http://www.scs.unr.edu/veronica. html>. To see a subject directory of Gopher files, go to "Gopher Jewels" at <http://galaxy.einet.net/GJ/index.html>.

2 Visiting FTP sites

FTP (short for "File Transfer Protocol") represents an archive of Internet sites. You can access FTP sources directly with addresses beginning "ftp://." A long list of these sites is available at <ftp://rtfm.mit.edu/pub/usenet/news/.answers/ftp-list/>. Better yet, investigate FTP sources through the Web at <http://www.info.net/Public/ftp-list.html>. Or access the FTP search tool, called Archie, at <http://scr.doc.ic.ac.uk/archie/archie.html>.

To learn more about both FTP and Gopher sites, read *World Wide Web: Telnet, Gopher and FTP* at <http://www.hsl.unc.edu/HSL/es/ntgftp.htm>.

3 Using WAIS

Pronounced "ways" and standing for Wide Area Information Service, WAIS enables you to search for key words in the actual text of files, thus increasing the likelihood that a document you've identified has information about your topic. WAIS addresses always begin "wais://." You can use WAIS to search World Wide Web and Gopher documents.

48e Use e-mail and discussion groups to communicate with people

1 Communicating by e-mail

When you send messages by e-mail, you turn the Internet into an electronic post office. Now you can communicate directly with experts and others involved with topics of interest or join group discussions of important issues. You might, for example, write to testing experts at a distant university to gather opinions about the presence of bias in standardized tests. With the "attachments" option built into most e-mailing software, you and your addressees can attach documents to e-mail messages and exchange files as part of your dialogue.

To send and receive e-mail messages, you and those you communicate with need a modem, a browser like Netscape Navigator or Internet Explorer, and an e-mail address, usually available through the service provider that connects you to the Internet. An e-mail address looks like this:

To send mail, you need e-mail software, which is usually a part of your browser. But one e-mail program called Eudora is available free over the Internet. Mac users will find it at <ftp://ftp.qualcom.com/quest/mac/eudora>. Windows users will find it at <ftp://ftp.qualcom.com/quest/Windows/eudora>. To search for e-mail addresses and locate people online, use a "finder" program such as Knowbot, Lycos People Find, or Switchboard. (Use the address under *Internet Searching* on p. 434 in Appendix A2 to take you to links to these tools.)

2 Participating in news groups

News groups are electronically connected groups of people and their collections of messages, called "postings." These postings are made available, usually for a week or so, to interested people through a network variously called Usenet or Netnews. If, for example, you are investigating overcrowding in US national parks and looking for visitor anecdotes and experiences, you might search for them on the World Wide Web with a Usenet search tool like DejaNews. With it, you can browse through menus of general-to-specific topics—in this instance, from "Recreation" to "Travel" to a specific discussion topic: "Should you visit the Everglades?" After the topic question, you would see responses to it grouped as a discussion "thread." You can simply read these responses or join the discussion yourself and, using your e-mail address, post a reply.

To find other discussions relevant to your topic, you might also conduct a key word search of the Usenet database. The many thousands of discussions are organized under broad topic headings. Here are seven of the major ones and their abbreviations used in addresses: (1) alternative topics that don't fit other categories (*alt*); (2) computer topics (*comp*); (3) miscellaneous topics related to the news itself (*misc news*); (4) recreational activities and hobbies (*rec*); (5) scientific topics (*sci*); (6) social, political, and religious topics (*soc*); and (7) opinions (*talk*).

To participate in a news group, you'll need news reader software, probably available as part of your browser. Or you can access news groups through the Web's "HyperNews" at <http://union.ncsa.uiuc.edu/

HyperNews/get/hypernews.html>. Or search for topics at DejaNews (<http://www.dejanews.com/>).

A cautionary note about news groups: Evaluate news group postings with great care. Anyone and everyone can join a newsgroup and add his or her two cents to a discussion. The quality of the contributions, therefore, varies widely from contributor to contributor. (For guidelines on evaluating information sources, see 49a and b.)

3 Subscribing to listservs

A **listserv** is a special kind of news group—a subscription-based e-mail discussion of a particular topic. The postings of each subscriber are sent by a list owner to the e-mail addresses of all other subscribers, who may then reply to one or more of these messages, creating a topic "thread." The many thousands of these groups are divided into "public" or "open" discussions, open to anyone who wishes to subscribe, and "private" or "closed" discussions. To subscribe to a "private" group, you must apply to a moderator for permission to participate and describe your interests.

To search for listservs, begin with the World Wide Web's "CataList Reference" site for public lists at <http://www.lsoft.com/lists/listref.html>. CataList allows you to search for discussion groups in a variety of ways. For example, to locate listservs focusing on US national parks, you might do a key word search using *Grand Canyon.* You'll discover a group called "Grand Canyon Chapter General Discussion" maintained by the Sierra Club and located at the e-mail address <GC-GENERAL@LISTS. SIERRACLUB.ORG>. If you wish, you can subscribe and receive the postings of the group members.

To join a listserv that interests you, send a subscription message to the listserv's subscription e-mail address, usually accompanying the name of the discussion list itself. If you want to join to the Grand Canyon listserv the subscription address is <LISTSERV@LISTS.SIERRACLUB.ORG>. In the body of the message, not the subject heading, include the word *SUB-SCRIBE* in all capital letters. For example, in your message subscribing to the Grand Canyon listserv, you'll type "SUBSCRIBE GC GENERAL" plus your name and e-mail address. To receive reference cards containing general user commands, or to ask questions, you'll include the words *HELP* or *INFO.*

Two cautions: (1) Never send a subscription message to the listserv e-mail address itself; that is reserved for the listserv discussion. Send your subscription queries to the subscription address. (2) Evaluate listserv contributions as carefully as you would the remarks in a news group posting, especially those that appear in public or unmoderated listservs. (For guidelines on evaluating information sources, see 49a and b.)

4 "Real-time" communicating via MOOs, MUDs, and IRCs

When you communicate by e-mail or join a news group or listserv, the recipients of your messages may not be online when you type them. Your communication is **asynchronous:** you send a message at one time and they receive it at another. But when you join a MOO ("multi-user domain, object-oriented") group, MUD ("multi-user domain"), or IRC ("Internet relay chat"), you enter an Internet space in which all writers are present at their computers. Here the communication is **synchronous:** in real time. Such Internet spaces are useful for classes, seminars, and special-interest groups whose members meet with one another at specific times.

If you are part of a MOO, MUD, or IRC, you will join the discussion using Telnet, an Internet language that lets you log on to another computer from your computer. Telnet addresses always begin "telnet://." To learn more about these spaces, see *How to Survive with Telnet* at <http://www.daedalus.com/net/telnet.html> and *The help@MOO Project* at <http://admin.gnacademy.org:8001/HyperNews/get/moo.html>.

A cautionary note: Evaluate MOO, MUD, and IRC groups with great care. Participants' remarks may or may not be trustworthy or authoritative. (For guidelines on evaluating information sources, see 49a and b.)

5 Writing effectively online

To communicate effectively, successfully, and happily on the Internet, observe the following guidelines, often referred to as **Netiquette.**

- Before you participate in a news group or listserv, spend time familiarizing yourself with the discussion. Read the FAQs that almost always accompany these groups to get an idea of the subject matter and level of conversation.

- Use the subject line of an e-mail file to identify your topic.

- Begin your message with a brief greeting to set the tone: *Hi Annie* or *Dear Dr. Masood.* Include a brief appropriate close: *Bye* or *Sincerely.*

- Keep your messages short and to the point.

- Adjust your formality to fit the occasion. Online messages addressed to friends and coworkers are often as informal as casual conversation, with all the slang, abbreviations, and sentence fragments you would expect to hear in speech. Online messages addressed to strangers or anonymous readers should sound somewhat more formal, suitable to your topic and purpose for communicating. For example, if you send an e-mail to an educational researcher, asking about the benefits of home-schooling, you would be more formal than when you discuss the same topic with friends in an online chat. To achieve the appropriate degree of formality for your messages, follow the guidelines in 27a–d.

- Send plain text only, avoiding tabs and other computer commands you would use to format print documents.

- Observe these punctuation guidelines:

  Underlining. Use a single underlining mark before and after text that you would italicize or underline in a print document.

  Henry David Thoreau's_Walden_recommends simple living but not poverty.

  Asterisks to replace italics and underlining. If your e-mail provider does not support italics or underlining, use asterisks.

  Poverty is *not* what Thoreau had in mind.

  Hyphens and Internet addresses (URLs). Never add a hyphen when you break an Internet address at the end of a line. The MLA guideline is to break only after a slashmark (/). (See also 48a5.)

  Angle brackets (< . . . >) and Internet addresses (URLs). In the text of your message, enclose Internet addresses, including e-mail, in angle brackets: <http://www.nps.gov>. Do not add additional punctuation within the angle brackets.

- Edit online communication as the occasion requires. Because online communication is often as spontaneous and informal as speech, readers are generally tolerant of minor errors and typos. But always reread your messages to see that you've said what you intended and that your formality fits the occasion. Then check to see that your writing is relatively free of error. And if your e-mail program has a spell checker, run it.

- Never send a message when you're angry or upset. Online name-calling and other outbursts, known as "flaming," are an especially vivid display of poor online manners. Avoid all-capital words for emphasis, a practice known as "shouting."

- For informal online messages, use the following emoticon symbols and abbreviations to convey the meanings behind your words:

:-)	smile	AFAIK	as far as I know
;-)	wink	IMO	in my opinion
:-(	frown	IMHO	in my humble opinion
<g>	grin	BTW	by the way
<vbg>	very big grin	OTOH	on the other hand
		CU	see you

49 Evaluating Print and Electronic Sources, Writing Research Notes

49a Evaluate sources with the "CASE" method

In 1a3, you learned to evaluate the quality of information and opinions before using them in your writing. At the same time, you should be evaluating your sources of information and opinion. Not all will be of equal value. Some may not suit your purposes; others may be flawed or unreliable. If you can't trust the quality of your sources, you can't trust their content.

As you evaluate sources, think of the word *case.* In order to make your case and support your thesis, be sure that each of your sources meets the standards represented by the letters C, A, S, E: Currency, Authority, Suitability, and Ease of use. To make an evaluation, answer the questions in the following sections.

1 Currency: Is this source up-to-date?

When was this source published? Is it a first edition, reprint, or revision? For most research topics, you want sources that contain the most recent information and opinion. Look for a recent publication or revision date, or an indication that a work has recently been reissued in a new edition. Currency is not always a relevant standard with literary and historical topics, however. You may be reading primary sources published hundreds of years ago, and secondary sources published decades ago may still provide valuable insights. But for technical and social science topics, in which information and opinion are changing rapidly, currency is an important standard of quality.

2 Authority: Is this source authoritative and trustworthy?

- What are the author's credentials for writing about this topic? Is this person an expert or eyewitness? What political, religious, or social beliefs may influence this person's view of the facts or objectivity? What organizational affiliations reveal this person's point of view? A biased source is not necessarily a bad source, but you need to know what the biases are and how they influence objectivity.

- Is the publication source (e.g., a university press, scholarly journal, major publisher) known for publishing reliable information? Are submissions to this publication source checked for their quality— "refereed"—by a panel of experts?

3 **Suitability: Does this source meet the needs of you and your readers?**

- Does this source contain the materials that you want and your readers need: facts, explanation, opinion, statistics, examples, eyewitness accounts, narratives? What are its main idea, thesis, and major supporting points? Will they lead you away from your topic?

- What is the purpose of this source: to inform, entertain, evaluate, or persuade? Does its purpose match your own or the needs of your readers? If a source aims to persuade, does it do so with facts, reasoning, or emotion? Which of these will help you make a case appealing to your readers?

- Do you and your readers share the point of view or outlook of this source? A source that your readers may reject as biased will probably not suit your purposes.

- What is this source's coverage of your topic? Is it broad in scope, presenting detailed background information? Is it narrow in scope, focusing on a specific topic? Does it present its topics in depth or superficially? Is it complete or partial in its coverage? Answering these questions will help you decide whether a source has the kinds and amount of information suitable for you and your readers.

4 **Ease of use: Will you and your readers find this source and its contents easy to use?**

- Can you locate this source, read it, and understand it in the time available for your project?

- Who is the audience for this source, experts or general readers? Is it written at a level appropriate for your readers? Will they be able to understand its contents if you quote or summarize it in your writing?

49b | Evaluate Internet sources with special care

To evaluate Internet sources, use the "CASE" standards (currency, authority, suitability, and ease of use) that you use to evaluate other sources. But with Internet sources, you will sometimes have difficulty finding what you need for an effective evaluation. The following information and tips will help you. (For more about evaluating Internet sources, see Appendix A3.)

🖥 *Computer Tip:* **Internet Evaluation Sites**

Some Internet sites claim to evaluate online sources, but they are often concerned with whether a site is "cool," "fun to use," or visually appealing, not whether its information is accurate or complete. Such standards aren't of much use to serious researchers.

1 Currency: Is this source up-to-date?

Most Internet sources have three dates associated with them: publication date, file date (when they are placed on a particular host computer), and revision date. Look at the beginning or end of a file for publication and revision dates. Prefer sites with the most recent dates.

2 Authority: Is this source trustworthy?

Because the Internet, news groups, and e-mail are open to anyone with a computer and a little technical knowledge, online sources vary widely in authority—the expertise of their authors. With few editorial review boards in cyberspace to vouch for quality, you must use these sources with care. To locate an author's name within a document, look at the beginning or end of the file. To decide whether an author is trustworthy, do the following:

- Examine addresses for their domain. An abbreviation in a site's URL identifies the type of organization that stands behind a source: *com,* a commercial source; *org,* a noncommercial, nonprofit organization; *gov,* a government source; *edu,* an educational institution; *mil,* a military source; and *net,* a network management source. Can you find a statement that a sponsoring organization approves of the site in question? The domain of a source doesn't guarantee quality, but it may suggest purpose or point of view, or the likelihood that a source has been checked for accuracy.

- Check an author's home page. Use an author's name to search for his or her home page, which may contain autobiographical information you can use to evaluate trustworthiness. Look for organizational affiliations that suggest point of view or bias. A "~" (tilde) in a URL indicates a personal Web site.

- Send an e-mail message. Online authors often include e-mail addresses with their names. Explore their qualifications or the background of their opinions. You can locate e-mail addresses with a people finder or "fingering" program. (See Appendix A2 for links to these programs.)

- Trace an author's postings. Evaluate the trustworthiness of an author by tracing his or her various contributions to a news group or listserv. Check whether the news group or listserv has a moderator to screen postings for quality and suitability.

- Follow hypertext links. See whether the source you are viewing is linked to other quality sites. Do these sites verify the claims of the source you are considering? Do they have the same outlook? Two sites connected by hypertext links are not equally authoritative. And one source does not necessarily authorize another. Evaluate each site separately.

- Check grammar, spelling, and punctuation. Poorly written sources may indicate a source with untrustworthy or incorrect information.

3 Suitability: Does this source meet the needs of you and your readers?

Like a print document, an Internet site should have a purpose and topic coverage suitable for you and your readers. To evaluate suitability, here's what to do:

- Identify the type of site. Is it informational, business or marketing, news, advocacy, or personal? Is this type of site likely to have the information you need? Do the purpose and outlook suit your readers' interests and outlook?

- Examine the body of the source. Does this source's coverage suit you and your readers?

4 Ease of use: Will you and your readers find this source and its contents easy to use?

To make this evaluation, answer the following questions.

- Do you, and if necessary your readers, have the equipment and software necessary to gain access to the source?

- Is the site user friendly? Do you understand how to gain access to the site and use it to its fullest capacity? Can you make your way through it easily, using hypertext links or key word searches?

- Is this site linked to other up-to-date, authoritative, and suitable sites?

- Do you and your readers have the background information necessary to understand the contents of the site?

How to . . . Evaluate Sources

Evaluate sources with the "CASE" method, checking for Currency, Authority, Suitability, and Ease of use. Follow these tips and guidelines.

1. Skim information at the beginning and end of a source.

   Print sources: For information about book authors, examine title pages, book jackets, author blurbs, and title pages. With periodicals, check the footnotes at the beginning or end of an article, or the list of contributors, usually appearing early in the periodical. For information about publication dates and editions, check the copyright pages of books (immediately following title pages) and the title pages of magazines.

   Internet sources: Examine the headers and footers of a file for information about authors, contact persons, institutional sponsors, home pages, and dates of creation, copyright, or revision. Use search engines or people finders to search for information about an author. (See Appendix A2.)

2. Read reviews, abstracts, and annotated bibliographies. Many print and Internet sources exist primarily to describe and evaluate other sources.

   Print sources: Check for book reviews in *Book Review Digest* or *Book Review Index.* Read author biographies in the various "Who's Who" biographical guides such as *Current Biography.*

   Internet sources: For reviews of Internet sites, use the Argus Clearinghouse at <http://www. clearinghouse.net/>, the Gale Research Cyber-Hound at <http://www.thomson.com/cyberhound/>, or the Internet Public Library at <http://www.ipl.org/>.

3. Note red flags that signal sources to avoid. One or two red flags may not prevent you from using a source, but more than a few should make you very cautious.

   - No publication date, no recent revision date, or an old date for information known to change rapidly.
   - Lots of negative reviews.
   - Counter-scenarios or explanations that spring readily to mind as you read a source. If you can think of other, more plausible explanations, then the reasoning of a source may be suspect.
   - Wild claims and broad generalizations. Most logical assertions sound reasonable, and trustworthy authors usually support their assertions.
   - Facts and statistics without source citations. Trustworthy authors usually give the sources for information they use.
   - Charged or biased language.
   - Poor writing; incorrect grammar, spelling, and punctuation.

49c Follow effective strategies for gathering information

1 Reading for research

As you read your sources, take notes on whatever seems relevant. If you're like most researchers, you'll end up taking more notes than you need, especially in the beginning. The deeper you dig into your subject, however, the more perceptive you'll become about what is right for you.

- *Where to begin.* Before you begin reading, arrange your sources according to difficulty. Read general or introductory sources first, as background for more specialized or technical sources.

- *Previewing your reading.* Before you begin reading a source, even if you're going to read only a chapter or a paragraph or two, put your reading in context by skimming the table of contents, the introduction, and surrounding paragraphs. See how the part fits into the whole document. Use the guidelines and questions in 1b1.

- *What to look for.* Look for facts, of course, but also for explanations or interpretations, expert opinions, evaluations, and examples that illustrate ideas. *A note on conflicts:* Take note of any controversies involved with your topic. If you already have an opinion, pay attention to the other side. Use this opportunity to test the quality of your opinion or to make up your mind.

- *Reading by the paragraph.* Finish reading a paragraph before taking a note about something you've found in it. In this way you'll see how the information that interests you fits into its context.

- *Thinking critically as you read.* To understand what you read, use the methods of critical thinking described in 1a: analysis (to see how things fit together), interpretation (to find the meaning of your reading), evaluation (to measure quality), and synthesis (to see how sources fit together and suit your purposes).

2 Gathering information with surveys and interviews

- *Conducting surveys.* Plan survey questions carefully to avoid personal bias or charged language. Avoid asking yes/no questions whenever possible; they are often not very informative. Guard against overly personal questions that may hinder respondents from answering truthfully. Ask one question at a time; don't combine two or more questions in one sentence.

- *Interviewing.* Make appointments with your sources and keep them promptly. Be clear about your purposes for the interview. Prepare your questions in advance using the preceding guidelines to surveys; ask clarifying or follow-up questions as necessary. As you listen, take careful notes; double-check quotations to be sure they're accurate. If necessary, ask your sources whether they are speaking "for the record" and may be cited by name. Tape-record sources only with their permission. Offer to send them a copy of your completed project.

49*d* | Take notes in an easy-to-use format

1 Taking notes on paper or with a computer

For brief papers drawing from only a few sources, you can gather information informally, photocopying or highlighting important information, jotting ideas marginally or on a sheet of paper. But if you have more than a few sources and if your paper is longer than a page or two, you'll have to take separate, individual notes to handle your information effectively.

- *Size*. Make note cards easy to sort by using only one size. Avoid cards too small for complete notes or so large you may write too much on one card. Buy a package of 4 × 6 inch cards, or make your own by dividing notebook sheets into four slips each. Cut the sheets into individual notes after you've finished your research.

🖥 *Computer Tip:* Taking Notes

Make a template for a "Notes" file by creating and saving properly sized columns or boxes. Adjust margins as necessary. Print and cut these computerized notes when you finish your research.

- *Length*. Generally, the shorter the note is, the better. Put one piece of information in each note. More than one idea makes a note difficult to sort and organize. When in doubt, divide an idea in two and put each idea in a separate note. Never write on the backs of cards. If you have a long note that won't fit on one card, write *Note 1 of 2, Note 2 of 2*, and so forth on the appropriate cards.

- *Plagiarism*. Use quotation marks around all word-for-word quotations. Compare summaries and paraphrases with the original to be sure you haven't quoted unintentionally. (See 50e.)

2 Formatting notes

Every note should contain the following information, which you'll use as you think about your topic, organize your paper, write your paper, and document your borrowing.

- A subject heading to identify the topic of the note.
- A reference citation for identifying the source of the note parenthetically in the text of your paper (the author and a short version of the title).
- A page number, if a print source.
- An introduction that provides a context for the note: *who, what, when, where, why,* or *how.*
- The note itself: quotation, summary, paraphrase, or a combination.
- Your comments on the note, if necessary, explaining it or telling how you intend to use it.

Here is a sample note card for an environmental research paper based on Aldo Leopold's *A Sand County Almanac:*

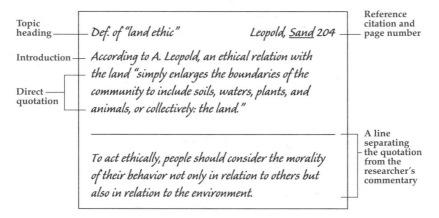

Topic heading — *Def. of "land ethic"*   *Leopold, Sand 204* — Reference citation and page number

Introduction — *According to A. Leopold, an ethical relation with the land "simply enlarges the boundaries of the community to include soils, waters, plants, and animals, or collectively: the land."*

Direct quotation

To act ethically, people should consider the morality of their behavior not only in relation to others but also in relation to the environment.

A line separating the quotation from the researcher's commentary

49*e* Take notes by an appropriate method: quotation, summary, or paraphrase

1 Note-taking by direct quotation

A direct quotation is a word-for-word reproduction of an original source. Quote often but briefly as you take notes. Remember that long quotations may be difficult to weave into a paper and difficult for readers to use. What to quote:

- *Key points.* Quote passages that sum up a key point in a condensed, emphatic way.
- *Expert opinions.* Quote sources when they offer an expert's opinion.

- *Powerful passages.* Quote dramatic, memorable, or well-known passages.
- *Subtle ideas.* Quote passages whose meaning may be lost in a summary.
- *Concise passages.* Quote passages whose meaning cannot be expressed in fewer words.

For a sample direct quotation note card, see 49d2. To quote effectively, you'll need to know how to use quotation marks (see 38a–d), commas and colons to introduce quotations (see 34g and 36a), brackets to insert editorial comments within a quotation (see 39c), and ellipsis points to signal omitted words (see 39d).

A note on quoting e-mail messages: If an e-mail message looks and functions like other quotations, correct any typographical errors. But if it observes the style of e-mail, quote exactly, including emoticons and e-mail abbreviations, punctuation meant to signal italics, all-capital words, and typographical errors. (See 48e5.)

2 Note-taking by summary

How to . . . Write a Summary

Follow these tips and guidelines to write effective summaries.

1. When you come to a passage you want to summarize, consider the surrounding sentences or paragraphs. Avoid taking information or opinions out of context; avoid distorting the author's purpose to suit your own.
2. Read the passage carefully and then look away to write your summary. In your own words and sentence style, present the author's main ideas and most important details. Usually omit examples, explanations, and statistics.
3. Compare your summary to the original to be sure that your words accurately and completely reflect the original.
4. Check to see whether you have quoted from the original. If you must quote single words or phrases from the original, enclose them in double quotation marks (see 38a and b).

A **summary** condenses an original in your own words, reducing a passage as short as a sentence or as long as a paragraph or a chapter to its central meaning and essential details. What to summarize:

- Background information
- Commentaries, explanations, and evaluations

- Arguments or a line of thinking
- Facts
- In literary works: description, events, episodes, and lengthy speeches or dialogue

Here is an original passage about the impact of pollution on national parks, followed by a note summarizing it.

> But scientists at Sequoia and other national parks are finding that forests, though enduring and resilient, are increasingly vulnerable to the influence of modern civilization. For example, plant and insect pests, often intro-duced by humans, have blighted and killed trees and forests in many parks, from conifers in California to palms in Biscayne Bay. Ozone, a common component of smog, is slowing tree growth at Virginia's Shenandoah Na-tional Park and along the Blue Ridge Parkway and threatens the health of conifers in Sequoia, Kings Canyon, and Yosemite National parks.
>
> (Steve Nash and Mike Spear, "Ghost Forest," p. 20)

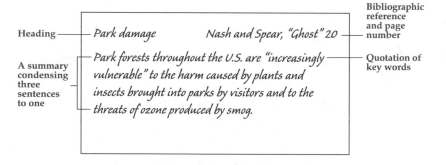

Heading ——— *Park damage*   *Nash and Spear, "Ghost" 20* ——— Bibliographic reference and page number

A summary condensing three sentences to one ——— *Park forests throughout the U.S. are "increasingly* ——— Quotation of key words
vulnerable" to the harm caused by plants and
insects brought into parks by visitors and to the
threats of ozone produced by smog.

3   Note-taking by paraphrase

A **paraphrase** restates a passage in your own words and phrasing. Usually about as long as the original, it includes examples and explana-tions from the original. Paraphrase what readers might otherwise misun-derstand. Avoid a word-for-word "translation" of the original into your words and phrases; that is plagiarism (see 50e). If you quote key words or phrases, enclose them in quotation marks. Here is an original passage about the role the land plays in the natural life cycle, followed by a note paraphrasing it.

> Land, then, is not merely soil; it is a fountain of energy flowing through a circuit of soils, plants, and animals. Food chains are the living channels which conduct energy upward; death and decay return it to the soil. The circuit is not closed; some energy is dissipated in decay, some is added by absorption from the air, some is stored in soils, peats, and long-lived

forests; but it is a sustained circuit, like a slowly augmented revolving fund of life.

(Aldo Leopold, *A Sand County Almanac*, p. 212)

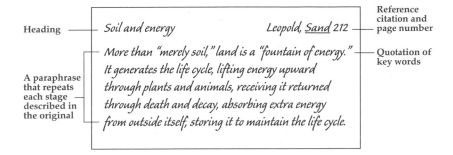

Heading — *Soil and energy*   *Leopold, Sand 212* — Reference citation and page number

A paraphrase that repeats each stage described in the original — *More than "merely soil," land is a "fountain of energy." It generates the life cycle, lifting energy upward through plants and animals, receiving it returned through death and decay, absorbing extra energy from outside itself, storing it to maintain the life cycle.* — Quotation of key words

50 Planning, Writing, Using Sources, and Revising

Planning and writing a research project are much like writing other kinds of papers. (See the guidelines to planning, writing, and revising in Chapters 3 and 4.) The following guidelines will give you tips for meeting the special challenges of research writing.

50*a* As you finish your research, take stock of it

Making planning notes

As you do research, your initial thoughts about your topic and paper will change. That's natural. You should expect to change your mind as the result of new information. To keep your thoughts straight and keep track of changing plans for your paper, write them down in planning notes. What should you write down?

- New ideas. Keep track of your new thinking as the result of research.
- New versions of key questions or statements of your problem.
- New versions of your thesis. Rewrite your thesis until it fits your research. Avoid overgeneral or incomplete thesis statements. *A report note:* If you're writing a formal report (see 61d), draw conclusions about the results of your research.
- Organizing plans. Write lists of ideas or brief sketch outlines to help you organize your research.

- Good lines. Write brief passages you might use to begin your paper, introduce parts, or explain key ideas.

Your aim is to write down as much as possible about your paper before you write it. The more you write now, the less you'll have to think of later as you write a draft.

50b | Plan a communications strategy

1 Organizing

One of the biggest challenges of a research paper is organizing all your materials to support your thesis or, if you're writing a report, to lead logically to your conclusion. Avoid organizing source by source, one after another. Your paper is about the point you want to make, not about your sources. Its design should support that point and reflect the logic of your thought. Here are organizing patterns traditionally used by researchers. See whether one is right for you.

- *Thesis support.* State your thesis early and then support it systematically, point by point.

- *Classical organizing patterns.* Arrange your ideas by *order of importance, classification, part by part (analysis), cause/effect,* or *comparison/contrast.*

- *Persuasion.* If you aim to persuade readers to change their beliefs or behavior, see the organizing patterns in 58a3.

- *Review of research.* If you're writing a survey of research, classify your sources into groups, explain their differing views, and then evaluate them to determine the most informative, insightful, and useful.

- *Problem/solution.* First describe the problem in detail; then pose a solution for it, if necessary explaining how the solution might be implemented.

- *Tracing a historical pattern.* Give necessary background information and then trace the unfolding of an event from one episode to the next. Be sure to show how one relates or leads to the next. Conclude by describing the consequences of the event.

- *Formal report.* For guidelines to organizing a formal report see 61d2. If your report will use in-text subject headings, see 46b.

A note on outlining: For a paper as complex as a research project, outlining is usually essential to discover an effective pattern of organization. (See 3c for guidelines.)

How to . . . Refocus Your Research Project

As you near the end of your research, write the following exercise to help yourself refocus your thinking and see your project more clearly.

1. I can now state my specific research topic as:
2. My key question or problem to be solved is now:
3. What I've discovered about my topic from my sources:
   a. What did I expect to find? What have I found instead?
   b. What are the controversies? Who agrees with whom?
   c. Which sources are the best? Why? What sources do I have left to check? (Reconsider the checklist in 47b4.)
4. My tentative thesis: "What I want to prove/explain/demonstrate/ show about [my topic] is that. . . . What I mean to say is that . . . " A report note: If you're writing a formal report, say: "My conclusion about [my topic] is that . . . "
5. I now have _____ days left to organize, write, and revise my paper.

2 Planning for readers

Focusing intently on their research, researchers sometimes lose sight of their audience, what their readers need to know, and what will interest them. (See 1c3.)

- *An introduction.* Many kinds of introductions are appropriate for research projects. (See 6c1.) Be sure that your topic and purpose are clear from the outset. Unless you have good reasons for doing otherwise, your opening should lead directly to your thesis, key question, or problem.

- *Illustrations.* Plan for examples and, if necessary, visual aids to explain or dramatize your ideas. (For more on visual aids, see 46b2–4.) Think of figurative language, especially analogies. (See 6b7 and 26c.)

- *Conclusions.* The following are appropriate ways to conclude research projects: warn about the need to act on your topic; pose solutions or make recommendations; show how your topic relates to some larger subject; identify a path that future researchers should take. (See 6d1 for other strategies.)

50c Blend source materials into your project

Your paper should weave other people's words and ideas so smoothly into your own that readers feel they are following one unbroken thread as they read. The following tips, based on the Modern Language Association style, will help you achieve this effect. (For tips to the American Psychological Association style, see 54a.)

1 Presenting borrowed material

Generally, presenting borrowed materials is a four-step process. With practice you'll learn to vary it in artful, interesting ways.

- Step 1: Use a signal statement. Whenever you quote, give another's opinions, or provide disputed information, write signal statements to introduce your borrowing. Use them to earn readers' acceptance of a source or to help readers understand or see the value of a source. To write a signal statement, do one or more of the following in an introductory phrase or sentence: identify the author or sponsor of the source; summarize the writer's credentials; give the title; announce the subject matter of the borrowing; provide its context; suggest the writer's purpose; evaluate the contents of the borrowing. Consider these sample signal statements:

Critic Mary Beth Pringle points out that . . .
[credentials, author, purpose]

Barry Herr, president of Bio-Systems International, assumes . . .
[author, credentials, purpose, and an implied evaluation]

The National Park Service has recently reported statistics on the alarming number of wild animals killed yearly by motorists on national parks roadways: . . .
[sponsoring source, purpose, subject matter, evaluation]

. . . warns Aldo Leopold in *A Sand County Almanac,* one of the most important documents of the environmental movement.
[purpose, author, title, evaluation]

To signal a writer's purpose accurately, choose from the following list of verbs. (See also 13b1.)

acknowledges	claims	emphasizes	objects	reports
adds	comments	endorses	observes	responds
admits	compares	explains	offers	reveals
advises	confirms	grants	opposes	says
agrees	considers	hints	points out	states
allows	contends	holds	presents	suggests
analyzes	criticizes	hopes	proposes	supports
answers	declares	illustrates	reasons	tells
argues	defines	implies	recognizes	thinks
asserts	denies	indicates	refutes	urges
assumes	describes	insists	regards	warns
believes	discusses	interprets	remarks	wonders
charges	disputes	notes	replies	

- Step 2: Present the quotation, summary, or paraphrase.

- Step 3: Document the borrowing. Provide enough information about the source to guide readers to complete publication information in the list of Works Cited or list of References at the end of your paper. (See MLA style, 52a and b; APA style, 54a and c; endnotes or footnotes, 55a; or the appropriate style manuals listed in 56b.)

- Step 4: Explain the borrowing. If readers may not understand the meaning or purpose of your borrowing, explain it. Don't assume readers will see what you do or get your message without assistance.

For example:

Signal phrase	The problems created by the popularity of U.S. national parks begin with the numbers themselves. As the nineteenth-century
Direct quotation	naturalist and author George Perkins Marsh warned, "Man is everywhere a disturbing agent. Wherever he plants his foot, the
Parenthetical documentation	harmonies of nature are turned to discords" (qtd. in Stegner 38). Each park has its own "carrying capacity" and can accommodate
Explanation	only so many visitors before their pleasures and the environment are adversely affected.

2 Taking credit for your ideas

Occasionally you'll have an idea about your topic and then find that a source has had a similar idea. To take credit for original thinking yet be fair to others, present your source's version of your idea, quoting if necessary, but also give your version, if necessary explaining how yours differs.

An idea that a writer shares with a source	Where overcrowding is most intense and harm to the environment greatest, officials should adopt the suggestion of former National Park Service director James M. Ridenour and adopt a
Citation of the source	reservations system for regulating entry ("Crocodiles" 71). This system need not be permanent or universal, nor operate throughout
The writer's version of the idea	the year. It would, however, permit the NPS to reduce the flow of visitors to the "carrying capacity" of individual parks and give harmed environments time to heal themselves.

3 Working with several sources at once

Occasionally, you will present several sources together.

- *Presenting one source at a time.* The standard procedure is to present your sources one at a time, documenting each as you borrow from it, as in the preceding examples.

- *Summarizing sources as a group.* A second method, useful when sources agree, is to summarize all of them at once, without mentioning names. After the summary, document them in one citation. But be aware that lengthy citations can be distracting.

> Throughout America's national parks, environmental damage from
>
> automobile air pollution is severe and well documented (McMahon 26; Coates,
>
> "Threat" 1; Craig 42).

- *Selecting a spokesperson.* A third method is to select a spokesperson to speak for all your sources. Document the person you quote or summarize.

> As many recognize, the great popularity of our national parks threatens, in
>
> James Coates's words, "to hit delicate natural resources particularly hard"
>
> ("Threat" 16).

4 Quoting briefly

Quote whenever you need a source's exact words. But be brief; use only the words you need. More may only mislead. Try to keep quotations to a sentence or less, punctuate them correctly, and connect them grammatically to your own words. (See 38b.) Here are two examples, the first quoting a phrase, the second a complete sentence.

> The cliff faces of many mountain parks are so covered by bolts drilled to make
>
> climbing routes that, according to Claire Martin, they are becoming the
>
> "equivalent of artificial climbing walls" (37).

> Most old growth forest has disappeared from the Northwest: "Less than one-
>
> fifth of the old growth that once covered the landscape of western Oregon
>
> and western Washington still stands" (Ervin 4).

A note on quoting excessively: Many people object to reading numerous quotations one after another, especially numerous long quotations. Such a pattern becomes monotonous. It may also suggest that you haven't thought carefully about the meaning of your borrowing or that you have failed to synthesize information to serve your purposes or support your thesis.

5 Using ellipsis points to signal omissions

Use three evenly spaced periods to signal the omission of words from a quotation. *A note on using brackets with ellipsis points:* The Modern Language Association requires that square brackets enclose ellipsis points inserted in quotations, as in the following example (see 39d).

- *The omission of less than a sentence.* Use ellipsis points for omissions within a sentence or at the end of a sentence. The remaining words must be grammatically complete. Do not use ellipsis points before or after fragmentary quotations or for an omission at the beginning of a sentence.

  Bruce Craig, a former park ranger, argues that "national parks [. . .] are not able to withstand the daily assaults of thousands upon thousands of visitors without experiencing change or degradation" (42).

  [The writer omitted the words *which preserve unique and delicate ecosystems and fragile historic treasures.* The remaining words make a grammatically complete statement.]

- *The omission of more than a sentence.* If you omit more than a full sentence, place a period before the three ellipsis points, as in the indented block quotation in 50d1.

6 Using brackets for insertions

Use typed or hand-drawn brackets (not parentheses) to insert your own words into a quotation to explain a reference or complete the grammar of the sentence (see 39c).

Nature writer Wallace Stegner believes that "recreation could be as dangerous [to wilderness areas] as logging or extractive use" (43).

50d Indent long quotations of prose and poetry

1 Indenting prose quotations

These are the Modern Language Association guidelines for long quotations. (For American Psychological Association guidelines, see 46d4.)

- *Length.* To make quotations longer than four typed lines easy to read, set them off in an indented block, separate from your words.
- *Introduction and punctuation.* Introduce the quotation in your own words. If your introduction is an independent clause that could be punctuated as a complete sentence, follow it with a colon. If it is a

signal statement such as *According to philosopher Susan Sontag,* follow it with a comma. If no grammatical break occurs between your words and the quotation, use no punctuation.

- *Indentation.* Indent 1 inch or 10 spaces from the left margin.
- *Quotation marks and spacing.* Do not enclose indented quotations with quotation marks. The block format signals word-for-word quotation. Double-space the quotation.
- *Paragraphing.* If you quote part of a paragraph or only one paragraph, do not indent the first line more than 1 inch or 10 spaces. To quote two or more paragraphs in block format, indent first line of each paragraph an additional quarter-inch or 3 spaces (a total of 13 spaces from the left margin). After a block quotation, begin a new paragraph of your own writing only if you change subjects.
- *Documentation.* One space after the punctuation ending the quotation, cite the source parenthetically. (For more on MLA in-text documentation, see 51b.)

The portrait of Thomas Gradgrind that Charles Dickens presents in <u>Hard Times</u> satirizes defects in the nineteenth-century philosophy of utilitarianism:

> Thomas Gradgrind, sir. A man of realities. A man of facts and calculations. A man who proceeds upon the principle that two and two are four, and nothing over, and who is not to be talked into allowing for anything over. [. . .] With a rule and a pair of scales, and multiplication tables always in his pocket, sir, ready to weigh and measure any parcel of human nature, and tell you exactly what it comes to. (2)

A note on omitted words: If you omit words from a quotation, signal the omission with ellipsis points. (See 39d.)

2 Indenting quotations of dialogue in fiction

If you quote dialogue between two or more speakers, use the indented format and follow the paragraphing of the original, even if you quote fewer than four typed lines. One space after the quotation, cite the source parenthetically (see 51b9).

3 Indenting quotations of dialogue in drama and film

If you quote dialogue between two or more speakers, use the indented quotation format. Indent 1 inch or 10 spaces from the left margin. Introduce each speaker by his or her name written in all capital letters followed by a period: *OTHELLO.* Use quotation marks only if they appear in the original. Indent subsequent lines in a character's speech an additional quarter-inch or 3 spaces. When a new character speaks, start a new line 1 inch or 10 spaces from the left margin. One space after the punctuation ending the quotation, cite the source parenthetically (see 51b9).

> As Iago incites him, Othello plots Desdemona's murder:
>
> > OTHELLO. Get me some poison, Iago, this night. I'll not expostulate
> >
> > with her, lest her body and beauty unprovide my mind again.
> >
> > This night, Iago!
> >
> > IAGO. Do it not with poison. Strangle her in bed, even the bed she
> >
> > hath contaminated. (4.1.200–04)

4 Indenting quotations of poetry

For quotations of more than three lines of poetry, use the indented quotation format.

- *Indentation.* Indent 1 inch or 10 spaces from the left margin. If the poem looks unbalanced on the page, indent it more or less as necessary.
- *Spacing and formatting.* Double-space the quotation and arrange the passage to look as much like the original as possible. If a quotation begins in the middle of a line, match the alignment in the original and do not shift the line to the left or right.
- *Line length.* If a long line of poetry would extend beyond the right margin, continue it on the next line, indenting an extra quarter-inch or 3 spaces.
- *Quotation marks.* Use quotation marks only if they appear in the original.
- *Line numbers.* Include line numbers in parentheses 1 space after the last line.
- *Omissions.* If you omit words or lines from a quotation, use ellipsis points. (See 39d.)

> William Blake's "The Tiger" questions the origins of that part of creation
>
> which is not innocent but not necessarily evil, either.
>
> > Tiger, Tiger, burning bright
> >
> > In the forests of the night,
> >
> > What immortal hand or eye
> >
> > Could frame thy fearful symmetry? (1–4)

A note on brief quotations: If you are quoting only two or three lines of poetry, incorporate them in your text, using a slash (/) to indicate the start of a new line (see 39e).

50*e* | Avoid plagiarism

When you use someone else's words or ideas or mention facts that are not common knowledge, you must credit your sources, first by giving in-text documentation and then by listing your sources in a Works Cited or Reference list at the end of your paper. Newspaper reporters and magazine journalists are not always required to document their sources of information, but in academic writing, you must acknowledge your sources.

Failure to document your borrowing is **plagiarism,** a form of theft and a serious breach of the researcher's code of ethics. Frequent, fair, and accurate documentation gives credibility and authority to your writing. (For the MLA style of documentation, see Chapters 51 and 52; for the APA style, see Chapter 54. For other styles, see Chapters 55 and 56.)

A note on recycled papers: Many instructors consider it unfair to resubmit in one course a paper that you previously submitted in another. Check with your instructor.

A note on collaborative writing: In school and on the job, writers are increasingly required to write collaboratively. This is especially true of work on electronic documents such as Web pages. Fairness, graciousness, and even policy statements require you to acknowledge the work of your collaborators and any other assistance you receive. You may do so in an acknowledgments page preceding the text of your writing or in a note at the end. In either case, acknowledge collaborators by name, identify their contributions, and thank them. (For an example of an acknowledgment, see the end of the Preface to this book, p. xi.)

1 Documenting common knowledge

Always document the sources of direct quotations, opinions, explanations, and interpretations. Facts and ideas are sometimes more difficult to handle. A fact or an idea is "common knowledge" if educated men and women could be expected to know it or if experts repeat it from one source to the next without documentation.

That Christopher Columbus first sailed to the Western Hemisphere in 1492 is a fact that requires no documentation. But what should a researcher do with the fact that automobile emissions are damaging vegetation in many U.S. national parks and forests? If many sources cite this development without documentation, it is common knowledge and need not be documented. However, if only one source presents it, the fact is original information and must be documented. When in doubt, document.

50e doc

A note on quoting or paraphrasing common knowledge: If you quote or paraphrase a writer's statement of common knowledge, you must document that.

2 Documenting quotations

Enclose direct quotations with quotation marks and document your borrowing.

- The original source:

  In Maine's Acadia National Park, needle rot on eastern white pines may be the result of acid fog and ozone pollution moving up the Eastern seaboard from the megalopolis to the south.

  (Steve Nash and Mike Spear, "Ghost Forest,"
National Parks, Mar.–Apr., 1991, p. 20)

- Plagiarism:

  In Maine, white pines are being killed by *acid fog and ozone pollution moving up the Eastern seaboard from the megalopolis to the south* (Nash and Spear 20).

  [Even though this example is documented, the writer has quoted half of the original without using quotation marks. Take care to prevent summaries from drifting into quotations without quotation marks.]

- Fair use:

  Steve Nash and Mike Spear declare that "in Maine's Acadia National Park, needle rot on eastern white pines may be the result of acid fog and ozone pollution moving up the Eastern seaboard from the megalopolis to the south" (20).

🖥 *Computer Tip:* Avoiding Internet Plagiarism

If you cut an excerpt from an Internet file and paste it into your paper, be sure to enclose it in double quotation marks (see 38a and b), introduce it with a signal statement (see 50c1), and document your borrowing at the end.

3 Documenting key words

Even if you take only one or two key words from a source, enclose them with quotation marks and document your borrowing.

- The original source:

  In short, a land ethic changes the role of *Homo sapiens* from conqueror of the land-community to plain member and citizen of it. It implies respect for his fellow-members, and also respect for the community as such.

  (Aldo Leopold, *A Sand County Almanac*, p. 204)

- Plagiarism:

  Americans must enlarge their concept of morality to include *a "land ethic"* to guide their relationship with the natural world.

  [Even though the borrowed words are enclosed in quotation marks, the writer has not documented the source.]

- Fair use:

  Americans must enlarge their concept of morality to include what naturalist Aldo Leopold calls a "land ethic" to guide their relationship with the natural world (204).

4 Documenting opinions

You must document an author's opinion or line of thinking. Writers have rights to their ideas as well as to their words.

- The original source:

  At the heart of the issue is the fact that the welfare of the national parks is inextricably linked to the lands around them.

  > (John Kenny, "Park Boundaries," *National Parks,* July–Aug., 1991, p. 22)

- Plagiarism:

  Unfortunately for U.S. national parks, they do not exist like islands in a sea, separate from urban America and its ecological threats. Their fate is shaped by the lands that surround them.

  [Although this passage is in the writer's own words and even imaginatively written, its ideas are based on those of the original source and must be documented.]

- Fair use:

  Unfortunately for U.S. national parks, they do not exist like islands in a sea, separate from urban America and its ecological threats. As John Kenny argues, their fate is shaped by the lands that surround them (22).

5 Documenting a paraphrase

To paraphrase effectively, restate the author's words and phrasing in your words and phrasing. Avoid the mere substitution of synonyms for the author's original.

- The original source:

  In the East, to "waste" water is to consume it needlessly or excessively. In the West, to waste water is not to consume it—to let it flow unimpeded and undiverted down rivers.

  > (Marc Reisner, *Cadillac Desert: The American West and Its Disappearing Water,* p. 16)

50e doc

- Plagiarism:

  Americans from the East say they "waste" their water when they consume it unnecessarily. In the West, however, water is wasted when it is not consumed but allowed to flow uninterrupted down rivers (Reisner 16).

  [The writer has documented the source of the original but has merely substituted synonyms for the original words and retained the original sentence structure.]

- Fair use:

  Americans define the "waste" of water in contradictory ways. To those in the East, waste means using water unnecessarily, while to those in the West, waste means leaving water in rivers, unused (Reisner 16).

How to . . . Revise and Edit a Research Project

Use the following questions to guide your revision and editing. Or ask peer reviewers to read your draft with these questions in mind and answer the most important. (For more on revision, see 4b and c.)

1. Does the paper's thesis appear somewhere in the introduction? Is it clear and complete? Does the introduction to a formal report describe a problem or pose a key question?
2. Does the paper include all the information, explanation, and interpretation needed to support its thesis or, in a formal report, to justify its conclusion? Will your support satisfy your readers' needs and interests?
3. Does the paper introduce and explain borrowed materials? Is the documentation complete and appropriate to the discipline in which the paper is written? Are all direct quotations enclosed by quotation marks?
4. Do the paper's ideas make sense and fit together logically and smoothly? Does the paper follow its outline? If it does not, which is more logically organized, the paper or the outline? Would another design improve the paper?
5. If the project uses subject headings, as in a report, are they formatted correctly? Do headings clearly identify the sections they introduce? (See 46b1.)
6. Is the language appropriate to research writing: accurate, precise, objective, and appropriately formal? (See 27a and c.) Is the style appropriate for the intended audience?
7. Does the paper include appropriately formatted drafts of a title page, outline page, acknowledgments, or abstract, if required? (See 46c for MLA format, 46d for APA format.) Has the writer prepared a Works Cited or Reference list? (See 52a to prepare an MLA Works Cited list, 54b to prepare an APA reference list.)

For a sample MLA research project with a title page and outline page, see Chapter 53.

PART **VIII.**

MLA
Documentation

MLA Documentation

VIII MLA

MLA Documentation

51 Writing MLA In-Text (Parenthetical) Citations

In papers for humanities courses, the preferred way to cite borrowed materials is the Modern Language Association (MLA) system of in-text citation. (For the American Psychological Association's author-date system, see Chapter 54. For footnotes or endnotes and a citation-sequence system, see Chapter 55 and 56a. For a list of style manuals used in various fields, see 56b.)

51a Follow MLA citation guidelines

As you write the first draft, document your borrowing at appropriate places in your paper.

- *In a signal statement.* Name your source in an introductory signal statement when you quote directly or borrow an explanation, opinion, interpretation, or disputed fact. Give the author's full name for first references and last name only thereafter. (See also 50c1.)

- *In a parenthetical citation.* In parentheses following your borrowing, provide enough information to guide readers to full publication information in the Works Cited list at the end of your paper. Give page numbers if your sources have them. Place the citation after the borrowing, following quotation marks, but before the period at the end of a sentence. *A note on indented quotations:* In block quotations, place the parenthetical reference 1 space after the last punctuation mark.

- *In the Works Cited list.* At the end of your paper, in a list titled "Works Cited," provide full publication or source information for each source you've used.

51b Follow parenthetical citation formats

The following guidelines will show you how to match signal statements with appropriate citation formats.

1 Naming an author in a signal statement

If you name an author in a signal statement and use only one source by that author, cite the page number of your borrowing in parentheses.

Ann J. Lane suggests that "The Yellow Wall-Paper" is the "most directly, obviously, self-consciously autobiographical" of all of Charlotte Perkins Gilman's short stories (16).

2 Naming a corporate author in a signal statement

Cite a corporate author as you would a person.

The Wilderness Preservation Society has proposed reservation systems to

regulate access at fourteen national parks (32).

3 Omitting the author name and signal statement

If you do not name the author in a signal statement and use only one source by that author, cite the author's last name and the page number in parentheses. No punctuation separates the author's name and the page number.

At the present time, vegetation at more than seventy national

parks is severely affected by automobile air pollution (McMahon 26).

4 Citing two or more sources by the same author

If your paper includes two or more sources by the same author, follow these guidelines for parenthetical citation.

■ *Author named in a signal statement.* If you name the author in a signal statement, give a short form of the title and the page number in parentheses. Enclose article titles in quotation marks; underline book titles.

Gene Rose has revealed that during 1991 the National Forest Service recorded

a net loss from timber sales in 69 of 120 forests ("Wood Cutting" 35).

■ *Author and title in a signal statement.* If a signal statement includes the author's name and the title of the source, give only the page number in parentheses.

In <u>A Sand County Almanac</u>, Aldo Leopold explains the necessity of a "land

ethic" to guide human relationships with the land (204).

■ *Author and title not named in a signal statement.* If you do not give the author or title in a signal statement, include both in the parenthetical citation, separated by a comma. Write brief titles in full; give shortened versions of longer titles.

In the Florida Everglades, picnickers have left behind the seeds of 221

nonnative species that are now driving out native species (Coates,

"Threat" 16).

5 Citing more than one author of a source

- If a source has two or three authors, name them in the signal statement or parenthetical citation.

  Campers who show up at national parks to claim the daily campsites may wait in line for hours (Adler and Glick 48).

- If a source has four or more authors, you may indicate multi-authorship in your signal statement (*Mary Peters and her colleagues reported . . .*) or give only the first author's name followed by *et al.* ("and others") in the parenthetical citation.

  Only recently have detailed proposals been made showing how to preserve spotted owl habitats without costing loggers their jobs (Peters et al. 48).

6 Citing an unknown author

If an author's name is not given in the source, use the complete title in a signal statement or the first key words in the parenthetical citation.

In Minnesota's Voyageurs National Park, snowmobilers have disturbed the habitat of the endangered gray wolf ("Shattering" 140).

7 Citing authors with the same last name

If you cite two or more authors with the same last name, include each author's first and last name in signal statements, or in parenthetical documentation include each author's first initial (full first name if the initial is shared, too) and last name.

Handsome park lodges entice visitors to such national parks as Mt. Rainier, Yellowstone, Bryce Canyon, and Grand Canyon (James Adams 19).

8 Citing a multivolume source

If you cite more than one volume of a multivolume source, give the volume number followed by a colon, 1 space, and the page number in the parenthetical citation.

Thoreau describes in his <u>Journals</u> how, in the natural world, humans "behave like oxen in a flower garden" (8: 110).

9 Citing literary works

Provide enough information in the parenthetical citation to enable readers to locate the material you are citing even if they use an edition different from yours. For **undivided** works such as short stories, include the page number in the parenthetical citation. For works **divided** into chapters, acts, and so forth, provide additional information.

- *Novels.* Parenthetically cite the page number in the edition you used, followed by a semicolon and the part, section, or chapter number.

   In <u>Light in August</u>, novelist William Faulkner traces the complex process by which his protagonist's childhood memories are transformed into knowledge and then belief: "Memory believes before knowing remembers" (104; ch. 6).

- *Poetry.* To cite poetry that is divided into books or other numbered sections, give the part and line numbers, as in this example from William Wordsworth's "Ode, Intimations of Immortality."

   Our birth is but a sleep and a forgetting:

   The Soul that rises with us, our life's Star,

       Hath had elsewhere its setting,

   And cometh from afar [. . .]. (5.59-62)

- *Plays.* Cite modern plays as you would a book, including page numbers. Cite verse and classic plays by act, scene, and line. Use Arabic numerals unless instructed otherwise.

   As Othello plots Desdemona's murder, he confesses her enduring power over him: "I'll not expostulate with her, lest her body and beauty unprovide my mind again" (4.1.200-01).

10 Citing an indirect source

If you quote a writer whose words appear in a source written by someone else, name the source you are quoting in a signal statement. Begin the parenthetical citation with *qtd. in* ("quoted in") and identify the source where you found the quotation.

   As historian Kenneth Clark has observed, "Nothing except love is so universally appealing as a view" of beautiful scenery (qtd. in McMahon 26).

11 Citing an entire work

To cite an entire work, give the author's name and the title, if necessary, in a signal statement or parenthetical citation.

Henry David Thoreau's <u>Walden</u> is the source of many of the attitudes

Americans hold about the value of wilderness.

12 Citing two or more sources in parentheses

When citing two or more sources in parentheses, separate the citations with a semicolon. Be aware, however, that multiple citations may be distracting. For other ways to document multiple sources, see 50c3.

Many who oppose restricting access to national parks profit economically from

that access (Coates, "Comfort" 14; Stapleton 34).

13 Citing an interview

To document an interview, name the source in a signal statement or parenthetical citation.

Raymond Marks, an official at Rocky Mountain National Park, reports that

visitors' most frequent complaints have to do with overcrowding.

14 Citing Internet sources

Cite Internet sources as you would print documents. Include enough information to direct readers to the appropriate citation in your Works Cited list. If an Internet source includes section headings, page numbers, or paragraph numbers, include them. (*Pars.* is the abbreviation for *paragraphs; chs.* for *chapters.*) Do not include page numbers from printouts because they may vary from one printout to another.

Tonnie G. Maniero, of the National Park Service, reports an alarming increase

in the death of national parks wildlife from heavy metal pollution ("Non-

acidic Particulates," pars. 2-3).

To cite Internet addresses in the text of your paper, see 48a5.

51c Include content and bibliography notes when necessary

Use notes in an MLA-style research paper only when you must provide additional information that cannot be worked into the text of your paper. Put raised, superscript numbers in your text to refer readers to a **footnote** at the bottom of the page or to an **endnote** on a page headed "Notes" immediately preceding the list of Works Cited. Number your notes consecutively throughout the paper. (For more on the use of notes, see Chapter 55.)

1 Writing content notes

Use content notes for definitions, formulas, explanations, and translations that would interrupt the flow of ideas if placed in the text of your paper.

- Text:

  In 1992, the 53 national parks received more than 58 million visitors, more than half, 35 million, visiting the 11 most popular parks.[1]

- Note:

  [1] The parks receiving the heaviest use were Great Smoky Mountains, 8.9 million visits; Grand Canyon, 4.1 million; Yosemite, 3.8 million; and Yellowstone, 3.1 million.

2 Writing bibliography notes

Use bibliography notes to cite several sources at once without a lengthy parenthetical citation, make cross-references, or refer readers to sources relevant to a topic.

- Text:

  Throughout America's national parks, environmental damage from automobile air pollution is severe and well documented.[3]

- Note:

  [3] For examples of this damage, see McMahon 26; Coates, "Threat" 1; "Haze" 95; "Tools" 14; and Craig 42.

Preparing the MLA Works Cited List

chapter 52

52a Follow MLA general guidelines

The list of Works Cited gives full publication information for all sources cited in an MLA-style research paper (see the example in Chapter 53). Your instructor may ask you to provide a works-consulted list that includes all the works you've read, whether you cite them parenthetically or not.

1 Placement of the Works Cited list

Begin the Works Cited list on a separate page at the end of your paper, after other concluding materials. (See 46c7 for the order of pages in an MLA paper.)

2 Works Cited–list format

- *Title.* Center the title "Works Cited" (without italics, underlining, or quotation marks) 1 inch from the top of the page. Continue page numbers from the text of your paper.
- *Spacing.* Double-space before the first entry and throughout all entries.
- *Indentation.* Begin each entry flush with the left margin. Indent second and successive lines one-half inch or 5 spaces.
- *Numbering.* Do not number the entries.
- *Alphabetical order.* Arrange entries alphabetically according to the author's last name as it appears on the title page of the sources you are borrowing from. Use square brackets to identify the true name when a pseudonym is given: *Mark Twain [Samuel Langhorne Clemens].* If an entry has no author, alphabetize according to the first word of the title, ignoring *A, An,* and *The.*

  McMahon, Edward T. "The Point of a View." <u>National Parks</u> Mar.-Apr. 1992:

      26-27.

  National Park Service Information Office (Rocky Mountain National Park).

      Telephone interview. 15 July 1993.

  "Parks Have Few Tools Against Air Pollution." <u>National Parks</u> July-Aug. 1992:

      14-15.

3 Citation formats

See 52b for sample MLA citations.

- *Two or more sources by the same author.* List two or more sources by the same author alphabetically by title. List the author's name for the first entry only. For the remaining entries, in place of the name type three hyphens followed by a period.

  Lane, Ann J., ed. <u>The Charlotte Perkins Gilman Reader: "The Yellow</u>

      <u>Wall-Paper" and Other Fiction</u>. New York: Pantheon, 1980.

---. Introduction. <u>Herland</u>. By Charlotte Perkins Gilman. New York:
Pantheon, 1979.

---. <u>To "Herland" and Beyond: The Life and Work of Charlotte Perkins Gilman</u>.
New York: Pantheon, 1990.

- *Punctuation of entries.* Place a period followed by 1 space after each part of a citation:

Author. Title. Publication information.

- *Publication dates.* For books, use the most recent publication date. For periodicals, abbreviate all months except May, June, and July.

- *Page numbers.* For inclusive page numbers, give only the last two digits unless more are necessary (e.g., *1–21, 88–93, 95–121, 141–61, 1198–213*). When a periodical or newspaper article is not printed on consecutive pages, give the first page number and a plus sign (e.g., *36+*).

- *Incomplete entries.* If an entry is incomplete, use the following abbreviations in the appropriate places: *n.p.* = no publisher given; *n.p.* = no place of publication; *n.d.* = no date of publication; *n. pag.* = no page numbers.

52*b* | Sample citations

1 Citing books

- The basic citation for a book

Author's last name, first name. Title and subtitle underlined or italicized. Place
of publication: Publisher, date of publication.

Shorten publisher names: Use the publisher's last name (e.g., *Knopf* for *Alfred Knopf*). Use the first last name if the publisher's name includes more than one person (e.g., *Farrar* for *Farrar, Straus and Giroux*). Or use the first key word (e.g., *Random* for *Random House*). Abbreviate *University Press* as *UP* (without periods).

- A book with one author

Tuchman, Barbara. <u>A Distant Mirror</u>. New York: Knopf, 1978.

- Two or three authors. List authors in the order in which they appear on the title page; reverse the name of only the first author. Use commas to separate three authors' names.

Fogel, Robert William, and G. R. Elton. <u>Which Road to the Past: Two Views of
History</u>. New Haven: Yale UP, 1983.

- Four or more authors. Cite all authors in the order in which they appear on the title page, or cite only the first author, followed by *et al.* ("and others").

  Frampton, Merle E., et al. <u>Forgotten Children</u>. Boston: Sargent, 1968.

- Corporate or institutional publication. Give the name of the corporation or institution as the author, even if it is also the publisher.

  American Friends Service Committee. <u>Who Shall Live?</u> New York: Hill, 1970.

- A book title within a title. If a book title appears within the title of another book, do not underline or italicize the shorter title. If the shorter title is normally enclosed with quotation marks, retain the quotation marks and underline the complete longer title.

  Golden, Catherine, ed. <u>The Captive Imagination: A Casebook on "The Yellow</u>

  <u>Wall-Paper."</u> New York: Feminist, 1992.

  Ruland, Richard, ed. <u>Twentieth Century Interpretations of</u> Walden. Englewood

  Cliffs: Prentice, 1968.

- An introduction, foreword, preface, or afterword. If you borrow from an introduction, foreword, preface, or afterword, begin with the author of the element being cited; then identify the element. Place the author of the book after the title.

  Duncan, Jeffrey L. Introduction. <u>Thoreau: The Major Essays</u>. By Henry David

  Thoreau. New York: Dutton, 1972.

- An author and an editor. Cite the author's name, the title, and then the editor. Use *Ed.* for one or more editors.

  Orwell, George. <u>1984</u>. Ed. Erich Fromm. New York: Harcourt, 1949.

- An editor or editors. Give the editor(s), followed by *ed.* or *eds.*

  Finch, Robert, and John Elder, eds. <u>The Norton Book of Nature Writing</u>. New

  York: Norton, 1990.

- An edition other than the first. Include the number of the edition after the title and after the name of the translator or editor (if any).

  Holman, C. Hugh, and William Harmon. <u>A Handbook to Literature</u>. 5th ed.

  New York: Macmillan, 1986.

- A republished edition. Give the original publication date before the place of publication.

  Roberts, Elizabeth Madox. <u>The Time of Man</u>. 1926. Lexington: UP of

  Kentucky, 1982.

- A book in a series. After the title, include the name of the series and series number.

  Howard, Lillie. <u>Zora Neale Hurston</u>. Twayne's United States Authors Ser. 381.

  Boston: Twayne, 1980.

- A translation. After the title, write *Trans.* ("translated by") and the name of the translator.

  Camus, Albert. <u>The Stranger</u>. Trans. Matthew Ward. New York: Knopf, 1988.

- A multivolume work. Give the number of volumes before the place of publication.

  Blotner, Joseph. <u>Faulkner: A Biography</u>. 2 vols. New York: Random, 1976.

- A volume in a series. If you borrow from only one volume of a multi-volume series, give its number and name the series to which it belongs (following *of*) before the place of publication. Give the total number of volumes following the date of publication.

  Durrell, Lawrence. <u>Mountolive</u>. New York: Dutton, 1959. Vol. 3 of <u>The</u>

  <u>Alexandria Quartet</u>. 4 vols. 1957-1960.

- A selection in an anthology. Give the author and title of the selection, followed by the title of the book, the editor's name, the edition if appropriate, and the publication information.

  Tolstoy, Leo. "The Three Hermits." <u>Short Shorts: An Anthology of the Shortest</u>

  <u>Stories</u>. Ed. Irving Howe and Ilana Wiener Howe. New York:

  Bantam, 1983. 3-10.

- A selection reprinted in an anthology. If a selection in an anthology was originally published elsewhere, cite the original source first. Follow with *Rpt. in* ("reprinted in") and a citation for the anthology. Original publication sources are usually listed on acknowledgment pages at the beginning or end of a book or at the bottom of the first page of a selection.

  Schorer, Mark. "With Grace under Pressure." <u>The New Republic</u> 6 Oct.

  1952: 19-20. Rpt. in <u>Ernest Hemingway: Critiques of Four Major Novels</u>.

  Ed. Carlos Baker. New York: Scribner's, 1962. 132-34.

- Cross-references to an anthology. If you cite more than one source from an anthology, provide full publication information for the anthology in its own citation. Cross-reference individual selections, giving author, title, editor's last name, and page numbers.

  Bone, Robert. "Ralph Ellison and the Uses of Imagination." Cooke 45-63.

Cooke, G. C., ed. <u>Modern Black Novelists</u>. Englewood Cliffs:

Prentice-Hall, 1971.

Tibble, Anne. "Chinua Achebe." Cooke 122-32.

- Anonymous or unknown author. Alphabetize the entry according to the first word of the title, ignoring *A, An,* or *The.*

<u>Sir Gawain and the Green Knight</u>. Ed. J. A. Burrow. Baltimore: Penguin, 1972.

- Encyclopedia or dictionary. Give the author (if any) of the entry, then the entry title, title of the encyclopedia or dictionary, edition number (if any), and the date.

"Mexico." <u>Encyclopedia Americana</u>. 1998 ed.

- Publisher's imprint. If a book was published by an imprint of a publishing company, give the name of the imprint followed by a hyphen and the publisher's name.

Selzer, Richard. <u>Mortal Lessons</u>. New York: Touchstone-Simon, 1976.

2 Citing periodicals and newspapers

- Article in a monthly magazine. Give the author's name, the title of the article enclosed by quotation marks, the name of the magazine underlined or italicized, the month and year of publication, and the page numbers on which the article appears. If the pages are not consecutive, cite the first page number followed by a plus sign (+).

McAuliffe, Kathleen. "The Undiscovered World of Thomas Edison." <u>Atlantic

Monthly</u> Dec. 1995: 80+.

- Article in a weekly magazine. Cite the full date of publication, not only the month.

Begley, Sharon. "The Puzzle of Genius." <u>Newsweek</u> 28 June 1993: 46-51.

- Article in a journal paged by volume. For scholarly journals paged consecutively throughout a volume, give the volume number after the name of the periodical and then the date in parentheses.

Rout, Kathleen. "Dream a Little Dream of Me: Mrs. May and the Bull in

Flannery O'Connor's 'Greenleaf.'" <u>Studies in Short Fiction</u> 16 (1979):

233-34.

- Article in a journal paged by issue. For scholarly journals paged separately by issue, give the issue number after the volume number.

Kasmer, Lisa. "Charlotte Perkins Gilman's 'The Yellow Wall-Paper': A

Symptomatic Reading." <u>Literature and Psychology</u> 46.3 (1990): 1-15.

- Signed newspaper article. Cite the author, title, name of the newspaper, and date of publication as you would an article in a weekly magazine. If an edition is given on the masthead of the paper, include it in your citation after the date. If each section of the paper is numbered separately, include the section number or letters before the page number.

  Coates, James. "Crowds Pose Threat to U.S. Park System." <u>Chicago Tribune</u> 21

  Apr. 1991, Chicagoland North, sec. 1: 1+.

- Unsigned magazine or newspaper article. If no author is given for an article, begin the citation with the title.

- Editorial. Identify the element by writing *Editorial* after the title.

  "Turning Nature On and Off." Editorial. <u>Los Angeles Times</u> 6 Sept. 1988,

  sec. 2: 6.

- Letter to the editor. Write *Letter* after the author's name.

  Stout, Michael. Letter. <u>Harper's</u> Feb. 1993: 5-6.

- Review of a book, movie, or play. After the author's name and title of the review, write *Rev. of* and then name the work reviewed. Give important information about the work reviewed such as the name of the author (preceded with *by*) or director (preceded with *dir.*).

  Rafferty, Terrence. "Fidelity and Infidelity." Rev. of <u>Sense and Sensibility</u>, dir.

  Ang Lee. <u>New Yorker</u> 18 Dec. 1995: 124-26.

3 Citing Internet sources

In a 1998 Internet posting, the Modern Language Association published a master template to guide students and scholars when citing Internet sources. As you prepare an MLA-style Works Cited list, include as many items from the following list as are relevant or can be found. The sample citations illustrate various applications of this template. For information about writing URLs, see 48a5. For tips to locating publication information in an Internet source, see 48c4. For more information about MLA Internet citations, see <http://www.mla.org/main_stl.htm> and the *MLA Sytle Manual and Guide to Scholarly Publishing,* 2nd ed. (MLA, 1998).

1. Author, editor, compiler, or translator of the source (last name first, followed by an abbreviation such as *ed.* or *trans.* when appropriate).
2. Title of article, short story, poem, or chapter (in quotation marks); or the title of a posting to a news group, listserv, or other discussion group (taken from the subject line and put in quotation marks), followed by the description *Online posting.*

3. Title of book or report (underlined).
4. Editor, compiler, or translator (if not cited earlier), preceded by an abbreviation such as *Ed.* or *Trans.* when appropriate.
5. Publication information for print versions of the source (arranged according to the guidelines in 52b1, 2, and 4).
6. Title of periodical, professional or personal site, database, or scholarly project (underlined); or for an untitled professional or personal site, a description such as *Home Page.*
7. Editor of the database or scholarly project (if available).
8. Volume number, issue number, or other identifying number for a journal; or the version number of a source when it is not part of the title.
9. Date of electronic publication, of the latest update, or of posting.
10. Name of the news group, listserv, or other discussion group.
11. The number range or total number of pages, paragraphs, sections, or chapters, if they are numbered.
12. Name of any institution or organization sponsoring or associated with the site.
13. Date when the researcher accessed the source. Do not use a period between items 13 and 14.
14. Electronic address (URL) of the source (in angle brackets, followed by a period). For guidelines to citing Internet addresses, see 48a5.

- A book or other lengthy document

Thoreau, Henry David. "Where I Lived and What I Lived For." <u>Walden</u>.

1854. <u>Project Gutenberg</u>. Jan. 1995. U of Illinois. 1 Sept. 1998

<ftp://uiarchive.cso.uius.edu/ pub/gutenberg/etext95/waldn10.txt>.

[This example includes the author, chapter title, title of the work, date of original publication, title of the scholarly project, date of electronic publication, organization sponsoring the site, date of access, and URL.]

<u>Reclaiming Our Heritage: What We Need to Do to Preserve America's National</u>

<u>Parks</u>. 1997. 5 chs. Natural Resources Defense Council. 31 July 1998

<http://www.nrdc.org/nrdc/nrdcpro/nrdcpro/roh/html>.

[This example includes the title of the work, publication date, total number of chapters, sponsoring organization, access date, and URL.]

- Articles in scholarly journals and magazines

Denman, Kamilla. "Emily Dickinson's Volcanic Punctuation." <u>Emily</u>

<u>Dickinson Journal</u> 2.1 (1993). 29 Jan. 1998. 33 pars. U of Colorado.

9 Sept. 1998 <http://www.colorado.edu/EDIS/journal/articles/

II.1.Denman.html>.

[This example from a scholarly journal includes the author, article title, print journal title, original publication date, latest Internet update, number of paragraphs, sponsoring organization, access date, and URL.]

Lawton, Millicent. "ETS Disputes Charges of Gender Bias." <u>Education Week</u>

14 May 1997: 1+. 3 June 1998 <http://www.edweek.org/we/vol-16/

33ets.h16>.

[This example from a magazine includes the author, article title, magazine title, print publication date, page number indicating nonconsecutive paging, access date, and URL.]

- Articles at professional, scholarly, business, and organizational sites

Connolly, Frank W. "Intellectual Honesty in the Era of Computing."

21 Oct. 1995. Loyola U of Chicago. 9 Aug. 1998

<http://www.luc.edu/infotech/sae/honesty.html>.

[This example includes the author, article title, latest revision date, organization sponsoring the site, access date, and URL.]

- Sources available through an online service like America Online

Gordon, Danielle. "The Usual Suspects." <u>Chicago Reporter</u> Sept. 1998:

88 pars. <u>Digital City Chicago</u>. America Online. 28 Sept. 1998

<http://chicagoreporter.com/09-98/0998main.htm>.

[This example includes the author, article title, title of periodical (underlined), date of publication, number of paragraphs, the name of the site (underlined), the name of the computer service, access date, and URL.]

- Professional, scholarly, business, or organizational site

<u>FairTest</u>. National Center for Fair and Open Testing. 1 July 1998. 30 Aug. 1998

<http://fairtest.org/>.

[This example includes the name of the site, the organization sponsoring the site, the date of last update, access date, and URL.]

- Newspaper articles

James, Frank. "U.S. Judges Reject Census Sampling." <u>Chicago Tribune</u>

25 Aug. 1998, sec. 1:1. 25 Aug. 1998 <http://chicagotribune.com/

news/nationworld/article/0,1051,ART-13624,00.html>.

[This example includes the author, article title, newspaper title, print publication information, access date, and URL.]

- Articles in a reference database such as an encyclopedia

"Jericho." <u>Encyclopedia of the Orient</u>. 1997. Centre d'Information Arabe

Scandinave. 4 Jan. 1998 <http://l-cias.com/e.o/jericho.htm>.

[This example includes the article title, title of the reference source, date of electronic publication, sponsoring organization, access date, and URL.]

- Posting to a newsgroup, listserv, or discussion forum (MOOs, MUDs, and IRCs)

> Doran, Brian T. "Re: Is Yellowstone Ever Closed to Overcrowding?" Online
>
> posting. 25 May 1997. The Total Yellowstone Chat Page. 31 July 1998
>
> <http://www.yellowstone-natl-park.com/wwwboard/messages/186.html>.

[This example includes the author, the title of the posting, the description of the posting, the posting date, the name of the forum, access date, and URL.]

- Literary works such as poems or short stories in a scholarly project or database

> Gilman, Charlotte Perkins. "The Yellow Wall-Paper." 1892. The "Yellow
>
> Wall-Paper" Site. Ed. Daniel Anderson and Nick Evans. 3 Sept. 1996.
>
> 1 May 1997 <http://www.cwrl.utexas.edu/~daniel/amlit/wallpaper/
>
> wallpapertext.html>.

[This example includes the author, the title of the short story, the original publication date, the name of the scholarly project, the editors of the project, the latest update, the access date, and URL.]

- Personal site

> Neumann, Kurt. Home Page. 27 Aug. 1998 <http://www.harper.cc.il.us/
>
> ~kneumann>.

- Electronic mail. To cite electronic mail, give the sender's name, a description of the document that includes the recipient, and the date of the document.

> Buss, Pauline. "Choosing a New Computer for Your Office." E-mail to Joseph
>
> Sternberg. 18 Jan. 1996.

4 Citing other electronic and print sources

- Periodical sources published on CD-ROM and also available in print. Many electronic sources are published at regular intervals, as magazines are, and also have print counterparts. For these, give the name of the author, if available; publication information for the printed source; the title of the database underlined; the publication medium (*CD-ROM*); the name of the vendor or distributor (if any); and the electronic publication date.

> Lacayo, Richard. "This Land Is Whose Land?" Time 23 Oct. 1995: 68-71.
>
> Academic ASAP. CD-ROM. Infotrac. Dec. 1995.

- Nonperiodical sources published on CD-ROM, diskette, and tape. Some CD-ROM sources and sources published on diskette or magnetic tape are issued only once, as books are. For these, give the author's name, if available; the title underlined or in quotation marks, as appropriate; the title of the product underlined; the edition, release, or version; the publication medium (*CD-ROM*); and the city of publication, publisher, and date of publication.

  "Grand Canyon National Park." Grolier Multimedia Encyclopedia. 1997 ed.

    CD-ROM. Danbury: Grolier Interactive 1997.

- Pamphlet. Cite a pamphlet as you would a book.

  Schubert, John. The Tandem Scoop: An Insider's Guide to Tandem Cycling.

    Eugene: Burley Design Coop., 1993.

- Government publications. The formats for government publications are many and varied. The order of an entry is as follows:

  Government body. Subsidiary body. Title of Document. Type and number of

    document. Publication information.

  If you know the author's name, place it at the beginning of an entry or after the title, following the word *By.*

  President's Commission on the Assassination of President Kennedy. Hearings

    before the President's Commission on the Assassination of President

    Kennedy. 26 vols. Washington: GPO, 1964.

  United States. Cong. House. Subcommittee on Science, Research, and

    Technology. Genetic Engineering, Human Genetics and Cell Biology.

    96th Cong., 2nd sess. Washington: GPO, 1980.

- Legal references. Do not italicize or underline the titles of laws, acts, or legal documents or enclose them with quotation marks; give the section and, if appropriate, the year. Italicize or underline the name of cases in the text of your paper but not in the list of Works Cited.

  Brown v. Board of Ed. 347 US 483. US Sup. Ct. 1954.

  US Const. Art. 2, sec 2.

- Published dissertation. Give the author and title as you would for a book, followed by the abbreviation *Diss.,* the university granting the degree, the date it was granted, the publisher, and date of publication. If the dissertation was published by University Microfilms, add the order number at the end of the citation.

  Smith-Hawkins, Elaine Yvonne. Ideals and Imagination in the Novels of Willa

    Cather. Diss. Stanford U, 1984. Ann Arbor: UMI, 1985. 8408359.

- **A dissertation abstract.** Give the author's name followed by the dissertation title in quotation marks, the abbreviation *Diss.*, the name of the university granting the degree, the date granted, the abbreviation *DA* or *DAI* (*Dissertation Abstracts* or *Dissertation Abstracts International*) as appropriate, the volume number, date of publication, and page number.

   DiPierro, Marianne Elizabeth. "The Utopian Vision in the Works of

   Wollstonecraft, Gilman, and Chopin." Diss. U of South Florida, 1994.

   DAI 54 (1994): 3737A.

- **Published proceedings of a conference.** Cite a selection from the published proceedings of a conference as you would cite a book. After the title of the publication, give information about the conference. Then give the editor's name if available, followed by the publication information.

   Peden, Margaret Sayers. "The Arduous Journey." The Teller and the Tale:

   Aspects of the Short Story. Proc. of the Thirteenth Comparative

   Literature Symposium, 23-25 Jan. 1980, Texas Tech U. Ed. Wendell M.

   Aycock. Lubbock: Texas Tech U, 1982. 63-86.

- **Lecture or speech.** Name the person making the speech, then the speech title in quotation marks, the name of the conference or sponsoring organization, the location, and date. If some of this information is not available, provide as much as possible.

   Fleenor, Juliann E. "Illinois Women: Quilt-Making--History-Making." Illinois,

   Beginning with Women . . . Histories and Cultures [Conference]. Urbana-

   Champaign. 26 Mar. 1993.

- **Interview.** To cite an interview that you conducted, name the person interviewed followed by *Personal interview* or *Telephone interview* and the date. To cite a radio or television interview, name the person interviewed followed by *Interview* or *Interview with* and the name of the interviewer.

   O'Connell, Edward J. Personal interview. 4 May 1993.

   Oates, Joyce Carol. Interview with Terry Gross. Fresh Air. Natl. Public Radio.

   WHYY, Philadelphia. 3 Aug. 1993.

   Paz, Octavio. Interview. Paris Review Interviews: Writers at Work. Ed. George

   Plimpton. 9th ser. New York: Viking, 1992. 81-108.

- **Personal letter.** Cite a letter addressed to you as follows.

   Linville, Troy M. Letter to the author. 4 June 1993.

- Radio or television program. When appropriate, identify those involved with the production preceded by these abbreviations: *Narr.*
  (narrator), *Writ.* (writer), *Dir.* (director), *Perf.* (performer), *Introd.* (in-
  troducer), *Prod.* (producer).

  "Hunger in America." CBS Reports. Narr. Charles Kuralt. Writ. Peter Davis.

  Prod. Martin Carr. WBBM, Chicago. 21 May 1968.

- Play performance. Give the title underlined, followed with *By* and the
  author's name, *Dir.* and the director's name, *Perf.* and the leading
  actor's name.

  The Tempest. By William Shakespeare. Dir. George C. Wolfe. Perf. Patrick

  Stewart. Broadhurst Theatre, New York. 24 Dec. 1995.

- Film or video recording

  Shall We Dance. Dir. Edward Everett Horton. Perf. Fred Astaire and Ginger

  Rogers. 1937. Videocassette. RKO Radio Pictures, 1987.

- Musical composition

  Mendelssohn, Felix. Symphony no. 4 in A Major, op. 90.

  Tchaikovsky, Peter. The Nutcracker Suite.

- Record, tape, or CD

  Ellington, Duke. "Harlem Airshaft." The Duke Ellington Carnegie Hall

  Concerts. Rec. 26 Dec. 1947. LP. Prestige, 1977.

- A work of art

  Hopper, Edward. Railroad Sunset. Whitney Museum of American Art,

  New York.

- Map or chart

  Mt. Rainier NP, Washington. Map. Reston: Dept. of the Interior, US Geological

  Survey, 1975.

- Cartoon. Give the cartoonist's name, then the name of the cartoon or
  its caption (if any), the label *Cartoon,* and appropriate publication
  information.

  Ziegler, Jack. "The Artist Who Wakes Refreshed." Cartoon. New Yorker

  25 Dec. 1995: 106.

MLA Research Project with Title and Outline Pages

The writer of the following problem/solution project was instructed to include title and outline pages. The paper follows MLA guidelines for parenthetical in-text documentation and the Works Cited list given in Chapters 51 and 52. Marginal notes indicate important features of research projects and MLA documentation. For an MLA paper without a title page or an outline page, see 4f.

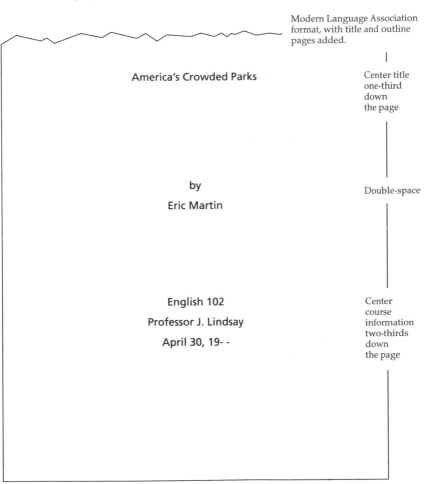

Modern Language Association format, with title and outline pages added.

America's Crowded Parks

Center title one-third down the page

by

Eric Martin

Double-space

English 102

Professor J. Lindsay

April 30, 19- -

Center course information two-thirds down the page

Outline

Thesis: At US national parks where overcrowding and harm to the environment are greatest, officials should adopt a reservation system to control park use and aid environmental recovery.

I. The popularity of US national parks is increasing.

II. Popularity has led to problems of overcrowding.

    A. Overcrowding causes problems for visitors.

        1. Visitors experience delays and inconveniences.

        2. Visitors are unable to enjoy the views.

    B. Overcrowding harms national park environments.

        1. Indirect harm: automobile air pollution damages vegetation.

        2. Direct harm: visitors cause erosion and pollution, deface natural sites, and disrupt ecosystems.

    C. Park Service budget cuts will increase the problems of overcrowding.

III. A reservation system is one obvious solution.

    A. A reservation system at the most threatened parks would reduce overcrowding.

    B. Opposing arguments are flawed.

        1. A reservation system is democratic, not elitist.

        2. Free access does not mean use without restrictions.

        3. Opponents make a faulty comparison of public lands and private property.

    C. A reservation system is an effective method to meet the threats to US national parks.

Use lower-case Roman numerals for preliminary pages.

Center heading 1 inch from top of page

Double-space throughout.

For guidelines on formal outlines, see 3c.

America's Crowded National Parks

As historian Kenneth Clark has observed, "Nothing except love is so universally appealing as a view" (qtd. in McMahon 26). And the views Americans seem to love most are views of the forests, mountains, and waters of the US national parks. In 1996, over 276 million people--a number equal to the total population of the United States--visited the more than 360 parks, monuments, and historic sites administered by the Park Service (<u>Reclaiming,</u> ch. 3). More than 58 million visited the 53 national parks alone, more than half, 35 million, visiting the 11 most popular parks. Each year, the Great Smoky Mountains and Grand Canyon are visited by the combined population equivalents of New York, Los Angeles, and Chicago (United States 2).

Title centered, double-spaced, if necessary, and typed 1 inch from top of page

Introduction: a dramatic quotation cited from an indirect source

Part I: Essential information about the topic

	1980	1984	1988	1992	1996
300 mil.					
275 mil.					
250 mil.					
225 mil.					
200 mil.					
175 mil.					
150 mil.					
125 mil.					
100 mil.					
75 mil.					
50 mil.					

Fig. 1. Annual visits to National Park Service sites, from "Funding Record: More Demand, Less Money," <u>Reclaiming Our Heritage,</u> 1997, 5 chs., Natural Resources Defense Council, 31 July 1998 <http://www.nrdc.org/nrdc/nrdcpro/nrdcpro/roh/ch3.html>.

Martin 2

These figures have increased nearly every year during the more than eighty years of the National Park Service (NPS) and will only continue to increase. By the year 2010, annual park visits are projected to reach 90 million (National). If these nature lovers were religious pilgrims, their journeys would constitute one of the great pilgrimages in human history.

The problem of such devotion begins with the numbers themselves. As the nineteenth-century naturalist and author George Perkins Marsh warned, "Man is everywhere a disturbing agent. Wherever he plants his foot, the harmonies of nature are turned to discords" (qtd. in Stegner 38). Each park has its own "carrying capacity" and can accommodate only so many visitors before their pleasure and the environment are adversely affected. Such is often the case at many of the most popular parks, which receive the most destructive use.

For visitors to these parks, overcrowding means just that, crowds of people instead of nature views. At Yosemite, the roads are filled with traffic. At Bryce Canyon, lines of sightseers along the canyon rim block other visitors' views. At Grand Canyon, 70,000 hikers annually trek down its steep sides, and its skies are filled with 400,000 who take airplane or helicopter overflights (Coates, "Creature" 1). In 1993, 90,000 mountain bikers rode the Slickrock Trail outside Moab, Utah, and in northern Minnesota's Boundary Waters canoe area, "the most popular lakes [. . .] resemble Walden Pond less than a summer camp in the Poconos, with a steady stream of paddlers never out of sight of one another." Those who show up at national parks to claim the daily campsites may wait in line for hours (Adler and Glick 48). Instead of what former park ranger Bruce Craig calls the "national park experience" (43), what too many visitors

Writer's name and the page number typed one-half inch from top of each page

Part I: Essential information about the topic

Part IIA: An expert source's warrant (see 57b2) introducing the first half of the thesis: the claim for an argument

Double-spacing throughout

Ellipsis points signaling the omission of part of a sentence

Citation of a source by two authors

experience, as Secretary of the Interior Bruce Babbitt has lamented, is "a bit like Times Square" ("Government").

A more distressing problem is the harm such numbers of visitors cause to the natural environment. As nature writer, poet, and novelist Wallace Stegner speculates, "Recreation could be as dangerous [to natural areas] as logging or extractive use" (43). Bruce Craig agrees: "National parks, which preserve unique and delicate ecosystems and fragile historic treasures, are not able to withstand the daily assaults of thousands upon thousands of visitors without experiencing change or degradation" (42).

The greatest danger is air pollution, caused in large measure by the vehicles that bring visitors into the wilds. Nearly seventy national parks and wilderness areas are affected (McMahon 26). At Acadia National Park and in Yosemite, air quality is so poor that the parks receive the same pollution warnings as Denver and Los Angeles (Coates, "Crowds" 1). Visitors to Tennessee's Great Smoky Mountains see smog instead of the views; visitors to many other parks see the gray skeletons of trees killed by ozone (Reclaiming, ch. 2).

Visitors also cause more direct harm. Hikers, horses, and mountain bikers are eroding trails and causing endangered species of raptors to abandon their nests (Martin 37). No matter how far one hikes into the Rocky Mountain National Park backcountry, rivers and streams are infested with giardiasis bacteria, largely produced by human waste (National). In Yellowstone each year, motorists kill hundreds of large park animals, including antelope, bighorn sheep, bison, bear, elk, and moose ("Hit"). The cliff faces of many parks are so covered by bolts drilled to make climbing routes that, according to Claire Martin, they are becoming "the equivalent of artificial climbing

Signal phrase citing an author and his credentials

Transition to Part IIB: Harm to the environment

Brackets used to insert an explanation within a quotation

Topic sentence

Examples supporting the thesis

An author named in the citation because he is not mentioned in the signal phrase

An Internet source without page numbers

Topic sentence

Martin 4

walls." Climbers have severely damaged park archaeological sites
in Texas, Arizona, Colorado, and Utah (37). In Death Valley, off-
road vehicles are destroying the habitat of the endangered desert
tortoise (Heacox 75). At high-altitude parks like Rocky Mountain,
the feeding of no-longer-wild animals has contributed to the
destruction of delicate Alpine vegetation, whose seeds are no
longer spread by these animals (Coates, "Threat" 16). In place
of natural vegetation grow noxious weeds and grasses, their
seeds deposited in the manure of passing horses (National). In
Florida, visiting picnickers have left behind the seeds of 221
nonnative species that now grow in the park (Coates, "Threat"
16). And in Minnesota's Voyageurs National Park, snowmobilers
have disrupted the habitat of the endangered gray wolf
("Shattering" 140).

Citation of an author who provides more than one source for this paper

Unfortunately, these conditions will only worsen. In
constant dollars, the NPS budget has fallen $635 million from
1978 to 1996 (Reclaiming, ch. 3). At the same time, to handle
the growing numbers of visitors, NPS spending has had to stress
visitor services over science, preservation, and maintenance.
The result is a $5.6 billion backlog of capital construction
needs, a figure that includes no money for natural resource
protection (Reclaiming, ch. 2). And while NPS funds have been
declining, overall spending on the environment has also declined
from 3% of the federal budget in 1980 to 1.9% in 1988 and 1%
currently (Craig 43). What money remains to the National Park
Service is obviously not enough to provide adequate services,
programs, and maintenance.

—Part IIC: Budget cuts

What should be done? The first nonnative American
visitors journeyed to what would become our nation's natural
monuments attracted by their wonders and beauties (Stegner 40).

Transition to Part III: The solution

In 1916, the National Park Act set aside these "pleasuring grounds" for contemporary visitors and "to conserve the natural and historic subjects in such manner as will leave them unimpaired for the enjoyment of future generations" (qtd. in Stegner 40). But many of America's national parks have been so severely damaged and the funds to repair the damage are so few that the promise of the National Parks Act is being broken. Many reforms are needed to rescue our parks from the excess of adoration they have received. But one reform would specifically meet the problem of overcrowding: where overcrowding and harm to the environment are greatest, officials should adopt the proposal of the Natural Resources Defense Council and institute a reservation system for regulating park access (Reclaiming, ch. 4). Such a system need not be permanent or universal, nor operate throughout the year. It would, however, allow officials to reduce the flow of visitors to the "carrying capacity" of individual parks and give harmed environments time to heal themselves.

Opponents argue that such a system is "elitist environmentalism" and that government lands belong to all tax-paying Americans. But such arguments spring from opponents like former Tucson mayor Don Hummel, a national park hotel operator, and others who benefit economically from unrestricted access to federal lands and their natural resources (Coates, "Creature" 14). What they do not admit is that the environments providing them with profits are being destroyed by their actions, that a reservations system is the simplest method for preventing damage to the parks, and that it is a democratic system applying equally to all, first come, first served.

A warrant (a federal law) that requires action to solve the problem

Part IIIA: The second half of the writer's thesis: a claim proposing action

Part IIIB: A rebuttal of opposing arguments: opponents' self-interest and the negative consequences of their actions

Freedom involves responsibilities. It is time for Americans to take what Aldo Leopold, one of the founders of the modern environmental movement, calls the next step in "ecological evolution," an "extension of ethics" into the human relationship with the natural world. As he explains in <u>A Sand County Almanac</u>, what is needed is a "land ethic":

> An ethic, ecologically, is a limitation on freedom of action in the struggle for existence. An ethic, philosophically, is a differentiation of social from anti-social conduct. These are two definitions of one thing. [. . .] A land ethic changes the role of <u>Homo sapiens</u> from conqueror of the land-community to plain member and citizen of it. It implies respect for his fellow-members, and also respect for the community as such. (202-04)

A national parks reservation system, limiting admission to environmentally threatened parks, pays respect to the land and to our membership in the community of nature. It is a gesture of cooperation and an ethical act that meets the "use without impairment" requirements of the National Parks Act.

Opponents of a reservation system have fallen into the fallacy of faulty analogy in a flawed comparison of national park lands to private property. They reason that just as private land owners pay property taxes and enjoy rights to their property, paying federal taxes gives them the right to use government lands as they wish. But the payment of property taxes does not convey land rights or ownership to taxpayers. And private land owners are bound by zoning laws restricting the uses they make of their property. Americans pay a portion of their taxes to preserve and maintain parks, not as the purchase price of

Margin notes:

A second rebuttal of opposing arguments: an expert opinion

A block quotation stating a warrant

A period followed by ellipsis points signaling the omission of a sentence or more

Documentation of a block quotation following the final punctuation

An explanation showing how the quotation supports the thesis

A third rebuttal of opposing arguments: explaining an error in reasoning

Martin 7

ownership but as a duty of citizenship. A parks reservation system is equivalent to a zoning regulation established for the common good.

In a time of crisis, such as during World War II, Americans have accepted rationing as a way to meet that crisis. Our national parks are in crisis. If a reservation system--entry rationing--were presented as a way to meet such a crisis, park visitors would accept it, especially when they understood the benefits they would receive from the reduced numbers of visitors. Fairly applied to all users of the most severely threatened parks, it would lighten the burdens on these parks, maintain and preserve the environment, and ensure that the pleasures of natural beauty that brought the first visitors long ago would remain to be enjoyed by new visitors when it was their time to visit.

Part IIIC: Conclusion, the benefits of adopting the writer's proposal

Martin 8

Works Cited

Adler, Jerry, and Daniel Glick. "No Room, No Rest." Newsweek
    1 Aug. 1994: 46-51.

Coates, James. "Creature Comforts Taking Toll on Park
    Wilderness." Chicago Tribune 22 Apr. 1991, sec. 1: 1+.

- - -. "Crowds Pose Threat to U.S. Park System." Chicago Tribune
    21 Apr. 1991, sec. 1: 1+.

Craig, Bruce. "Diamonds and Rust." National Parks May-June
    1991: 41-44.

"Government Plans to Ban Most Cars from Major National
    Parks." Hannibal Courier-Post 28 Nov. 1997. 30 July
    1998 <http://www.courierpost.com/stories/112897/
    yosemite.html>.

Heacox, Kim. "A Poet, a Painter, and the Lonesome Triangle."
    Audubon May 1990: 66-78.

"Hit Your Brakes, Not the Bison." Yellowstone Today Summer
    1998. Rpt. in Yellowstone Net Newspaper 5 June 1998.
    25 July 1998 <http://www.yellowstone.net/newspaper/
    news/060598.htm>.

Leopold, Aldo. A Sand County Almanac and Sketches Here and
    There. 1949. New York: Oxford UP, 1987.

Martin, Claire. "Set in Stone." National Parks Nov.-Dec. 1990: 37-38.

McMahon, Edward T. "The Point of a View." National Parks
    Mar.-Apr. 1992: 26-27.

National Park Service Information Office (Rocky Mountain
    National Park). Telephone interview. 15 July 1998.

Reclaiming Our Heritage: What We Need to Do to Preserve
    America's National Parks. 1997. 5 chs. Natural Resources
    Defense Council. 31 July 1998 <http://www.nrdc.org/
    nrdc/nrdcpro/nrdcpro/roh/html>.

"Shattering the Snowy Silence." Sierra Jan.-Feb. 1991:
    139-40.

Title centered 1 inch from top of page

A source with two authors

Two sources by the same author: alphabetical arrangement, double-spacing throughout

First lines flush left, second and successive lines indented 5 spaces.

An Internet source with no author given

An Internet source re-published from a print source

A citation of a book

A citation of an interview

An Internet source published by a professional organization

Martin 9

Stegner, Wallace. "It All Began with Conservation." <u>Smithsonian</u>
Apr. 1990: 34-43.

United States. Dept. of Interior. National Park Service Socio-
Economic Studies Division. <u>National Park Service Statistical</u>
<u>Abstract</u>. Denver: US Dept. of Interior, 1993.

PART **IX.**

APA and Other Documentation Styles

APA Documentation

Other Styles

APA Documentation

54 Using the APA In-Text Citation Style

The American Psychological Association (APA) recommends an author-date style of documentation for papers written in the social sciences. This style is also used in anthropology, the biological sciences, business, economics, education, linguistics, and political science.

54a | Follow APA citation guidelines

1 Citing a summary or paraphrase

To summarize or paraphrase a source, use a signal statement containing the author's last name followed by the publication date in parentheses, or give the last author's name and the date in parentheses at the end of the borrowed material, preceding the period. Use the past tense with signal verbs: *explained, reported,* and *argued* (see 13b1).

- *Author and date preceding the borrowing:*

Sanchez (1993) reported that students from small, often rural schools do not fare as well on standardized tests as students from urban areas with large economic bases.

- *Author and date in parentheses following the borrowing.* Use a comma between items in parentheses.

Students from small, often rural schools do not fare as well on standardized tests as students from urban areas with large economic bases (Sanchez, 1993).

2 Citing a quotation or specific reference

To quote directly or refer to a specific part of a source, include page numbers in the parenthetical citation, preceded by *p.* or *pp.* ("page" or "pages").

In its statistical sense used in standardized testing, bias refers to "constant or systematic error as opposed to chance errors" (Anastasi, 1988, p. 194).

3 Citing authors' names

- *A source by one author.* Follow the examples given in 54a1 and 2.

- *A source by two authors.* For a source by two authors, give both last names in all signal statements and parenthetical citations. In parentheses, join the two authors' names with an ampersand (&).

  Aptitude tests have assisted "students who vary in significant respects from the traditionally academically successful students" (Tyler & Wolf, 1974, p. 47).

- *A source by three to five authors.* For a source with three to five authors, give all last names in the first signal statement or parenthetical citation.

  Elder, Lopez, Smith, and Breen (1993) have systematically documented the social bias in standardized tests.

  In later citations, give the last name of the first author, followed by *et al.* ("and others").

  Elder et al. (1993) have proposed greater minority involvement in the design of standardized tests.

- *A source by six or more authors.* When a work has six or more authors, give the last name of the first author followed by *et al.* in signal statements and parenthetical citations.

- *Corporate authors.* Generally, spell out corporate names. Always spell out all corporate names in the reference list at the end of your paper. If a corporate name has a well-known abbreviation, spell out the name in the first citation and abbreviate thereafter:

  First citation: (National Educational Association [NEA], 1982)
  Subsequent citations: (NEA, 1982)

- *Unknown author.* When the author of a work is not identified in the source, use the complete title in a signal statement or the first few words of the title in a parenthetical citation.

  Standardized testing puts students from rural, often poor areas at a great disadvantage ("Opportunity for All," 1995).

- *Two or more sources in parentheses.* To cite two or more sources in parentheses, put the citations in the order in which they appear in the list of references at the end of the paper. Separate them with semicolons.

  (Anastasi, 1988; "Test Bias," 43; Tyler & Wolfe, 1974)

  If two or more sources are by the same author, give the author's last name once followed by the dates of publication in chronological order.

  (Anastasi, 1988, 1991)

- *Authors with the same last name.* When two or more authors have the same last name, include initials in all signal statements and parenthetical citations:

  (G. B. Dukes, 1991)

  (L. K. Dukes, 1989)

- *Personal communication.* To cite personal communication such as a letter or e-mail, give the author's initial(s) and last name, followed by the words *personal communication* and the date.

  W. Hine (personal communication, October 8, 1998) has proposed three

  reforms for standardized tests.

54b | Prepare the APA reference list

The reference list gives full publication information for all sources cited in a research paper. See the sample citations in 54c and the complete reference list at the end of the sample research project in 54d.

1 Placement of the reference list

Begin the reference list on a separate page at the end of your paper.

2 Reference list format

- *Title.* Center the title "References" (without italics, underlining, or quotation marks) at the top of the page. Continue page numbers from the text of your paper.
- *Spacing.* Double-space throughout, unless instructed to single-space within entries.
- *Indentation.* Begin each entry flush with the left margin. Indent second and successive lines up to one-half inch or from 3 to 5 spaces. In projects sent to APA journals for publication, first lines are indented and successive lines typed flush left. If you are uncertain which format to use, ask your instructor. (For more on indentation see the APA *Publication Manual,* 4th ed., pp. 251 and 331–32.)
- *Alphabetical order.* Arrange entries in alphabetical order according to the last names of first authors or corporate names. If the author is not given, alphabetize by the first word of the title, ignoring *A, An,* and *The.*
- *Two or more works by one author.* If you use two or more works by the same author, arrange them by date of publication, with the earliest first.

3 Citation formats

- *Author names.* Invert the names of all authors: write the last name first, followed by a comma and the person's initials, separated by 1 space. When there are two or more authors, use an ampersand (*&*) instead of *and*. Separate three or more names with commas. Write the names of all authors; do not use *et al.*

- *Date of publication.* Put the date of publication in parentheses after the author's name.

- *Punctuation.* Space once after punctuation within an entry. Underline periods and commas following the titles of books, the names of periodicals, and volume numbers.

- *Capitalization.* Capitalize the names of periodicals as you would ordinarily. Capitalize only the first word of article and book titles, the first word of a subtitle (if any) usually following a colon, and proper nouns.

  Journal: <u>Journal of Personality and Social Psychology</u>

  Article: Pollution damage in America's national forests

  Book: <u>National park environments: An ecological guide</u>

- *Quotation marks and underlining.* Do not enclose article titles in quotation marks. Underline book titles and the names of periodicals. Underline the volume number of periodicals.

- *Abbreviations.* Use standard bibliographic abbreviations when appropriate: *chap.* (chapter), *Ed.* (editor), *ed.* (edition), *n.d.* (no date), *p.* or *pp.* (page or pages), *Rev. ed.* (revised edition), *Trans.* (translator), *Vol.* (a single volume), *Vols.* (a number of volumes), *No.* (number).

- *Publisher names.* You may shorten publisher names, so long as they remain recognizable.

- *Page numbers.* Write out inclusive page numbers completely: *341–344* (not *341–44*).

54c Sample APA citations

1 Books

- One author

  Berman, J. (1985). <u>The talking cure: Literary representations of psychoanalysis.</u>
  New York: New York University Press.

- Two or more authors

  Mack, K., & Skjei, E. (1979). <u>Overcoming writer's block.</u> Los Angeles: Tarcher.

- Corporate or institutional author

  American Medical Association. (1990). The American Medical Association
  handbook of first aid & emergency care (Rev. ed.). New York: Random
  House.

- An unknown author

  Justice: Alternative political perspectives (2nd ed.). (1992). Belmont, CA:
  Wadsworth.

- Edited book

  Kamerman, S. B., & Hayes, C. D. (Eds.). (1982). Families that work. Washington,
  DC: National Academy Press.

- An edition other than the first

  Strunk, W., Jr., & White, E. B. (1979). The elements of style (3rd ed.). New York:
  Macmillan.

- Source in an anthology or a chapter in an edited book

  Hocket, C. F., & Ascher, R. (1968). The human evolution. In Y. A. Cohen (Ed.),
  Man in adaptation: The biosocial background (pp. 237-256). Chicago:
  Aldine.

- Translation

  Fanon, F. (1963). The wretched of the earth (C. Farrington, Trans.). New York:
  Grove. (Original work published 1961).

- Multivolume work

  Shepard, L. A. (Ed.). (1991). Encyclopedia of occultism and parapsychology
  (3rd ed., Vols. 1-2). Detroit: Gale Research.

2 Periodicals and newspapers

- Journal article, one author, journal paged by issue

  Kraft, R. J. (1992). Closed classrooms, high mountains and strange lands: An
  inquiry into culture and caring. Journal of Experiential Education, 15(3),
  8-15.

- Journal article, two authors, journal paged by volume

  Gilula, M. F., & Daniels, D. N. (1969). Violence and man's struggle to adapt.
  Science, 164, 396-405.

- Journal article, three, four, or five authors

    Nickle, M. N., Flynt, F. C., Poynter, S. D., & Rees, J. A., Jr. (1990). Does it
    make a difference if you change the structure? School-within-a-school.
    Phi Delta Kappan, 72, 148-152.

- Magazine article

    Gagnon, P. (1995, December). What should children learn? The Atlantic
    Monthly, 65-78.

- Signed newspaper article, discontinuous pages. If an article appears on
  discontinuous pages, give all page numbers, separated by commas.

    Kilborn, P. T. (1990, December 23). Workers using computers find a supervisor
    inside. The New York Times, pp. 1, 18.

- Review

    Kermode, F. (1996, January 29). Beat the devil [Review of the book The death
    of Satan: How Americans have lost the sense of evil]. The New Republic,
    214, 36-39.

- Letter to the editor

    Levy, P. S. (1993, September 8). Abuse and illness [Letter to the editor]. The
    Chicago Tribune, sec. 1, p. 18.

3   Internet sources

The following guidelines and examples are based on the American
Psychological Association's *Publication Manual,* 4th ed., (APA, 1994), and
"How to Cite Information From the Internet and the World Wide Web,"
available at <http://www.apa.org/journals/webref.html>.

1. For sources with print counterparts, cite the print publication and the
   location of the Internet version.
2. When necessary, identify the type of document or source in square
   brackets [. . .].
3. Do *not* enclose Internet addresses (URLs) with angle brackets (<. . .>); do
   not end URLs with periods.
4. *A note on breaking URLs:* As of 1998, the APA had not given guidelines on
   breaking URLs at the end of a line. Others who have applied the APA
   style to electronic sources recommend that punctuation such as hyphens
   and slashes be retained at the end of a line. For more information about
   URLs, see "Web Extension to American Psychological Association Style"
   at <http://www.beadsland.com/weapas/>.

- An electronic text such as a book

  London, J. (1905). The people of the abyss. Retrieved September 2, 1998 from

  the World Wide Web: http://sunsite.berkeley.edu/~emorgan/

  text/literature/american/1900-/london-people-205.txt

  [This example includes the author, date of original publication, title, and a retrieval note identifying date of retrieval, Internet space, and URL.]

- A report from a government body, university, or private organization

  National Center for Fair & Open Testing. (1998, January 21). FairTest fact sheet:

  The SAT [Online service textfile]. Cambridge, MA: Author. Retrieved July

  31, 1998 from the World Wide Web: http://fairtest.org/facts/satfact.htm

  [This example includes the name of the organization, publication date, title of the report, type of source in brackets, place of publication, publisher (*Author* indicates that the organization is the publisher), and a retrieval note identifying date of retrieval, Internet space, and URL.]

- An article in a periodical

  Fine, M. A., & Kurdek, L. A. (1993). Reflections on determining authorship

  credit and authorship order on faculty-student collaborations. American

  Psychologist, 48, 1141-1147. Retrieved August 12, 1998 from the World

  Wide Web: http://www.apa.org/journals/amp/kurdek.html

  [This example includes two author names, date of original publication, article title, journal title, type of source in brackets, volume number, original pages, and a retrieval note identifying date of retrieval, Internet space, and URL.]

- A newspaper article

  Booth, W. (1998, September 2). California to buy ancient redwood grove. The

  Washington Post, p. A1 [Newspaper, selected stories on line].

  Retrieved September 2, 1998 from the World Wide Web: http://www.

  washingtonpost.com/wp-srv/Wpcap/1998-09/02/058r-090298-idx.html

  [This example includes the author, original publication date, title, name of the newspaper, page number, type of source in brackets, and a retrieval note identifying date of retrieval, Internet space, and URL.]

- A source in an Internet information service or database

  National Center for Health Statistics. (1998, July 30). Health in America tied to

  income and education [Online textfile]. HHS News. Washington, DC: U.S.

  Department of Health and Human Services. Retrieved August 4, 1998 from the World Wide Web: http://www.cdc.gov/nchswww/releases/

98news/98news/huspr98.htm

[This example includes the name of the organization that produced the informa-tion, the date of publication, title, type of source in brackets, name of the site, place of publication, publisher, and a retrieval note identifying date of retrieval, Internet space, and URL.]

Ascher, Carol. (1990). Can performance-based assessments improve urban

schooling? [Digest]. ERIC Clearinghouse on Urban Education. Retrieved

July 31, 1998 from the World Wide Web: http://eric-web.tc.

columbia.edu/digests/dig66.html

[This source includes the author, date of publication, title, type of source in brack-ets, name of the site, and a retrieval note identifying date of retrieval, Internet space, and URL.]

- An abstract of an article

Weingardt, K. R., et al. (1998). Episodic heavy drinking among college

students: Methodological issues and longitudinal perspectives [Abstract].

Psychology of Addictive Behaviors, 12, 155-167. Retrieved September 2,

1998 from the World Wide Web: http://www.apa.org/

journals/adb/998ab.html#1

[This example includes the name of the first of six authors, publication date, title, type of source in brackets, journal title, volume, page numbers, and a retrieval note identifying date of retrieval, Internet space, and URL.]

- Discussion group posting

Neumann, K. (1998, July 15). The rhetoric of effective business communication

[Discussion list posting]. Retrieved July 20, 1998 from listserv discussion

group: BUSCOMP@HARPER.CC.IL.US

[This example of a subscription-based discussion group includes the author, post-ing date, title of the message, type of source in brackets, and a retrieval note identi-fying date of retrieval and listserv e-mail address.]

Hamilton, K. (1998, August 12). Forget nature vs. nurture--Do parents

matter? [Online news posting]. Deja News. Retrieved September 1,

1998 from the World Wide Web: http://www.dejanews.com/

[ST_chan=soc]/channels/soc/soc_fp1.shtml

[This example of a news group posting includes the author, posting date, title of the discussion group, type of source in brackets, the owner of the site, and a retrieval note identifying date of retrieval and listserv e-mail address.]

54c APA

- E-mail. Because e-mail is not easily recoverable, it is not cited in the reference list. Cite e-mail and other personal communications only in the text of your paper. (See 54a3.)

4 Other sources

- Abstract on CD-ROM

    Rubin, D. (1992). Cultural bias undermines assessment [CD-ROM]. Personnel Journal, 71(5), 47-50. Abstract from: Infotrac File: Academic ASAP Item: 12422735

- Data file or database on tape or CD-ROM

    National Council of Teachers of English. (1987). On writing centers [Electronic data tape]. Urbana: ERIC Clearinghouse for Resolutions on the Teaching of Composition, II. SilverPlatter [Producer].

- Computer software

    Herrmann, B. C., Pointer, R. A., & Vogler, D. E. (1992). PEAKS ExamBuilding software (Version 2.01) [Computer software]. Eden Prairie, MN: Instructional Performance Systems.

- Government reports

    Chilman, C. (1966). Growing up poor (Welfare Administration Publication 13). Washington, DC: U.S. Department of Health, Education, and Welfare, U.S. Government Printing Office.

- Source from an information service such as NTIS or ERIC. To cite a source from the National Technical Information Service (NTIS) or Educational Resources Information Center (ERIC), include the name of the information service and the number assigned to the source at the end of the citation.

    U.S. Forest Service. (1992). Leave no trace! An outdoor ethic: A program to teach skills for protecting wilderness environment. Washington, DC: U.S. Department of Agriculture. (ERIC Document Reproduction Service No. ED 354 112)

- Published proceedings of a conference or symposium. Present the regularly published proceedings of a conference as you would a periodical.

    Aguilar, A. (1984). Communication of emotion. Proceedings of the 23rd International Congress of Psychology, 5, 79-103.

- Dissertation abstract

    Gilyard, R. K. (1985). Voicing myself: A study of sociolinguistic competence (Doctoral dissertation, New York University, 1985). <u>Dissertation Abstracts International, 46</u>, 3636A.

- Videotape

    Peters, W. (Producer), & Peters, W., & Cobb, C. (Writers). (1985). <u>A class divided</u> [Videotape]. Washington, DC: Public Broadcasting Service Video.

54d Sample APA research project

The following report has been written in the APA manuscript format for student papers (see 46d), with APA author-date in-text documentation and a reference list. (For more on reports, see 61d. For more about the headings often used in reports, see 46b1.)

Standardized Testing   1

American Psychological Association (APA) Format

Page header and page number 1 inch from top of page

The Problems of Standardized Testing

Ashley Sheffer

English 201: Advanced Composition

William Rainey Harper College

October 13, 1998

Number pages consecutively from the title page to the end of the paper, including references

Center title, author, and other identifying information

Standardized Testing   2

Abstract

This report investigates social bias in standardized educational placement tests such as the SAT and ACT. According to the most recent sources, such tests are being required by a diminishing number of colleges and universities. Whether expert sources favored or opposed standardized testing for college admissions, they generally agreed that these tests are flawed. They measure only a narrow range of skills; they do not accurately predict student success; and they are biased against minorities, women, students of low socioeconomic status, and students from disadvantaged backgrounds. Recommendations include decreasing reliance on test scores for admission purposes, an expanded definition of academic preparedness, and reform of standardized tests to eliminate bias.

An abstract is a block paragraph of 100–150 words.

The Problems of Standardized Testing

Each year, out of the millions applying to college, many are denied admission to the school of their choice because of poor performance on entrance examinations like the SAT and ACT. Have these students not done well because they are not as gifted as those who are accepted? Or have disadvantaged or nontraditional backgrounds failed to provide many with the skills necessary to do well on admissions tests? What do these tests measure, exactly? Are they fair? How well do they predict college success?

(1) Background

(2) History

(3) The Scholastic Aptitude Test (recently renamed the Scholastic Assessment Test). Among the 127 million students who take education achievement tests each year, the largest number take the SAT. First used in 1926, it was developed by the Educational Testing Service to measure "developed abilities" (Anastasi, 1988, p. 330) in reading comprehension, vocabulary, and math. Taken by 12th graders in one of several new forms introduced each year, it is used for college admissions and counseling (Dejnozka & Kapel, 1982, p. 456).

The American College Test. Founded in 1959, the American College Testing Program (ACT) is currently the second largest testing organization in the country. Overlapping traditional aptitude and achievement tests (Anastasi, 1988), the ACT Assessment Battery measures preparedness in English, math, the social sciences, and natural sciences (Geisinger, 1985, p. 11).

Important Definitions

Achievement test. A standardized test measuring what students have actually learned.

Annotations (right margin):

1-inch margins; page header 1 inch from top of page

An introduction that states a problem and poses research questions

Headings: (1) primary centered, (2) secondary flush left, (3) tertiary run-in

APA citation of a source not mentioned in a signal statement

Citation of a source with two authors, names linked by ampersand

Page numbers to refer to a specific part of a source

Aptitude test. A standardized test measuring "the capacity or potentiality of an individual for a particular kind of behavior" (Nairn, 1980, p. 55).

A quotation identified by a specific page number

Bias. In the popular sense, a biased test favors some test takers and penalizes others. In its statistical sense, bias designates "constant or systematic error as opposed to chance errors" (Anastasi, 1988, p. 194).

Reliability. A test is reliable when the same test taker earns consistent scores on the same or equivalent versions of the test.

Standardization. Preparing a "standardized test" to make it a reliable and valid measure for all test takers. When a test has been "standardized," the value of an individual's score can be determined by comparing it to established norms (Anastasi, 1988, pp. 25-26).

Validity. "The extent to which a test does the job desired of it" (Lyman, 1971, p. 196), whether "a test actually measures what it purports to measure" (Anastasi, 1988, p. 26). If an aptitude or achievement test measures class membership or economic status instead of educational preparedness or achievement, it is invalid.

Results and Discussion

Reduced Reliance on Standardized Tests

Even though standardized tests continue to be popular college admissions tools, they are beginning to lose favor at all kinds of institutions, from small colleges like Bates and Bowdoin, to public universities like those in California and Oregon (National Center for Fair & Open Testing, 1997), to highly selective institutions like Harvard and Princeton. College officials state that they are paying less attention to standardized tests and more to the personal qualities vital to academic performance (Elkind, 1991, p. 173). What are the reasons for these changing admissions standards?

Cause/effect organization of the body of the report: The writer examines why standardized tests are losing favor as a method for determining college admissions.

The Skills Measured by Standardized Tests

One reason standardized tests now receive failing grades is that they measure only a narrow range of skills, factual recall, and theoretical knowledge (Willie, 1985, p. 627), not such qualities as judgment, motivation, academic commitment, honesty, and altruism. These are the qualities that, according to a survey of 300 teachers reported by Nairn, have most to do with college success (1980, p. 71). Ernest Boyer, president of the Carnegie Foundation for the Advancement of Teaching, indicated that "with few exceptions, standardized testing ends up evaluating what matters least" (cited in Willie, 1985, p. 628).

Predictive Failures

Perhaps because standardized tests measure so few traits essential to academic success, they are not particularly accurate predictors of it. According to Persell, "considerable evidence refutes the predictive validity of . . . aptitude testing" (cited in Willie, 1985, p. 626). Even the Educational Testing Service admitted that the correlations between some ETS tests and academic success are "near zero" (Nairn, 1980, p. 63). According to the National Center for Fair and Open Testing (1997), the ACT and SAT "acknowledge that high school grade-point average (GPA) or class rank are the best predictors of first-year grades, despite huge variation among high schools and courses. The SAT predicts other outcomes, such as graduation rates, even more poorly."

Bias

A third cause of the decline in popularity of standardized tests is their bias against test takers who might be considered "different." Nairn (1980) showed that among those taking the SAT, "the more money a person's family makes, the higher that person tends to score . . . ; people from white collar homes tend

A topic sentence to introduce a paragraph

A quotation integrated into the writer's sentence

Ellipsis points to signal omission of part of a sentence

A topic sentence that introduces a multiparagraph section

Ellipsis points followed by a semicolon to complete a grammatical unit

to score higher than people from blue collar homes" (p. 200).

The reason is, according to Weaver (1996), that "standardized tests are biased in favor of those whose culture and upbringing most closely resemble that of the test makers--typically white middle-class males who live in metropolitan areas." Lyman (1971) explained that "because tests are usually developed by upper-middle-class people who have upper-middle-class criteria in mind, the tests naturally are most likely to favor the upper- and upper-middle-class groups" (p. 165).

Involved with this economic bias, as both symptom and result, are ethnic, gender, and geographic bias that "stack the deck" against women, minorities, and rural students (Northwest Regional Educational Laboratory Equity Center, 1997). Steelman and Powell (1985) discovered that "the composition by sex, the composition by race, and the average family income of the test-taking population . . . affected state averages" of scores (p. 604). And Sanchez (1993) reported that students from small, often rural schools lacking economic and educational resources do not fare as well on standardized tests as students from urban areas with large funding bases and access to a wider variety of educational offerings. "Simply put, states that tend to spend more money on education generally have higher corrected average SAT scores" (Steelman & Powell, 1985, p. 606).

Conclusions

The narrow focus, predictive failures, and significant bias of standardized tests make them unreliable instruments for evaluating students. This fact is recognized by the more than 1,000 colleges and universities that no longer require the SAT or ACT as an admissions requirement. Because such tests contribute so little to our national goal of excellence in education, other

Author named in a signal statement

The writer's conclusion, based on information and expert opinion in the "Results and Discussion" section

Standardized Testing 7

schools should follow their lead. Instead of using standardized test scores, admissions officials should adopt assessment tools such as essay questions, portfolios, and observations that focus on the achievements and personal traits shown to predict success in college and afterward (Northwest Regional Educational Laboratory Equity Center, 1997). As postsecondary education is increasingly required of greater and greater numbers, the emphasis should change from measuring students to fit a particular pattern to enlarging the pattern to accommodate diverse student needs (Gordon, 1974, p. 59).

The writer's proposal of a solution to the problem uncovered by the report

Standardized Testing 8

References

Anastasi, A. (1988). <u>Psychological testing</u> (6th ed.). New York: Macmillan.

Dejnozka, E. L., & Kapel, D. E. (1982). <u>American educators' encyclopedia.</u> Westport, CT: Greenwood.

Elkind, D. (1991, October). Applying to college. <u>Parents, 66</u>(10), 173.

Geisinger, K. (1985). The ACT assessment. In D. J. Keyser & R. C. Sweetland (Eds.), <u>Test Critiques,</u> (pp. 11-20). Kansas City, MO: Test Corporation of America.

Gordon, E. W. (1974). Toward a qualitative approach to assessment. In R. W. Tyler & R. M. Wolf (Eds.), <u>Crucial issues in testing</u> (pp. 58-62). Berkeley, CA: McCutchan.

For APA Reference list guidelines, see 54b.

Magazine article

Standardized Testing   9

Lyman, H. B. (1971). Test scores and what they mean. Englewood
Cliffs, NJ: Prentice-Hall.

Nairn, A. (1980). The reign of ETS: The corporation that makes up
minds. Washington, DC: Ralph Nader.

National Center for Fair & Open Testing. (1997, September 26).
FairTest fact sheet: The SAT [Online service textfile].
Cambridge, MA: Author. Retrieved July 31, 1998 from
the World Wide Web: http://fairtest.org/facts/satfact.htm

Northwest Regional Educational Laboratory Equity Center. (1997,
September 7). Educate America: Student assessment and
testing [Online service textfile]. Portland, OR: Author.
Retrieved September 2, 1998 from the World Wide Web:
http://nwrel.org/cnorse/booklets/educate /11.html

Sanchez, C. (1993, September 28). Bates College takes issue with
SATs. All Things Considered. National Public Radio.

Steelman, L. C., & Powell, B. (1985, May). Appraising the
implications of the SAT for educational policy. Phi Delta
Kappan, 66, 603-606.

Weaver, C. (1996). Facts: On standardized test and assessment
alternatives [Online service textfile republished from a
printed source]. In C. Weaver, L. Gillmeister-Krause, &
G. Vento-Zogby (Eds.), Creating support for effective
literacy education. Portsmouth, NH: Heinemann. Retrieved
September 2, 1998 from the World Wide Web: http://
homepage.tinet.ie/~seaghan/articles/10.htm

Willie, C. V. (1985, May). The problem of standardized testing in a
free and pluralistic society. Phi Delta Kappan, 66, 626-628.

Book with
one author

Internet
source by
a corporate
author

Radio
broadcast

Periodical
source by
two authors

Internet
source
republished
from a
printed
source

Other Styles

55 Using Endnotes or Footnotes (The Chicago Style)

The preferred style for papers in the humanities is the in-text parenthetical system of documentation of the Modern Language Association (see Chapters 51 and 52). But in business, the humanities, and the fine arts, endnotes and footnotes—a system of documentation sometimes referred to as the Chicago style or CMS (after the University of Chicago Press's *Manual of Style*)—are often used to cite the sources of borrowed materials. If you use endnotes or footnotes, you may not need a bibliography; check with your instructor. If a bibliography is required, see 55c.

55a Choose an endnote or footnote format

Use endnotes at the end of your paper unless you are instructed to place footnotes at the bottom of a page of text.

- *Numbering.* Number notes consecutively from the beginning to the end of your paper. Do not assign each source its own number. Use a new number for each citation even if several notes refer to the same source. In the text, at the first break after a summary, paraphrase, or quotation, write a raised, or superscript Arabic numeral outside all punctuation except dashes.

  Charlotte Perkins Gilman described her nomadic childhood as "thick with railroad journeys."[14]

- *Placement.* Endnotes appear on a separate "Notes" page at the end of your paper, following the text and preceding the bibliography. Double-space between and within endnotes. If you must use footnotes, quadruple-space after the last line of text and place them at the bottom of the page. Single-space footnotes; double-space between them. If a footnote continues onto the next page, skip two lines below the text on the new page and type a solid line across the page; then double-space and continue the note. Place new notes immediately after it.

- *Indentations.* Indent the first line the same number of spaces as you are indenting paragraphs in your paper, generally one-half inch or 5 spaces. Make second and succeeding lines flush with the left margin.

- *Formatting note numbers.* The number preceding each note should *not* be a superscript. Use the same numerals that you use elsewhere in your text, for dates and so forth. After the number, put a period and leave 1 space.

- *The first reference to a source.* When you cite a source for the first time, give complete publication information in the note. Begin each note with a capital letter and end with a period. Do not use internal periods. Give the author's name in normal word order. For books, enclose the place of publication, publisher, and date of publication in parentheses. Always give the exact page number(s) of a borrowing.

  1. Aldo Leopold, <u>A Sand County Almanac</u> (New York: Oxford University Press, 1987), 204.

- *Subsequent references to a source.* In second and later references to a source, give the author's last name, or a short form of the title if no author's name is given, followed by the page numbers of the borrowing. This information will allow readers to locate complete information for a source in an earlier note or in the bibliography.

  2. Leopold, 169.

  3. "Report," 14.

- *Subsequent references to an author of more than one source.* If you use more than one source by an author, use the author's last name and a short form of the title in subsequent references to distinguish one source from another.

  23. Coates, "Crowds," 16.

  24. Coates, "Creature Comforts," 14.

- *A reference to the source in the preceding note.* Use *Ibid.* (an abbreviation of *ibidem,* "in the same place") to refer to a source cited in the immediately preceding note. Follow with a page number if different from that in the preceding note.

  24. Coates, "Creature Comforts," 14.

  25. Ibid., 15.

55_b_ Make a full first reference to a source

1 Citing books

- Basic reference to a book. Cite two or more authors in the order given on the title page of the book. Use commas to separate the names of three or more authors. Use *and* before the second or final author's name. For a corporate publication, cite the corporation as the author. After the book title, include information such as the names of translators or editors (if any), the number or description of the edition (if other than the first), and the series name (if any). Cite a pamphlet as you would a book. Note that the Chicago style uses complete publisher names (*Random House*) and old-style state abbreviations with periods (*Del., Fla., N.J.*).

> 1. Barry Lopez, <u>Arctic Dreams: Imagination and Desire in a Northern Landscape</u> (New York: Scribner's, 1986), 104.

- An introduction, foreword, preface, or afterword

> 2. Jeffrey L. Duncan, introduction to <u>Thoreau: The Major Essays,</u> by Henry David Thoreau (New York: Dutton, 1972), xi.

- One volume from a multivolume work. Place the volume number after the general title. If a particular volume is titled separately, include the individual title after the volume number.

> 3. Joseph Blotner, <u>Faulkner: A Biography,</u> vol. 2 (New York: Random House, 1976), 426.

- Titled parts of a book

> 4. Anne Tibble, "Chinua Achebe," in <u>Modern Black Novelists,</u> ed. G. C. Cooke (Englewood Cliffs, N.J.: Prentice-Hall, 1971), 128.

- An encyclopedia or dictionary. Begin with the name of the reference work followed by the edition, the abbreviation *s.v.* (for *sub verbo,* "under the word"), and the item cited, which is capitalized if a proper noun and otherwise written in lowercase letters.

> 5. <u>Encyclopaedia Britannica,</u> 11th ed., s.v. "Mexico."

2 Citing periodicals and newspapers

Write out the names of months in publication dates. Do not capitalize the names of seasons: (*fall 1996*).

- Article in a weekly or monthly magazine

> 6. Sharon Begley, "The Puzzle of Genius," <u>Newsweek,</u> 28 June 1993, 50.

- Article in a scholarly journal. If the periodical is paged by issue, include the issue number after the volume number of the journal.

> 7. Lisa Kasmer, "Charlotte Perkins Gilman's 'The Yellow Wall-Paper': A Symptomatic Reading," <u>Literature and Psychology</u> 46, no. 3 (1990): 14.

- Review of a book, movie, or play

> 8. Stanley Kauffmann, "Stars in Their Courses," review of <u>One True Thing</u> (Universal movie), <u>New Republic,</u> 19 October 1998, 30-31.

- Newspaper article. To cite a signed newspaper article, begin with the author's name. To cite an unsigned newspaper article, begin with the title. When appropriate, include the edition, section number, and page number.

9. James Coates, "Crowds Pose Threat to U.S. Park System," <u>Chicago Tribune,</u> 21 April 1991, Chicagoland North edition, sec. 1, p. 1.

3 Citing electronic sources

The Chicago Manual of Style, 14th edition, provides only brief instructions for citing Internet sources. Its publisher, University of Chicago Press, recommends that writers use the more detailed guidelines presented by Andrew Harnack and Eugene Kleppinger in *Online! A Reference Guide to Using Internet Sources* (New York: St. Martin's, 1998) as a supplement. The following examples are based on Harnack and Kleppinger's guidelines.

- An Internet document. Provide the author's name (if known), the title of the document in quotation marks, the title of the complete work (if applicable) in italics or underlined, date of publication or last revision (if known; otherwise use *n.d.*), the URL in angle brackets, and date of access in parentheses.

  10. Leslie A. Schwalm, "Sweet Dreams of Freedom: Freedwomen's Reconstruction of Life and Labor in Lowcountry South Carolina," <u>Journal of Women's History,</u> Spring 1997, <http://www.indiana.edu/~iupress/journals/jwh-art5.html> (26 October 1998).

- Internet information service. Provide the author's name (if known), the title of the document in quotation marks, the name of the service, identifying numbers of the document, the URL in angle brackets, and date of access in parentheses.

  11. Ruth Axman Childs, "Gender Bias and Fairness," <u>ERIC Digest,</u> December 1990, ED328610, <http://www.ed.gov/databases/ERIC_Digests/ed328610.html> (31 July 1998).

- Electronic mail. Provide the author's name (if known), the author's e-mail address in angle brackets, the subject line from the posting in quotation marks, date of publication, type of communication (personal mail, distribution list, office communication), and date of access in parentheses.

  12. Jennifer Loster, <jenlos@nps.gov>, "History of Grand Canyon National Park," 3 June 1998, personal e-mail (3 June 1998).

- Listserv message. Provide the author's name (if known), the author's e-mail address in angle brackets, the subject line from the posting in quotation marks, date of publication, address of listserv in angle brackets, and date of access in parentheses.

  13. Raymond Greenberg, <rgreen@email.msn.com> "Native Americans in WWII Service," 1 September 1997, <amhist@kcsu.edu> (13 March 1998).

- Newsgroup message. Provide the author's name (if known), author's e-mail address in angle brackets, the subject line from the posting in quotation marks, date of publication, the name of the newsgroup in angle brackets, and date of access in parentheses.

> 14. Ethel L. Flores, <eflores@aol.com> "Undocumented Immigrants in Illinois," 15 August 1997, <soc.books.reviews> (29 August 1997).

- Synchronous communication (MOOs, MUDs, IRCs). Provide the name of the speaker (if known) or the name of the site, title of the event (if appropriate) in quotation marks, date of event, type of communication (group discussion, personal interview) if not indicated elsewhere in the entry, address (using a URL in angle brackets or command line directions), and date of access in parentheses.

> 15. Jerome Stone, "Seminar on Environmental Ethics and Eco-Terrorism," 1 November 1997, <telnet://kcsumoo.edu:8888> (1 November 1997).

4 Citing other sources

- Government publications. The format for government publications follows this sequence: government body, subsidiary body, title of document, individual author if given, identifying numbers, publication information (in parentheses), page number(s). Include as much information as you have available.

> 16. House Subcommittee on Science, Research and Technology, <u>Genetic Engineering, Human Genetics and Cell Biology,</u> 96th Cong., 2nd sess., 14 May 1980, 47.

- A dissertation. If you are citing an unpublished dissertation, follow the title with *Ph.D. diss.*, the institution granting the degree, the date it was granted, publication information, and page number. If you are citing an abstract, follow the title with a reference to *Dissertation Abstracts* or *Dissertation Abstracts International.*

> 17. Marianne Elizabeth DiPierro, "The Utopian Vision in the Works of Wollstonecraft, Gilman, and Chopin" (Ph.D. diss., University of South Florida, 1994), abstract in <u>Dissertation Abstracts International</u> 54 (1994): 3737A.

- A letter

> 18. Troy M. Linville to Peter Sherer, 4 June 1999.

- Lecture or speech. To cite the printed version of a lecture or speech, give the page numbers from which you have borrowed.

> 19. Carl A. Battaglia, "Filmmaking and the Composing Process" (paper presented at the Forty-Seventh Annual Conference on College Composition and Communication, Milwaukee, Wis., 30 March 1996), 4-6.

- Interview

> 20. Joyce Carol Oates, interview by Terry Gross, <u>Fresh Air,</u> National Public Radio, 3 August 1993.

- Film or videocassette

> 21. <u>Shall We Dance,</u> prod. Pandro S. Berman, 116 min., RKO Radio Pictures, 1937, reissue, Fox Hills Video, Los Angeles, 1987, videocassette.

- Recording

> 22. Edward Kennedy ["Duke"] Ellington, "Harlem Airshaft," on <u>The Duke Ellington Carnegie Hall Concerts,</u> Prestige 24075.

55c Prepare a bibliography

If a bibliography is required to accompany your project, follow these guidelines.

- *Placement.* Start the bibliography on a new page immediately following the endnotes or, if you used footnotes, following the text of the paper. Center the heading "Bibliography" 1 inch from the top of the page. Continue page numbering from the notes page or text of the paper.

- *Spacing.* Double-space throughout.

- *Indentation.* Do not indent the first line of an entry. Indent following lines one-half inch or 5 spaces.

- *Alphabetical order.* Do not number the entries of a bibliography. Arrange them in alphabetical order according to the author's last name or the first word of the title, ignoring *A, An,* and *The.*

> Lau, Beth. "Coleridge's Reflective Moonlight." <u>Studies in English Literature</u> 24 (autumn 1983): 533-48.
>
> Radley, Virginia. <u>Samuel Taylor Coleridge</u>. New York: Twayne, 1966.

- *Punctuation.* Separate the major parts of an entry with a period and 1 space.

- *A titled part of a book.* Cite the pages of the part immediately after the title and the editor.

> Tolstoy, Leo. "The Three Hermits." In <u>Short Shorts: An Anthology of the Shortest Stories,</u> edited by Irving Howe and Ilana Wiener Howe, 3-11. New York: Bantam, 1983.

56 Using the CBE Style and Other Styles

56a Use the CBE style for scientific writing

The Council of Biology Editors (CBE) recommends two styles for writing in the life sciences—biology, botany, zoology, anatomy, and physiology. One is an author-date system similar to the APA style (see Chapter 54). The other, a citation-sequence system, uses numbers in the text of the paper to refer to numbered entries in a reference list at the end of the paper. Following are guidelines to the citation-sequence system.

1 Citing sources in the text of your writing

- Use raised, superscript numbers after each use of source material to refer readers to entries in the reference list. Begin with "1" and give each source its own number.

  The increase of childhood asthma during the last twenty years is attributed to environmental rather than genetic factors.[1] Chief among these factors is air pollution.[2]

- If you cite two or more sources at once, place a comma but no space between citation numbers. If you refer to a source cited earlier, reuse the original number.

  Studies of asthma in developing nations have noted that exposure to firewood smoke is a frequent cause of obstructive airways disease.[2,3]

2 Preparing the reference list

At the end of your paper provide a list of all sources that you refer to in your paper, including sources cited in notes, tables, and figures. Follow these format guidelines:

- *Heading.* Use the heading "References."
- *Spacing.* Single-space each entry; double-space between entries.
- *Arrangement.* Arrange entries in the numerical order of their first citation in the paper, not alphabetically.
- *Indentation.* Type the number of each entry on the line of type (not raised) and flush with the left margin (not indented). Follow with a period and 1 space. Indent the second and successive lines of an entry to align beneath the first word in the first line.
- *Author names.* Invert all author names, typing last name first followed by 1 space and initials for the first and middle names. Do not use pe-

riods or spaces between initials—for example, *Conroy LB*. If a source has two or more authors, place a comma between author names—for example, *Conroy LB, Jameson RN*.

- *Punctuation.* Use a period and 1 space to separate major parts of an entry: "Author name. Title. Publication information."

- *Titles.* Do not underline, italicize, or use quotation marks for the titles of books and articles. Capitalize only the first letter of the first word and proper nouns.

3 Sample citations

- A book. Use a colon and 1 space between the place of publication and the publisher. Use a semicolon and 1 space between the publisher and year. Conclude with the total number of pages in the book.

  1. Gould SJ. The panda's thumb: more reflections in natural history.

     New York: Norton; 1983. 343 p.

- An article in a scholarly periodical. After the journal title, provide the year of publication, a semicolon, the volume number, a colon, and inclusive pages. No space precedes or follows the semicolon and colon.

  2. Metzger R, Delgado JL, Herrell R. Environmental health and Hispanic

     children. Environmental Health Perspective 1995;103:25-32.

- An article in a newspaper. Provide the date, the newspaper section number, and the page.

  3. Van, J. Biochips power medical research. Chicago Tribune 1998 Oct 26; Sect

     4:1 (col 2).

- An Internet document. Provide the author's name, title, description of the source (in square brackets), date of publication and other publication information (if available), the words "Available from" followed by a colon and the online location of the source, the URL in angle brackets, and the access date.

  4. Eggieston P, Malveaux FJ, Butz AM. Medications used by children with asthma

     living in the inner city. Pediatrics [serial online] 1998 Mar 11; 101:349-54.

     Available from: Asthma Information Center. <http://www.ama-assn.org/

     special/asthma/library/readroom/medscful.htm> Accessed 1998 May 5.

- E-mail message. Provide the author's e-mail address in angle brackets, the date of the message, the subject of the message, the type of communication in square brackets, and the access date.

  5. Winegarden O. <owine@medtronix.org> 1998 Oct 25. Hodgkins disease

     [personal e-mail]. Accessed 1998 Oct 26.

56b Choose a style manual appropriate for your subject

Every scholarly field has a preferred manuscript form and system of documentation. Here is a list of style manuals for a variety of fields.

- *Biology.* Council of Biology Editors. *Scientific Style and Format: The CBE Manual for Authors, Editors, and Publishers.* 6th ed. New York: Cambridge UP, 1994.

- *Chemistry.* American Chemical Society. *The ACS Style Guide: A Manual for Authors and Editors.* Washington: ACS, 1997.

- *English and the humanities.* Gibaldi, Joseph. *MLA Handbook for Writers of Research Papers.* 5th ed. New York: Modern Language Association, 1999.

- *Engineering.* Michaelson, Herbert B. *How to Write and Publish Engineering Papers and Reports.* 3rd ed. Phoenix: Oryx, 1990.

- *Geology.* United States Geological Survey. *Suggestions to Authors of the Reports of the United States Geological Survey.* 7th ed. Washington: GPO, 1991.

- *Law. The Bluebook: A Uniform System of Citation.* Comp. Editors of Columbia Law Review et al. 15th ed. Cambridge: Harvard Law Review, 1996.

- *Linguistics.* Linguistic Society of America. *LSA Bulletin,* Dec. issue, annually.

- *Mathematics.* American Mathematical Society. *A Manual for Authors of Mathematical Papers.* 8th rev. ed. Providence: AMS, 1990.

- *Medicine.* Iverson, Cheryl, et al. *American Medical Association Manual of Style.* 9th ed. Baltimore: Williams, 1997.

- *Music.* Holoman, D. Kern, ed. *Writing about Music: A Style Sheet from the Editors of* 19th-Century Music. Berkeley: U of California P, 1988.

- *Physics.* American Institute of Physics. *AIP Style Manual.* 4th ed. New York: AIP, 1990.

- *Psychology.* American Psychological Association. *Publication Manual of the American Psychological Association.* 4th ed. Washington: APA, 1994.

- *General. The Chicago Manual of Style.* 14th ed. Chicago: U of Chicago P, 1993. United States. Government Printing Office. *Style Manual.* Rev. ed. Washington: GPO, 1984.

PART **X.**

X argument

Argument *and Persuasion*

Argument and Persuasion

Argument and Persuasion

57 Creating Logical Arguments

In most people's minds, argument involves anger and other heated emotions. But here, and in most academic writing, it is nothing more—and nothing less—than a process of reasoning about an issue whose truth or plausibility is in doubt. In its simplest form, **argument** consists of an assertion supported by factual information and logic.

Consider, for example, two friends planning a vacation. One says, "If it's real wilderness you want, let's go to Capitol Reef National Park, in Utah. You'll see few tourists, fewer RVs and buses, and no souvenir stands cluttering the landscape. That's about as close to my definition of wilderness as we're going to get." What we have here is a capsule argument (and note that in its classic definition an argument requires only one participant):

- *Assertion.* "If it's real wilderness you want, let's go to Capitol Reef National Park, in Utah."

- *Factual information.* Capitol Reef has "few tourists, fewer RVs and buses, and no souvenir stands cluttering the landscape."

- *Logic.* A definition of *wilderness* shows that the factual information supports the assertion.

As you will see in this chapter, this process of reasoning in a more fully developed form is a feature of many kinds of writing you do, in school, on the job, in public. In essays, reports, business writing, and elsewhere, it provides a way to determine the truth, make sound judgments, and decide on the best course of action.

57a Write arguable claims

1 Identifying the point of an argument

An argument begins when someone makes an assertion—a claim—needing support before others will accept it. Like the thesis of an essay, a **claim** is the point of an argument, what it is all about. Just as the content of an essay provides support for the thesis, the factual information and logic of an argument provide support for the claim. There are four kinds of claims. Knowing what they assert will help you see how to support them.

- A **factual claim** asserts that something about a subject is true or plausible. For example: *Standardized achievement tests are biased against racial minorities, the poor, and rural students.* The subject of this claim is *standardized tests.* The claim asserts that these tests are biased. To prove the truth of this claim, an argument would have to provide factual information about standardized test scores and logic showing that these scores reveal bias.

- A **cause/effect claim** makes an assertion about the causes of an effect or, conversely, the effects resulting from a cause. For example: *Television advertising targeted to children raises unattainable expectations and promotes their unhappiness.* This claim asserts that a cause, television advertising, has two effects on children. An argument supporting it would have to show that young viewers of television advertising are affected in these ways.

- A **value judgment** is a claim that evaluates a subject for its usefulness, beauty, desirability, or rightness or wrongness. For example: *The Dynacomp Personal Computer has the internal memory, disk space, and speed to meet the needs of most college students.* An argument supporting this evaluation of a computer's usefulness would have to present information about the needs of college students and then show that the features of this computer meet those needs.

- A **proposal** is a claim advocating a course of action or a policy. It may assert a need for action, the benefits of action, or both. For example: *To protect endangered park environments, the National Park Service should begin restricting admissions at parks most threatened by visitor overcrowding.* An argument supporting this proposal would have to show a need for action with information about the conditions of national parks, the benefits of reduced park use, and the practicality of restricting admission.

2 Writing a tentative claim

When you have a project requiring an argument, begin by writing a tentative claim that you hope to support. Write it as you would a tentative thesis, beginning with the words *My point is that* (see 2d).

> My point is that bilingual education is the most effective and economical method for teaching English to nonnative speakers.

As you gather support for your claim, revise the claim to fit that support. Later, as you write the actual argument, remove the formula phrase. For example: *Bilingual education is the most effective and economical method for teaching English to nonnative speakers.*

3 Converting a tentative claim to an arguable assertion

As you write a claim, make it an arguable assertion, one whose truth or plausibility is in doubt but which can be supported by factual information and logic. Follow these guidelines.

- Avoid subjective assertions of personal preference. An arguable claim is more than an expression of personal preference or taste.

  Our   so overcrowded that visitor enjoyment and the environment are suffering.
  I think our national parks are too crowded.

  [The original claim may have meant only that the writer doesn't like all those other visitors visiting national parks. The revision makes a value judgment claim that can be supported by factual information and logic.]

- Avoid easily verifiable statements of fact. Statements that are obviously true or easily shown to be true do not require argument.

  killing the forests of many national parks.
  The smog from auto pollution is as bad in many national parks as in

  downtown Los Angeles or Denver.

  [The original claim is an easily verifiable statement of fact. The revision is a cause/effect claim whose truth must be established by an argument showing that smog is killing the forests.]

- Use exact, specific language. You and your audience must know exactly what your words refer to.

  devote more funds to protect wildlife and restore historic monuments.
  The U.S. Park Service must act now to save the treasures of our national

  parks.

  [The meaning of the words *save* and *treasures* is imprecise and vague. The revision makes a proposal in which the subject of the argument is well focused and clear.]

57*b* Gather two kinds of support for your claim

1 Collecting evidence

Evidence consists of factual information presented to support a claim. (For methods of research to help you gather evidence, see Chapters 47, 48, and 49.) You'll probably collect three kinds.

- **Data** may be facts, statistics, experimental data, research findings, or reliable observation.

- **Examples** are specific instances or illustrations of the point being made.

- You may use as evidence the **opinion of an expert** based on an examination of the facts, unless the opinion is challenged. In that case, the truth must be established independently.

2 Establishing warrants

A **warrant** makes a connection between evidence and a claim, showing how or why the two connect. For an argument to be effective, there must be a link, and it must be clear and logical. Suppose two people are driving down a busy street, late for a concert. As they approach an intersection, the passenger says, "Here, turn right on Highland Avenue. There's less traffic, and it's shorter." In a diagram of this passenger's argument, the evidence is connected to the claim by the warrant, an assumption travelers make when choosing a route.

Evidence: Highland Avenue is the shorter route and has less traffic

Unspoken implicit warrant: The best route is the shortest one with the least traffic.

Claim: Turn right on Highland Avenue.

In simple arguments like this, the logic is so clear that the warrant need not be explicitly stated. In other arguments, however, the link between evidence and claim may not be clear or more than one warrant may be at work, and people who have trouble following the line of reasoning will say, "I don't see the connection."

Consider another argument:

EVIDENCE

During the last fifty years, canals have been dug through the Florida Everglades and vast amounts of water have been diverted for human consumption. The result is that many species of animals, fish, and birds have disappeared, vegetation is dying, and the region is beginning to resemble a desert.

CLAIM

The National Park Service should allocate resources to repair damage to the Everglades and restore the park as much as possible to its original state.

Even if the claim is one you could agree with, it may not be clear why the evidence calls for the action the claim proposes, so the link must be identified. Here is the way this argument looks written out, with several warrants connecting the evidence to the claim.

> [*Evidence*] During the last fifty years, canals have been dug through the Florida Everglades and vast amounts of water have been diverted for human consumption. The result is that many species of animals, fish, and birds have disappeared, vegetation is dying, and the region is beginning to resemble a desert. [*Partial claim*] Something must be done. [*Warrant 1: an ecological principle*] After all, if the Everglades is destroyed, the surrounding environments will also suffer. [*Warrant 2: the principle of self-interest*] Our way of life may be threatened. [*Warrant 3: an assumption*] Besides, the natural world is beautiful and valuable in itself, and deserves protection. [*Warrant 4: a law*] And there's no alternative, really, because the National Parks Act requires that parks should be preserved "unimpaired for future generations." [*Complete claim*] So the National Park Service should allocate resources to repair damage to the Everglades and restore the park as much as possible to its original state.

Singly and together, these warrants reveal the logic of the argument, showing how evidence and claim are related.

As this example shows, we take warrants from many sources: natural laws (like gravity or photosynthesis), scientific and mathematical formulas (πr^2), theories (evolution), human laws, institutional policies, standards of artistic taste, moral values, principles of human nature, rules of thumb, proverbs ("Waste not, want not"), basic assumptions ("All people are created equal"), and precedent (the assumption that past events may be a guide to future events).

3 Building logic into your argument

As you construct an argument and look for warrants linking evidence to your claim, follow these guidelines.

- *Writing a claim based on evidence.* If you're unsure what to claim about a body of evidence, ask yourself what laws, policies, principles, assumptions, or procedures apply to that evidence. They will act as warrants leading you to a logical claim.

- *Identifying the link between evidence and claim.* If you already have a claim and evidence and need the link tying the two together, ask what laws, policies, principles, assumptions, or procedures explain the connection. These are your warrants.

- *Stating warrants in an argument.* As you design an argument for an audience, ask whether the connection between evidence and claim is clear and logical. If you have doubts, express your warrant or warrants directly in your argument. If you're certain the relationship is clear, they can remain unstated.

57c Test your argument; modify it, if necessary

1 Testing an argument

Throughout the process of building an argument, check its accuracy, logic, and strength by applying the following critical thinking tests (see also 1a). Some will apply only to certain parts or to certain kinds of arguments. But the more tests your argument can pass, the more confident you can be that your reasoning is sound.

- *The truth test.* Is everything supporting your claim true or plausible? Facts must be facts, opinions must be accepted as true, and assumptions must be plausible. If your evidence and warrants are unreliable, you cannot be confident your claim is true.

- *Relevance.* Do your evidence and warrants actually apply to the case you're arguing? Your support must be relevant to your claim. Evidence about tourist overcrowding in the state parks of Virginia, for example, may not be relevant to an argument about overcrowding in national parks.

- *Timeliness.* Do your evidence and warrants represent the most recent or up-to-date information? Statistics about the number of visitors to Yosemite National Park in the 1950s are not very useful for an argument about overcrowded national parks in the 1990s.

- *Sufficiency.* Do you have enough support to make your claim convincing? Evidence for the destruction of forests in Acadia National Park is not sufficient to prove a threat to forests throughout the National Park system.

- *Representativeness.* Have you gathered your support from a variety of sources—more than just one or a few? Your support should broadly represent the facts of your case. One National Park Service official speaking about overcrowding in national parks will not be as convincing as three park officials, a U.S. senator, and several park visitors just returned from vacations.

- *Occam's razor.* Named for a medieval theologian, *Occam's razor* is the principle that the simplest argument is usually the best. What is the simplest case you can make for your claim and still support it convincingly?

- *Utility.* Apply this test to proposal arguments. Is your proposal practical and workable? How confident can you be that it will achieve your aims?

2 Modifying an argument

As you apply the preceding tests, you may find that an argument has fatal flaws of truth or logic. To be reasonable, you'll have to abandon it in favor of a better alternative. But you may find that although an argument is weak, it can be improved. The following modifications will help you clarify or strengthen your case.

- *Citing sources.* If your audience may not accept the truth of your evidence or warrants at face value, citing their sources may improve your credibility. In academic writing especially, cite your sources by name and document them appropriately. (For MLA citations, see Chapter 51; for APA citations, see Chapter 54.)

- *Adding qualifiers.* Qualifiers are words that indicate degrees of strength, confidence, or certainty: *may, must, certainly, probably, necessarily, it is unlikely, as far as the evidence goes, it seems, as nearly as I can tell,* and so forth. Rarely will you be able to argue with ironclad proof and reach absolute certainty. Add qualifiers to assertions to show the degree of confidence you have in their truth or logic.

  may be
  Tourists ~~are~~ responsible for the loss of Alpine vegetation in Rocky

  Mountain National Park.

  [The original version expresses complete confidence in the truth of the assertion; the revision reflects incomplete or inconclusive evidence.]

- *Identifying exceptions.* Rarely will an argument apply to all situations, so explain where it applies and where it doesn't by stating the exceptions. An argument that appears to cover many situations when it really covers only a few will lack credibility.

  To protect national park environments, the National Park Service

  should begin regulating park admissions/ *at those parks most affected by*

  overcrowding.

  [The original seems to apply to all parks without exception. The revision limits the case to parks needing protection; others are exceptions to the claim.]

- *Adding rebuttals.* Most arguments have counterarguments that can be made against them. You will strengthen your case if you summarize opposing arguments and answer them with a rebuttal. Apply the tests in 57c1 to discover their weaknesses and describe what you find.

57d Identify logical fallacies

You'll improve your ability to test an argument if you can recognize errors in reasoning, known as **logical fallacies.** The following are the most common.

- *Against the person (ad hominem).* Attacking a person instead of rebutting an argument, often through name-calling, as in "those weak-kneed, do-good liberals." Attacking a person's character is justified only when self-interest or incapacity may affect that person's ability to argue truthfully or logically.

- *Appeal to the people (ad populum).* Appealing irrelevantly to the attitudes of an audience instead of convincing them with argument. "Reelect Representative Hamm! Born and raised here in Pleasantville, in the good old USA, he's a freedom-loving veteran who will oppose every attempt to pick your pocket with new taxes." Evidence should support a claim rather than play to an audience's personal sympathies.

- *Bandwagon.* Arguing that one should accept a claim because everyone else does. Consider: "You still don't have a Dynacomp 68040 Computer? Why, you're the only person in the dorm without one!" The value of a claim does not depend on how widely it is supported.

- *Begging the question.* Assuming the truth of a statement without proof, arguing in a circle. "State U. should drop its literature requirement. So much literature is bad for growing minds, filled as it is with sex and violence." This argument uses as evidence the unproven— "begged"—statement that literature containing sexual subjects and violence is bad for growing minds. Until a statement has been proven to be true or plausible, it cannot be used to support a claim.

- *Either/or.* Arguing that only two alternatives exist when there may be more and, often, rejecting one as inappropriate. "Either we provide weapons for the freedom fighters of Santa Costa, or we abandon them to dictatorship." In fact, there are many kinds of aid one country can give to another. The alternatives in argument are often more than two.

- *Faulty analogy or comparison.* Comparing two subjects that are not really similar in order to force a conclusion. "We must reform schools to make them more like businesses. In business, employees are held accountable for the products they produce. The same should be true of schools, whose product is educated youngsters." Students are more than raw materials to be shaped into products, so the analogy is false.

- *False cause (post hoc).* The post hoc fallacy (which comes from the Latin *post hoc ergo propter hoc,* "after this, therefore because of this") assumes that because one thing precedes another, the first caused the second. But sequence does not always signal a cause/effect relation. "Most people who succeed in business wear suits. If you want to succeed, you'll wear a suit, too." Events may be coincidental, or one may only be an insignificant cause of another.

- *Hasty generalization.* A generalization about a group is hasty when based on insufficient, unrepresentative, or irrelevant evidence. "Walking around campus, I see students with stereo headphones on, students reading comic books or playing computer games, students lying on the grass sunning themselves. Obviously, today's students are illiterates!" A generalization this broad must depend on more evidence than the casual observations of one person.

- *Irrelevant emotional appeals.* Appealing to emotion rather than reason. "Please don't give us a final exam, Professor Moore. It's been a long semester. We've worked so hard, and we're tired. Besides, you're such a hard grader." Irrelevant appeals to fear, pleasure, or pity (as in the "sob story") are used to coerce, seduce, or mislead rather than persuade.

- *Irrelevant authorities (testimonial).* Using an opinion that comes from outside that person's area of expertise. Consider political ads in which actors endorse politicians or other ads in which athletes sell motor oil or clothing. This fallacy of irrelevancy attempts to transfer prestige and authority from one area to another.

- *Non sequitur ("it does not follow").* Making false assumptions based on signs or symptoms. "Fred loves to read. I see him in bookstores and the library all the time. With his thick glasses, he even looks like the studious type. He must get straight *A*'s." These traits do not necessarily signal a person's academic success. The support for an argument must lead logically to the claim.

- *Red herring.* Hunters long ago used to drag strong-smelling herring across the path of dogs to divert them from their prey. An arguer uses a red herring when he or she purposely introduces irrelevant issues to divert an audience from the real issues. "Sure, you support raising admission fees to U.S. national parks. You're wealthy and retired, your children all grown, and you have no financial worries." The status of the audience has nothing to do with support for the claim. A red herring is a way of ducking issues.

58 Arguing Persuasively

If the audience for an argument were all like Mr. Spock, the thoroughly rational Vulcan of *Star Trek* fame, a logical argument would be persuasive by itself. But audiences naturally bring their own interests, understanding, and priorities to an issue, which means that they use more than reason alone to make up their minds. To win your audience's agreement involves adapting an argument to their priorities, building their trust in you, and rousing their desire to accept your position.

58a | Adapt your argument to your audience's needs and interests

1 Knowing your audience

Arguments often fail because people make cases that would persuade themselves but not necessarily their audiences. As you build an argument, think of your audience and what it will take to persuade them.

- *Audience profile.* Construct a profile of what you know about your audience (see 1c3).

- *Audience knowledge.* Decide what your audience knows or believes about your subject. Are they opponents or potential allies, skeptical or merely undecided?

- *Interests and priorities.* Identify your audience's interests and priorities. Where your subject is concerned, are your readers interested in fairness, justice, effectiveness, efficiency, health, safety, pleasure, or some other priority? Do they have a hidden agenda about your topic—fears or motives they may be reluctant to acknowledge?

2 Building a persuasive argument

As much as possible, make a claim that respects your audience's interests, needs, and capacities. Be clear about what, exactly, you want from them. Avoid claims that may leave them asking, "So? What should be done? By whom? How?" An effective claim answers these questions.

> *Because visitor overcrowding*
> ~~Overcrowding~~ threatens plant and animal life in our most popular
> *parks,*
> national ~~parks.~~ *environmentally minded tourists should take their vacations elsewhere.*

[The original claim does not involve the audience. The revision proposes their action in response to the environmental threat.]

As you build your argument, avoid issues that may distract your audience or work against you. For example, if you intended to persuade people concerned with fairness that visits to overcrowded national parks must be reduced, you would probably avoid a quota system as one solution. This audience may become resentful at the thought of being denied access to a park their tax dollars support.

How to . . . Argue Persuasively

1. As you build your argument, construct an audience profile of those you want to persuade (see 1c3). Be sure to note their priorities or a hidden agenda influencing their response to your case.

2. Write a specific claim tailored to their interests and capacities for action. (See 57a.)

3. From the support for your claim, choose the evidence and warrants most persuasive for this particular audience. Don't distract or alienate them with irrelevant appeals. Arrange your argument for greatest clarity and power. (See 58a3.)

4. Decide what opposing arguments your audience may find appealing. Build a rebuttal of these positions, making concessions or proposing compromise where appropriate.

5. Plan an introduction that will earn your audience's trust. Present your credentials, establish common ground with your audience, create a persona they'll find easy to listen to, and demonstrate your fairness. (See also 6c.)

6. Plan a conclusion that will rouse your audience's feelings in support of your claim. Consider an emotionally compelling story that proves your point, vivid description of something having to do with your subject, or a powerful quotation. (See also 6d.)

3 Organizing persuasively

Organize your argument for greatest clarity and logical impact on your readers. You can adapt or combine the following common patterns of argument.

- *Thesis/support.* Putting your claim first, followed by your support, is an effective strategy if your claim is especially strong.

- *Emphatic order.* Generally, the most emphatic arrangement of ideas from a reader's point of view is to place the most important last, the next most important in the beginning, the least important in the middle.

- *Warrants first (deductive order).* Begin with the warrants linking your evidence to your claim, follow with the evidence covered by them, and conclude with your claim. This design is effective when an audience may not understand how your evidence supports your claim or when they will accept your warrants without question. If they accept these warrants without question and if you can show that your evidence is covered by them, you've made your case.

- *Evidence first (inductive order).* Place your evidence before your claim. Use this pattern when your evidence is dramatic and leads clearly and logically to your claim, or when your audience might reject your claim if you put it first.

- *The pro/con pattern.* Begin by summarizing the arguments for and against a position, follow with a claim that chooses between the positions, and conclude by defending your claim as the best choice.

- *The classical argument.* Begin with a summary of the problem and at least a partial statement of the claim. Follow with an argument supporting the claim, a rebuttal answering opponents, and a conclusion that makes new appeals or summarizes your case.

- *The needs/benefits and problem/solution patterns.* First, show that change is necessary. Follow with a claim proposing change or a solution. To conclude, show the benefits of your proposal, explain why it is the best, and, if necessary, explain how to implement it. (See the sample essay in 58d for an illustration of this pattern.)

- *The narrative pattern.* An argument in story form is most effective when you are offering your own experiences as proof for your claim. But be sure your audience keeps sight of your claim, and remember that anecdotal evidence is the weakest, least convincing kind. If you can add evidence from other sources as you tell your story, you'll strengthen your case.

- *Rogerian argument.* This model of argument proposed by psychiatrist Carl Rogers aims at building understanding between opponents when no agreement is currently possible. Begin by summarizing your opponents' position fairly in words they can accept. Then summarize your position in words that won't alienate them while at the same time being fair to your beliefs. Point out key differences dividing you and your opponents, what common ground (values, priorities, interests) you share. If possible, conclude by proposing interim activities to foster relations, maintain communication, and lead to eventual resolution.

58b In your introduction, present yourself as trustworthy

An argument may be entirely logical, but if an audience doesn't know or trust the person making it, it will not, by itself, be persuasive. For this reason most persuasions open with what the philosopher Aristotle called *ethos,* an introduction of the person making the case. If you present yourself in the beginning as someone your audience can trust, you'll have an easier time winning them to your position. Here are ways to build trust in your introduction.

- *Presenting your credentials.* Present your credentials for writing about your chosen subject. What knowledge, experience, or expertise qualifies you? How can you work these qualifications into your opening without seeming to brag?

- *Establishing common ground.* If yours is a "friendly persuasion," addressed to people with whom you share values and experiences and who are likely to become your allies, plan an introduction that establishes common ground with them. Identify common experiences or values creating a bond between you. Show that you speak their language; create a persona they will feel comfortable listening to. (See 2c.)

- *Being fair.* If you're addressing people with whom you have little in common, win their trust by showing fairness to all involved, concern for others instead of yourself, willingness to compromise, and respect for others' opinions.

- *Building trust in academic audiences.* Most academic writing does not require special efforts to build trust. Your knowledge of your subject, fairness, and documentation of your sources will build academic readers' trust. (For more on introductions, see 6c.)

58c Conclude with suitable emotional appeals

Most academic writing has little room for emotion; objectivity is the required point of view. But when the occasion permits—in school or out—you can give an argument additional power by including relevant emotional appeals to audience feelings, which Aristotle called *pathos.* Persuasions often conclude with such appeals. Aim to make your position attractive or your opponents' position unattractive. How can you rouse an audience's feelings? Use the following strategies.

- **Anecdotes.** Tell a moving story that illustrates your point.

- **Description.** Describe an emotionally charged scene that helps your audience see things as they were, are, or could be.

- **Quotations.** End with a dramatic quotation, especially a quotation by someone your audience finds sympathetic.

- **Figurative language.** End with a fresh, vivid metaphor or simile that expresses feeling and understanding (see 26c).

A note on irrelevant emotional appeals: Appealing irrelevantly to your readers' feelings, as in a "sob story" or name-calling, is a logical fallacy (see 57d).

How to . . . Revise and Edit Persuasive Writing

Use these questions to guide your revision and editing. Or ask peer reviewers to read your draft with these questions in mind and answer the most important. (For more on revision, see 4b and c.)

1. Does this paper have a clearly identifiable and arguable claim? What revisions would make the claim clearer or more arguable? (See 57a3.)
2. Does the paper support the claim with factual, relevant, timely, representative, and sufficient evidence? Does the paper supply warrants showing the connection between the evidence and claim? What changes will strengthen its argument? (See 57c.)
3. Who is the audience for this paper? Will its argument appeal to their interests and priorities? What changes would strengthen its appeal? (See 58a1.)
4. What does this paper do to earn readers' trust? Consider the writer's credentials, persona, establishment of common ground, and fairness. What changes would increase readers' trust? (See 58b.)
5. What does this paper do to make its case emotionally appealing? Look for moving stories, description, and figurative language. Are they relevant to the argument? What changes would improve the appeal of this case? (See 58c.)

58*d* | Sample persuasive essay

The student author of the following persuasive essay, Eric Martin, wrote his paper in a composition course focusing on argument and persuasion. He first conducted research into the issue of overcrowding in US national parks and wrote a research project (see the paper in Chapter 53). For his persuasive paper, he was assigned to use this research in an argument attractive to a clearly identifiable audience. In the earlier paper, Eric wrote objectively about the environmental threats to national parks and the need for a reservations system to regulate use. Here he writes more personally, addresses outdoor enthusiasts like himself, and tries to persuade them to change their vacation plans and, in so doing, reduce the problems of overcrowding in national parks. The general subjects of the two papers are similar, but the differing purposes and audiences have led to distinctly different projects. (See 46a for guidelines to the manuscript form for academic writing. See 46c for the Modern Language Association documentation format used in this paper and appropriate for college English classes. See 46d for the American Psychological Association documentation format.)

On Not Seeing the Forests for the People

An anecdote that dramatizes a problem and presents the writer as an eyewitness

What a disappointment! For months my friend Peter and I had been planning a trip to US national parks in Utah and Colorado. Our high point was to be Rocky Mountain National Park and Trail Ridge Road winding across the summit of the Rockies at over 12,000 feet. The air might be thin and the weather chill, but what views! Snowy peaks. Subalpine valleys. Forests and streams. Arctic tundra. Wildlife. What we didn't anticipate was how many others had the same plans.

Emotionally charged language to describe the effects of over-crowding

Trail Ridge Road was jammed bumper to bumper with cars and RVs. Medicine Bow Curve, the visitor center at Fall River Pass, and the Gore Range Overlook might as well have been New York City at rush hour. I could see the mountains, all right—through a forest of other people's heads, elbows, and camera straps. Peter and I ended up as two of the 2.9 million visitors who yearly stand where we stood and like us, probably, wondered whether there were more people than trees in these mountains. One of my keenest memories is of two park workers straining to lift a barrel of garbage into their truck as the wind sent candy wrappers and hamburger bags scudding in an ugly blizzard across the snow fields. This was the high point of my vacation? Next year I'm doing something different.

Ethos: the writer's values that establish common ground with the audience and establish a warrant

Now, I'm no hermit. People and the pace of city life suit me fine. But from time to time I want something underfoot besides concrete—I long for the wind in trees, wildflowers, colors that are not dyed, the feel of rock and leaf and moss, the sight of animals not tamed into pets. And, like most people these days, I consider myself an environmentalist and believe with Henry David Thoreau that "in wildness is the preservation of the world" (qtd. in Stegner 37).

MLA in-text citation of sources

The writer's credentials: research

Evidence: statistics

So my disappointment at Rocky Mountain National Park comes from more than irritation that I wasn't first in line at the sightseeing overlook. Since my vacation I've done some reading, and what I've discovered is that my experience is not uncommon. Our fifty-three national parks, America's most popular nature preserves, are overcrowded and becoming more so each year. In 1992, 58 million people visited them (United States 2), more than two for each of the National Park System's 24.6 million acres. This figure will swell to 90 million by 2010 (Coates, "Crowds" 16). Consider the

Warrant: a definition of "carrying capacity" used to link evidence to the claim

consequences: Each park has what ecologists call a "carrying capacity." That is, each can accommodate only so many visitors before they and park environments begin to suffer. And that is what is happening at the most popular national parks, which are crowded beyond capacity. Increasingly, America's "pleasuring grounds," as Yellowstone National Park was once called, are no longer providing pleasure, and the environment is being devastated.

A factual claim

At Yosemite, as in Rocky Mountain National Park, the roads are filled with traffic ("Crocodiles" 70). During peak season at Denali, finding space on the shuttle bus that takes visitors through the park may require waiting as long as two days (Chadwick 80). At Bryce and Grand Canyons, streams of hikers along the canyon rims block other visitors from the views. In northern Minnesota's Boundary Waters canoe area, "the most popular lakes [. . .] resemble Walden Pond less than a summer camp in the Poconos, with a steady stream of paddlers never out of sight of one another" (Adler and Glick 48). According to a Park Service official at Rocky Mountain National Park, most visitors now feel that crowds are reducing the quality of their visits (NPS). They lose what former park ranger Bruce Craig calls "the national park experience" (43).

Factual evidence cited from sources: one consequence of national parks' popularity

Citation of authorities

To meet the needs of these visitors, more and more of our national parks are being transformed into "destination resorts" like Disney World (Coates, "Creature" 14), no longer nature parks but "theme parks," filled with stores, hotels, and amusements. George Siehl, natural resources specialist at the Congressional Research Service, predicts that in the coming years visitors will "demand even more high-impact amenities," more "canyon flights, warm hotel rooms, groomed snowmobile trails, dirt bike race courses, and fast food" (qtd. in Coates, "Creature" 14). Even now, Park Service rangers increasingly report vacationers "more concerned with the amenities of the park than they [are] with the scenic and cultural wonders they [are] experiencing" (Coates, "Crowds" 16).

Evidence: a second consequence of national parks' popularity (their transformation into "theme parks")

What many distracted visitors may not see are the environmental consequences of their increasing numbers and the "amenities" they demand. Former ranger Bruce Craig warns, "National parks, which preserve unique and delicate ecosystems and fragile historic treasures, are not able to withstand the daily assaults of thousands upon thousands of visitors without experiencing change or degradation" (42). Automobile air pollution from visitors' vehicles is destroying national forests (McMahon 26). Hikers, horses, and mountain bikes are causing national park trails to erode. The water in park streams and lakes is everywhere polluted. Climbers are destroying rock faces. Other visitors are destroying vegetation, disrupting habitats, and endangering wildlife (Martin 37). As the nineteenth-century naturalist and author George Perkins Marsh declared, "Man is everywhere a disturbing agent. Wherever he plants his foot, the harmonies of nature are turned to discords" (qtd. in Stegner 38).

Evidence: a third consequence of national parks' popularity (environmental damage)

58d aud/dev

Transition to the writer's second claim

Enough! America's national parks, "the best idea America ever had," according to Britain's Lord Bryce, deserve better. They need funds restored to National Park Service budgets so that preservation projects can continue. They need our votes for environmentally aware legislators who will change government funding priorities. And they need a rest from at least some of us nature lovers.

Claim: a proposal for action

The next time I plan a vacation, I'm going to leave national parks out of my plans—at least the most popular, most crowded ones during their most popular seasons. I urge you to do the same. Oh, I'll get there someday. But for now, I say, give the harried park staff, the trampled landscape, and the threatened wildlife a rest. With reduced pollution and use, the air will clear, the scars will heal themselves, the plants will regenerate, the animals re-turn. Where to go instead? Consider state parks, Bureau of Land Management lands, or National Forests. Any good map, atlas, or

Explanation to enable readers to act on the claim

travel guide will identify them. Instead of the Great Smoky Mountains, there is the Joyce Kilmer Wilderness in North Carolina ("Lesser-Known Parks"). In Alaska, instead of Denali National Park and Preserve, consider Denali State Park, 324,240 acres, with a "fine trail system, [. . .] abundant wildlife and spectacular views of the Alaska range" (Chadwick 64). There's the important point. Most alternative vacation spots offer their own attractive vistas and activities made more so without all those other vacationers to block the view or clog roads and trails. What will you find off the beaten track? Here's an example.

This summer, after nearly a week of weaving through crowds at Utah's Zion and Bryce Canyon National Parks, my friend Peter and I headed across Utah toward Arches National Park. Along the way, east of Escalante, we happened upon Dry Hollow, the tiny town of Boulder (population 65), and Boulder Mountain. Before we arrived, they were just names on a map, unremarked by us and most other vacationers. But surprise! This became the best part of our trip. Except for the welcoming residents of Boulder glad for two new faces, we were alone, away from the crowds, the entice-ments of *un-natural* "theme park" activities, and the souvenir stands packed with trinkets stamped out who knows where.

Emotional appeal: description to make the writer's proposal attractive to the audience

Over two days a wonderful experience opened to us. The cliffs of the hollow were as sheer and deeply red as Zion or Bryce, the textures of rock as sharp to the touch and the eye, the rush of wind as constant, the road even steeper in its hairpin turns drop-ping to the canyon floor. On the floor of the hollow, not dry at all, rippled a muscular ribbon of creek flowing into the Escalante River. Everywhere were flowers: desert marigold, thornapple, Sego lily, desert paintbrush, blue flax, Tahoka daisy, and wild rose. Up on Boulder Mountain, aspens shimmered, streams sang, snow glistened. And there was this: in purple dusk, in the middle of Boulder, deer bounded in silent arcs from the playground of the one-room school, across a meadow, over a fence, and into the evening. Above them in the distance, like sentinels watching over our two-days' travel, stood the Henry Mountains. To be in such a

A concluding quotation from a sympathetic source to emphasize the value of accepting the writer's proposal

place and have such experiences was, in the words of Chief Luther Standing Bear of the Oglala Sioux, to live "surrounded with the blessing of the Great Mystery" (qtd. in Stegner 35). The pleasure of this mystery is there for you, too, out there somewhere along a road less traveled.

Works Cited

MLA documentation of the writer's sources

Adler, Jerry, and Daniel Glick. "No Room, No Rest." *Newsweek* 1 Aug. 1994: 46–51.

Chadwick, Douglas H. "Denali: Alaska's Wild Heart." *National Geographic* Aug. 1992: 62+.

Coates, James. "Creature Comforts Taking Toll on Park Wilderness." *Chicago Tribune* 22 Apr. 1991, sec. 1: 1+.

———. "Crowds Pose Threat to U.S. Park System." *Chicago Tribune* 21 Apr. 1991, sec. 1: 1+.

Craig, Bruce. "Diamonds and Rust." *National Parks* May–June 1991: 41–44.

"Crocodiles vs. Condos: Can We Protect Our National Parks?" *Business Week* 20 Aug. 1990: 70–71.

Internet source

"Lesser-Known Parks: Doorways to Adventure." *NatureNet* 25 June 1998. National Park Service. 10 Aug. 1998 <http://www.nps.gov/pub_aff/lesser/lesser_frames.htm>.

Martin, Claire. "Set in Stone." *National Parks* Nov.–Dec. 1990: 37–38.

McMahon, Edward T. "The Point of a View." *National Parks* Mar.–Apr. 1992: 26–27.

National Park Service Information Office (Rocky Mountain National Park). Telephone interview. 15 July 1993.

Stegner, Wallace. "It All Began with Conservation." *Smithsonian* Apr. 1990: 34–43.

United States. Dept. of the Interior. National Park Service Socio-Economic Studies Division. *National Park Service Statistical Abstract*. Denver: US Dept. of the Interior, 1993.

PART **XI.**

Special Writing Projects

XI projects

Writing about Literature

59 Writing about Literature

You're reading literature in college for the same reasons you might read while relaxing at home, for the pleasures of escape, vicarious experience, suspense, and surprise. But you're also reading for the deeper pleasures that come from an enlarged understanding of yourself and the world. The writing you do in response to your reading may be notebook or journal entries, in-class writing, essays, reviews, research projects, or creative assignments. Their form will depend on your focus, whether on the work itself, on your responses, or on the context (historical or biographical) in which the work was written. In any case, you are writing to enlarge your understanding, explore your feelings, develop your creative powers, and share your responses with others.

59a | Reading the elements of literature

See 1b for general guidelines for critical reading. The following additional guidelines will help you increase your pleasure in reading literature and add to your insights. As you read, look for the literary elements that writers use to create their art. These elements open a doorway to response and understanding.

- *Characters.* Greet literary characters as you greet real people you're meeting for the first time—with healthy skepticism. Don't believe everything they say. What do they know, exactly? Are they reliable observers? Compare words to deeds and to other characters' remarks.

- *The narrator.* Every work of fiction and poetry has a narrator, a person who tells the story or presents the poem, even if there is no *I* in the work. Narrators do not necessarily speak for the author. Unless they earn your trust, view narrators with the same healthy skepticism with which you view any other character in the work.

- *Stylistic devices.* Look for the stylistic devices writers use to dramatize their message: **irony** (discrepancies between words and deeds, between your expectation and what actually happens, between what a character says and what you know to be true), **symbols** (things, places, or people that have meaning beyond themselves), and **figurative language** (metaphor and simile). (See 26c.)

- *Mood.* As you read, be sensitive to the feeling expressed in the work toward the subject (serious, humorous, mocking, amused, and so forth). Mood is expressed by the narrator's point of view, details of characterization, the course of events, and the way events and setting are described.

- *The title.* Decide what the title suggests about the mood, subject, or message of the work.

- *Key passages.* Look for key passages in which the narrator or another character seems to step back and comment on the subject or action.

- *Layout and staging.* Consider white space between passages and stanzas as clues to structure or meaning. *A drama note:* Use stage directions and descriptions of set design to help you imagine setting, events, and the personality of the characters. Note the instructions for characters' actions or speeches that suggest personality, motivation, and conflict.

59*b* Choose your options for writing about literature: analysis and interpretation

Readers use analysis and interpretation to understand a work, their response, or the historical context. **Analysis** is the systematic description of literary elements (character, setting, plot, imagery, and so forth) and the way they work together to form your opinions as you read. **Interpretation** focuses on elements that are not immediately apparent (for example, the hidden causes of an event or the reasons for two characters' conflict) and then, using evidence and logic, tries to clarify these elements (see 1a1 and 2).

1 Selecting literary elements to analyze and interpret

Adapt the questions after each of the following elements to your chosen literary work. Your answers will provide materials for your writing.

- *Character.* Explain your opinion of a character by answering one or more of these questions: What kind of person is this? Consider appearance, dress, speech, action, thoughts, feelings, flaws, relationships, and motives. Does this character change? If so, how? What is the secret of the relationship between this character and another? Why do these characters engage in conflict? How are conflicts resolved? What is this character's role in the work: main character (protagonist), antagonist, confidant(e), or foil (a minor character whose personality sheds light on a main character's personality)?

- *Setting.* Describe the setting of the work—natural, social, political, or cultural. What does setting contribute to the mood, your understanding, or your evaluation? What force does it exert on the characters?

- *Plot and structure.* Describe the change taking place in the course of the narrative. What are the causes and consequences of this change? What mood or message is expressed by the arrangement of events? Consider the use of flashback. What patterns of imagery, language, dialogue, or poetic form do you see? What does each contribute to mood or message?

- *Symbols.* Identify and explain literary symbols. What characters or details of setting seem to be symbolic? What ideas, values, or conditions do they symbolize?

- *Mood.* Explain the overall feeling or attitude expressed in the work about its subject. What do the characters, setting, plot, imagery, and style contribute to this mood?

- *Style.* Describe the style of the work and the contributions of this style to the work's mood or theme. Consider formal or informal word choice (see 27a), metaphor and simile (see 26c), and complex or simple sentence structure (see 10c).

- *Point of view.* **Point of view** is the narrator's vantage point for presenting the action of a literary work. Who is the narrator: an actual character in the work (an *I* telling his or her story or someone else's) or a disembodied voice writing in the third person (*he* or *she*)? What does the narrator know or not know? Do you trust the narrator? Why or why not? How do the narrator's knowledge, values, and relationships with other characters affect the structure, mood, and message of the work?

- *A key passage.* Explain how a brief key passage sums up the mood or message of a work.

2 Defending a theme

In a broad sense, a **theme** is the message of a work but more than simply a moral. A moral says, "Do this; don't do that." A theme says, "Life is like that." Theme is a message or judgment a work dramatizes about its subject. Present the theme of a work and show how it is embodied by the characters, plot, imagery, mood, and style—for example, *Eudora Welty's short story "Death of a Travelling Salesman" portrays materialistic human beings prevented by fear, mistrust, and materialism from fulfilling their desire for human companionship.*

Follow these guidelines for writing theme statements:

- *A formula for writing theme statements.* Use this formula to write a tentative theme statement: "The message of ___(the name of the work)___ is that . . . "

- *A generalization.* A theme is a generalization about life; therefore, it does not identify characters by name but makes statements about people in general or certain types of people.

- *A complete sentence.* A theme is a complete declarative sentence, not a fragment or question.

- *A stated or implied theme.* A theme may sometimes be located in an actual statement in a work. Or it may only be implied, and you'll express it in your own words.

- *An insightful statement.* A theme statement for a serious work of literature will always be more insightful than pronouncements on "the moral of the story" or a trite saying ("Love conquers all").

- *A unifying statement.* As a unifying statement, a theme should not be contradicted by any major details of a work.*

59c | Choose your options for writing about literature: the review

Analysis and interpretation *explain* a literary work or some part of it. A **review** *evaluates* a work or some part of it. But a review does more than present one reader's personal preferences. Skillful reviewers rely on widely shared standards of value and recognized points of comparison to decide the value of their subjects (see 1a3).

1 Applying standards of value

There are three kinds of standards for evaluating literature.

- Reviewers apply **technical and aesthetic standards** to judge how well a work achieves its intended effects. Is a humorous story humorous; is a tragedy tragic? What explains a work's success or failure in achieving its aims: point of view, structure, plot, characterization, style? How well constructed is a work in comparison with others of its type?

- Reviewers use **psychological and social standards of personality and behavior** to evaluate the plausibility of characters and their world. How "real" are these characters? Or how well do they express the conventions of their literary type?

- Reviewers use **ethical standards** to evaluate the morality of a work and its contents. What values does this work seem to endorse? Do you share them?

---

*For these guidelines to theme statements, I am grateful to Laurence Perrine's *Literature,* 7th ed. (New York: Harcourt, 1997).

2 Writing a review

The thesis for a review is your dominant impression, your overall judgment of the work or the feature you've chosen to evaluate. You may focus your review in two ways, drawing from the standards described in 59c1 to make your judgment.

1. Evaluate a literary work or some feature of it. How effectively does the writer handle characters, setting, plot, structure, or style? Is the work believable, consistent, appropriate to its type, well constructed?

2. Evaluate the ideas or values expressed in a literary work. What does the work dramatize as useful, valuable, desirable, or virtuous? What does the work suggest about the way things should be? Consider description, dialogue, and the narrator's comments. Do you agree with what the work seems to favor? Why or why not?

59*d* | Choose your options for writing about literature: the personal or creative response

1 Writing a personal response

- *The responsive essay.* Write an essay in which you explain your responses to a literary work. Answer these questions: What in the literary work prompted your responses? What were your feelings, memories, or associations as you read? What personal experiences, observations, or beliefs explain these responses?

- *The relation between art and life.* Explore the relationship between art and life by writing a comparison. Use your experiences to help you explain something in a literary work: character, setting, plot, theme. Or use something from the work to help make sense of something in your own life.

- *Then and now.* Responses and opinions change as readers reread and discuss a literary work. Trace the evolution in your thinking by answering these questions: What did I originally think or feel and why? What made me change? What do I now think and feel?

2 Writing a creative response

Use literary techniques to dramatize your feelings or opinions about a work or some part of it. Imagine a revealing scene that the author has not presented. Or dramatize the thoughts of a character in a soliloquy (a monologue in which a character expresses thoughts or feelings that would otherwise be unspoken). Or narrate events that might have occurred "offstage." Or present an episode in a character's life from before or after the events described in the literary work. Whichever strategy you choose, try to remain faithful to the characters, plot, mood, theme, and style as the original author expressed them.

59e Choose your options for writing about literature: the research project

Many literature classes require some form of research paper. (For guidelines, see Chapters 47–50.)

- *Writing a review of research.* Your project may expand on one of the preceding options, using scholars' interpretations to enrich your own. With whom do you agree? Why? How has your research changed your thinking?

- *Writing a biographical project.* Investigate a writer and his or her work. How does this writer's work reflect his or her life? How did he or she come to write this work? What is the history of the work's reputation?

- *Writing about historical context.* Investigate the historical context of a work or some part of it. What does this work reveal about the culture and period in which it was written? How accurately does it present historical figures, conditions, or events?

59f Write a literary paper, using these guidelines

1 Preparing to write

- *Focusing.* Write a key question about your topic or a tentative thesis to provide focus as you reread your chosen work and gather ideas for your paper. (See 2b3 and 2d.)

- *Taking notes.* To support your thesis, take notes as you reread. Provide a context for each note: Who is speaking to whom? What is happening where and when? (See 49d and e.)

- *Refocusing your thesis.* When you've finished rereading and taking notes, reconsider your thesis to see whether it fits what you've discovered. (See 3a.) Beware of "So?" statements, incomplete assertions. Revise to make assertions about the causes, consequences, or importance of your topic.

Laura Sheridan, in Katherine Mansfield's short story "The Garden

Party," lives in a dream world/ *until her visit to the grieving Scott family, when she*

awakens from her dream and discovers what it means to be fully alive.

[The original is a "So?" thesis: So what's the point about Laura and her dream world? The revision answers the question.]

- *Organizing to support your thesis.* In an important sense, your paper is not about your chosen literary work. It's about your thesis. Organize so that everything in your paper follows from or leads to your thesis.

2 Writing and revising

- *Identifying author and title.* Identify the author and title of your literary work early in your essay, even in the first sentence. Use quotation marks around the titles of poems and short stories ("The Garden Party"). Italicize or underline the titles of novels, plays, and films (*Hamlet* or <u>Hamlet</u>). (For quotation marks, see 38d; for italics or underlining, see 41a.)

- *Avoiding an all-summary paper.* Unless instructed otherwise, assume that the audience for your paper is your instructor and the other members of your class. They've probably read your chosen work and won't want to read a book report–style summary. But they may not understand the work as you do or remember the small details you have in mind. Summarize briefly to present evidence supporting your opinions.

- *Using the present tense for summaries.* Use the present tense to write about an author's work and to summarize action in the work. The original may read: *As Laura walked up to the workmen, she blushed and tried to look severe.* But you would write: *As Laura **walks** up to the workmen, she **blushes** and **tries** to look severe.* Events occurring before the opening of a work should be summarized in the past tense. (See 13b1.)

- *Using quotations.* Quote often but briefly to explain and illustrate. (See 38a and b.) Indent long quotations of more than four typed lines. (See 50d.) Use ellipsis points to signal omissions from quotations (see 39d) and brackets to insert clarifications (see 39c).

- *Following the proper format.* Format the final draft of your paper according to Modern Language Association guidelines for writing in the humanities (see 46c).

417

How to . . . Revise and Edit a Literary Essay

Use the following questions to guide your revision and editing. Or ask peer reviewers to read your draft with these questions in mind and answer the most important. (For more on revision, see 4b and c.)

1. A question for peer reviewers: Describe the thoughts and feelings you had as you read this paper. Do your responses to the literary work agree with the writer's? If not, where do you differ? Can you explain the differences?
2. What is this paper's purpose: analysis, interpretation, evaluation, or personal response? Point out any passages that may not fit this purpose.
3. Point out or summarize the thesis of this paper. Does it seem to be a "So?" thesis? Does the paper include another version at the end? Is that statement clearer? Does it better fit the evidence of the paper? (See 4b4.)
4. Does the paper present enough evidence (quotation, summary, and explanation) to support the thesis? Point out places where more support is needed.
5. Can readers follow this essay from beginning to end? Does its design follow the order of events in the original literary work (summary order) or the order of ideas in the thesis (logical order)? What design is clearest and most appropriate?
6. Does this paper follow the format for literary essays? (See 59f.)

59g Sample literary essay

The following essay was written by student-author Leslie Kelly in an introduction to literature course. Her assignment was to write a character study of the narrator of William Stafford's poem "Traveling Through the Dark." To make her interpretation, she considers the narrator's personality and the poem's setting, imagery, and style. She concludes by explaining how the narrator embodies the poem's theme. (For guidelines to the format of a literary essay, see 59f2.)

"Traveling Through the Dark" by William Stafford

Traveling through the dark, I found a deer
dead on the edge of the Wilson River road.
It is usually best to roll them into the canyon:
that road is narrow; to swerve might make more dead.

By glow of the tail-light I stumbled back of the car
and stood by the heap, a doe, a recent killing;
she had stiffened already, almost cold.
I dragged her off; she was large in the belly.

My fingers touching her side brought me the reason—
her side was warm; her fawn lay there waiting,
alive, still, never to be born.
Beside that mountain road I hesitated.

The car aimed ahead its lowered parking lights;
under the hood purred the steady engine.
I stood in the glare of the warm exhaust turning red;
around our group I could hear the wilderness listen.

I thought hard for us all—my only swerving—
then pushed her over the edge into the river.

Dark Necessity

An opening that identifies the author and title of the literary work

A general statement of the thesis

On a first reading of William Stafford's "Traveling Through the Dark," the narrator of the poem appears admirable, a hero, even. He is a good Samaritan, sensitive but in control of his feelings, thoughtful, and capable of decisive action. Who wouldn't trust him to be the driver on a journey down a dark, dangerous, lonely road? And yet a careful rereading reveals that there is more to this man and his actions than first appears.

Topic sentence introducing the first part of the essay

Make no mistake. He is a good man doing the right thing for the right reasons. From the first stanza, as soon as he sees the dead deer, he shows his concern for others and their safety. You or I might whiz by, unseeing, indifferent, or pressed for time. But he sees that if he does not act, because the "road is narrow; to swerve might make more dead." Other travelers might swerve to avoid the carcass and turn into the path of oncoming traffic or over the edge into the river.

The use of brackets to insert a clarification into a quotation

Three times he acts. He "dragged her [the dead doe] off the road." He "thought hard for" "our group" about what should be done after he discovers that the dead doe's unborn fawn is alive. Then, deciding what must be done, he "pushed her over the edge into the river."

Quotations from the poem woven into the text of the essay to support the writer's interpretation

He acts decisively, in part, because he thinks so clearly. Nearly every stanza reveals his logic. In the first, he reasons about what he has discovered—the dead deer, the narrow road, and the potential consequences of a swerve. In stanzas 2 and 3 he reasons inductively. Already stiffened, "almost cold," the deer was a "recent killing." But "large in the belly," "her side [still] warm," "her fawn lay there waiting." He knows from common sense that there is no saving this fawn. Reasoning by analogy, he knows that to pause in pity is a "swerving" as dangerous as the actual swerve of a car.

A topic sentence to introduce another trait of the narrator's personality

Throughout, however, his logic is tempered by sensitivity. "Her fawn lay there waiting, alive, still, never to be born." The word "still" seems to mean both "yet," as in "yet alive," and "quiet" or "unmoving," as one might expect of an animal connected by umbilical cord to its dead mother. There is paradox and enormous awareness in these lines. As he thinks of what to do, he personifies the silence of the wilderness into listening attention. In these connections between life and death, self and wilderness, he understands

An interpretation of poetic language

419

the importance of his decision. How often do we think and act so decisively but with such understanding and awareness?

A transition to the second part of the essay

And yet . . . even if the narrator is as admirable as these details make him appear, there are other details to be accounted for. Consider the title. The narrator is not driving through the dark; he's "traveling." This word suggests more than a drive in the country, not the fact of a journey so much as its condition. He may be driving his car, but to no near destination.

An interpretation of a key word from the title

An interpretation of the setting that reveals a contrast between the narrator's civilized world and the natural world

Here is a man whose condition is being in the dark. In such darkness, some things are difficult to see. One is the world of the poem. It is a pair of parallel universes existing simultaneously in the same space. There is, first of all, the natural world of night, mountain, river, canyon, dead doe, and dying fawn. The other world penetrates, dominates, and finally destroys the former. Its features are the human name for the river, the road, the man, the darkness of the poem's title that refers to more than night, and, most vivid of all, the narrator's car. In contrast to doe and fawn, it lives in images of "the steady engine" that "purred" "under the hood," in the breath of "warm exhaust turning red," in its readiness for purposeful action as it "aimed ahead its lowered parking lights." Given these powerful differences, the human, technological world must displace the natural as it does in the narrator's last, symbolic act, when, with an energy not called for in the first stanza, he does not "roll" the [deer] into the canyon, he *"pushed* [emphasis added] her over the edge into the river."

The narrator's behavior explained in terms of the values of his world

He pushes despite his feelings for the fawn because he stands apart from the natural world. His first response, in stanza 1, is to the social code covering such encounters with the natural world: "It is usually best to roll them into the canyon." The deer is a "heap" *before* it is a "doe" ("the heap, a doe"), the descriptive word suggesting debris more than a "recent killing." He does not perceive the presence of the fawn directly. Instead, "my fingers touching her side brought me the reason," as if his fingers were intermediaries between the natural world and human world of reason and technology. Throughout, of course, he thinks and acts "by the glow of the tail-light." The only sound the wilderness can hear as he thinks and it listens is the purr of the car, the sound of the life that directs his life and decides his choice.

A conclusion that states the theme of the poem as the writer of the essay understands it.

Given his character and the nature of his world, what other choice does he have? He may think hard, but his concern for the fawn is only a "swerving"—a dangerous reflex from a civilized point of view. Viewed in the dim taillights of the car, "roll" comes naturally to "push," and "shove" is not far behind. "Traveling Through the Dark" dramatizes the force of civilized life in the natural world. However much human pity may give it pause, its effects are inevitably disregarding, brutal, destructive. For travel through the dark must continue.

—Leslie Kelly (student)

Essay Examinations

60 Essay Examinations

Essay exams usually ask you to demonstrate three skills:

- *Recall.* You'll show your grasp of the facts by recalling information.

- *Clarification.* You'll demonstrate your understanding of facts (their meaning, causes, consequences, sequences, relationships, points of comparison, and priorities) by clarifying and organizing information.

- *Argument.* You'll apply your knowledge to new situations by constructing arguments that use factual information to prove a point (see Chapter 57).

A note on instructors as examination readers: Your instructors may know what you do about the subject of the examination. But don't take their knowledge for granted and leave out information because you assume they know it. Treat them as intelligent, curious readers interested in your subject. Provide them with what they need to understand you.

60a Deciding what a question calls for

When you receive an essay exam, study each question carefully before you begin writing.

- Look for **topical terms** identifying the subjects you'll cover in your answer. Frequently nouns, they identify people, events, issues, and concepts.

List the most prominent abolitionists of the pre–Civil War era. Discuss their contributions to the abolitionist movement.

[Topical terms here are *abolitionists, pre–Civil War era, contributions,* and *abolitionist movement.*]

- Locate **operators** to decide what skills the question calls for. Frequently verbs, these terms will tell you what to do with your information: inform, clarify, or argue. In the sample question above, students are asked to *list* (recall) and *discuss* (recall and clarify)—in other words, to describe what each abolitionist did, identify influence, and evaluate achievement or importance. Here is a list of operators that appear frequently on essay exams. Note the accompanying definitions and synonyms:

Analyze: divide into parts, explain features, describe the structure or operations.

Argue: make a point and prove it with evidence.
Classify: divide into groups based on shared characteristics.
Comment: describe, analyze, or explain.
Compare: show similarities.
Contrast: show differences.
Criticize: evaluate positively or negatively, giving your reasons.
Defend: support a statement with facts, statistics, authorities, and logic.
Define: tell what something is, how it works.
Describe: present features, parts, or details about a subject.
Develop: explain, analyze, or present details involved with the subject.
Discuss: explain, trace, analyze, or make a subject clear.
Enumerate: list.
Evaluate: present and defend a judgment about a subject.
Exemplify: present examples that illustrate or explain a subject.
Explain: make clear by description, definition, or enumerating.
Identify: describe, list, explain, or offer examples.
Illustrate: present examples.
Interpret: analyze, explain, or present and defend your opinion.
Judge: evaluate.
Justify: explain, prove, or defend.
List: recall.
Outline: give steps or stages; identify major points or topics.
Persuade: argue; support a statement with evidence and reasoning.
Prove: argue.
Provide information: give facts and figures.
Rebut: oppose a statement with evidence and reasoning.
Refute: oppose.
Review: summarize, explain, or provide information.
Show: explain, illustrate, or prove.
Summarize: give the main points of your reading, observation, or study.
Trace: identify the steps or stages in a process; describe causes or effects.

- Look for **modifiers** indicating how to organize or focus your answer. Usually these will be adjectives or adverbs: *most important, primary, briefly, thoroughly,* and so forth. In the sample question above, *most prominent* indicates that students must decide who were the most important abolitionists and focus on their *contributions*.

- Here are some more essay questions. Before you read the accompanying analysis of each question, try to identify their topical terms, operators, and modifiers.

Describe the operation of the adrenal glands.

[This recall question requires students to define the adrenal glands before describing their operation.]

Briefly define and illustrate the concept of determinism.

[This question's first word, *briefly,* provides a clue that this is primarily a test of recall and understanding. Students are being asked to state the meaning of a key
term—presented in class discussion or a textbook—and summarize examples that
illustrate the way determinism works.]

Analyze the characters of the Duke and Duchess of Ferrara in Robert
Browning's poem "My Last Duchess." Trace the Duke's growing
disenchantment with his wife; evaluate his reasons for his actions.

[To answer this question successfully, students must do more than summarize the
poem. To *analyze,* they must describe the personalities of the Duke and Duchess and
then support their opinions with details from the poem. To *trace,* they must describe
a process. To *evaluate,* they must judge the quality of a character's reasoning.]

60*b* | Planning and writing your answer

If scratch paper is available, use it. Even if you're well prepared, the
answer to a complex question may not spring to mind fully formed.

- *Brainstorming and freewriting.* Make lists, jot down ideas, freewrite.

- *Noting your main idea or thesis.* Write out the main idea or thesis of
  your essay. Be sure that this most important part of your essay includes key topical terms from the question to keep you on course as
  you write. Consider this thesis:

  Determinism is the philosophical doctrine that every event, human
  or natural, can be explained as the result of earlier events. Everything
  is caused; there is no such thing as free will; no event is purely
  accidental.

  [This thesis gives the definition called for by the question. The following explanatory sentence clarifies the definition by telling what *determinism* is not and lists the
  areas from which the writer will draw the examples called for by the question: examples of causality, the absence of free will, and the absence of chance.]

- *Writing a sketch outline.* To complete your plans, sketch an outline of
  your answer. Think of your answer as a pyramid with the thesis or
  main idea at the top and your facts and explanations spreading out
  beneath, following a line of reasoning and providing support.

- *Manuscript form.* If permitted, write in pencil so that you can erase.
  Write on every other line, allowing generous margins. *A note on writing with computers:* Check with your instructor before bringing a laptop computer to the exam.

- *Organization.* Don't waste time with introductions. Get to the point.
  Follow your outline.

- *Rereading.* If you have time, read your answer twice—once to make
  sure you've actually answered the question, a second time to check
  grammar, punctuation, spelling, and legibility.

Business Writing

chapter
61 Business and Professional Writing

Computer Tip: Creating Templates for Business Documents

> Your word processing program may already have a "templates file," containing a variety of templates for familiar business documents such as letters and memos. You can customize them to suit your needs. Or you can create your own templates using the fonts, styles, header, and format commands of your word processor. Note, however, that ornate, "over-produced" documents will distract readers.

61a | Write effective business letters

1 Following the conventions for writing business letters

- *Paper.* Use good-quality, heavy, white bond paper. Letterhead paper makes the best impression.

- *Typescript.* Type your letters or use a computer. Use a black ribbon and standard typeface. If you use a computer, note that many readers object to dot matrix printers. (See 46a.)

- *Length.* When possible, limit letters to one page. If you write a longer letter, put second and successive pages on plain white paper. One inch from the top, type a heading: the addressee's name flush left, the page number centered, and the date flush right.

- *Balance.* Make your letter look easy to read by centering it on the page. Keep paragraphs relatively brief; double-space between them. Provide ample white space surrounding your text. To help readers keep track of important information, use indented lists, bullets, or enumeration. (See 46b2.)

- *Format.* Among letter formats, one of the most common and attractive is the modified block, illustrated by the sample letter that follows. Near the right margin, place the return address (unless you're using letterhead stationery), the date, complimentary close, and signature section. All other parts begin at the left margin.

- *Nonsexist address.* Use nonsexist forms of address. Address readers by name or specific title: *Dear Mr., Ms., Mrs., Dr., Professor,* and so forth. Call ahead to find out your readers' names. When you do not know their names, address them by title alone: *Dear Editor, Service Manager, Director of Admissions,* and so forth. Do not use first names unless you know your reader personally. (See 27e.)

- *Envelopes.* Mail business letters in standard business-size envelopes, 4 × 9½ inches.

2 Conveying your personality to readers

Whatever your reasons for writing, your readers will usually be reading as part of their jobs. They'll appreciate anything in your letter that makes their work easier, including layout, detailed information, and style. Be businesslike. Don't sound stuffy, but be as serious as the occasion requires. Avoid the features of an informal style: slang, most contractions, sentence fragments, and inappropriately charged language. (For more on persona, see 2c and 27a.)

Whenever possible, adopt what business writers call a "you" attitude. Try to see things from your readers' point of view, keeping their interests, needs, and benefits uppermost in mind. Most public letters are, after all, persuasive. You'll be persuasive if your readers know you're thinking of them as you write. (See 58b.)

3 Organizing business letters

Make your letters easy to follow by adopting the standard three-part design. In your opening paragraph, identify your subject and purpose and provide necessary background. In your middle paragraphs, provide information, explanation, and reasons. Close with a brief paragraph describing the action you want your audience to take. If you have bad news, save it until you've presented all the information and reasons explaining it.

4 Using electronic communication

- *Faxes.* Because faxes are easily lost, advise the recipient that one is coming. Include a cover sheet that gives the recipient's name, company, fax number, date, time, subject, your name, fax number, and the total number of pages, including the cover sheet.

- *E-mail.* E-mail messages are less formal than business letters or even memos; sometimes they seem closer to speech than writing. But as you write, keep your readers in mind: their knowledge, their positions, and your relationship with them. Be courteous—say "please" and "thank you"—and take the time to be sure your language is accurate and that your message will be clear to its reader. Headings for e-mail depend on the network you're using, but you can still address your reader by name and sign off with your name. Finally, remember that e-mail is not confidential. (See also 48e1 and 5.)

1201 W. Chase Avenue, Apt. 2C
East Lansing, MI 48824
April 14, 199-

Maria L. Garcia
Director of Student Services
Harley Williams School
Institute of Child Psychiatry
709 W. Greenleaf Avenue
Chicago, IL 60626

Dear Ms. Garcia:

Professor Gerald Ashby, Chair of the Psychology Department at
Michigan State University, has informed me that you have three
openings for Child Care Worker-Summer Interns. I wish to apply
for one of these positions.

As my enclosed résumé indicates, I am now a college sophomore
studying for a degree in child psychology. I plan a career as a
child psychologist working with institutionalized children. Most
of my work so far has been with children.

For two years I worked as a summer counselor at a camp for
children with developmental disabilities. My responsibilities
were to provide tutoring, physical therapy, and recreational
supervision.

For one year I worked as a Boys Club Recreation Supervisor.
Besides my supervisory and coaching duties, I was assigned to
five boys to act as their "big brother."

My current position as a hospital orderly not only helps me
pay for tuition, books, room, and board but also provides a
valuable introduction to institutional work.

I believe I am qualified by education and work experience to be a
Child Care Worker-Summer Intern at Harley Williams School. I can
be available for an interview at your convenience; if you wish, I
will have my references and academic records sent to you. I can be
reached by mail at the above address or at (517) 555-1541
weekdays from 9 to 11 a.m. I look forward to hearing from you.

Sincerely,

Matthew Leigh

Matthew Leigh

Enclosure: Résumé

Margin annotations:

Modified block business letter format

Heading (return address omitted with letterhead stationery) and date

Inside address

Salutation followed by a colon

Itemized information

Block paragraphs

Complimentary close

Reference area: enclosures, typist's initials, copies, and so forth

61b Write effective résumés

A **résumé** presents important information about your background, education, experiences, achievements, and references. It is the proof of your qualifications.

1 Preparing a résumé

As you prepare a résumé, be brief but complete. If possible, limit the résumé to one page. Use clipped phrases rather than complete sentences: *Career Objective: To become a child psychologist working with autistic children in an institutional setting.* Group related information to make it easy to locate, and make headings grammatically parallel, such as all nouns or noun phrases: *Education, Experience, References,* and so forth (see Chapter 19). Never send a résumé without a cover letter.

2 Formatting a résumé

The formats for résumés are varied; make yours look professional and easy to read. If you have important achievements, list them first. Follow a chronological order, most recent job first; or describe the functions of your job, most important first. If you're a recent graduate or still in school, place your education first, beginning with your most recent schooling. See the sample résumé on page 428.

61c Write effective memos

A **memo** is a written document sent within an organization to specific persons or departments. Its purposes are to inform, summarize, record, or call for action. Successful memos are usually sensitive to writer-reader relations. (See 1c3 for questions about audience; see 2c for guidelines to creating a persona.) Often customized to suit the needs of a particular organization, memos vary widely in their formats. The sample memo on page 429 illustrates standard memo parts and a common pattern of organization.

61d Choose your options for writing an effective report

A **report** is a systematic presentation of information to a specific audience for a specific purpose. The reports you'll write in college and on the job may take several forms: informal memo or letter reports, technical field or lab reports, informative reports, problem/solution reports, progress reports, proposals, and case studies.

MATTHEW R. LEIGH
1201 W. Chase Avenue,
East Lansing, MI 48824
(517) 555-1541

Position Desired:	Child Care Worker-Summer Intern
Career Objective:	To become a child psychologist working with autistic children in an institutional setting

Education:

199- to present: Michigan State University
Major: Child Psychology
Minor: English
Grade Point Average: 3.75 (Possible 4.0)
Honors: Dean's List, 199- to 199-
    Leonard E. Frank Scholarship

Academic history to highlight training

Honors listed

199- to 199-: William Rainey Harper College
Phi Theta Kappa Honor Society
Editor, <u>The Harbinger</u>, Campus Newspaper
Basketball and Track Teams,
199- and 199-

Experience:

199- to present: Orderly, Weldon Memorial Hospital, East Lansing, MI
199- and 199-: Camp Counsellor, Camp Onewata, Schroon Lake, NY
Tutored and supervised recreation at this camp for developmentally disabled children, ages 8-14

Experience listed in reverse chronological order

199- to 199-: East Lansing Boys Club, East Lansing, MI
Supervised group recreation

References: References and credentials available on request from the Placement Office, Michigan State University, East Lansing, MI 48824

Relevant activities or accomplishments

TO:	Laura Chin, Selection Committee, State College Student Anthology	Block format memo
FROM:	Beth Logan, Editor *BL*	Writer's initials
DATE:	December 10, 199-	

SUBJECT: Reading this year's submissions to the student literary anthology

Enclosed are the submissions to be evaluated for the next issue of the anthology. Read them in the usual way:

1) Award each entry from 1 to 5 points (1 low, 5 high).

2) If you discover incomplete or misassembled entries, let me know, and I'll try to get you good copies.

3) Record your votes beneath your initials on the enclosed alphabetized list.

We'll meet to discuss our evaluations at the end of January. Thanks for all your efforts on last year's issue. It was first-rate. I know we can make this year's even better.

Enclosures: Anthology submissions
Author list

Triple-space after the subject line and begin the body of the memo flush left.

Do not indent memo paragraphs. Single-space within paragraphs, double-space between.

Whenever possible, use lists for clarity and emphasis

Reference area

1 Preliminary activities

Your preliminary preparations will be similar to those for other investigative writing: surveying the situation (see 1c), posing key questions or describing the problem, and identifying your purpose (see 47a2). You will gather the information for your report from appropriate sources: interviews, minutes, letters, questionnaires, surveys, experimentation, direct observation, published reports, and other documents. (For guidelines to research, see Chapters 47–49.) When you finish your investigation, write out your **conclusion,** the point of your report supported by your information (see 2d4).

2 Organizing a report

Prepare an informal report as you would a letter, memo, or essay, with an appropriate beginning, middle, and end. Formal reports generally consist of (1) prefatory parts such as a cover, title page, letters of authorization or acceptance, acknowledgments, a table of contents, an abstract, and an executive summary; (2) the text of the report, including an introduction, body, and conclusion; (3) supplementary parts such as an appendix, bibliography, or index. Include all parts relevant to your report and required by your readers. Follow these guidelines to organize the text of your report:

- *Introduction.* The introduction includes all elements necessary to orient your readers and help them understand your information: a statement of the problem or key questions, a description of materials and methods, background or history, definitions, a review of relevant published research, or an overview of the presentation to follow.

- *Body.* The body of a report is often labeled *Results, Data, Findings,* or *Discussion.* The results and discussion may be separated or combined, depending on their relationship, the length of the report, and your readers' needs. Organize the body of a report according to topics, chronology, importance, or other logical patterns. (See 6b.)

- *Conclusion.* A conclusion summarizes information, makes generalizations about it (comparisons, causes and effects, classifications, estimations, predictions), poses solutions to problems, makes evaluations and recommendations, or proposes action.

- *Inductive or deductive organization.* For readers who need detailed explanation or who may resist your recommendations without a full presentation of the case, organize the text of your report in an *inductive* or conclusion-last order: introduction, body, conclusion. For busy readers who may not read the entire report, who will agree with you, or who want your opinion promptly, use a *deductive* or conclusion-first order: introduction, conclusion, body.

3 Formatting and style

- *Headings.* Informal reports are usually written as continuous documents, undivided except for paragraphing. The text of formal reports is usually divided by headings into clearly labeled parts: *Introduction, Background, Discussion, Conclusion,* and so forth. (For guidelines to effective headings, see 46b1.)

- *Visual aids.* Use lists, tables, and graphics to illustrate and group information as well as to help your readers understand it (see 46b2–4).

- *Style.* Generally write in the present tense unless you have a good reason for using the past tense: *This report recommends . . .* (see 13b1). Choose concrete, specific words as specialized as the subject requires and reader understanding will allow (see 26a and b). Except in conclusions, avoid generalities. Also avoid emotionally charged words that may make your report sound biased (see 25b).

- *Documentation.* Cite the sources of borrowed information in an appropriate format. (For Modern Language Association guidelines, see Chapters 51 and 52; for American Psychological Association guidelines, see 54a–c; for other formats, see the style manuals listed in Chapter 56.)

4 Sample formal report

For a sample formal report written in the American Psychological Association style, see 54d.

PART **XII.**

Appendix

A List of Internet Sources

Internet Resources

🖥 *Computer Tip:* Locating Missing Internet Sources

If you are unable to locate a resource listed in this appendix, it may have moved to another site. Try deleting parts of the URL that you typed in the address box of your browser, beginning at the right and stopping at each slashmark. If you still can't find the resource, search for another by typing in key words for the resource in the query window of your browser's default search engine. If, for example, you want to locate resources on researching the Internet, type in "Internet AND searching."

1 Learning the Internet and the World Wide Web

- *Advanced Searching: Tricks of the Trade.* Peggy Zorn, Mary Emanoil, and Lucy Marshall's guidelines for practiced Internet users.

  <http://www.onlineinc.com/onlinemag/MayOL/zorn5.html>

- *ICYouSee Guide to the World Wide Web.* Three basic lessons for beginners, from the Ithaca College Library.

  <http://www.ithaca.edu/library/Training/where.html>

- *Internet Help Desk.* A list of hypertext links to Internet guides, references, and search tools.

  <http://www.strife.com/helpdesk.html>

- *Searching on the Internet.* A brief guide to search tools from the Hampton, Virginia, public library, with links to tutorials and Internet tours. Excellent for beginners.

  <http://www.hampton.va.us/hpl/search.htm>

- *Sink or Swim: Internet Search Tools & Techniques.* A detailed guide to search tools and strategies.

  <http://www.sci.ouc.bc.ca/libr//connect96/search.htm>

- *TERENA Guide to Network Resource Tools.* A comprehensive guide to Internet search tools and research, by Margaret Isaacs. Excellent for intermediates.

  <http://www.terena.nl/libr/gnrt/>

- *Understanding WWW Search Tools.* A description and evaluation of major search tools, by Jian Liu.

  <http://www.indiana.edu/~librcsd/search/old/>

2 Search tools

To search the Internet for information, you'll rely on four kinds of search tools:

- Search engines such as AltaVista, Excite, Lycos, HotBot, and InfoSeek scan texts looking for key words. These are good tools if you know your topic.
- Subject directories such as Argus Clearinghouse, Magellan, or Yahoo! arrange topics for browsing according to hierarchical menus. These are good tools if you're unsure of your topic.
- Multi-search tools such as Dogpile or Metacrawler use multiple search tools to search for sources.
- People finders are search tools that look for e-mail addresses, phone numbers, and businesses.

Following are the names and addresses (URLs) of central sites that will link you to these search tools. Click on the names of these tools and begin your search. Be sure to make bookmarks for any that you want to use again and again.

- *Evaluation of Selected Internet Tools.* A good site for intermediate Internet users who want to see at a glance how the most popular tools operate, from Northwestern University.

  <http://www.library.nwu.edu/resources/internet/search/evaluate.html>

- *Internet Searching.* December Communications' excellent and exhaustive list of new or noteworthy sites; resource lists; subject directories; search engines; protocol search tools for searching the Web, gopher space, and ftp sites; and people finders.

  <http://www.December.com/cmc/info/internet-searching.html>

- *Introduction to Search Engines.* A brief description of the most popular search tools, from the Kansas City Public Library. Good for beginners.

  <http://www.kcpl.lib.mo.us/search/srchengines.htm>

3 Evaluating information on the Internet

- *Evaluating Quality on the Net,* by Hope N. Tillman, of Babson College.

  <http://www.tiac.net/users/hope/findqual.html>

- *Evaluating World Wide Web Information,* from Purdue University. A brief checklist of questions about sources.

  <http://thorplus.lib.purdue.edu/library_info/instruction/gs175/3gs175/evaluation.html>

- *Testing the Surf: Criteria for Evaluating Internet Information Resources,* by Alastair G. Smith. Included is a useful "toolbox of criteria" for evaluating sources.

  <http://info.lib.uh.edu/pr/v8/n3/smit8n3.html>

- *Why We Need to Evaluate What We Find on the Internet,* from Widener University. A comprehensive guide to Internet source evaluation, with checklist questions for each type of Web page and a hypertext bibliography linking other evaluation sources.

  <http://www.science.widener.edu/~withers/cklstlnk.hktm>

4 Desktop references

- *Acronym and Abbreviation List.* Searchable list of acronyms; also reversible to search for acronym from a key word.

  <http://www.ucc.ie/info/net/acronyms>

- *CIA World Factbook.* Every hard fact about every country in the world.

  <http://www.odci.gov/cia/publications/factbook>

- *Hypertext Webster Interface.* A searchable dictionary.

  <http://c.gp.cs.cmu.edu:5103/prog/webster>

- *Quotations Page.* Search for that quotation by key word.

  <http://www.starlingtech.com/quotes>

- *Scholes Library Electronic Reference Desk.* An index of "ready reference" sources.

  <http://scholes.alfred.edu/Ref.html>

5 Writing help

The Internet contains many, many sites with information to help writers write.

- *Allyn and Bacon's CompSite.* An interactive meeting place for teachers and students to share resources and work on projects.

  <http://www.abacon.com/compsite>

- *Resources for Writers and Writing Instructors,* by Jack Lynch, a detailed list of hypertext links to writing instruction sites, dictionaries and other reference works, grammar, punctuation, and usage sites.

  <http://www.english.upenn.edu/~jlynch/writing.html>

- *LEO: Literacy Education Online.* Help with "what's bothering you about your writing."

  <http://leo.stcloud.msus.edu>

- *English as a Second Language.* Bills itself as the starting point for learning English as a second language online. Includes visual and auditory resources, as well as a 24-hour help center.

  <http://www.lang.uiuc.edu/r-115/esl>

- *Main Writing Guide.* Three complete online handbooks for writing.

  <http://www.english.uiuc.edu/cws/wworkshop/mainmenu.html>

- *Non-Sexist Language.* Tips for avoiding sexist language, based on National Council of Teachers of English guidelines.

  <http://mickey.la.psu.edu/~chayton/eng202b/nonsex.htm>

- *Purdue On-Line Writing Lab.* An extensive source of online help for writers, including professional help to specific questions by e-mail.

  <http://owl.english.purdue.edu>

- *Researchpaper.com.* An impressive compendium of research-paper help, including live chat rooms.

  <http://www.researchpaper.com>

- *Writers' Workshop: Online Resources for Writers.* A directory of online writing help at the University of Illinois at Urbana-Champaign.

  <http://www.english.uiuc.edu/cws/wworkshop/writer.html>

- *Writing Papers of Literary Analysis: Some advice for student writers.* From Western Michigan University.

  <http://www.wmich.edu/english/tchg/lit/adv/lit.papers.html>

6 Specialized Web sites (an alphabetical topic list)

- Art and film

  Internet Movie Database. A key word–searchable database of everything you ever wanted to know about movies.

  <http://us.imdb.com>

  World Wide Arts Resources. A searchable gateway to the arts online, plus a directory of Web sites, chats, and bulletin boards.

  <http://wwar.world-arts-resources.com>

- Business

  The Business Communication World Wide Web Resource Center. A guide for business writing, with links to other online resources.

  <http://idt.net/~reach/Lance/lance-cohen.html>

  Nijenrode Business Webserver. Searchable guide to online business resources, focused on the needs of students, faculty, and researchers.

  <http://www.nijenrode.nl/nbr/index.html>

- Education

  ERIC Clearinghouse on Information and Technology. The WWW starting point for the Educational Resources Clearinghouse.

  <http://ericir.syr.edu>

  National Center for Education Statistics. Department of Education site containing statistics on education in the United States.

  <http://nces.ed.gov/pubsearch/index.html>

- Government and law

  Fedworld Information Network. The searchable gateway to the huge information resources of the federal government.

  <http://www.fedworld.gov>

  GPO Access Databases. Another guide to government publications, online and print versions (with instructions for ordering print documents).

  <http://www.access.gpo.gov/su_docs/aces/aaces002.html>

  Thomas. A searchable database of all bills before the most recent sessions of the House of Representatives.

  <http://Thomas.loc.gov>

  U.S. Senate. A guide to business of the U.S. Senate.

  <http://www.senate.gov>

  United States Census Bureau Home Page. A gold mine of statistics about the U.S. population.

  <http://www.census.gov>

- History

  Essays in History—University of Virginia. Full text of the journal *Essays in History* since 1990.

  <http://www.lib.virginia.edu/journals/EH/EH.html>

- Humanities

  Voice of the Shuttle: Web Page for Humanities Research. An amazingly comprehensive directory of humanities-oriented Web pages.

  <http://humanitas.ucsb.edu>

- Language

  The Human-Languages Page. A huge compendium of links to resources in language.

  <http://www.june29.com/HLP>

- Literature

Alex: A Catalog of Electronic Texts on the Internet. A listing of full-length texts available on the Internet.

<http://www.lib.ncsu.edu/staff/morgan/alex/alex-index.html>

American Poetry Hyper-bibliography. A Web-based guide to American poetry, searchable by author or title.

<http://www.hti.umich.edu/english/amverse/hyperbib.html>

A Glossary of Rhetorical Terms with Examples. Forty-five rhetorical terms (*Alliteration* to *Zeugma*) with links to classical text for examples.

<http://www.uky.edu/ArtsSciences/Classics/rhetoric.html>

Online Literary Resources. A searchable, categorized directory of academic sources of information in English and American literature; extensive.

<http://www.english.upenn.edu/~jlynch/Lit>

Project Gutenberg. The continuing project to make text versions of public domain classic literature available online; currently nearing 1,000 titles.

<http://www.promo.net/pg>

University of Virginia Electronic Text Library. Provides access to the University of Virginia's extensive collection of digitized texts and images.

<http://etext.lib.virginia.edu/uvaonline.html>

- Philosophy and religion

Religion. A starting point for studies in world religions.

<http://sunfly.ub.uni-freiburg.de/religion>

- Science and medicine

NASA Spacelink. NASA's fulfillment of its obligation to disseminate all the information it gathers through space exploration.

<http://spacelink.msfc.nasa.gov>

National Center for Health Statistics. The repository of the Centers for Disease Control's data.

<http://www.cdc.gov/nchswww/default.htm>

- Social Sciences

Social Science Information Gateway. A comprehensive listing of social science information sources available electronically worldwide.

<http://sosig.esrc.bris.ac.uk>

7 Current events

- *CNN.* Multimedia, up-to-the-minute online news source; not adequately archived for searches.

<http://www.cnn.com>

- *InfoSurf: E-Journals and E-Zines.* A categorically arranged list of magazines and journals available electronically.

  <http://www.library.ucsb.edu/mags/mags.html>

- *The* New York Times *on the Web.* Requires registration, but free.

  <http://www.nytimes.com>

- *Newsstand.* Links to over 4,200 Web sites of print publications—newspapers, magazines, computer publications. Searchable by publication name.

  <http://www.ecola.com/news>

- San Francisco Chronicle. Online version; searchable.

  <http://www.sfgate.com/cgi-bin/chronicle/list-sections.cgi>

- Time *Magazine.* An online version of *Time* magazine; search feature searches *Time* and many other magazines; also provides access to bulletin boards and chats.

  <http://pathfinder.com/time>

8 Bibliographic citation guides

- *American Psychological Association (APA) Guide to Style.* Online version of the APA guide; abridged.

  <http://www.wilpaterson.edu/wpcpages/library/apa.htm>

- *Bibliographic Styles Handbook: APA.* A hypertext index to the APA publication style, from UIUC.

  <http://www.english.uiuc.edu/cws/wworkshop/apamenu.htm>

- *MLA Style.* The authoritative Modern Language Association guide to citing Internet sources.

  <http://www.mla.org/main_stl.htm>

- *Modern Language Association (MLA) Guide to Style.* Online version of the MLA guide; abridged.

  <http://www.wilpaterson.edu/wpcpages/library/mla.htm>

- *Publication Manual FAQ:* Frequently Asked Questions About the *Publication Manual of the American Psychological Association (4th ed.).* Contains a link to "How to Cite Information from the Internet and the World Wide Web."

  <http://www.apa.org/journals/faq.html>

Index

443

445

A Guide to Correction and Editing Symbols

Numbers refer to chapters in the book

abbr	incorrect abbreviation, 42
adj	incorrect adjective, 18
adv	incorrect adverb, 18
agr	faulty agreement: subject-verb, 14; pronoun-antecedent, 15
art	incorrect articles (ESL), 30
aud	audience unclear, 1c3
awk	awkward: emphasis needed, 20; variety needed, 21; mixed and incomplete messages, 22
case	incorrect case form, 17
cap	incorrect capitalization, 40
cliché	cliché, 26d
coh	coherence needed, 7
cs	comma splice, 12a–b
comp	incorrect comparisons, 18d
coord	ineffective coordination, 20c, 21b2
dm	dangling modifier, 23b
d	ineffective diction (word choice): exact words, 25; vivid words, 26; appropriate words, 27
db neg	double negative, 18e
dev	inadequate subject development, 6
det	concrete details needed, 6a; concrete and specific words, 26a–b
doc	incorrect documentation: MLA, 51a–b; APA, 54a–c; CMS, 55a–c; CBE, 56a
emph	emphasis needed, 20
exact	imprecise or inexact word, 25
fig	inappropriate figure of speech, 26c–d
frag	sentence fragment, 11
fs	fused sentence, 12c
hyph	misused hyphen, 44
ind quot	indirect quotation: 24e; ESL, 32c
-ing	*-ing* error (ESL), 31f
ital	italics: 41; for emphasis, 41e
jar	jargon, 27c
lc	lower case: 40; misuse of capitals, 40d
log	incorrect or faulty logic (fallacies), 57d
mixed	mixed construction, 22b
mm	misplaced modifier, 23a
ms	incorrect manuscript form (format): 46a; MLA format, 46c; APA format, 46d
nonst	nonstandard: 27b; nonstandard reflexive pronouns, 17g
num	incorrect use of numbers, 43
org	ineffective organization, 3